I0762821

# ADIRONDACK VERNACULAR

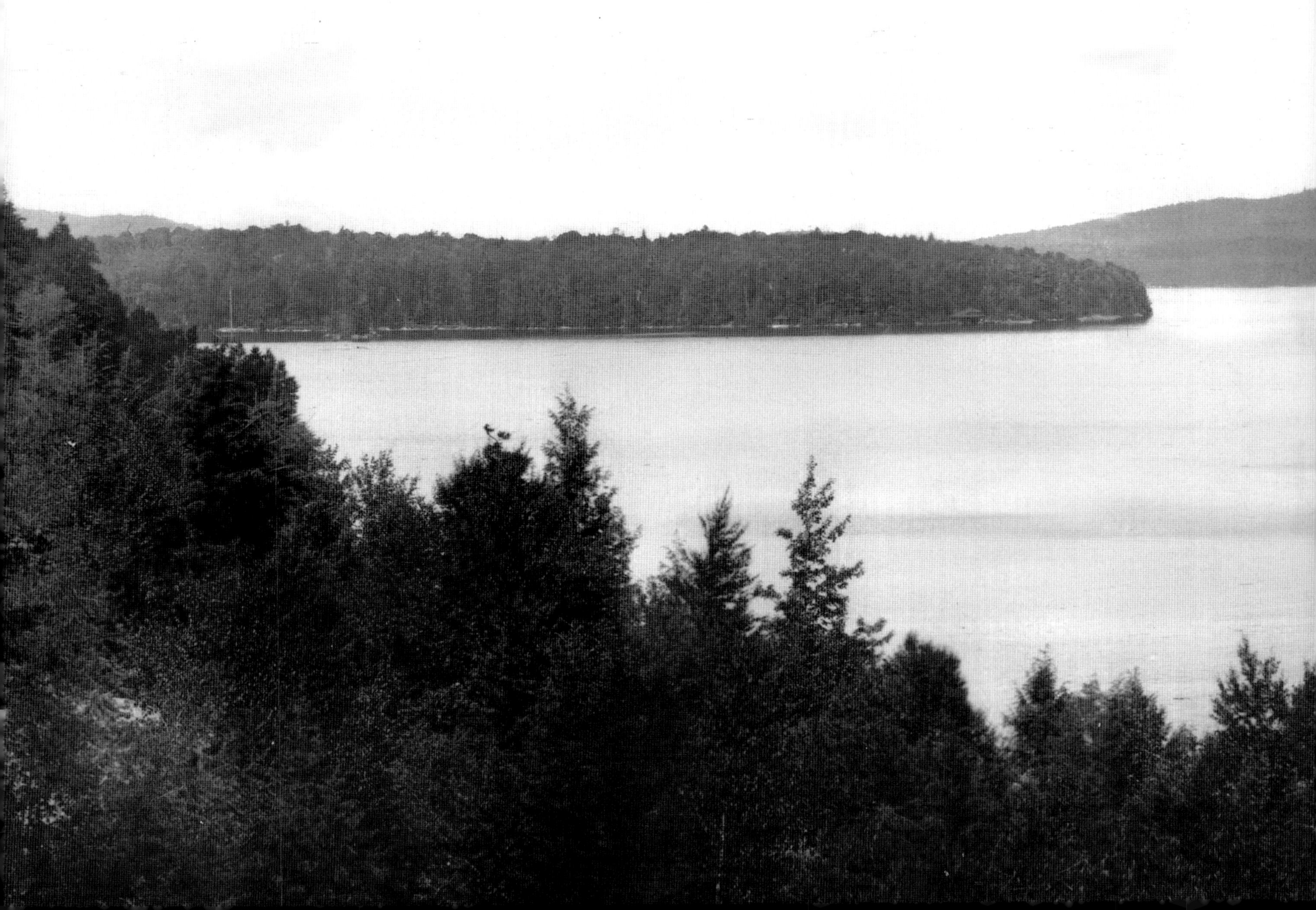

# ADIRONDACK VERNACULAR

## The Photography of Henry M. Beach

Robert Bogdan

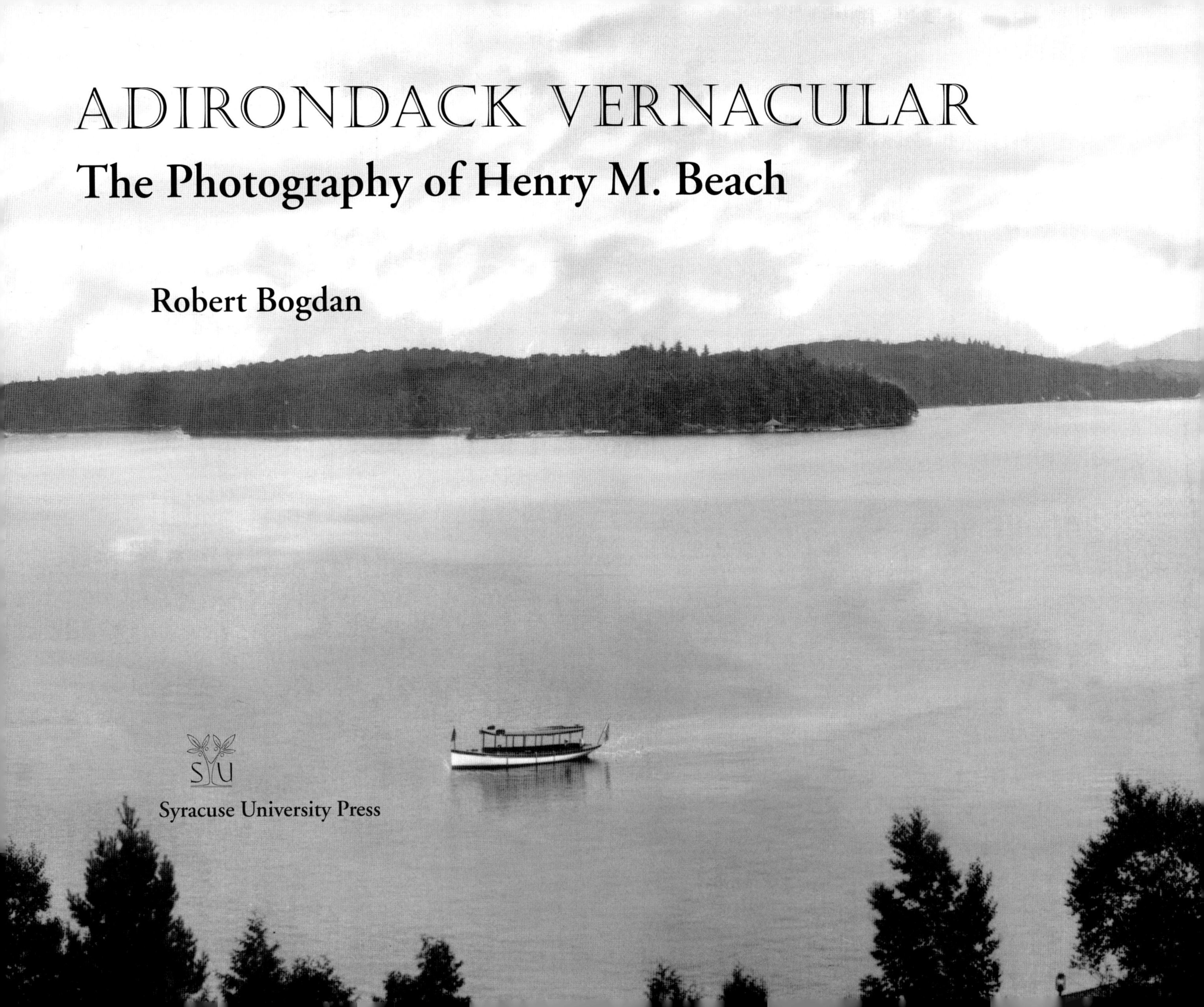

SU

Syracuse University Press

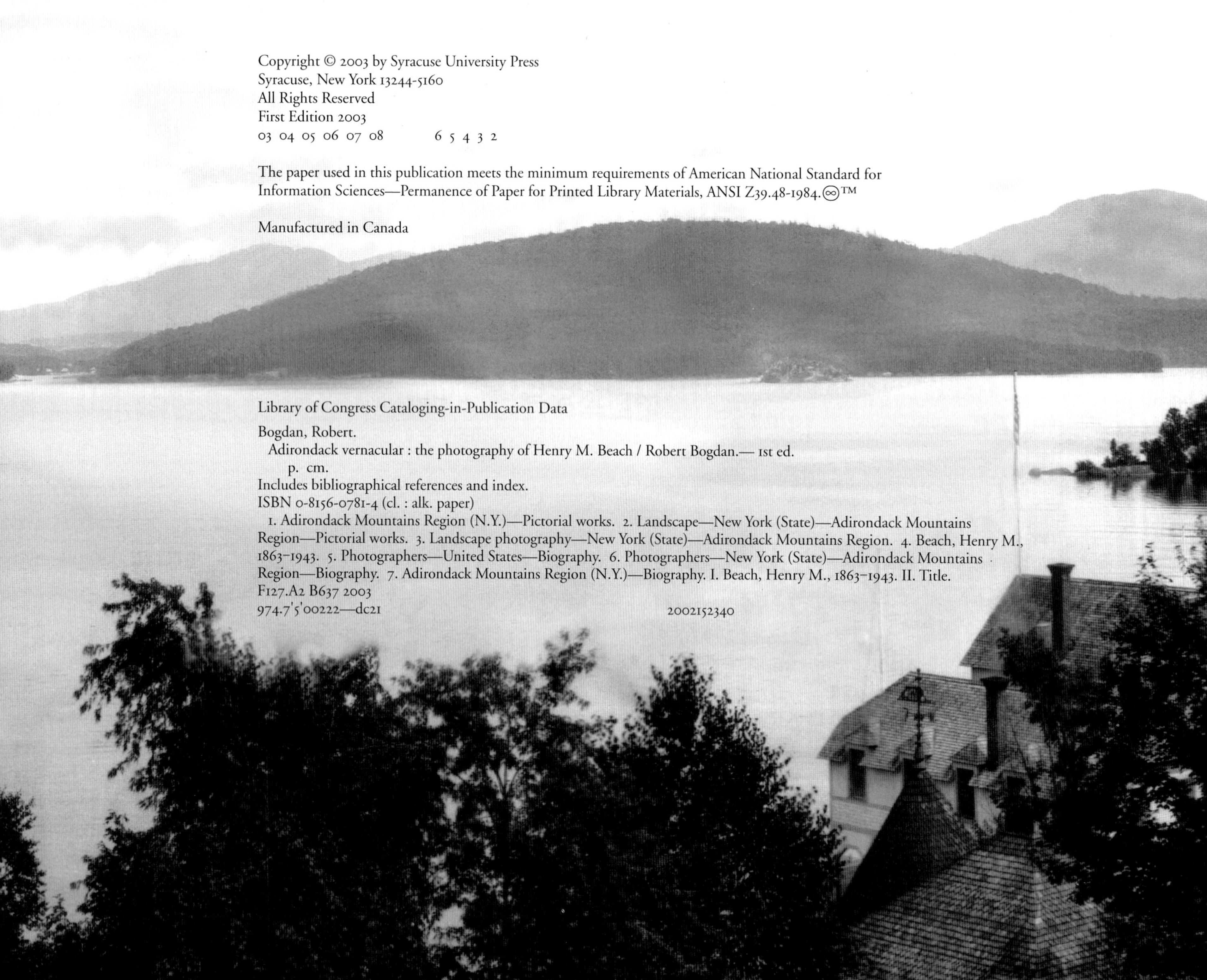


Syracuse, New York 13244-5160

First Edition 2003
03 04 05 06 07 08 6 5 4 3 2

The paper used in this publication meets the minimum requirements of American National Standard for Information Sciences—Permanence of Paper for Printed Library Materials, ANSI Z39.48-1984.∞™

Manufactured in Canada

Library of Congress Cataloging-in-Publication Data

Bogdan, Robert.
Adirondack vernacular : the photography of Henry M. Beach / Robert Bogdan.— 1st ed.
p. cm.
Includes bibliographical references and index.
ISBN 0-8156-0781-4 (cl. : alk. paper)
1. Adirondack Mountains Region (N.Y.)—Pictorial works. 2. Landscape—New York (State)—Adirondack Mountains Region—Pictorial works. 3. Landscape photography—New York (State)—Adirondack Mountains Region. 4. Beach, Henry M., 1863–1943. 5. Photographers—United States—Biography. 6. Photographers—New York (State)—Adirondack Mountains Region—Biography. 7. Adirondack Mountains Region (N.Y.)—Biography. I. Beach, Henry M., 1863–1943. II. Title.
F127.A2 B637 2003
974.7'5'00222—dc21 2002152340

*To my family—Chet, Jono, Meg, Yinka, and Janet*
*Remembering those camping trips to the Fulton Chain!*

**Robert Bogdan** is distinguished professor of sociology and cultural foundations of education at Syracuse University. He was awarded the Syracuse University Chancellor's Citation of Distinguished Academic Achievement in 1990. In 1996, he was a visiting Fulbright scholar at the University of Stockholm. He is the author of *Exposing the Wilderness: Early-Twentieth-Century Adirondack Postcard Photographers* (1999), also published by Syracuse University Press, and *Freak Show: Presenting Human Oddities for Amusement and Profit* (1990), and coauthor of *Qualitative Research for Education* (1998) and *The Social Meaning of Mental Retardation* (1994). He has also written more than ninety articles.

# Contents

# Illustrations

**Panoramics**

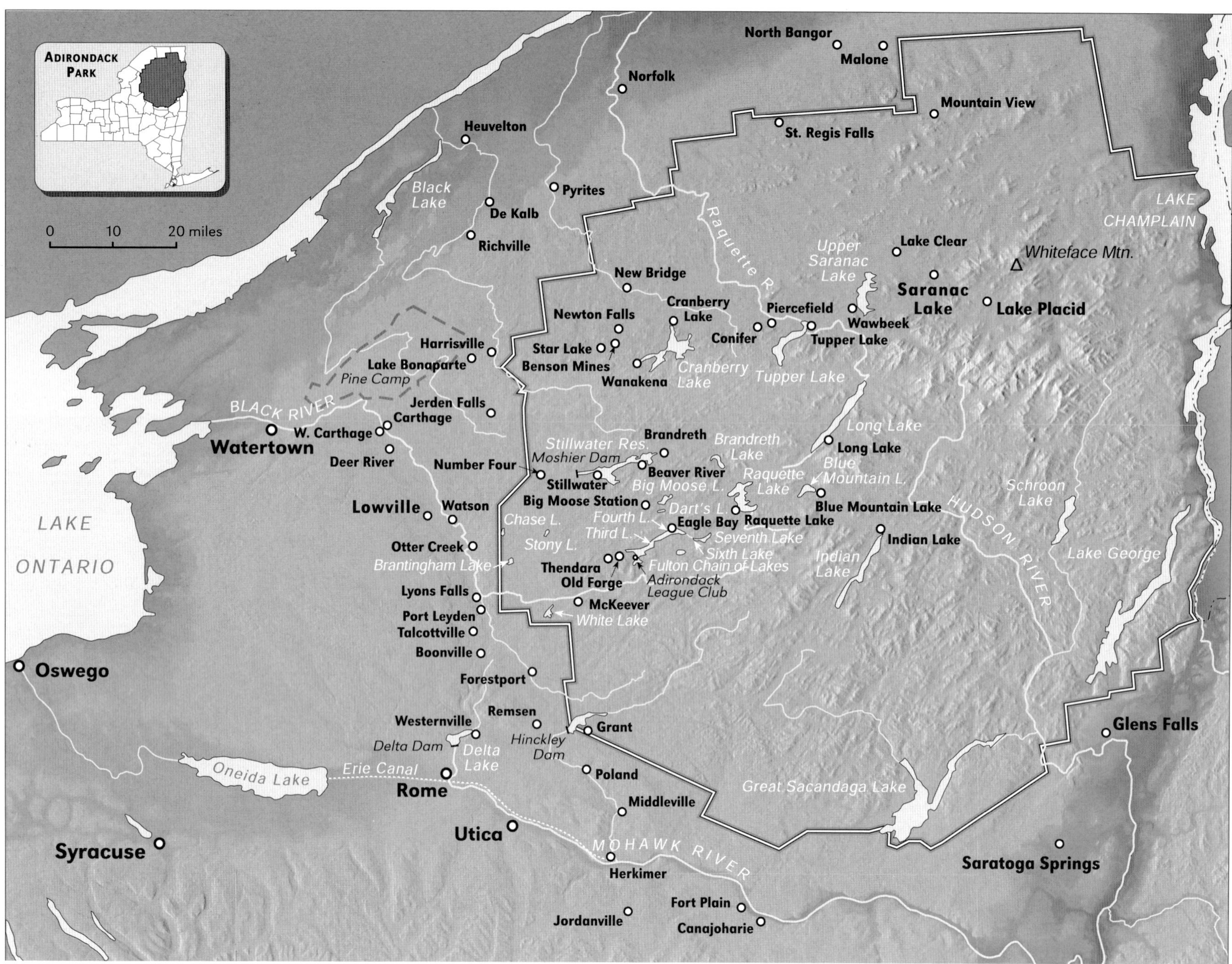

Adirondack Park
0
10
20 miles
North Bangor
Malone
Norfolk
Mountain View
St. Regis Falls
Heuvelton
Pyrites
Black Lake
De Kalb
Richville
Raquette R.
Lake Champlain
Upper Saranac Lake
Lake Clear
Whiteface Mtn.
Saranac Lake
Lake Placid
New Bridge
Cranberry Lake
Piercefield
Wawbeek
Newton Falls
Conifer
Tupper Lake
Harrisville
Star Lake
Benson Mines
Lake Bonaparte
Wanakena
Cranberry Lake
Tupper Lake
Pine Camp
Jerden Falls
Black River
Carthage
W. Carthage
Watertown
Deer River
Number Four
Long Lake
Long Lake
Brandreth
Brandreth Lake
Stillwater Res.
Moshier Dam
Beaver River
Raquette Lake
Blue Mountain L.
Stillwater
Big Moose L.
Big Moose Station
Dart's L.
Blue Mountain Lake
Schroon Lake
Lowville
Watson
Fourth L.
Eagle Bay
Raquette Lake
Hudson River
Lake Ontario
Chase L.
Third L.
Seventh Lake
Indian Lake
Stony L.
Sixth Lake
Indian Lake
Lake George
Otter Creek
Brantingham Lake
Thendara
Fulton Chain of Lakes
Old Forge
Adirondack League Club
Lyons Falls
McKeever
Port Leyden
White Lake
Talcottville
Boonville
Oswego
Forestport
Remsen
Westernville
Hinckley Dam
Grant
Glens Falls
Delta Dam
Delta Lake
Oneida Lake
Erie Canal
Poland
Rome
Great Sacandaga Lake
Middleville
Utica
Syracuse
Mohawk River
Herkimer
Saratoga Springs
Fort Plain
Jordanville
Canajoharie

# Preface
## Tracking Henry

This is the first book to present the work of Henry M. Beach (1863–1943), a prolific, talented, and creative commercial photographer from rural northern New York State. Beach was born, lived, and practiced his craft in and on the edge of the Adirondack region of New York. Although he occasionally photographed other sections of the state, most notably Albany and the southern tier, the North Country was where he focused his lens. I concentrate on that work.

I use the terms *North Country, North Woods,* the *Adirondacks,* and the *Adirondack region* interchangeably, consistent with my broader definition of the Adirondacks that extends the region's boundaries beyond the confines of the Blue Line (the demarcation on New York maps of Adirondack Park) and includes contiguous towns and counties as well. My use is consistent with late-nineteenth and early-twentieth-century definitions and with common local usage. I use *central Adirondacks* to include the areas around the Fulton Chain, Big Moose, Beaver River, Raquette Lake, Blue Mountain Lake, and Long Lake.

Because postcards were central to Beach's photographic business, they dominate this book, but I do not exclude his other work. Most notable are his expansive panoramic photographs, some of which are more than forty inches long.

I studied many Beach photographs in order to write this book. In addition to examining the extensive collection at the Adirondack Museum, I poured over the holdings of dozens of collectors and dealers. I even accumulated a small Beach archive of my own. I do not know how many photographs Beach produced. I estimate that I have examined more than ten thousand different Beach images, and I am sure there are many more.

With so many and such a variety of Beach's work to choose from, on what basis did I pick the ones included here? I sought photographs that were aesthetically and in other ways interesting, clearly focused, and well printed: in other words, the best of Beach's work. I was also looking for a group of pictures that represented the range of Beach's subject matter, geographic area, and time period. Because he photographed most in the central and western areas of the Adirondack region, they are widely represented. Beach was most prolific and at his best during the period he lived in the town of Remsen (approximately 1906 through 1916). Therefore, I favored the photographs he took then. I chose a few pictures to include because even though they might not be as good visually as others, they were historically important. They are images that document something undocumented, or tell about an aspect of the region to which we have paid scant attention.

When I started this project, I was adamant that I would focus on Beach's work, not his biography or on the history of the region. As I proceeded, though, it became difficult for me to separate his work from his life and from the region. Finding the proper balance between the person and his or her work is a challenge to anyone producing a book on an accomplished photographer's work. It is especially so with Beach because he was so closely tied to the land and the people he photographed. Thus, in addition to a chapter on his life, I refer to his biography and related matters throughout the discussion of his photographs.

*Adirondack Vernacular* is the result of my collaboration with many people from a range of backgrounds and with a variety of interests. Some are the same people who helped me with *Exposing the Wilderness.* They feel like old friends now, and the relationships I have developed through these Adirondack projects have been the most gratifying part of this work.

George Davis has remained steadfast with his historical curiosity and support. He has shared his collection of Adirondack photographs with me as well as the excitement of the chase as we looked for new information on Beach's life. It is George who kept encouraging me to go back to Lowville in pursuit of the missing history of local photographers. George's father was the principal of Lowville Academy when Beach was still a commercial photographer. One year, when George was very young, he sat on his father's lap when Beach took the annual school picture. George was too young to remember the event or to describe the photographer in action. Although George has no personal recollections of Beach, he was able to direct me to a few people in the Lowville area who do. I am grateful to him and them for their help. Clayton and Bertha Bailey kindly continued being helpful in sharing their knowledge of the Beach family and information and photographs from the Beach Family Papers.

Besides letting me borrow images and searching through their collections, dealers and collectors of Beach photo postcards have assisted me in a variety of ways. They have given information and insights that can be derived only from careful study and devotion to the objects they pursue: postcards. Ed Biederbecke has repeatedly shared his vast knowledge, insights, and images. Tom Gates has gone out of his way to find information and share his collection with me. Others who helped in a multitude of ways include: Mary Teal, Wanda Martin, Derwin "Doc" Jones, Holly Slusarczyk, B. J. Slusarczyk, Frank Carey, Gerv Hartle, Susan Smeby, Larry and Mary Myers, Ruth Jones, Ted Comstock, Jim Keebler, Bill Scheffler, Ida Winter, Jose Rodriguez, Dorothy King, Fred Rollins, Evelyn and Melville Edwards, Ken Seeber, Ed Fynmore, Hank Burhans, Bunnie Moses, Brenda and David Jones, Jonathan Holstein, Ed Pierce, George J. Getman, James Spring, David Pierce, Sandy Drake, Peter Clark, Jim Pitcher, Terry Perkins, Andreas Brown, Ray Hanlon, Morgan Williams, Brenda Jones, and Charlie Kiefer. Donald Chapman, a person with extensive knowledge of the history of the automobile, helped by dating some cards.

A special thanks to Ted Comstock, Peg Hanousek, Richard Loder, Tom Gates, Doug Biklen, and Janet Bogdan, who read an earlier draft and commented as editors and critics. As might be expected, although in most cases I agreed with their suggestions and made appropriate changes, I did not always follow their thoughtful advice. The inadequacies in the manuscript lie with the author.

Employees and volunteers at various libraries, historical associations, and museums as well as local historians have been generous with their time and knowledge. They include: Peg Masters of the Town of Webb Historical Association; Lisa Becker of the Lewis County Historical Society; Fred Rollins of the Jefferson County Historical Society; James Neville of the Fort Drum Historical Collection; Sandra Cronkhite, Village of Fort Plain; Laura M. Prievo, village historian, Carthage; Dave Manclow, Fort Plain; Mary J. Centro, Westernville; Sister Monica, Ursuline Convent, Malone; Mia Fineman and Jeff Rosenheim, Department of Photography, Metropolitan Museum of Art; and Todd Gustavson, George Eastman House, Rochester.

For their extensive help on numerous occasions, I owe a special note of thanks to the people at the Adirondack Museum, most notable Jerry Pepper, Jane MacKintosh, Caroline Welsh, and Jim Meehan. I am especially grateful to Jim for his help and foresight. Early in his tenure at the museum he realized the importance of Beach's work. He devoted much thought and labor into preserving and organizing the Beach holdings. His index of that collection was invaluable to me and will be a necessary resource for anyone who wants to understand the scope of Henry Beach's work.

People I have come to know through this project are not the only ones to whom I am grateful. I have another group of supporters closer to home that includes my family, friends, and members of the Syracuse University community. Thank you, Diana Biro, John Palmer, Gary Spencer, David Tatham, Sari Knopp Biklen, Doug Biklen, Jerry Grant, Dixie Carlisle, Aimee Delman, Ben Ware, Mary Olszewski, Diane Swords, Stephanie Schreven, and Janet Bogdan.

David Broda of the Photo and Imaging Center at Syracuse University shared his extensive knowledge of photographic history and processing with me. He has helped me on a number of projects, and I have been blessed having him as part of my university community.

Special thanks go to Bill Scheffler and Ann Sheffer for financial support for this project.

# Abbreviations

| | |
|---|---|
| Adirondack Museum | Adirondack Museum Photographic Collection, Blue Mountain Lake, N.Y. |
| ALC Coll. | Adirondack League Club Collection, Old Forge, N.Y. |
| Author's Coll. | Robert Bogdan Collection, Syracuse, N.Y. |
| Bailey Coll. | Bertha (Beach) Bailey Collection, North Western, N.Y. |
| B. J. Slusarczyk | B. J. Slusarczyk Collection, Remsen, N.Y. |
| Burhans Coll. | Henry Burhans Collection, Los Corrales, N.M. |
| Carey Coll. | Frank Carey Collection, Califon, N.J. |
| Comstock Coll. | Edward Comstock Jr. Collection, Old Forge, N.Y. |
| D. Jones Coll. | Derwin "Doc" Jones Collection, Phoenix, N.Y. |
| D. Pierce Coll. | David P. Pierce Collection, Carthage, N.Y. |
| Davis Coll. | George Davis Collection, Lowville, N.Y. |
| E. Pierce Coll. | Ed Pierce Collection, Brewerton, N.Y. |
| G. Jones Coll. | Gaylord Jones Collection, Remsen, N.Y. |
| Gates Coll. | Thomas A. Gates Collection, Barneveld, N.Y. |
| Getman Coll. | George J. Getman Collection, Manlius, N.Y. |
| H. Slusarczyk Coll. | Holly M. Slusarczyk Collection, Remsen, N.Y. |
| Holstein Coll. | Jonathan Holstein Collection, Cazenovia, N.Y. |
| Keebler Coll. | Jim Keebler Collection, Pittsford, N.Y. |
| Martin Coll. | Martin Collection, Big Moose Lake, N.Y. |
| Myers Coll. | Larry and Mary Myers Collection, Boonville, N.Y. |
| Rollins Coll. | Fred H. Rollins Collection, Watertown, N.Y. |
| Scheffler Coll. | William Scheffler Collection, Westport, Conn. |
| Seeber Coll. | Dr. Kenneth Seeber Collection, Lowville, N.Y. |
| Smeby Coll. | Susan Smeby Collection, Potsdam, N.Y. |
| Spring Coll. | James Spring Collection, Schenectady, N.Y. |
| Teal Coll. | Mary Teal Collection, Lyons Falls, N.Y. |
| Winter Coll. | Ida Ainsworth Winter Collection, Big Moose, N.Y. |

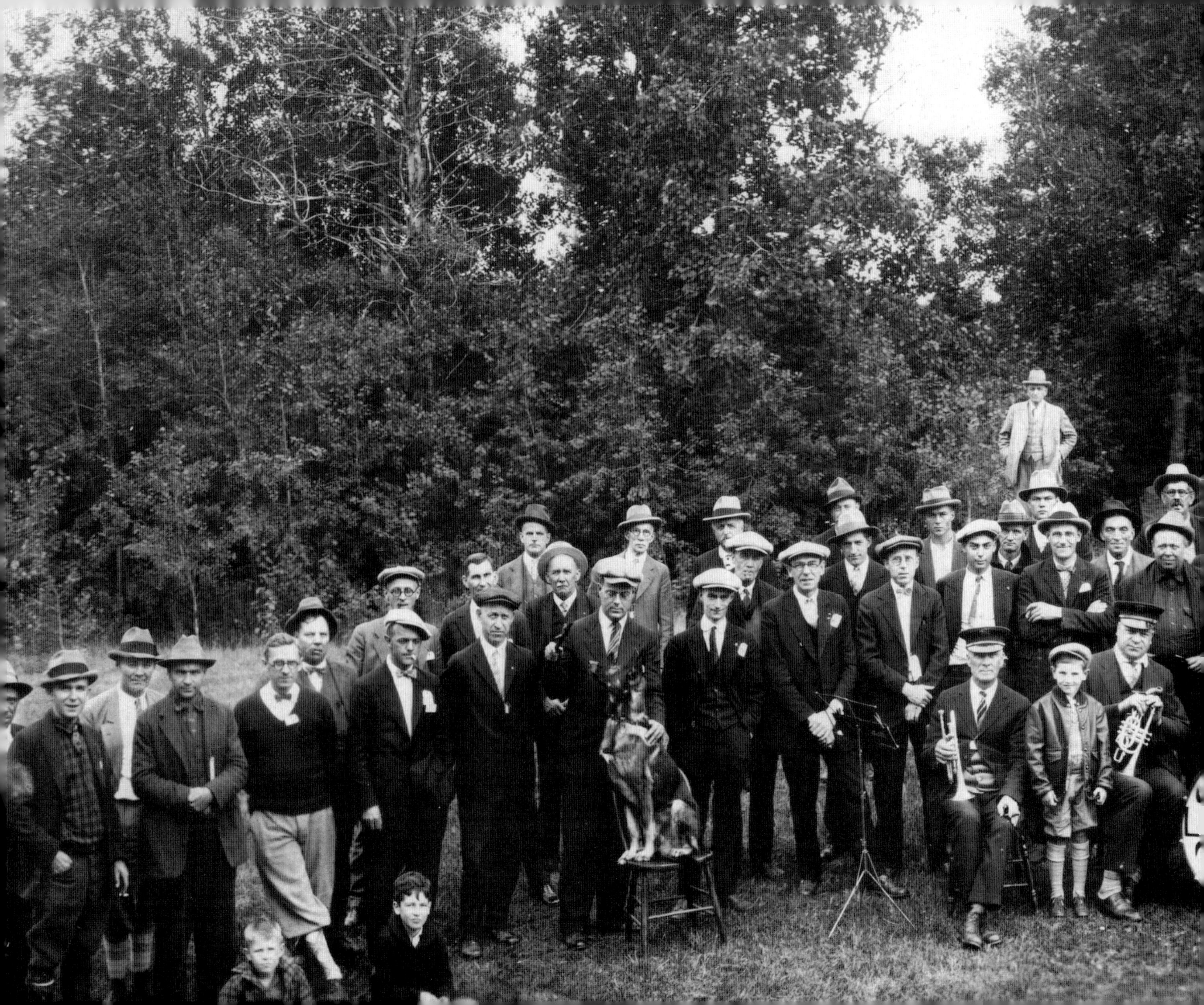

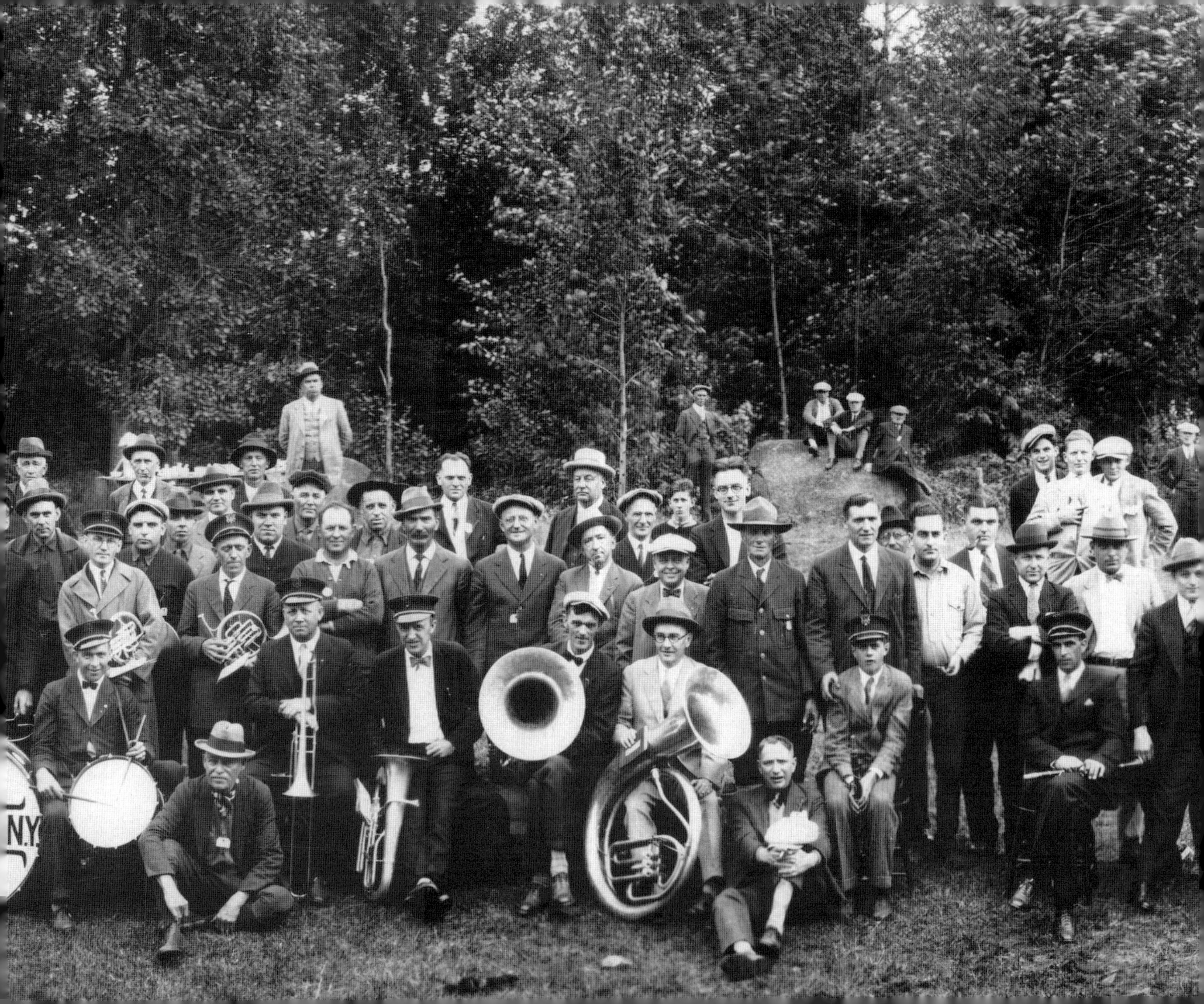

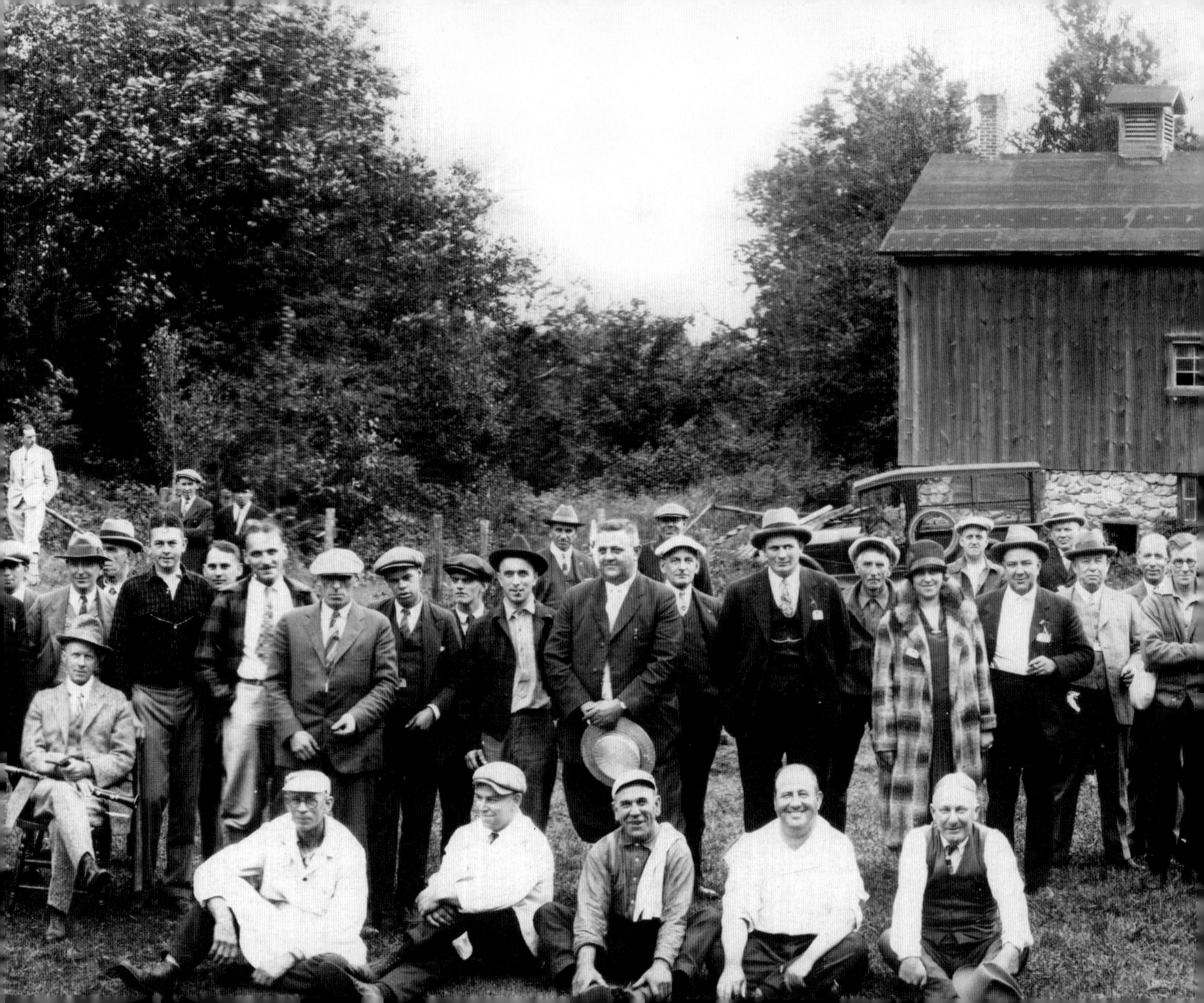

# PART ONE Time, Place, and Format

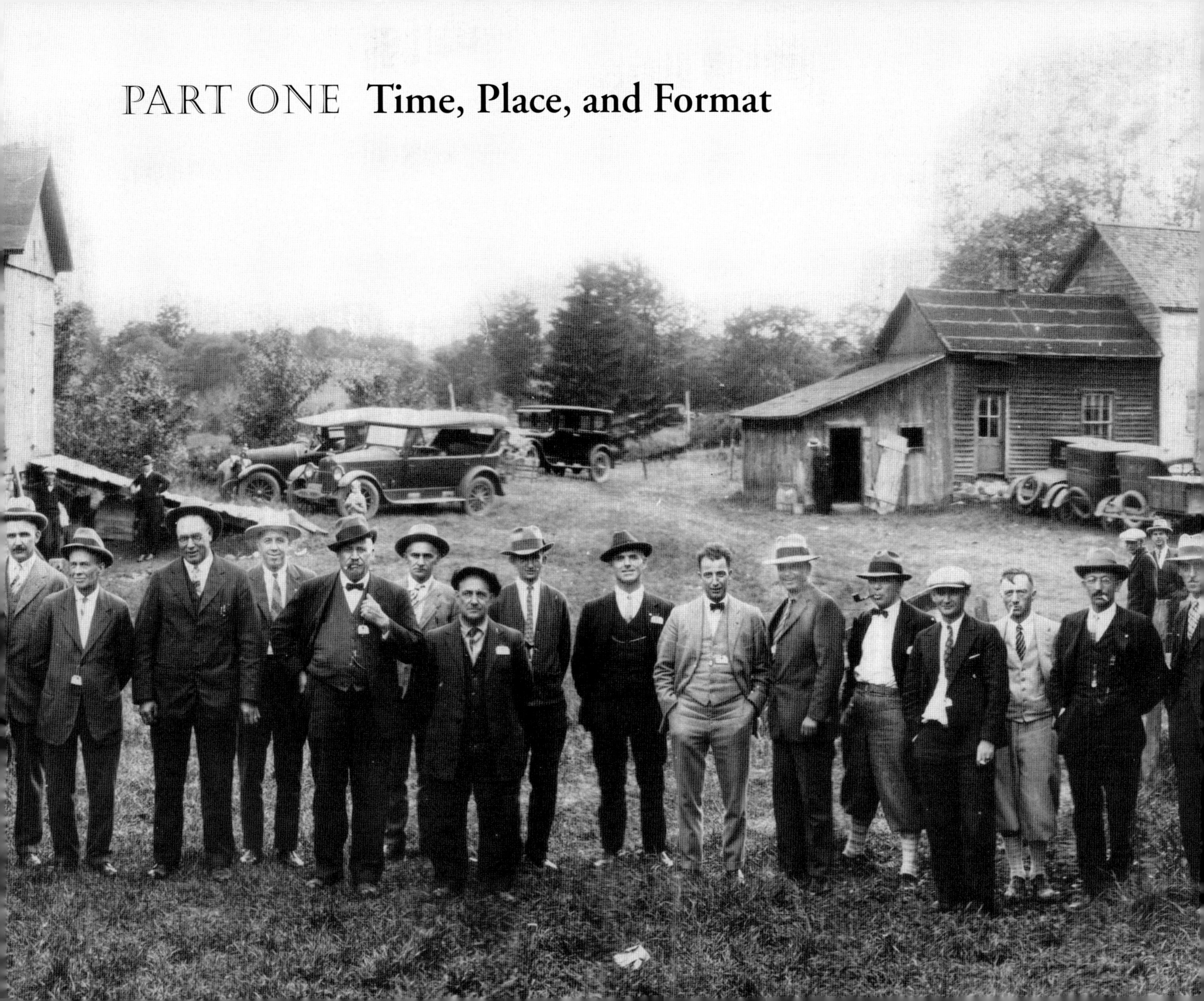

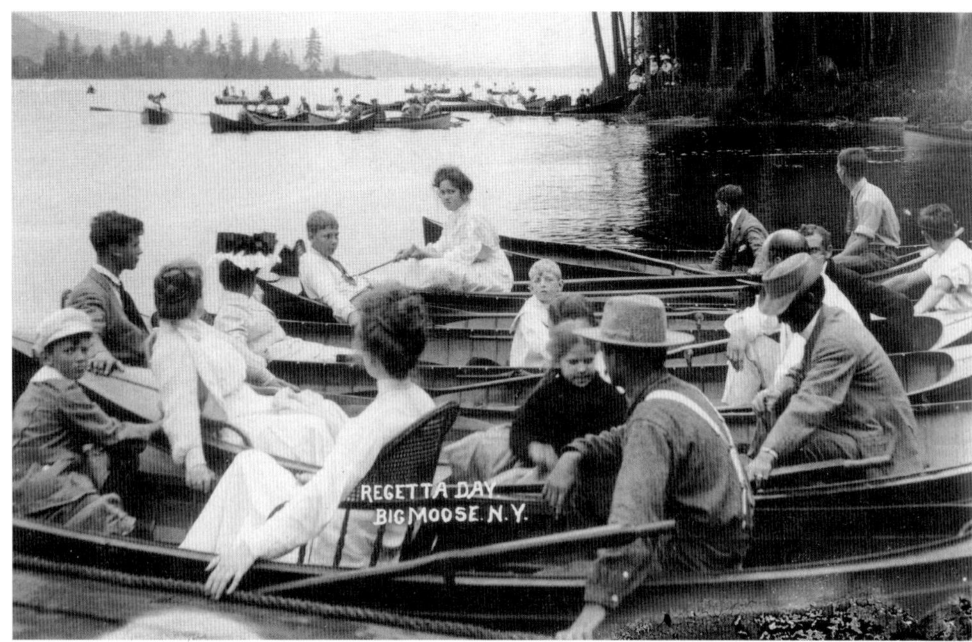


1.1. Regatta day, Big Moose, N.Y., ca. 1908. Courtesy of the Adirondack Museum.

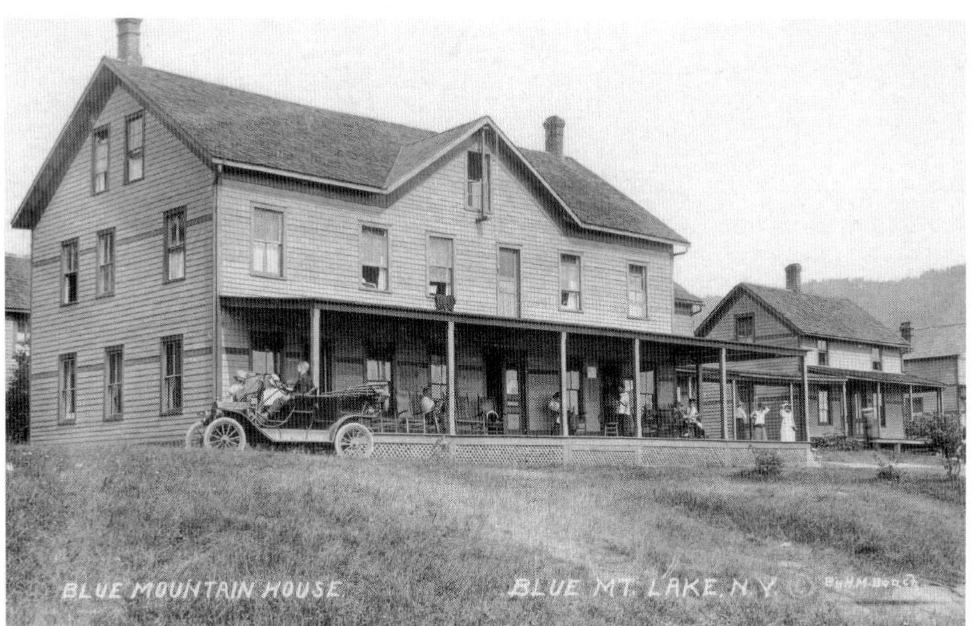


1.2. Blue Mountain House, Blue Mountain Lake, N.Y., ca. 1912. This location is the present site of the Adirondack Museum. Davis Coll.

1

# Introduction
## Did You Take That Picture, Henry?

Blue Mountain Lake is in the heart of New York's North Woods and the home of the Adirondack Museum. That facility is a treasure trove of regional relics, and it showcases engaging displays that make the area's past come alive. The antique boat exhibit is always a hit with visitors. On one wall, in a prominent place, hangs a three-by-five-foot enlargement of a 1908 photograph with the imprinted caption "Regetta [*sic*] Day, Big Moose Lake, N.Y." (illus. 1.1).[1] This sharp, well-composed image captures the ambience of the exhibit and provides a glimpse of what was happening on that summer day almost a century ago. Although there is no inscription that tells who took the picture, Henry M. Beach (1863–1943) was the photographer.[2]

Many Adirondack aficionados have admired Beach's images without knowing whose work it is. Only regional experts who specialize in such matters and ardent postcard collectors know the extent, superior quality, and uniqueness of Beach's photography. Henry M. Beach, like many small-time local image makers of the first third of the twentieth century, is a forgotten contributor to the region's past. Dismissed simply as local commercial photographers, Beach and his ilk are neglected in the history of photography as well. My hope is to rectify this oversight by telling you about Beach and his work, and I also want to please you with his pictures.

1. The picture is a blown-up version of what was originally meant to be a postcard-size print. Of course, *regatta* is the proper spelling.

2. All the illustrations in this book, except the ones that are noted otherwise, are by Henry M. Beach. The regatta photo comes from the Beach Collection at the Adirondack Museum.

Henry Beach grew up in Watson, approximately thirty miles from Big Moose Lake whose shoreline he walked many times. He probably knew the folks in his regatta picture. Blue Mountain was part of his rounds too, so he stood on the very spot where his regatta picture now hangs (illus. 1.2). But that time was long ago, long before there was a museum or, for that matter, campgrounds, motels, electricity, and many more of the conveniences that people who flock to the area now take for granted. Beach produced his images at a time when it was normal for people to attach themselves to an occupation such as photography and perfect their skills over time. He and others like him devoted their lives to making a living creating useful and occasionally beautiful products that became a meaningful part of ordinary people's everyday lives.

We can only guess what Henry might think of the new, imposing rustic-style Adirondack building (Gilborn 2000; O'Leary 1998) that serves as the entrance and gift shop to the Adirondack Museum. How would he react to the multilevel garage that affords parking space for the hundreds of visitors' cars there on a summer day? And what would he think about seeing his photograph displayed?

In many ways Henry was ahead of his time. He embraced new technology and incorporated it into his photography. Beach was enthralled with the changing face of the North Country and eager to capture the arrival of the commercialism of the modern twentieth century that was heralded by the invasion of the automobile. Perhaps he would applaud the proliferation of commerce and the wave of upscale "camp" construction made affordable by profits from the high-tech expansion of the U.S. economy. But Beach was a product of nineteenth-century rural life. He was grounded in skepticism about the benefits of urban living and trendsetting innovations and styles. Although he welcomed the tourists and produced thousands of postcards and other photographs to sell to them, his ties and ideas were local. Beach loved the mobility that went along with owning a car and loved fussing with his complex panoramic cameras, but he clung to an older, simpler Adirondacks. He was grounded in the great upstate forests his grandfather found when he arrived in the area in the early nineteenth century. After all, Henry was only a generation removed from an Adirondacks of crudely built cabins where the forest loomed larger than people did.

Copies of many of Henry Beach's photos are displayed at the museum as embellishments to exhibits depicting early life in the region. Thousands of his images reside in their archives, and private collectors hold many more. The variety and number are overwhelming, exceeding the work of any of his contemporaries.[3]

## Henry M. Beach and Seneca Ray Stoddard

Mention "Adirondack photographer" to anyone familiar with the history of the North Country, and the name Seneca Ray Stoddard (1843–1917) will be the immediate response (Adler 1997; Crowley 1982; DeSormo 1972; Horrell 1999). Stoddard was born in 1843 in Wilton, which lies between Saratoga Springs and Glens Falls, New York, on the eastern edge of what is now the Adirondack Park. Using his studio at Glens Falls as his base, Stoddard extensively photographed the Adirondack region until his death in 1917. A number of Stoddard's nineteenth-century views are icons, symbols of the early days in the Adirondacks (Adler 1997), a time that many area enthusiasts hold on to as the golden years. Stoddard himself is an Adirondack standard. His fame as a nineteenth-century landscape photographer transcends the region. Stoddard's images are on the walls of the Adirondack Museum too, but unlike Beach's they are celebrated and always have proper attribution.

3. His career spanned fifty years, much longer than most photographers. The nature of his business required that he produce in volume. The Eastern Illustrating Company rivals Beach in the number of postcard images they produced (Bogdan 1999).

There are some similarities between Beach and Stoddard. Both were prolific, and, although each preferred to photograph close to their homes, Stoddard in the eastern part of the Adirondacks and Beach in the western, each traversed the North Woods and beyond, producing pictures that cover a wide area. Photography was their craft, but they were also businesspeople, entrepreneurs who made a living selling their photographs to the mass consumer market.[4]

There were also important differences between the two. Stoddard was widely recognized and highly regarded by the wealthy and influential, whereas Beach did not know people outside his immediate business contacts, neighbors, and family. Seneca Ray chased fame and moved comfortably among the wealthy and well educated. Henry shirked attention and avoided social situations; he was most comfortable among common people. Seneca Ray regularly talked

4. My discussion of the differences between the two men is not exhaustive. There were other similarities; for example, both men were inventors who dabbled with photographic technology.

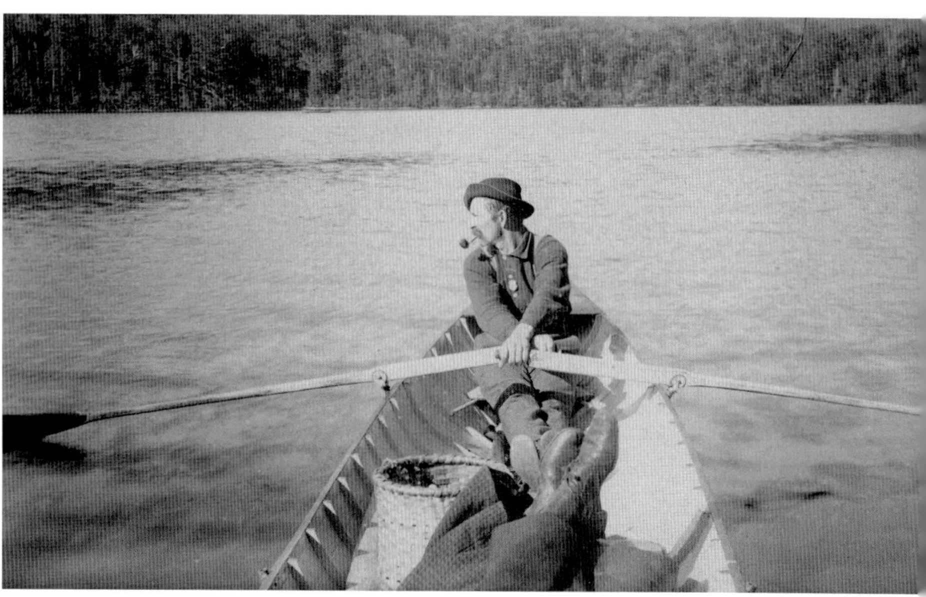

1.3. Although there is no caption on the photo itself, Stoddard's title was: "The Way It Looks from the Stern Seat," ca. 1885. Courtesy of the Adirondack Museum.

with practicing artists and intellectuals. Beach was isolated from such influences. Stoddard was well read and a published author. Although Beach loved to read, he had no literary talent, and, as the "regetta" photo illustrates, he struggled to spell the captions on his postcards correctly. In short, although he was far from being part of the elite art world of New York City, compared to Beach, Stoddard was cosmopolitan. Compared to Stoddard, Henry was a country bumpkin.[5] Although Beach had an ambitious photographic agenda and sold many photographs, he never rose above his rural origins or strayed too far from his home area of Watson in Lewis County, New York.

Essential to understanding the differences between the two men's work is that Beach was twenty years younger and died twenty-five years after Stoddard. Stoddard's best work was done in the last third of the nineteenth century, before the automobile and before a host of other changes that transformed the Adirondacks from a relatively isolated region that served as a retreat for the rich and the upper middle class to a tourist mecca for a wider range of people, including ones of modest means. Beach's significant images were produced in the first third of the twentieth century, during the coming of the automobile. He recorded the old Adirondacks, its transition, as well as the posthighway North Country.[6]

Emblematic of the differences in the subject matter of the two photographers are illustrations 1.3 and 1.4. The first is Stoddard's well-known "The Way It Looks from the Stern Seat." It shows a guide rowing an Adirondack guide boat. The second, by Beach (and never published before), is also of a man in a boat, but here the boat is powered by an internal combustion engine (Bond 1995). It is titled "The Motor Boat."

In keeping with the photo technology and fashion of his time, each photographer produced in different formats. Stoddard specialized in stereographic cards as well as large stiff board-mounted views. He also gave public lectures illustrated with magic-lantern slide shows of his own images. When postcards emerged as a favored format Stoddard was in his declining years and did not

5. Stoddard served on government survey projects and worked for railroad companies. A public speaker of some repute, he was an active promoter of the Adirondack region. In 1891 he presented his popular "Adirondacks Illustrated" lantern-slide lecture to the state legislature in support of establishing the Adirondack Park.

6. There is also a good deal of overlap in the subject matter of their photographs.

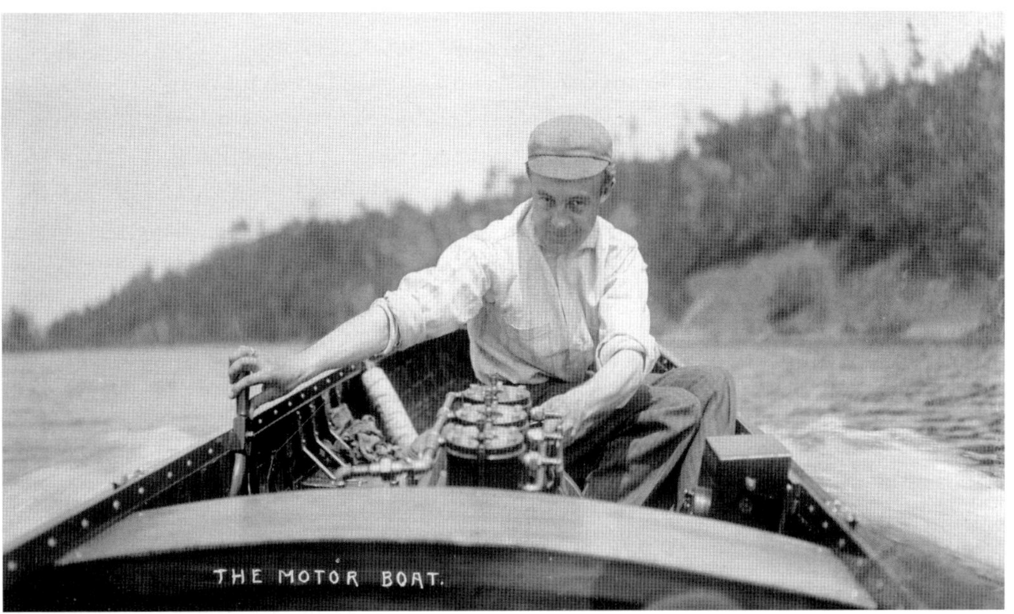


1.4. Motorboat, ca. 1912. Courtesy of the Adirondack Museum.

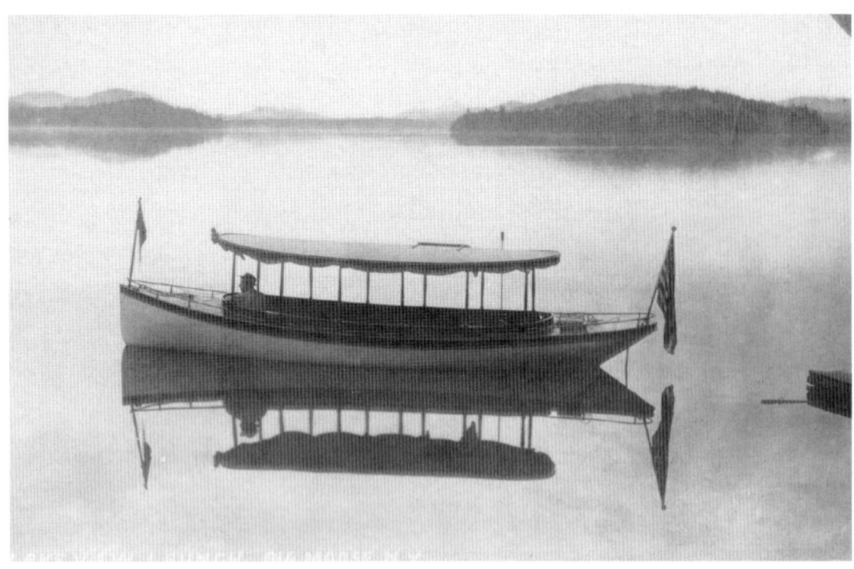

1.5. Lake View launch, Big Moose, N.Y., ca. 1913. Comstock Coll.

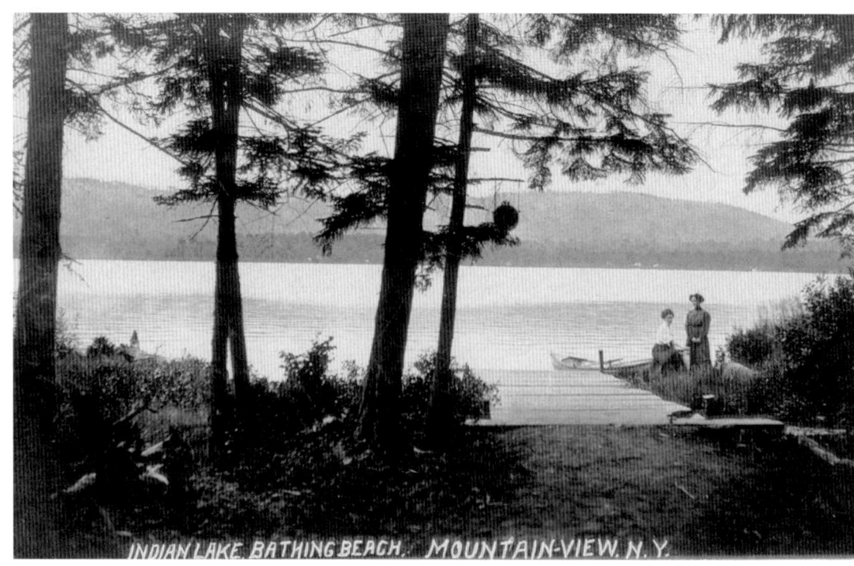


1.6. Indian Lake bathing beach, Mountain View, N.Y., ca. 1914. H. Slusarczyk Coll.

make the transition into the new postcard market. He manufactured a few printed postcards, but they are either poor-quality reprints of earlier work or uninteresting scenic views. Although Beach practiced studio photography earlier in his life, took a stereo card or two, and did some large-format outdoor groups and scenes, he specialized in postcard and panoramic photography.

In comparing the work of the two men we need to pay attention to how changes in the mechanical and chemical processes involved in taking pictures affected the images produced. Between 1870, when Stoddard began producing in earnest, and 1905, when Beach's postcard business took off, all aspects of photo production from camera technology and plate production to the chemicals and paper used changed. Some differences between the two men's work—how and whether subjects were posed, tones and visual effects, contrast between various parts of the picture—are a function of the technology involved.

Comparing their photographs we see some similarities, but their styles and subject matter were basically different. Stoddard's approach to image making was to create artlike representations, pretty pictures that emphasize the creation of the mood of the setting rather than capture its details. Authors link him with the Hudson River school of landscape painting and "luminism" (Adler 1997; Horrell 1999; Naef 1980), a style concerned with the "textures of nature and the poetic effects of light and atmosphere" (Adler 1997, 21). Typical of writers who review Stoddard, Adler, who is his leading biographer, describes his work as "converting real places into little glimpses of heaven" and as investing people and objects with "a special and partly spiritual meaning" (28).

Given what I have said about Beach and his down-home country ways, Adler's art-conscious description of Stoddard's work may sound like the antithesis of the type of photographs you would expect from Henry. Overall that depiction is true, but some of Beach's photographs do have qualities that resemble Stoddard's beautiful pictures. Beach's fondness for reflections in lakes and dark foregrounds against sky and water will remind you of Stoddard photos (illus. 1.5, 1.6).

But Henry did not emulate any particular style, especially any approach associated with a sophisticated art scene. That assertion does not mean he did not have an approach to photography that can be recognized in his work. Early in the century he abandoned his formally posed studio-photographer approach

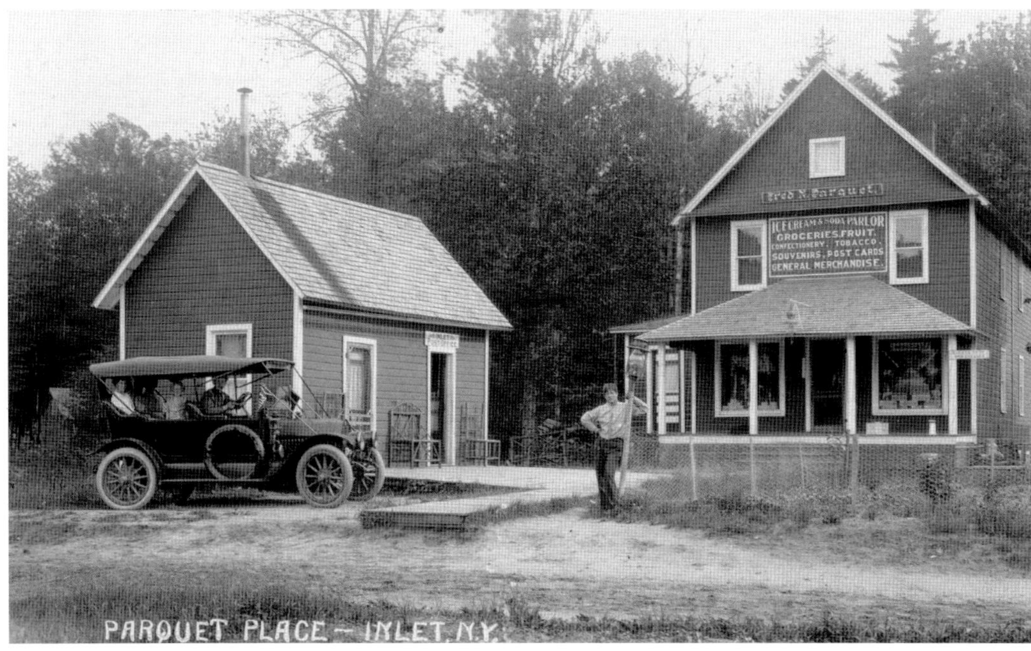


1.7. Parquet Store, Inlet, N.Y., ca. 1914. Martin Coll.

and experimented with a range of subject matters and modes. His images evolved into a vernacular documentary style: plain pictures, clearly focused, with extensive detail that clearly aimed to capture the location or what was going on (Galassi 1995). He was not trying to produce someone else's version of art.[7] In addition, compared to Stoddard, Henry's work is more unpredictable and eccentric. This point is true not only in his outlandish montage work but in his other pictures as well. They contain quirky elements that are distinctively Beach (illus. 1.7, 1.8). For example, if you look carefully at illustration 1.4, you can see that he touched up that photograph to add a more pronounced wake.

Arguing whether Stoddard's work is superior to Beach's or vice versa is not the point here. To a large extent it is a matter of taste and how you like the Adirondacks represented. In my way of thinking, Henry M. Beach's work is as important to the twentieth-century Adirondacks as Seneca Ray Stoddard's is to the nineteenth century. Each photographer's style best suits the era they photographed, and both are exemplars of the approach they practiced.

## Why Has Beach Been Slighted?

If Beach was so prolific and his photographs so good, why isn't he famous? Part of the answer lies in the format of the photographs he produced. Another is the time in which he worked.

Postcards and panoramics were immensely popular during the first quarter of the century. A nickel apiece and cheaper when you bought postcards by volume and a dollar and less for huge panoramics, Beach and other photographers produced as many as the market would take. Their pictures were so commonplace that they were not taken seriously, especially in exclusive art-world circles where one-of-a-kind and limited editions ruled (Becker 1982). In addition, some people dismissed work like Beach's as consumer-driven, routine com-

7. By studying the original print of illustration 1.7 for details you can see the Wrigley Spearmint window display, as well as the sign on the top of the store: "Fred N. Parquet." Underneath is a list of the items carried, including postcards. To the right of the store there is a sign: "Barbershop Downstairs." On an open porch of the building on the left are rustic-style chairs flanking a door with a sign over it that says "Inlet Post Office."

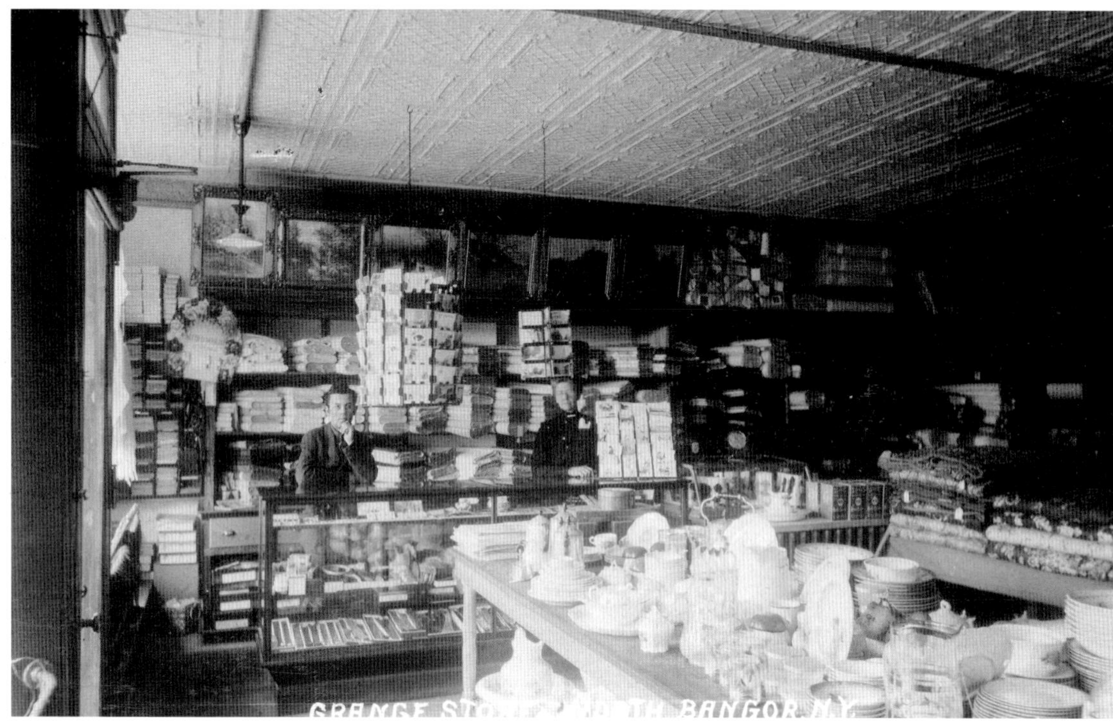


1.8. Grange Store, North Bangor, N.Y., ca. 1912. Note the postcard racks on the counter in the back of the store. Courtesy of the Adirondack Museum.

mercial products rather than expressions of artistic vision. The postcard's and panoramic photograph's status as being for artistically low-class clientele lingers today (Blake and Lasansky 1996).

Other factors besides snobbery have to be taken into account in understanding why Beach remains unknown. Beach and others like him could shoot, develop, and print fastidiously, resulting in images of the finest quality. Given the low prices their work brought, being too careful undermined profit. They needed to turn the work out. Quality suffered. Beach and other commercial photographers' best work may have been terrific, but much of it is humdrum and technically below refined standards.

The unassuming formats and uses of postcards and panoramics also contribute to their lack of respect. Postcards are small and inconspicuous, easily stacked or stored in albums or shoe boxes. It is difficult to put them on public exhibit. Although many were bought to keep, message writers and postal workers mutilated most of them. The clumsy panoramics were often rolled up and stored out of sight, or framed and hung as souvenirs until people grew tired of them and retired them to basements and attics. Both the postcard and the panoramic were considered personal mementos—definitely not art.

Commercial photographers of Beach's generation engaged in other practices that undermined their status among the dignified. Unlike in earlier formats, they scrawled crude captions directly on the negatives, so they showed boldly on the prints. Photographers who aspired to be artists considered this convention defacement. The quality of the lettering often contributed to the low rank of the postcard. Even with the more accomplished letterers, one finds many misspellings, misshapen letters, and grammar mistakes. Beach's work provides many such examples.

Stoddard produced in cheap formats, too—after all, the stereo card was the nineteenth-century equivalent of the postcard. Why does Stoddard get all the attention? First, attention to Stoddard as a photographer is rather recent, and he would probably have been more revered if he had not been a commercial photographer. But when Stoddard was rediscovered in the 1960s his commercialism was forgiven (DeSormo 1972). Part of the reason he overcame the stigma was that he had traveled in higher circles and attracted a cadre of people who admired and promoted him as a central figure in the history of the Adirondacks. Furthermore, he was a nineteenth-century photographer. Practicing in that century distanced him from the taint of modern popular culture, which some associate with the decline of the Adirondacks. Likewise, many people prefer Stoddard's nineteenth-century romantic representations of the wilderness to Beach's more direct, unsentimental down-home rendering.

Although there are many reasons critics might ignore Beach's work, we live in an era of art appreciation where we are not as categorical about what is art and what is not. There is a new enthusiasm for the vernacular (Hambourg et al. 2000; Lesy 1997; Nickel 1998; Rosenheim 2000; Rosenheim and Eklund 2000), and many people question the exclusionary practices of some in the art establishment. Some aspects of Beach's work that may have undermined his reputation in the past may now enhance it. His crude captions, for example, do not have to be seen as a flaw in his work; rather, they are a quality of it. Such idiosyncracies give his images a folk quality that adds to their interest and brings us closer to what he was photographing.

## Significance

Henry's work is significant not just because of its volume and its value in documenting the region during an interesting time in its history. It is significant because his best work consists of wonderful photographs, images that stir the heart and provoke the imagination.

Although Beach's postcard pictures and other photographs were taken to sell in bulk to retailers who in turn sold them to the general public, they are not just mass-produced stylized, pretty pictures. Yes, some are of bubbling brooks and shady woodland paths, but he also photographed paper mills belching pollution and factory boomtowns. He photographed dandy visitors at play, but he also documented the manual laborers sweating in the forest, logging camps, factories, mines, and construction sites. Although he took some images of "great camps," his pictures of structures were most often of modest abodes, small stores, and family-owned resorts. He took pictures of trains in scenic surroundings as well as mangled wrecks after tragic railroad accidents. There are Bambi-like wildlife images as well as a plethora of pictures of hunters with their kills. In addition to standard-view cards he produced whimsical montages and advertisement postcards. He engaged in serious visual commentary as well as lighthearted picture play. Some of Beach's views reinforce the cliché "pretty as a picture," whereas others violate and contradict that line.

His panoramic photographs—many more than three feet long—expand the dimension of his contribution. The panoramic photograph's unique features and Beach's innovative use of them are worthy of attention. As you will see, Beach's panoramic views provide a detailed and captivating picture of Adirondack life available only through this format.

Henry was a local, an insider to the world he photographed, a person intimate with the region's people and geography. Beach was a common person with an uncommon talent. It was from that position that he photographed the Adirondacks. In addition to shooting as a local, he had little formal education and did not seem to be professionally trained in his craft. He lived far enough away from mainstream society that his work was not dominated by national photographic styles and trends, and was unencumbered by art-world pretense (Becker 1982). He was free to focus on different subject matters, add quirky elements to his pictures, experiment with form and composition, and do things with his images that other photographers would not. The result is a vernacular documentary style that is unique, engrossing, and significant.

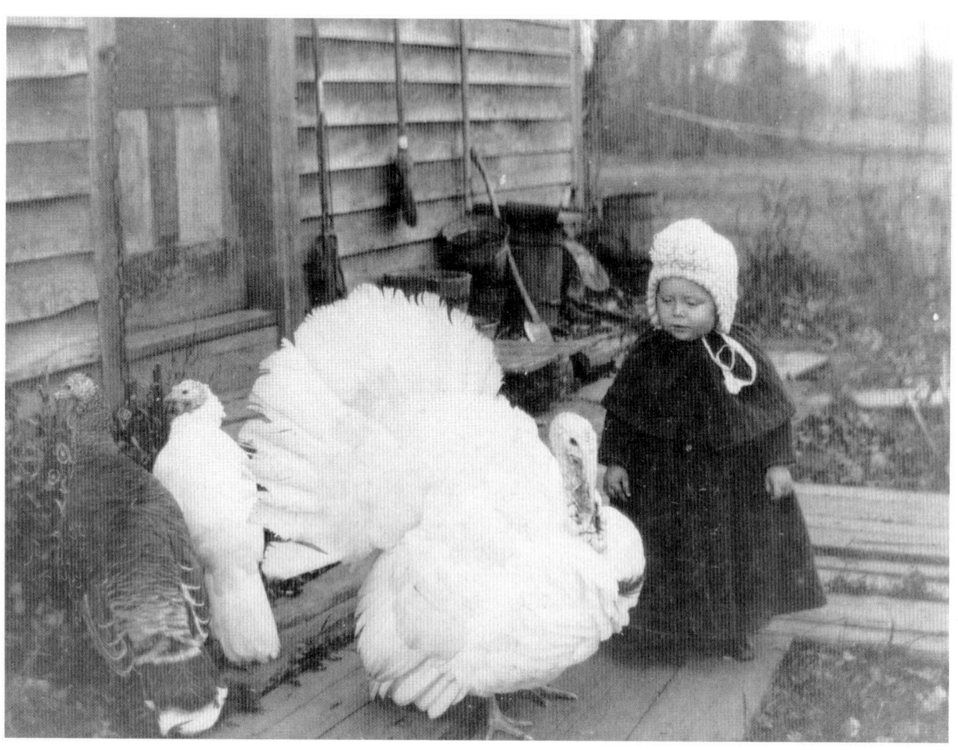

2.1. Henry's son Harry with turkeys, ca. 1892. Bailey Coll.

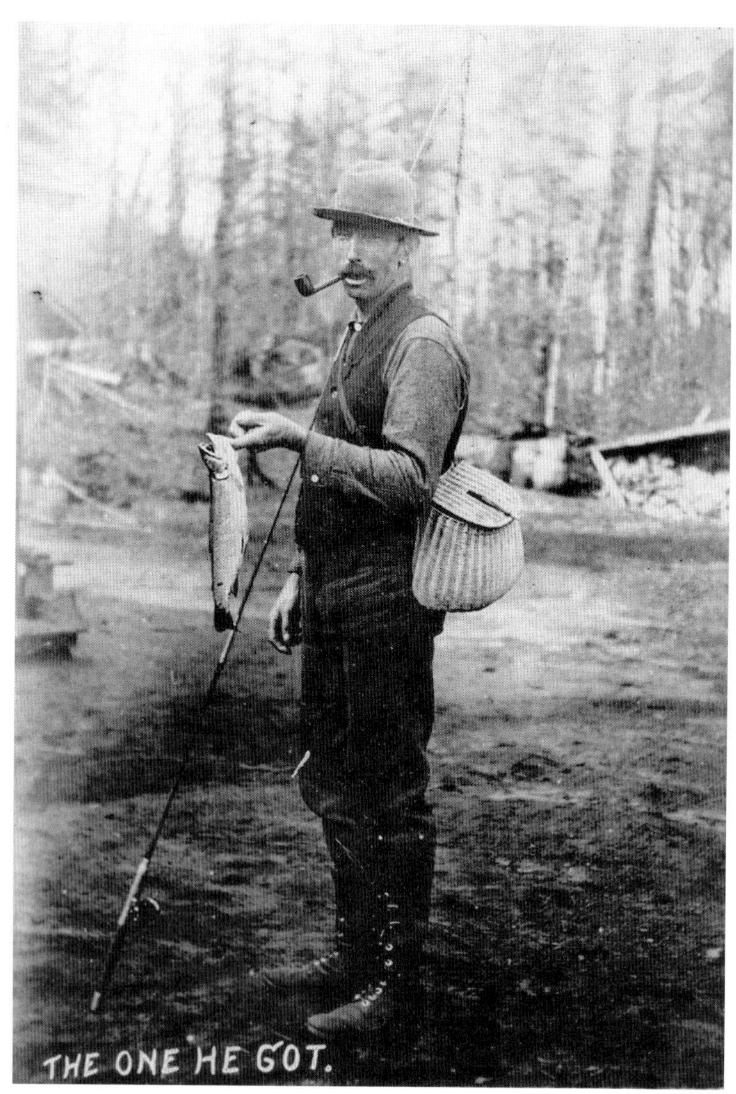


2.2. Self-portrait postcard of Henry M. Beach, ca. 1910. Getman Coll.

2

# Life and Times of Henry M. Beach

## Is That You, Henry?

Unlike "Regetta Day," illustration 2.1 by Henry Beach has never been on public display. The young child is Henry's firstborn son, Harry, and the picture was taken at the family home in the North Country around 1892. In addition to being an interesting example of his early handiwork, the photograph symbolizes how little we know about Beach's life and work.

Until recently, Beach was a puzzling figure without a past (Bogdan 1999). People who are usually well informed about such matters did not even know that Henry was his first name.[1] Beach is difficult to trace. When he was in his middle years he lived in two different communities where he had weak and short-lived ties. For this consequential period of his life he left few clues about his business and domestic affairs. In his declining years Henry withdrew from public life and returned to the place of his birth, a relatively isolated rural community. He died approximately sixty years ago, so people who knew him are either dead or find it difficult to recall their encounters with the man. No one did the primary research required to construct an in-depth biography when more information was available.

I spent months digging before I came up with the clues that would allow me to write even a brief account of his life and locate photographs such as the one of Harry and the turkeys (Bogdan 1999). I am still in pursuit of Henry. Here I share with you what I know about this gifted, subdued, and intriguing character (illus. 2.2).

1. I still do not know what the initial *M* in his name stands for!

### The Times

Henry M. Beach was born in 1863 when the Civil War was raging and Abraham Lincoln was president. Franklin Delano Roosevelt was in office and World War II was destroying Europe when Henry died in 1943. He lived a long life, seventy-nine years, and was a photographer all his working years.[2] Although he started taking pictures in the early 1880s, he did his most significant work, the work I celebrate here, during the twenty years between 1905 and 1925.

Beach's lifetime covered a period of tremendous change. He experienced the rise and fall in the popularity of the postcard and the panoramic photo, the formats that sustained him. These changes that occurred during his lifetime were minor, however. He was born in the horse-and-buggy days, before there were automobiles, paved highways, gasoline stations, motorboats, airplanes, indoor plumbing, electricity, telephones, phonographs, radios, or motion pictures. Over the most productive years of his career, all these innovations and more came to pass, altering the American landscape and transforming its citizens into a mass consumer society. With one foot in the nineteenth century and

2. The 1900 census enumerators' report gives 1863 as his birth date, which is also the date marked on his gravestone. The family genealogy gives his year of birth as 1862 (Beach 1923). His January 7, 1943, obituary in the *Lowville Journal and Republican* states that he was eighty at the time of his death. Using the 1863 date, he was seventy-nine, approaching his eightieth birthday when he died.

the other in the twentieth, and with his lens focused on New York's North County, he documented the old days as well as the new, the changes, and their consequences.

## The Automobile Arrives

Beginning around 1906, just about the time that Beach became a postcard photographer in earnest, the first automobiles began traversing the Adirondack region of New York State (Hochschild 1962b, 99) (illus. 2.3). The arrival of the automobile is a momentous benchmark in the history of the North Country (White 1985, 230). Before the turn of the century, in addition to permanent residents scattered in modest hamlets and loggers working in the forest, the Adirondacks had been largely the domain of the wealthy camp owners and people who could afford long hotel vacations. Part of the nineteenth-century lure of the North Woods had been its inaccessibility. As trains and steamers improved access, tourists and summer people of more modest means began visiting in large numbers. The automobile accelerated that trend, bringing more transients with less money to spend who sought a different kind of Adirondack experience from earlier visitors. By 1915, the roads were being improved, and some had even begun to be paved. General stores and liveries were selling gasoline and catering to tourists. Filling stations and service stations began appearing (Margolies 1993). By the early 1930s, the time when Beach was leaving commercial photography, there was an extensive system of good roads, public and private campsites, tourist homes and cabins, hamburger stands, ski resorts, and a host of other roadside accommodations, services, eateries, and amusements.

Automobiles changed the lives of year-round residents in ways that were not just tied to the tourist trade. Having a car meant you could travel into town to shop rather than be completely dependent on the hamlet general store. With the advent of the internal combustion engine, logging operations changed radically. For example, loggers' camps became less important and then obsolete when workers could commute to harvest sites (Bethke 1981). The legendary river drives transporting logs to mills via rushing waterways declined and were then eliminated as alterative means of transport became available (McMartin 1994). Small lumber companies were bought by larger operations as the processing of logs at mills became increasingly mechanized. Many other industrial and commercial activities were altered fundamentally by the new technologies.

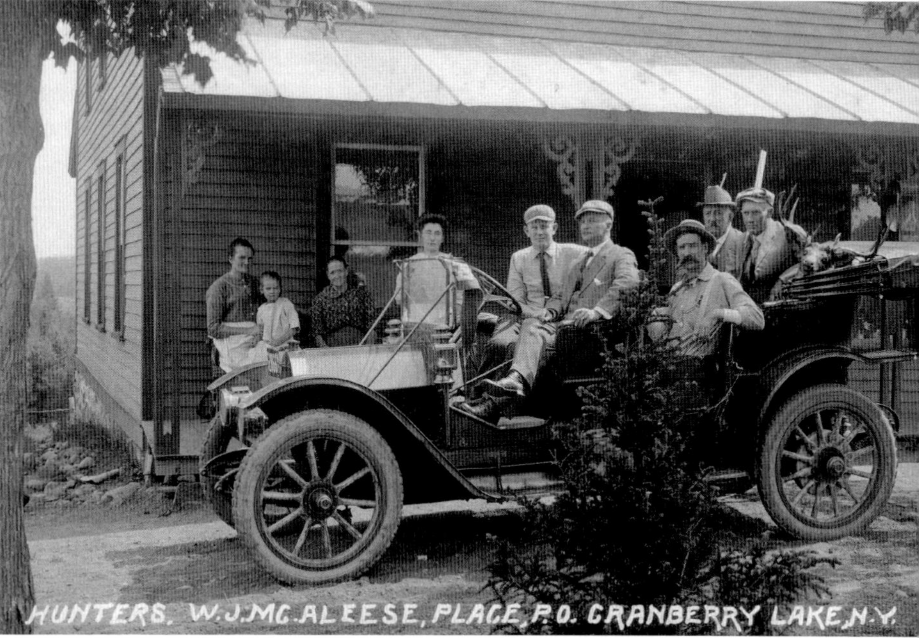


2.3. Hunters, W. J. McAleese Place, Cranberry Lake, N.Y., ca. 1910. Early automobile visiting the Adirondack wilderness. Smeby Coll.

The Adirondacks had changed, especially along the roads. But through the thirties, and even today, an older Adirondacks remained, a North Woods of secluded hotels, camps, and clubs as well as backwoods lumber operations and pristine forest. The postcard and the automobile appeared on the scene at approximately the same time. Beach was taking photo postcards immediately before and during the coming of the automobile-consumer age to the North Country. After that era arrived he photographed the range of Adirondack scenes from the paved highway to the backwoods camp.

Beach produced his views for a variety of customers: summer people, tourists and other seasonal recreational visitors, transient workers, and locals. Although not regular customers, wealthy visitors occasionally hired him to photograph their retreats. He contracted with a few managers of upper-end hotels to stock his views, and private clubs such as the Adirondack League Club occasionally

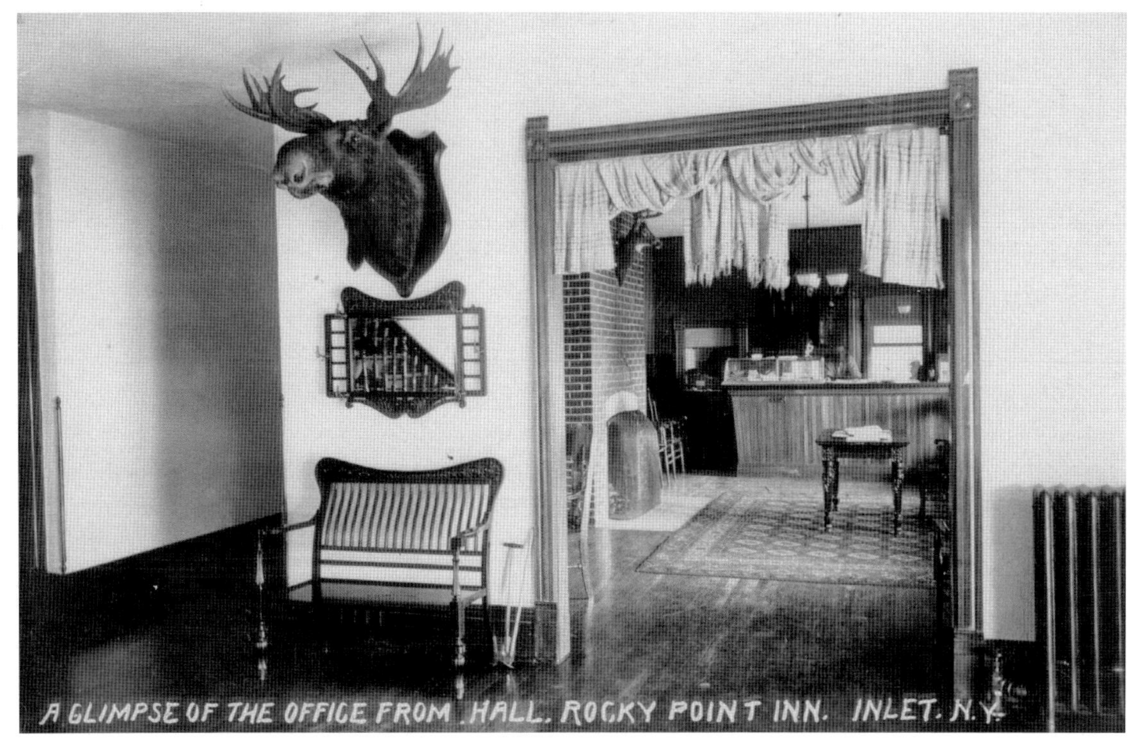


2.4. Glimpse of the office at Rocky Point Inn, Inlet, N.Y., ca. 1910. Beach photographed small hotels and resorts throughout the central Adirondacks. The proprietor, Arch Delmarsh, who was a guide as well as a hotel manager, is behind the desk. Gates Coll.

made use of his services (Gilborn 2000). But Beach felt more at home with mom-and-pop establishments—people of lesser means. This ease is reflected in the overall content of his portfolio (illus. 2.4).

## The Family Tree

Henry's family lineage in North America goes back to 1635 when his ancestors arrived from England and settled in Connecticut (Beach 1923). Beaches were early arrivals to New York's North Country—originals, you might say. In the early 1800s, they were among the first settlers of Watson, in Lewis County. Although "Remsen, New York," is printed on the backs of most of his postcards, Henry Beach was born in Watson, died in Watson, and spent more than sixty years of his life in that township.

Watson now straddles the Blue Line on the western extreme of the Adirondack Park close to Lowville, the county seat. Farmers and lumbermen settled the region. The development of the territory went hand in hand with the construction of the Black River Canal that stretched from Carthage to Boonville and south to the Erie Canal at Rome. Tall spruce and hemlock and stands of pine interspersed with maple, ash, beech, and birch covered the land (Samson 1971). Agricultural goods produced on the cleared land and lumber products taken from the forests to the East were shipped to market via that waterway (Landon 1932).

Henry's great-grandfather's brother was an early visitor to eastern Lewis County. In the 1820s Henry's grandfather followed his uncle to the area and prospered. In addition to farming fifty acres, he owned and operated a saw- and shingle mill. Among his holdings was a timber tract of three thousand acres that he managed and harvested (Hough 1883).

Maps of Lewis County are dotted with references to Henry's relatives, including Beach's Bridge, Beach's Cemetery, and Beach Mill Pond.[3] Some Beaches farmed, but their contribution to the area and their livelihood came from the development of commerce on the Black River Canal and from the lumber industry. If Henry was a boastful man, he could have pointed with pride to his relative Nelson J. Beach who served in the New York State Assembly, and from 1847 to 1851 was a canal commissioner and supervised the construction of the Black River Canal.[4] One of Henry's uncles owned and logged large timber holdings within what is now the Adirondack Park. A cousin who was in the lumbering business nearly all of his life owned Beach's Mill. The Beaches were among the best-known barge builders in the area, and they used the vessels they built to ship the lumber from their mills to the markets in Rome, Utica, Troy, and Albany (Bowen 1970).

George Nelson Beach, Henry's father, was a lumberman and a farmer too, but judging by the size of his home and the amount of land he owned, he was less prosperous than his father had been. Henry's mother was Esther E. Hall Beach. George and Esther married in Watson in 1855 and lived in a modest family house on Chase's Lake Road a few miles east of Lowville all of their married lives.

## Young Henry

Henry was born in the family home on August 10, 1863. Family, fields, and forest surrounded him in childhood. He contributed to the household by working on the family farm, on the canal, and in the woods. Accompanied by his cousins, he hunted and fished around Chase Lake, which was a short distance from where he lived. Venison and trout were quite often on the family table. Although he gave up hunting later in life, he remained an avid trout angler. He was a strong student, but as was the custom at the time, he left school sometime before his sixteenth birthday. He grew up with an older sister. When he was seventeen, she, along with her new husband, accidentally drowned in a local pond. His other siblings, a sister who was four years younger and a brother, Louis, sixteen years Henry's junior, remained in the North Country all of their lives.

## Henry and Bertha

Henry was more than six feet tall, a lanky Ichabod Crane–like figure with a long, narrow face and a slim nose. As he aged his shoulders stooped, and although still long and slim, he developed a paunch. In his early twenties he sported a trim, light mustache (illus. 2.5). As he matured it became thick, dark, long, and straggly, a defining feature that dominated his profile (illus. 2.6).[5]

At age twenty-three, on September 4, 1886, Henry married the pert Bertha W. Brown of Philadelphia, New York, a small town thirty miles north of the Beaches' home.[6] Although nothing is known about their courtship or how they met, it is plausible that they got together while he was working in Carthage, a town approximately halfway between Watson and Philadelphia.

Bertha was five years younger than Henry. Although little is known about her family, the number of photographs Henry took around the area of his wife's birthplace suggests that she and Henry remained in close contact with her relatives. The couple had four children. The first, Harry, was born three years after their marriage. The succeeding children, Wellington, Welta, and Lyle, were born approximately five years apart (illus. 2.7).

Henry preferred suits, ties, and stiff-collared shirts when engaged in his photographic trade. Although he dressed down when working around the house, he never wore the clothes of a woodsman or manual worker. He smoked a pipe and read with exuberance, a passion he shared with his wife. Not very sociable, Henry would only reluctantly accompany Bertha to church socials. He was impatient with small talk. When he did speak, he was often opinionated and dismissive of people who had ideas that varied from his own. Henry was a little out of step with other locals. But his neighbors respected him for being

3. Brandreth Lake in Hamilton County was at one time named Beach's Lake (Pilcher 1992, 54). Whether it was named after Matthew Beach or Nelson J. Beach, Henry's relative, is unknown.

4. Whether Matthew Beach, one of the first settlers at Raquette Lake, was Henry's relative is unknown (Pilcher 1992, 51).

5. In *Exposing the Wilderness* (1999) I said he never wore eyeglasses. That information was provided by relatives and is apparently wrong. Since then, I have come across a picture of him wearing eyeglasses.

6. The family genealogy gives September 4, 1887, as the date, but the party invitation for their fiftieth wedding anniversary celebration gives 1886 as the year.

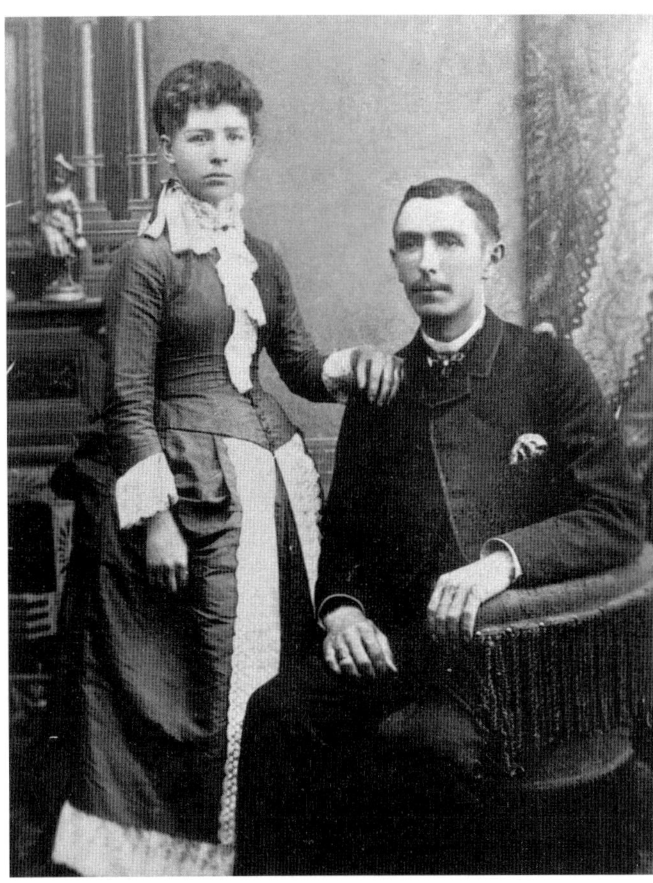

2.5. Bertha and Henry Beach, wedding picture, 1886. Bailey Coll.

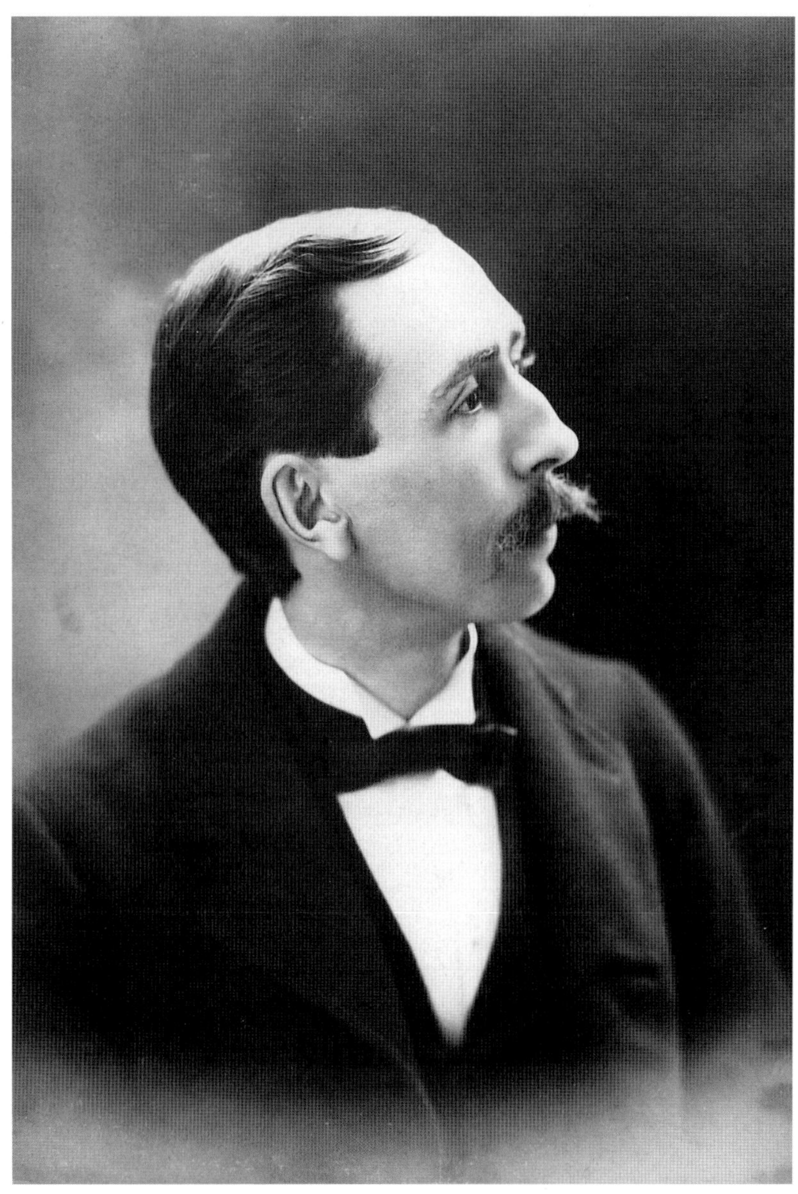

2.6. Henry Beach self-portrait, ca. 1900. Author's Coll.

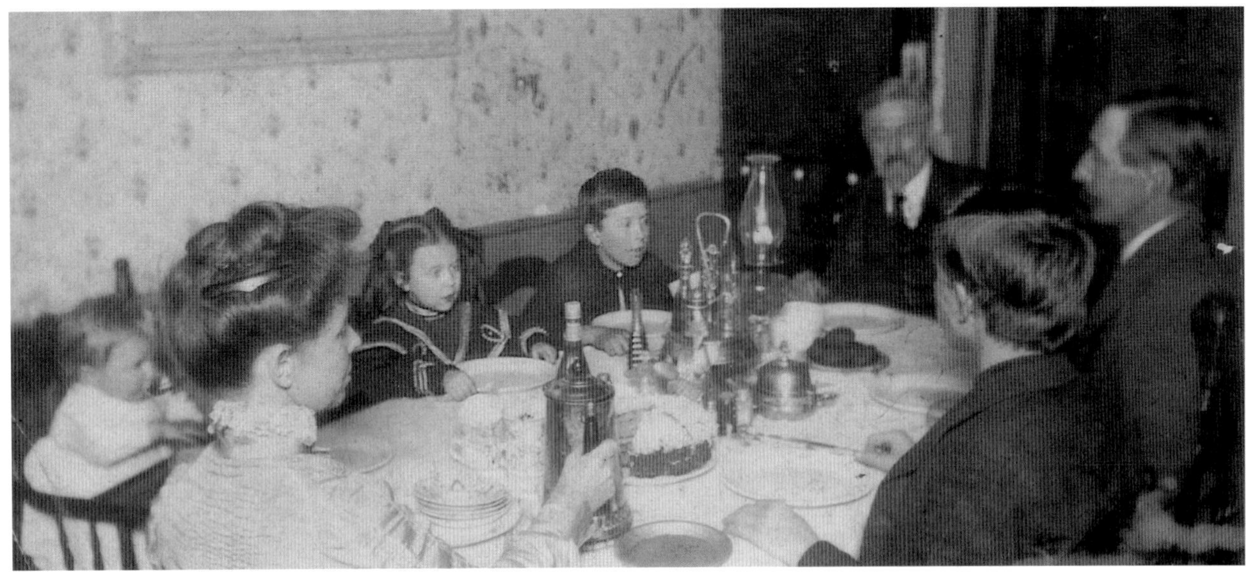

2.7. Beach family around the table, ca. 1904. Henry is on the far right. Bailey Coll.

smart, or, as they put it, "for knowing how to figure things out." They were intrigued by the workshop behind his house where he toiled on secret projects. Known to be intense when he was focused on his work, Henry had an enterprising attitude toward his calling and was aggressive in pursuit of his photographic business. He also liked to travel. Usually, his journeys were confined to frequent picture-taking sojourns around northern and western New York State.

In the early years he traveled by horse and buggy or by train. Around 1912 he purchased his first automobile, and although he still relied on the train for some picture taking, he began using his car for business.[7] He occasionally took short trips to other states, visiting his son Harry in Colorado and Florida. Henry took photographs on his trips. The few that remain are the only evidence of his travels.

When Henry was on his picture-taking excursions, Bertha stayed at home and took care of the household and children. He would leave home without notice and be gone for weeks, even months.

## Early Years as a Photographer

How did Henry Beach learn his trade? Who were his mentors? There were commercial photographers active in the Lowville area when Henry was growing up, but there is no evidence that Henry apprenticed with any of them. An early 1880s cabinet card from Carthage, a town fifteen miles north of Lowville, suggests that Beach might have learned the photography trade from Fred K. Hart, who ran a studio in that town. The logo at the bottom of the cabinet portrait in question indicates it was taken at "Hart Studio" but also declares "Beach and Hart" as the photographers.

The date when Henry went into business is unknown. Tracking his career in its early years is complicated because Henry's younger brother, Louis, was also a photographer. The logo on L. E. Beach's work is similar to Henry's, and both men marked their work "Beach's Studio" but did not always provide their ini-

7. A car with New York license plate number B782 1913 appears in a number of Beach's photographs. In one, Wellington is at the wheel. This automobile was probably Henry's.

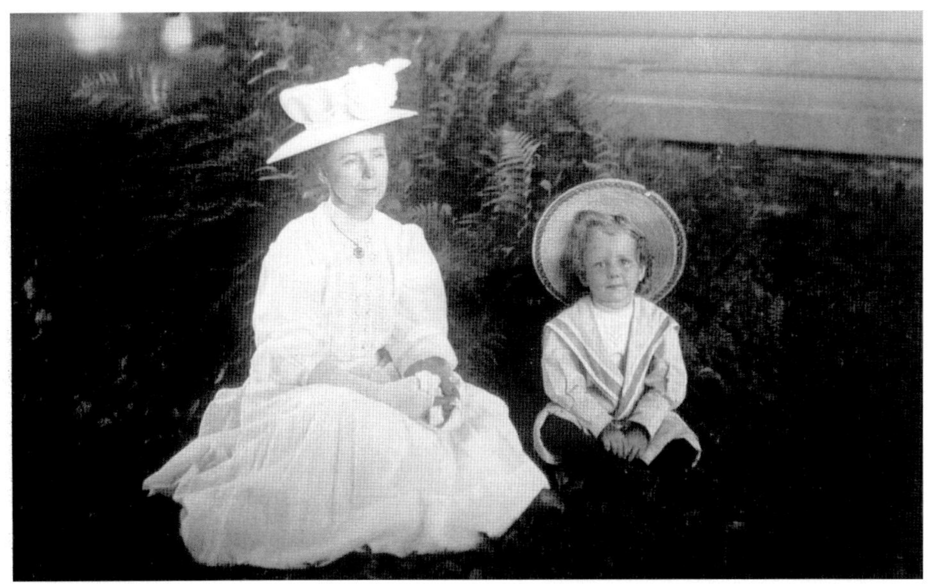

2.8. Bertha with Lyle, ca. 1906. Bailey Coll.

tials. The brothers probably shared a studio for a time. Louis Beach left Lowville around the turn of the century, worked out of Beaver River as a hunting and fishing guide, later moved to Eagle Bay, and finally settled in nearby Old Forge. In addition to guiding, Lou was a lumberjack, a logging-camp cook, a skilled house builder, and a hotel manager. He died in 1963 in Old Forge.

Pictures with Henry's name and trademark on them date back to the 1880s. Most are studio portraits of local people, suggesting that this form of photography was his major source of income. But even in his early years, he took many outdoor photographs, or at least more than was typical for a studio photographer of the time. Many are those lumber camps and logging operations near Watson. Some of the people in the pictures are Beach's relatives, indicating that they were taken in family-owned logging camps and were of people working for his relatives.[8]

8. In 1902 Henry took a series of photographs of a small lumber company, Page, Fairchild & Co., located in Lewis County and compiled an album that he offered for sale. This company apparently was not owned by a relative.

In addition to his commercial work, Henry took pictures of his family. Although most of them are lost to us, a few remain, including the splendid photograph of his firstborn child, Harry, taken with turkeys, outside an old clapboard building that was likely Henry's or a relative's home (see illustration 2.1). Illustration 2.8 is a picture of Henry's wife, Bertha, and their last-born child, Lyle, taken around 1906. It is one of the early family pictures printed on postcard stock.

At the turn of the century Henry was not yet settled in the direction of his photographic career. Looking for a niche in the market, he tried aggressively marketing low-priced studio photographs as a formula for success. One advertisement, printed on the back of a studio portrait, illustrates his heavy-handed approach to promotion. He boasted about winning prizes at the Lewis County Fair. In addition to an assertion about the quality of his work, he proclaimed: "I can save you money on any kind of work." The ad ends with riddle, "TAEN DNA PAEHC," which spelled backward reads, "CHEAP AND NEAT." Henry remained a bold spinner of advertising hyperbole throughout his life.

In 1900 Henry, Bertha, and their three children, ages one to eleven, lived in a rented house on Railroad Street in Lowville. A 1904 advertisement published in the business directory of Carthage and West Carthage suggests that he was operating studios in both Lowville and Carthage. According to his 1904 ad Henry then specialized in pictures of "family groups and wedding parties."[9]

At the turn of the century Lowville was a western port for launching trips into the Adirondack forest (Bowen 1970; Donaldson 1921). The Lowville area had some tourists, summer residents, and hotels that catered to people traveling onward, but it was never primarily a tourist or summer town. The Adirondack Mountains are visible from Lowville, but the land surrounding the village, especially to the west, is relatively flat and fertile. The fields and pastures supported dairy herds that provided the backbone of the area's economy. The town was the government, transportation, and commerce center of rural Lewis County whose western end extends into the Adirondack Park.

Lowville residents hunted, fished, camped, picnicked, boated, and summered in the mountains. Although Lowville is not part of the Adirondack Park and not economically dominated by it, the townspeople thought of themselves as being part of the Adirondacks. As we will see, many family and commercial connections exist between the Lowville area and the central Adirondacks, and Henry capitalized on them later in his career (Higby 1974, 17, 34).

Lowville had a number of photographers at the turn of the century. They included George Carter, Frank Duflo, and the talented William Mandeville (Bogdan 1999). These men were village photographers who stuck close to home and remained predominately studio photographers who sold their products mainly to locals rather than to tourists. When postcards arrived on the scene they dabbled in the genre, but that format was not their primary source of revenue.

Beach started out as a village studio photographer but was restless in the confines of that role. By 1900, many people owned a camera, and amateur snapshot photographers were changing the business of commercial photographers. For early photographers, studio work—local people coming in to pose for portraits—was their economic mainstay. By the turn of the century many potential customers were taking informal portraits themselves, thereby undercutting a substantial part of the professional trade. The revenue from portraits could no longer sustain a typical business.

Photo postcards and large panoramic group photos, turn-of-the-century innovations in the United States, provided an opportunity for the small-town commercial photographer. Although Kodak was soon making cameras for the amateurs to take postcards (Morgan and Brown 1981), the convenience of buying quality views on the spot created a demand for postcards from the rack. Many professionals embraced photo postcards as a way of giving a boost to lagging business. Similarly, the arrival of the Cirkut camera, an instrument that took large panoramic photographs, allowed photographers to take large group pictures that were beyond the capabilities of the snapshot amateur's skills (Burleson and Hickman 1986). Although many professionals incorporated the postcard and the panoramic into their ongoing work, thus making only modest alterations in their practices, others seized upon the new formats in a more enterprising way. They took to the road to do their work, marketing to larger audiences and in some cases neglecting individual customers who sought studio portraits. Beach was one of them.

Henry began producing photo postcards in and around Lowville by 1904. Rather than just catering to walk-in trade, he courted local business and civic leaders, selling them multiple copies of photographic-montage advertising and business cards consisting of letters and pictures. Before Beach produced this promotional work in postcard format, he tried his hand at it in other forms. Illustration 2.9 is an advertising photograph he made for Frank Hews's dry goods store. Although the photograph was mounted on cardboard that had printed marketing text on the back, it is strikingly similar in composition and style to the advertising postcards that became one of his hallmarks. He began taking regular postcard views too, first in the Lewis County area, then gradually expanding his territory in all directions. Henry aggressively wholesaled his scenic views to dry goods stores and other commercial establishments.

During the first decade of the century competition among photographers in Lowville was considerable, which must have been a factor in Henry's decision to leave. Given his inclination to travel and his entrepreneurial spirit, he probably chose to move in order to be in a place that offered better access to the tourist market in the central Adirondacks and to the urban clientele in the more densely populated Mohawk Valley. He had postcards on his mind.

9. At around this time the Beach family moved to a house on Pine Grove Road, in Watson. It was there that their fourth and last child, Lyle, was born in 1903.

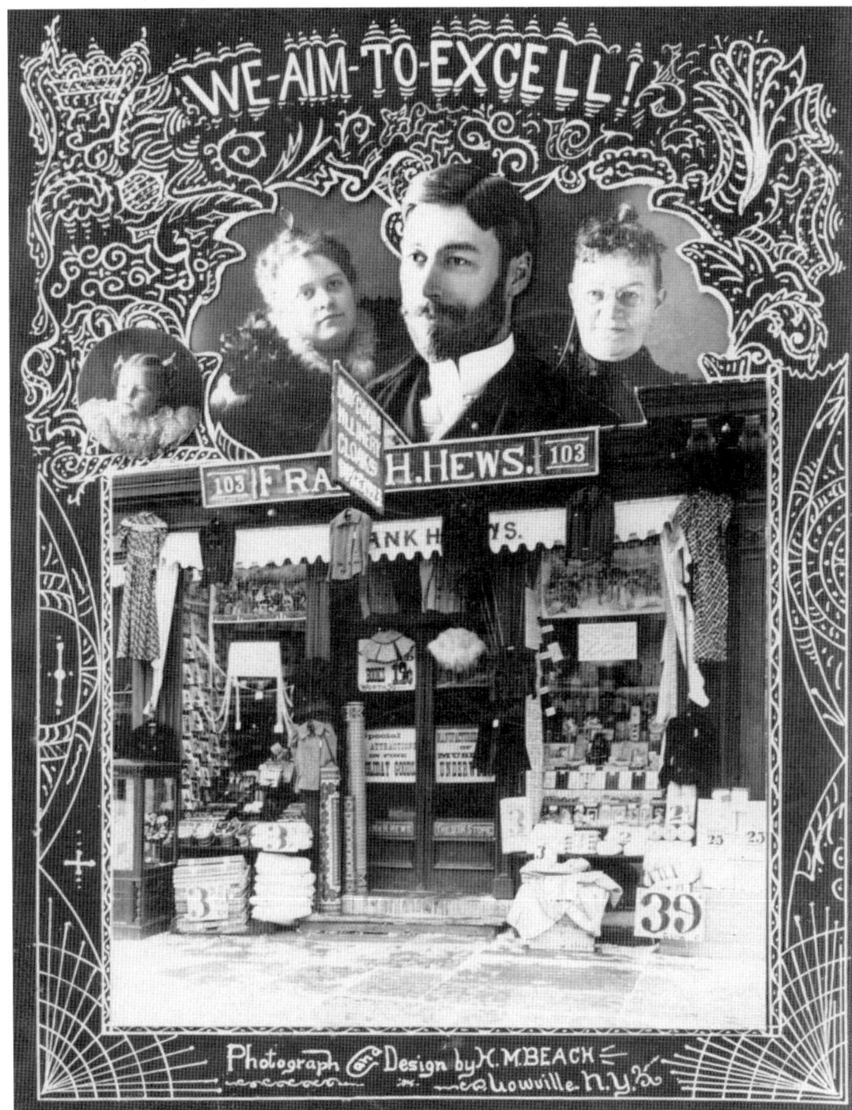


2.9. Advertising photograph produced by Henry Beach for Frank Hews dry goods store in Lowville, N.Y., ca. 1900. Gates Coll.

## Remsen

Around 1906 Beach closed his studio in the Lowville area and with his family moved thirty-five miles and four stops southeast on the railroad to Remsen where they lived and Henry conducted his business. Although the distance may not seem great, the move must have been risky and unsettling. After all, Henry had four children, was forty-three years old, and had never lived far from his place of birth. Beach must have experienced some success before the move, because starting over in a new town took more than courage and self-confidence. He had to have some capital, especially to start production as aggressively as he did.

Remsen is a village on the southwestern edge of the Adirondack Park, north of Utica. Beach operated his photographic business there for about ten years. With photo postcards as his major product, supplemented with panoramic work, these years were his most prolific and the time of his best work.

Exactly where he relocated immediately after the move is unknown. When a census enumerator made his rounds in 1910 the Beaches were living at 71 Maple Avenue. On April 30, 1914, the Beaches bought a home next to the tracks of the Adirondack Division of New York Central off Maple Avenue.

Remsen was a small but thriving business and transportation center when Beach moved there (Kudish 1996, 390). Trains serving many North Country locations stopped at the busy railroad station. The tracks that lined his property were the preferred route to the central Adirondacks. Beach could jump on a train and comfortably arrive in Fulton Chain (now Thendara), Big Moose, and Beaver River in a short time. A longer ride would take him to Childwold and Tupper Lake, and a transfer at Lake Clear would get him to Saranac Lake and Lake Placid. Another train that stopped at Remsen went through Boonville and on to Lowville and Carthage where he could make connections to Benson Mines, Newton Falls, and Wanakena (Kudish 1996). Beach photographed all of these sites as well as many other North Country locations accessible by the trains that ran by his door (illus. 2.10).

When Henry became an automobile owner in around 1912 he began using his car for business. It made lugging heavy equipment easier and allowed him to reach places trains did not go, but he continued to rely on rail travel for longer journeys and to places close to the tracks.

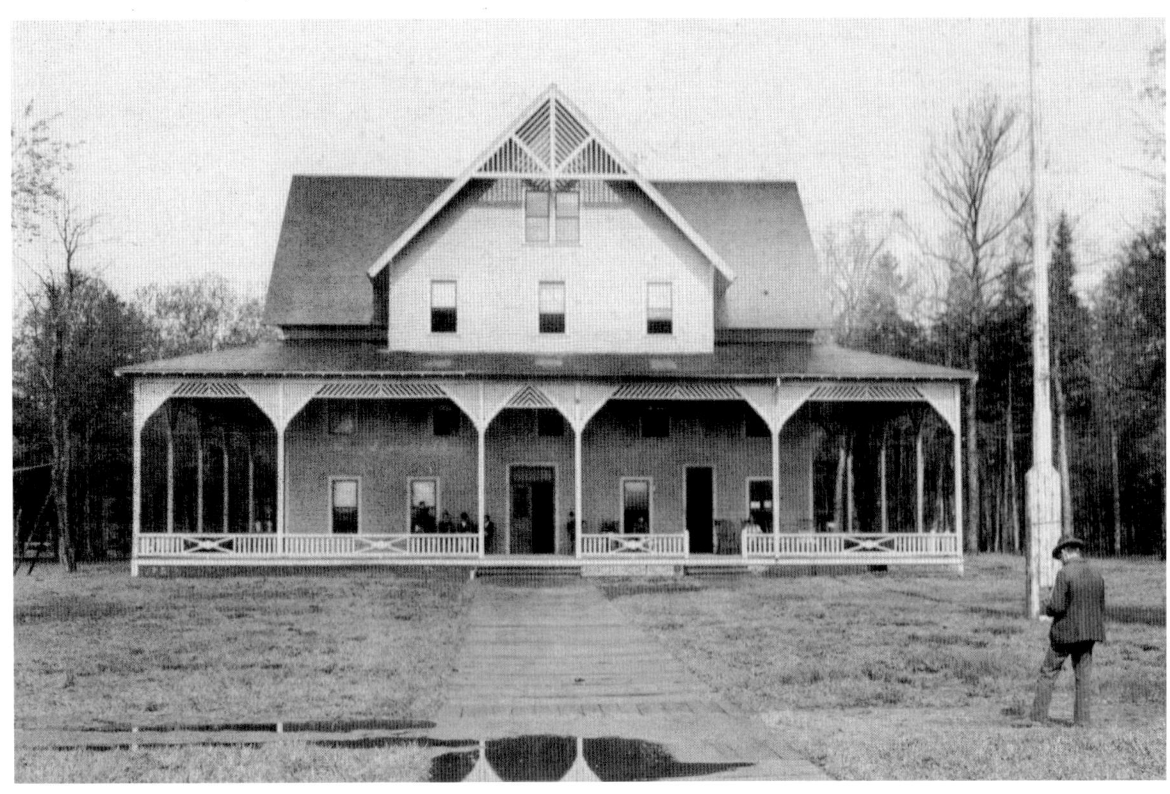

2.10. Beach photographing the Norridgewock Hotel at Beaver River, ca. 1910. Author's Coll.

Considering the large number of Beach's cards surviving today, Henry must have been outfitted for high production at his Remsen workshop. He referred to his facilities as a factory, but that wording is misleading. His house was small, and the largest outbuilding was no bigger than what would now be an oversized two-car garage. There is no record of his owning or renting additional real estate. At least during the busy summer season, Henry hired employees. But we do not know how many or how his shop was organized. Whatever the details, he worked in cramped quarters.

Chief among his workers was Leroy Thomas, a twenty-two-year-old practicing Remsen photographer when Beach moved to the village. Henry hired Leroy and relied on his skills in photo production. Thomas returned to his own photography business when Beach moved away from Remsen.

Thomas's contribution to the Remsen operation must have been considerable. When you compare the lettering in the captions on Thomas's cards that he produced when he was an independent with many of the cards printed on stock with the Beach logo they appear identical. Thomas's photographs are well composed and of high quality. He likely wrote many of Beach's captions and may have taken some of the photographs we attribute to the master. Thomas's career was short-lived. He died in Remsen when he was only forty-one years old.

Jud Davis was another Remsen resident who worked for Beach. Henry's children helped as well. That experience was how his two sons learned the photography trade and went on to become commercial photographers.

There are many unknowns about the mechanical operations of Beach's Remsen factory. For example, it is not clear whether all the Beach prints were done

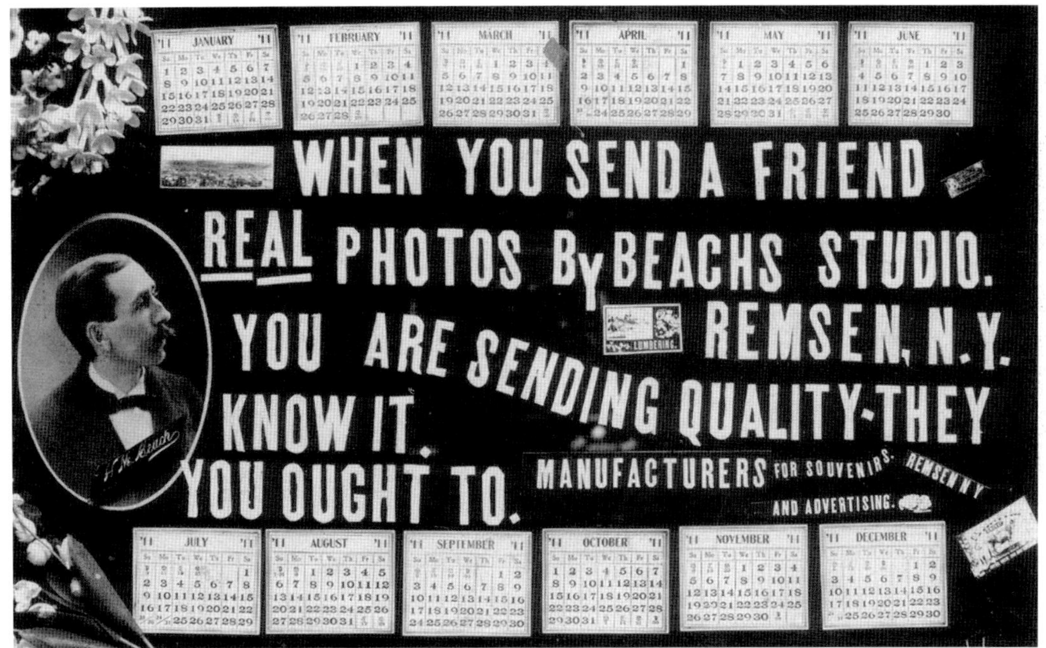


2.11. Beach's advertisement with calendar and portrait, ca. 1911. Teal Coll.

individually or with the aid of mechanized printing devices (printing machines) that became available around 1908. Given his high-volume production, an assembly line–like routine must have been in place. There needed to be a large dark room and high-capacity tanks of developing fluid and other liquids, in addition to a drying and finishing area as well as packing facilities. Although some of the orders were sent through the mail, Beach personally delivered many in conjunction with his shooting schedule.

Beach's operation in Remsen exceeded the technology and level of production of a typical small-town photography studio, but it was far from being a high-tech factory. Beach and his employees were exclusively engaged in photo production. In addition to printing pictures, Henry served his costumers by making postcards from negatives and prints they had taken. Although there is no way to tell for sure, it appears that Beach printed pictures his customers took on plain stock, not on the paper with the Beach logo on it. Beach did not sell cameras and photographic supplies to amateurs, an aspect of the photography business that other photographers embraced after the turn of the century when they were losing their studio customers.

Beach created advertising postcards to promote his own business (illus. 2.11). By studying them, aspects of his marketing approach become clearer. The more retailers bought, the cheaper they were, but Henry always reminded his would-be customers that they were buying quality. As illustration 2.12 shows, real photograph souvenir postcards as well as advertising cards were his specialties.

At the same time, he took and sold panoramic photographs. Those huge photos, as long as forty-five inches and as wide as ten inches, were of both scenery and groups. Beach bought his first panoramic camera, a Kodak Cirkut, around the time he moved to Remsen and began taking commercial pictures

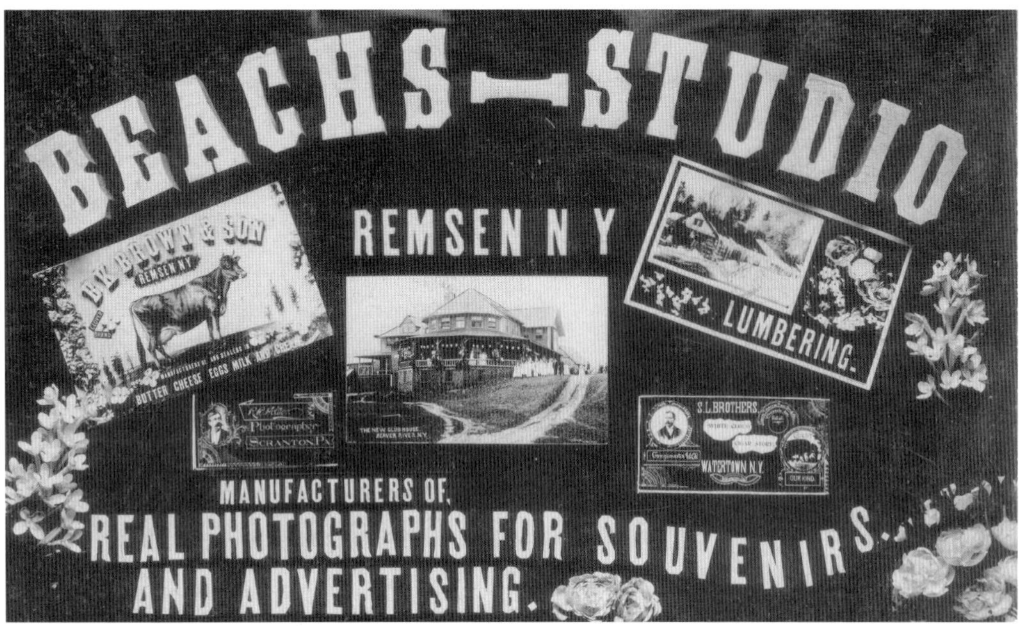


2.12. Beach postcard advertisement, ca. 1907. Teal Coll.

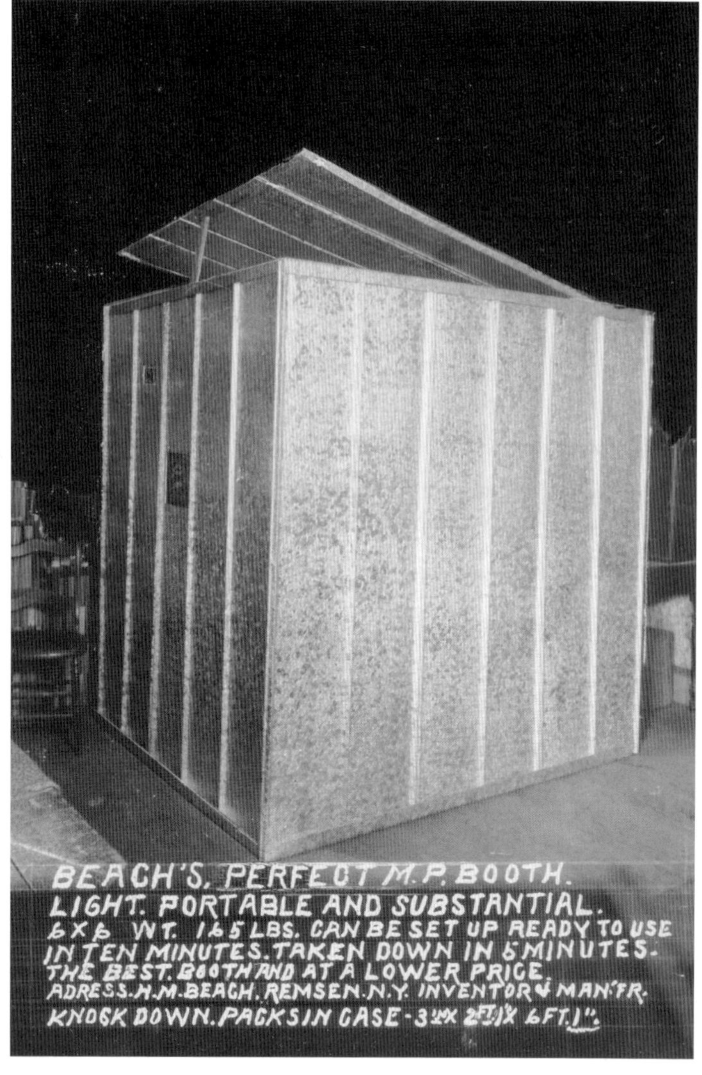


2.13. "Beach's Perfect M.P. Booth," ca. 1912. Courtesy of the Adirondack Museum.

with it immediately. Given the large size of the prints, the production of the panoramics must have cramped his workshop. One neighbor remembered that he washed his large prints in the stream that flowed past the house.[10]

Beach's inquisitive and inventive mind also led him to design new products. One story has it that Henry had invented the movie camera but was swindled out of the invention by another man. Another invention some claim for Beach was a postcard vending machine. It is difficult to determine the accuracy of these stories, but there is evidence that he was an inventor. He advertised "Beach's Perfect M.P. Booth" on a postcard (illus. 2.13). Just what the product is is unclear. "M.P." may stand for multipurpose and manufactured to be a folding, traveling dark room. It is interesting that on the caption Henry identifies

10. First in 1910 and then again in 1911 and 1912 Henry sent copies of his panoramic photographs to the Library of Congress to register for copyright protection. He submitted a total of thirty-six. (A few were sent later.) These photographs are the only ones he sent to Washington, as far as I know.

himself as an inventor and manufacturer. Although there are indications that he was an inventor, I found no record of how successful he was in producing and marketing what he created.

## Beach's View of His Work

During his most productive years, what did Beach think of his craft and the photographs he was producing? Typical of photographers who came of age in the late nineteenth century, part of his identity was as an "artist-gentleman" (Battani 1997). In self-portraits he used for advertisements he dressed formally, struck a contemplative pose, and looked toward the heavens with a facial expression that said, "I am a person with aesthetic sensitivities." He used the term *artist* in some of his business literature and the word *studio* as well. But his identification as an artist must be understood in the context of early-twentieth-century rural upstate New York. *Artist* did not mean that he related to elite urban photographers who were laying claim to that honorific title. In fact, the elite urban photographers were status seekers who were making fun of local commercial photographers for their use of the term *artist* (Stieglitz 1980). For Beach, *artist* was an assertion that he was more than a mechanic operating a machine called a camera. It was a declaration of his talent, a talent that he directed toward producing photos that not only were technically superior but also met a high aesthetic standard, even if those standards were his own.

But "artist" was only one self-identifier. When the enumerator from the census came knocking on his door in 1910, he gave "traveling photographer" as his occupation. He never abandoned his "artist" title completely, but after his move to Remsen, he began using an industrial and business vocabulary in his self-description as well. He considered his photographic studio at Remsen a "factory" and himself a "manufacturer" of postcards. He also saw himself as an inventor, and from the way he conducted his business it is obvious that "entrepreneur" fitted his self-concept as well. Although he remained a small-town operator, he was not bashful about casting himself as a modern businessperson. This apparent contrasting combination of artist and businessman may seem like a difficult role to juggle, but Beach's success lay in his ability to integrate the two while still maintaining his rural orientation (illus. 2.14).

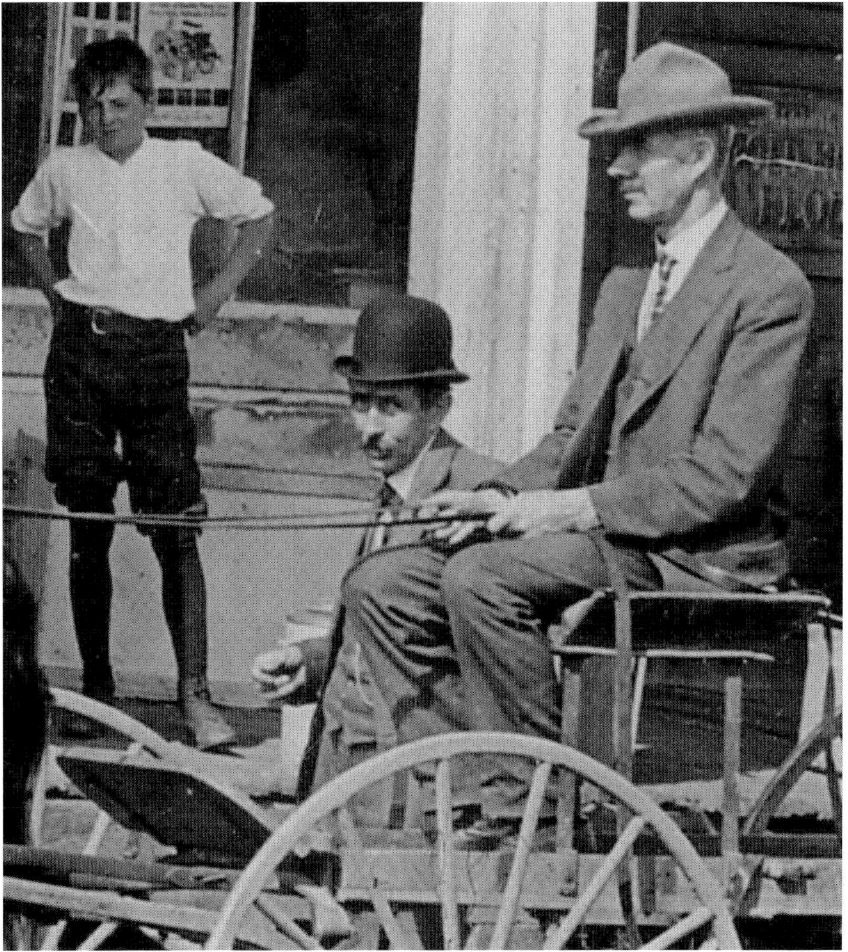

2.14. The man in the center of the picture is Henry Beach, ca. 1908. It is a close-up from one of his postcards. Author's Coll.

Who or what outside influences might have affected his photographic style? All we can do is speculate! He did not attend photographers' conventions, and there is no indication that he met with other photographers. As was pointed out earlier, in some of the text that he stamped on the backs of his pre-Remsen portraits he bragged about winning photographic prizes at the Lewis County Fair. This piece of information indicates that his work was peer reviewed and that he probably engaged in discussion with others about his work, but all in rural Lewis County. Henry received photography manufacturers' mailings and saw trade publications and other photography literature. He subscribed to general-audience periodicals that were extensively illustrated, such as *National Geographic.* Undoubtedly, it all influenced the pictures he took. Although stylized elements taken from national trends were part of his work, Beach developed his photographic eye while working with locals in rural surroundings. Although we do not know exactly where, or from whom, he learned the basics of the trade, his aesthetic was more local than national.

What is striking about Henry's photographs is their down-to-earth directness. He was a commercial photographer, but there are elements in some of his work that give it a folk quality. By this description I mean he related straightforwardly to locals and spontaneously produced innovative elements in his compositions. Though not uniformly absorbing—he took his share of commonplace views—a high proportion of his images is striking, involving, whimsical, and unconventional. He broke standard photographic protocol by adding quirky elements to the compositions and commentary to his captions. Of course, his natural talent, lack of professional training, and folksy photographic eye can easily explain this superior quality, but there are other points to consider.

Henry was slow and methodical in his approach to photography. Rather than moving rapidly from place to place and taking the easily available shots, he spent time in a location, figuring out and waiting for better, more satisfying photo opportunities. Because of the expense and work involved in making and printing from glass-plate negatives, he could not afford to take many shots and then throw out the ones that did not suit him. He photographed as if each click mattered. He was not socially aggressive, but with camera in hand he had no trouble getting people to pose before his lens and inserting himself into places that other photographers might skip. In addition, Henry was familiar with the ways of the people of the North Country, and had personal relationships with many of the Adirondackers he photographed. As we will see, this fact was especially true in the central and western Adirondacks. Many of the late-nineteenth- and early-twentieth-century settlers of those regions originally hailed from the Black River Valley where Henry was born and raised (Higby 1974, 23).

## Fort Plain

In 1916, Henry Beach was approaching his midfifties and apparently doing quite well as a photographer. For reasons that are not clear, he and his family packed up and moved to Fort Plain, New York, an Erie Canal town halfway between Utica and Albany. Thinking he could continue to expand his business even beyond what he had done in Remsen, perhaps Henry was seeking a place closer to population centers. One clue to his business activities in Fort Plain is an advertisement postcard dated March 1917 that shows two stores that Henry was operating on Main Street.[11] One was labeled "Beach's Studio," the other "Beach's Art Shop and Amateur Supplies." The caption on the postcard reads, "Beach's Studio, Fort Plain, N.Y., Better Than Ever. Electric Printing for Amateur Trade, Enlargements, etc." It appears that Beach was attempting to expand into new areas of production by entering the retail photo-services and photo-supply trade.

In July 1917, Henry and Bertha's only daughter, Welta, eighteen at the time, died in a car accident ("Killed in Auto Wreck" 1917). She was killed instantly when the automobile in which she was riding with her mother and two brothers skidded off a road, turned over three times, and landed in a ditch. Bertha sustained a compound fracture of the left leg that left her with a permanent limp. Lyle fractured his right leg. The driver, Wellington, twenty-three years old at the time, escaped injury. Welta's death was an enormous tragedy for the family.

The Beach home in Remsen was not sold until 1919. In 1920 the Beaches were living in a modest house they owned in Fort Plain.[12] Other information about Henry's activities during this period of transition in his life adds confu-

11. This photo postcard is in the collection of Jose Rodriguez.

12. On July 14, 1920, Henry and Bertha bought property at the corner of Home and Washington Streets in Fort Plain. On September 27, 1920, he sold the property to Saint Paul's Lutheran Church of Fort Plain.

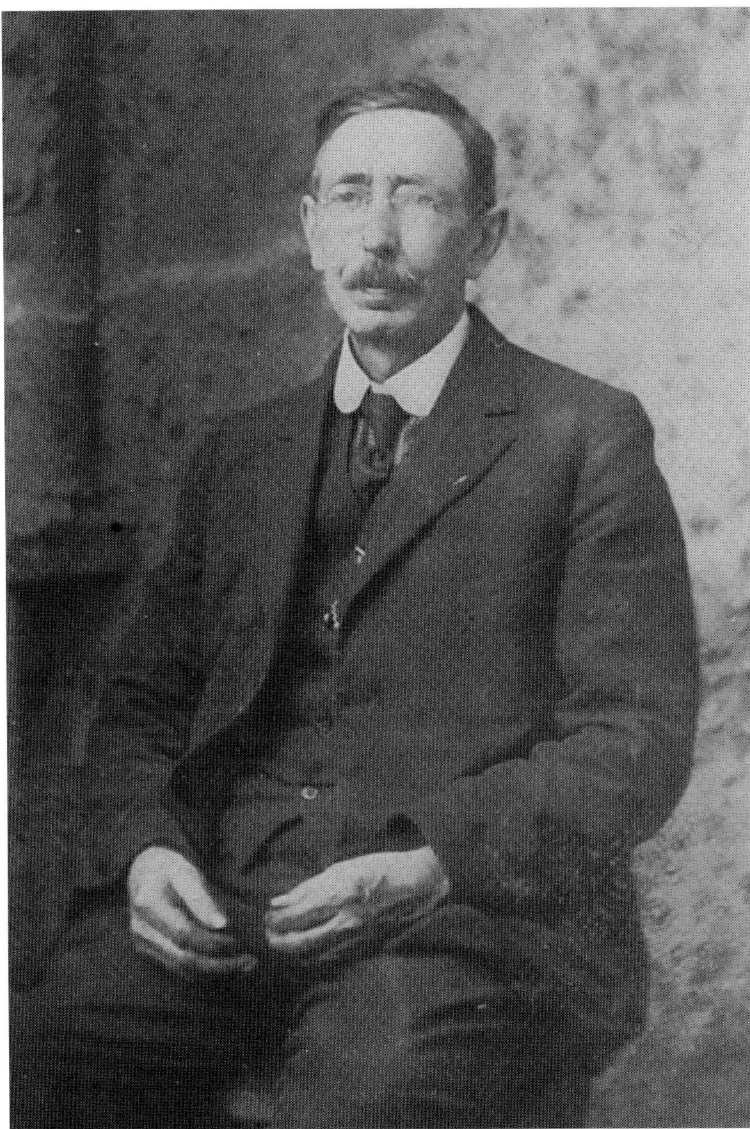

2.15. Picture of the aged Henry from a Beach family album, ca. 1930. Bailey Coll.

sion to the story. An advertisement he produced in 1921, emphasizing portrait photography, states that his studio was in Canajoharie, a village a few miles east of Fort Plain. His panoramic photographs of a United States Army training camp during World War I in South Carolina suggest that Henry might have spent some of the war years traveling in the Southeast producing photographs of the troops in basic training. Whatever Henry was up to, he did not stay in the Fort Plain area long.

## Back Home

Henry's father had died before Henry left Watson for Remsen. His mother continued to maintain the family home on Chase Lake Road in Watson, although she lived with Henry and Bertha off and on. In 1921 Henry and Bertha bought a large farm, with a substantial house just three houses away from his mother's place, and moved back to Watson. The property was known as the Gazin Farm, and in addition to the large house and outbuildings there were 148 acres of land.[13] When his mother died in 1922, Henry inherited her place. He rented his mother's house to a young couple whose children became close to the Beaches. The land on the Gazin place was leased to a neighboring farmer who harvested the hay. Henry and Bertha settled into a rural lifestyle in which Bertha maintained a large garden and raised chickens and rabbits for the family's own consumption. Behind the house was an outhouse, in front a well that ran low in the summers. Electricity did not come to their homestead until the 1940s. Although they were far from wealthy, they appear to have been comfortable, at least compared to their neighbors. Whether they could afford the farm and to live as they did because of Henry's business success or from inherited money from his father and mother is not known.

The photographic record reveals that Henry continued to take pictures in and around the Fulton Chain and in other sections of the North Country after he returned to Watson (illus. 2.15). His productivity was a fraction of what it had been earlier. He reprinted from his earlier negatives but engaged in new

13. This number is a revised figure from the one given in *Exposing the Wilderness* (Bogdan 1999). An elderly neighbor conveyed the earlier figure. This one comes from the deed.

projects, too. Henry kept his automobile, a big touring car, and used it extensively in his photography business, traveling about taking postcard pictures and panoramics. When the Northeastern Power Corporation expanded their power facilities after construction of the Mosier Dam on the Beaver River near Stillwater, Henry entered some arrangement with the company management to photograph the construction. His last-known panoramic photograph was taken in 1936.

Just where Henry had his office and photo-processing shop during this time is not clear. A letterhead dated 1927 gives Lowville as the location of his business. Some of his postcards have *Glenfield* printed on them, but he did not live or have a shop there, Glenfield being merely his post office delivery station (Mihalyi 1998). Henry owned two houses on Pine Grove Road in Watson and used one of them as a workplace in the 1920s. Later he sold those properties and appears to have operated solely out of his home on Chase River Road. His neighbors remember him doing his work in a large outbuilding near the main house, which he kept exclusively for his own use. It was there that he did photographic processing and worked on his inventions.

Although Henry slowed as he aged, he continued to travel, most often without Bertha. In 1937, when he was in his early seventies, Henry took a trip to Florida to visit his sons.

## The Sons

Henry's firstborn, Harry, born February 22, 1889, had a love for travel that exceeded even his father's. Two photographic postcards taken by Henry around 1907 show Harry and a friend with a tandem bicycle (illus. 2.16). The boys look to be about eighteen years old and set to embark on a trip to the Gulf of Mexico.

Harry left home in his late teens and moved from place to place until after his father's death. He married a woman from Brooklyn in 1911, and served in World War I. Over his lifetime he lived in Brooklyn, New Jersey, Michigan, Virginia, Colorado, Florida, Vermont, and various places in New York State. While residing in Colorado Springs in the 1920s he ran a small Kodak photographic supply, developing, and printing store he called "Kodocraft." For a short time he had a photo studio in Old Forge.

Wellington, born in 1893, was the second child. He served in World War I as a government photographer. He married Harry's wife's sister and moved to Palm Beach, Florida, where he owned and operated a small photography studio. Bud, as he was called, rarely traveled north to see his parents.

The youngest, Lyle, was born in 1903, when Henry was forty-one (illus. 2.17). Unlike his outgoing brothers, Lyle was nervous and shy. He lived at home until his early thirties. He too married a woman from New York City. Their first child, Bertha, was named after her grandmother.

## The Later Years

Later in life, Henry liked to sit by the kitchen table in a captain's chair and smoke his pipe, which he rested on a Firestone miniature rubber-tire ashtray. The neighbor's blue-point hound, Nickie, was a regular at the Beach place. Henry was fond of animals and took a special liking to Nickie, who was bothered by ear mites. To the dog's pleasure, Henry would lift Nickie's ear and blow a thick puff of pipe tobacco smoke deep into the canal. The dog begged for the treatment. Some mornings Henry would fix pancakes for the dog.

On Friday evening, September 4, 1936, the Beach home was filled with visitors who came to celebrate Henry and Bertha's fiftieth wedding anniversary. Bertha had sent postcardlike invitations that Henry had designed with the couple's 1886 wedding picture incorporated into the layout.

In the late thirties Henry began suffering from stomach pains. Taking bicarbonate of soda mixed in a tall glass of water seemed to offer relief, or at least he drank many glasses of the mixture. In November 1942, Henry was feeling so badly that Bertha telegraphed Harry to come to Watson immediately. Harry arrived to find his father improving. This first bout of sickness started Henry's decline. A few months later Henry was hospitalized with stomach and bowel pain.

With Bertha at his side, Henry died at home, in his sleep, on January 5, 1943 ("Obituary" 1943). He was seventy-nine. His death certificate lists the cause of death as a number of conditions associated with old age, including heart failure. When he heard the news of his father's death Harry immediately rushed home over ice-covered roads and twenty-below-zero temperatures from Vermont to be with his mother.

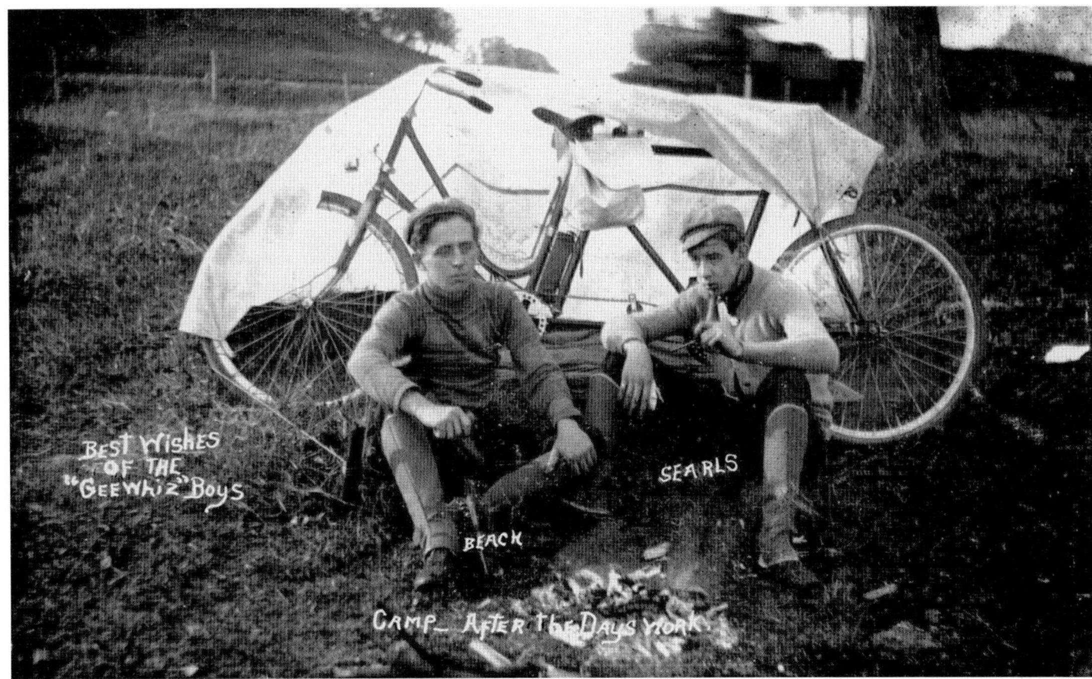


2.16. "Best Wishes of the 'Gee Whiz' Boys," ca. 1907. Note the train in the background. Harry Beach is on the left. Author's Coll.

In about 1945, Harry and his wife moved from Vermont to the family homestead on Chase Lake Road where they lived during the warm months of the year (winters were spent in Florida). Bertha lived with them until she died in 1955.

Henry is buried in the large family plot at Beach's Bridge Cemetery in Watson. A short obituary appearing in the *Lowville Journal and Republican* identified him as a "veteran photographer."

## Scattered Photographs

Most of the original glass negatives that Henry used to print his postcards as well as the prints and equipment were stored in the family house after he died. Thinking the older cards worthless, Bertha burned most of them, but the remainder of Henry's photography eventually became Harry's. Harry collected antiques and occasionally sold items to dealers. He rarely threw anything out. He understood and appreciated the importance of his father's photographic work. This understanding combined with his pack-rat tendencies ensured the safekeeping his father's remaining prints, negatives, and photographic equipment. Sometime after his mother died, in the late fifties, Harry sold five thousand of his father's glass-plate negatives to the then newly established Adirondack Museum.

Harry died on June 16, 1971, at the age of eighty-four ("Funeral Held" 1973). He too is buried in Beach's Bridge Cemetery. Soon after Harry died the Beach family house in Watson burned to the ground, leaving only a few traces of the family in its ashes.

Exactly where the remains of Henry Beach's photographs and equipment went after Harry's death is unknown. Although some may have been destroyed in the fire, most of Henry's remaining photographs, including postcards, early motion pictures, and equipment, are alleged to have gone to a young friend of Harry who helped him in his declining years.

## The View from Billy's Bald Spot

Around the same time that Henry Beach shot the regatta photograph that hangs in the Adirondack Museum he climbed to a favorite site of Big Moose–area hikers, Billy's Bald Spot. He lugged his bulky photographic equipment with him. A large rock outcropping in the woods high above Big Moose Lake, Billy's Bald Spot offered an expansive view of the lake and its surroundings (Scheffler and Carey 2000). Perched on the massive rock, surveying the world below, you could get a good sense of the North Woods and your relationship to them. You could see for miles. Moreover, one could spot boats, camp buildings, docks, and clearings like the ones in the regatta photo. You felt that you were in the sky, invisible, and could comfortably spy on the Adirondack landscape and its visitors. Changing your focus back and forth from the details to the expansiveness, Billy's Bald Spot provided a broader, more intense sense of place than other spots near the lake. So it is with Beach's photographs. His views allow us to see the particulars of daily life, while not losing the bigger picture of what those times might have been like. His images help us feel what it was like to be there.

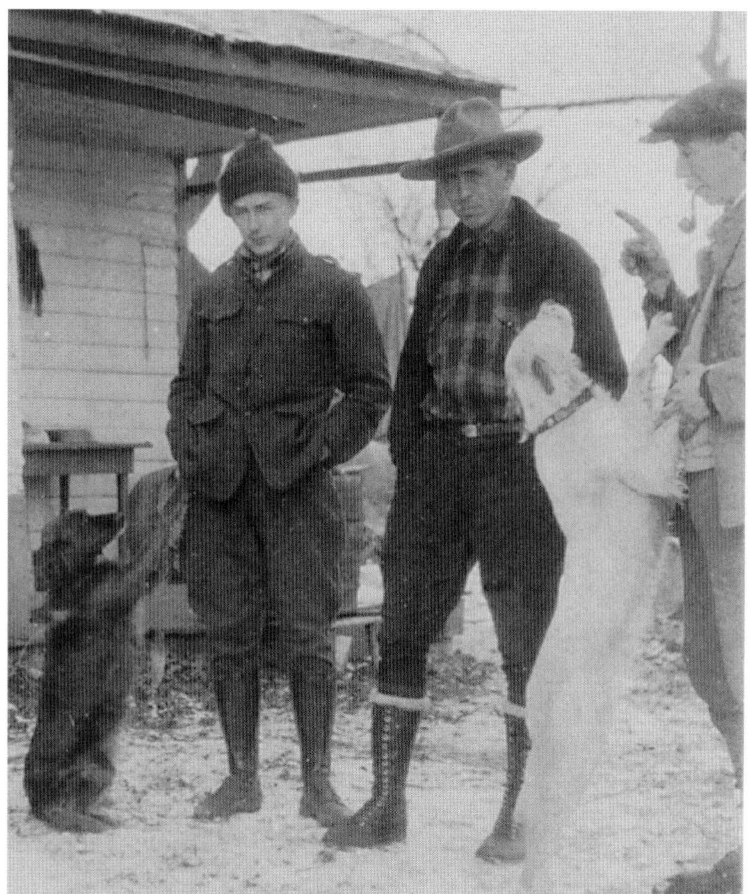

2.17. A picture from the Beach family album taken in front of the family home, ca. 1932. *Right to left:* Henry M. Beach, his son Harry, and son Lyle. Bailey Coll.

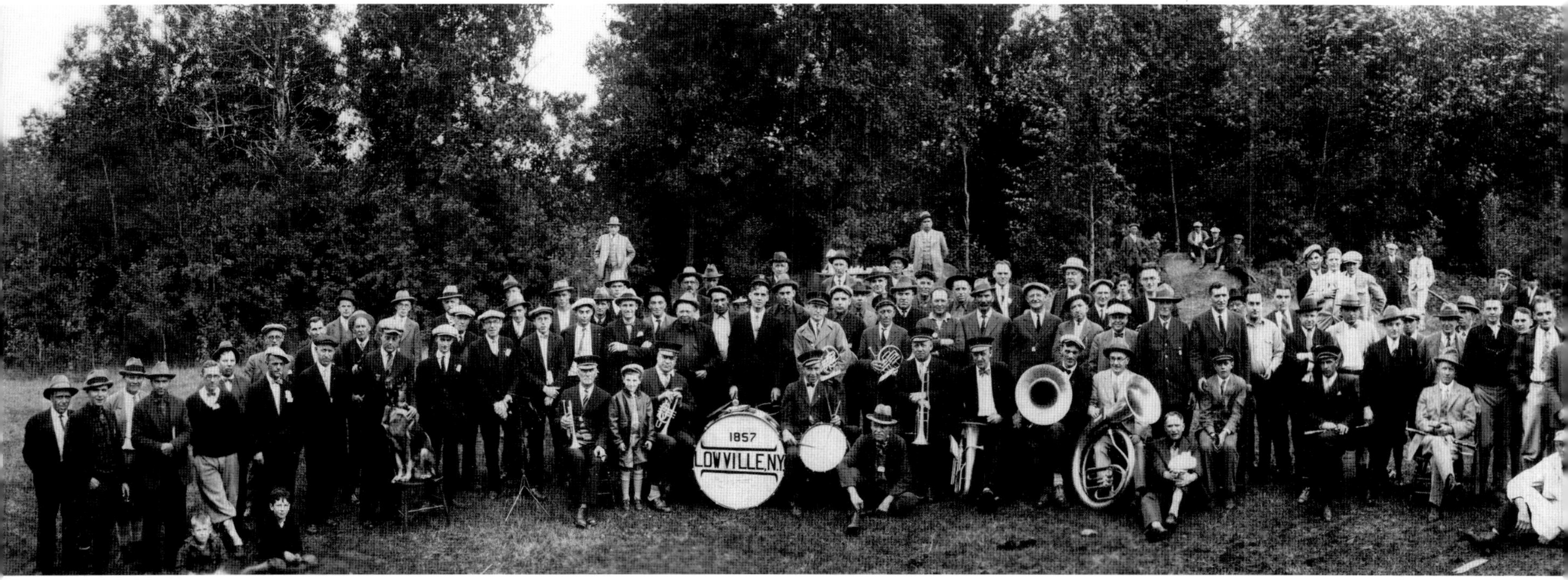

1. Lowville Fish and Game Club clambake, Number Four, N.Y., 1927. Author's Coll.

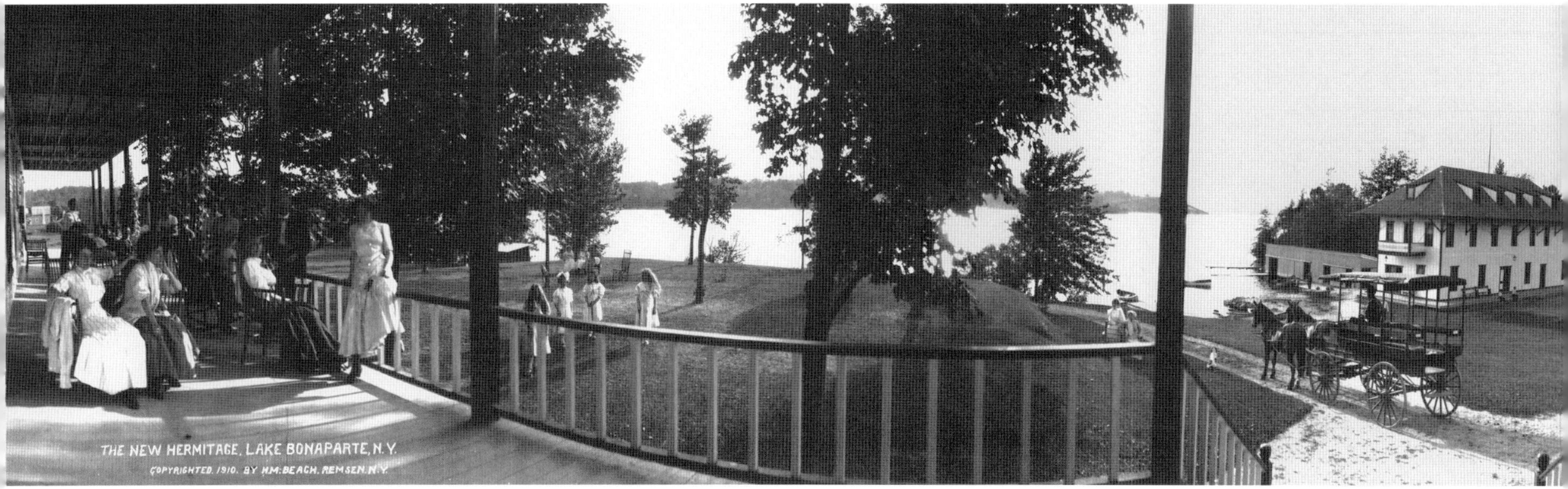

2. The New Hermitage, Lake Bonaparte, N.Y., 1910. Actual photo size is 6½ by 36 inches. Seeber Coll.

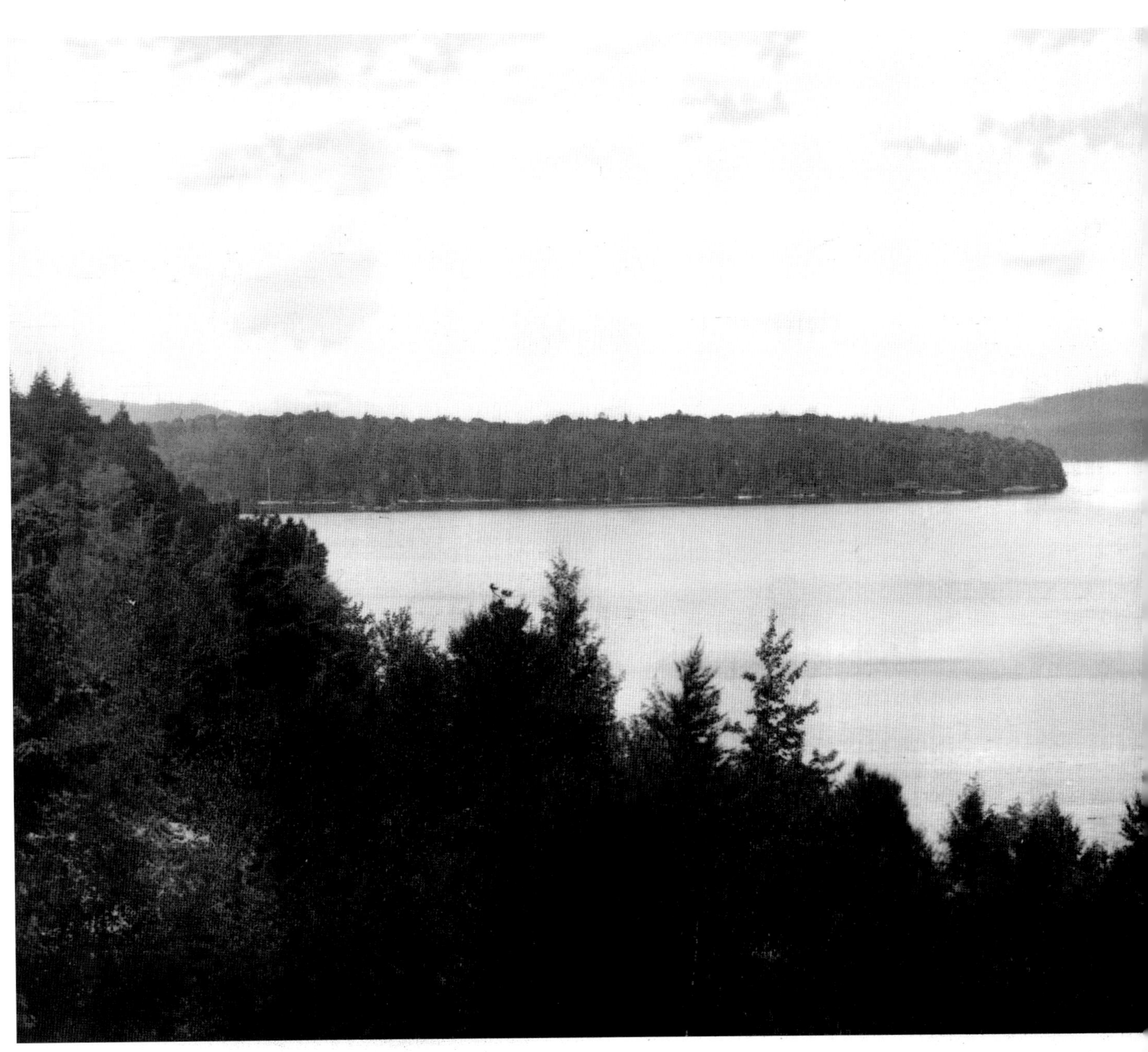

3. Upper Saranac Lake, 1911. Actual size is 6½ by 33½ inches. Seeber Coll.

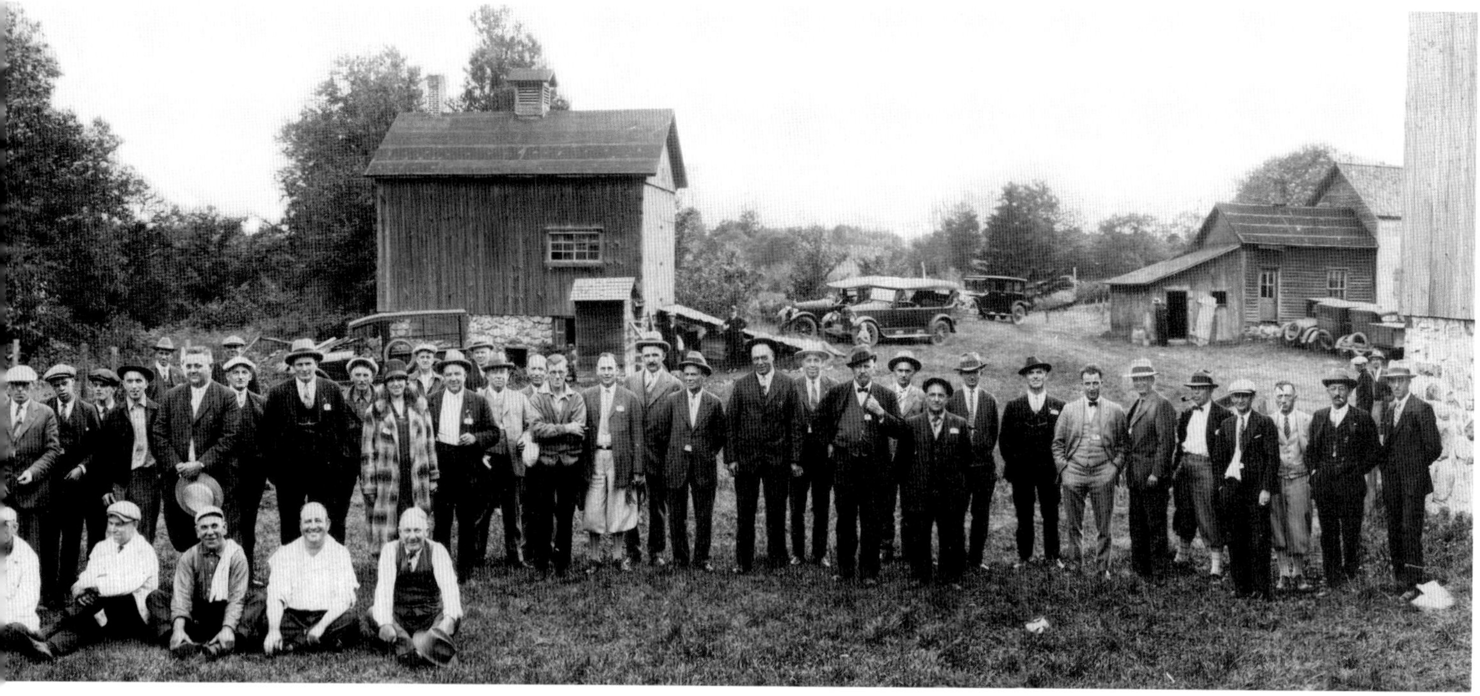

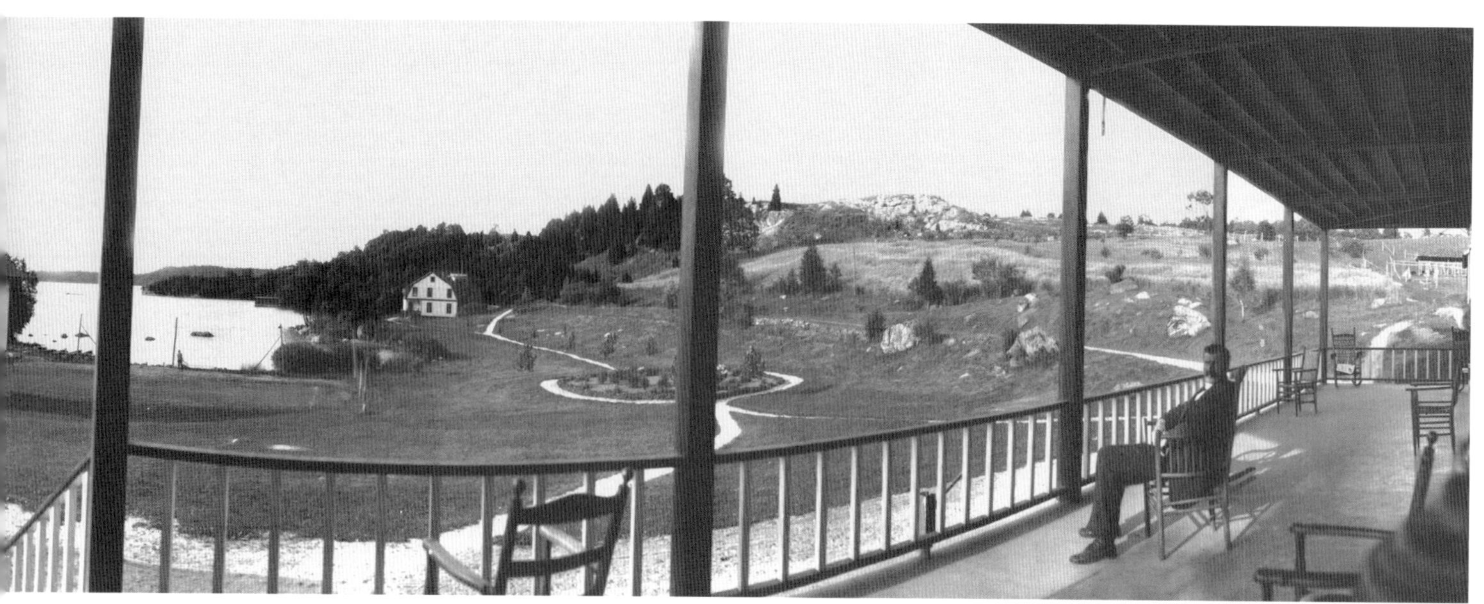

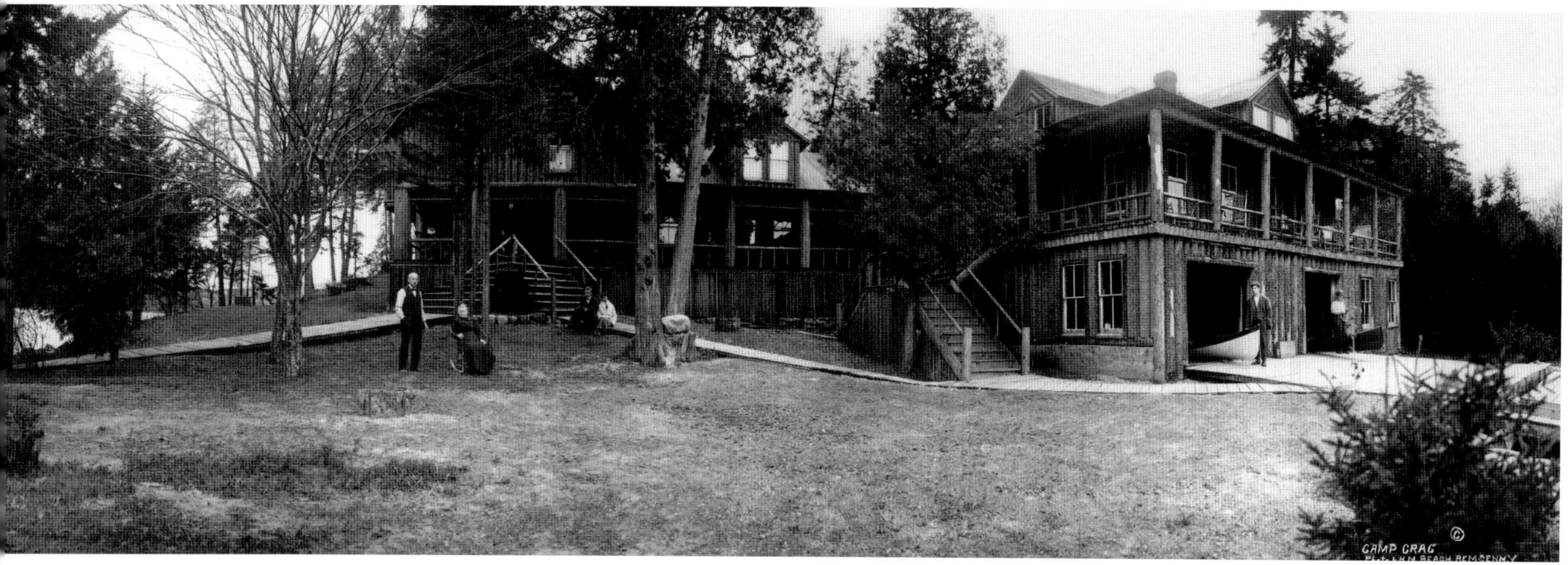

ches. Courtesy of the Adirondack Museum.

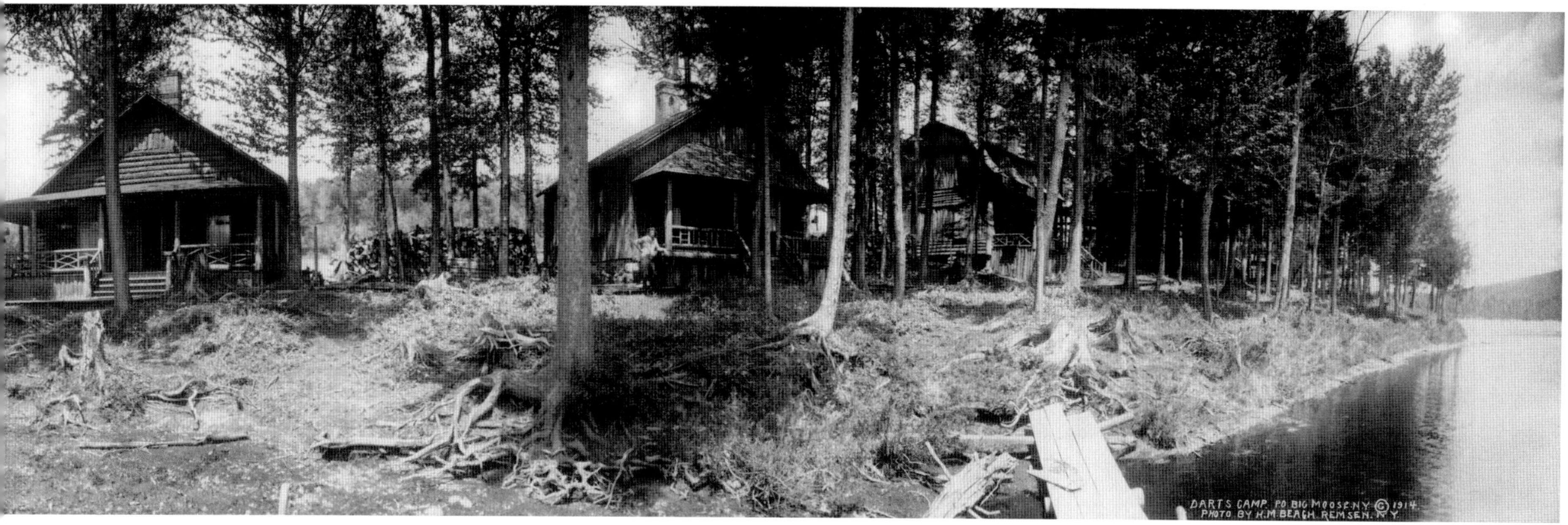

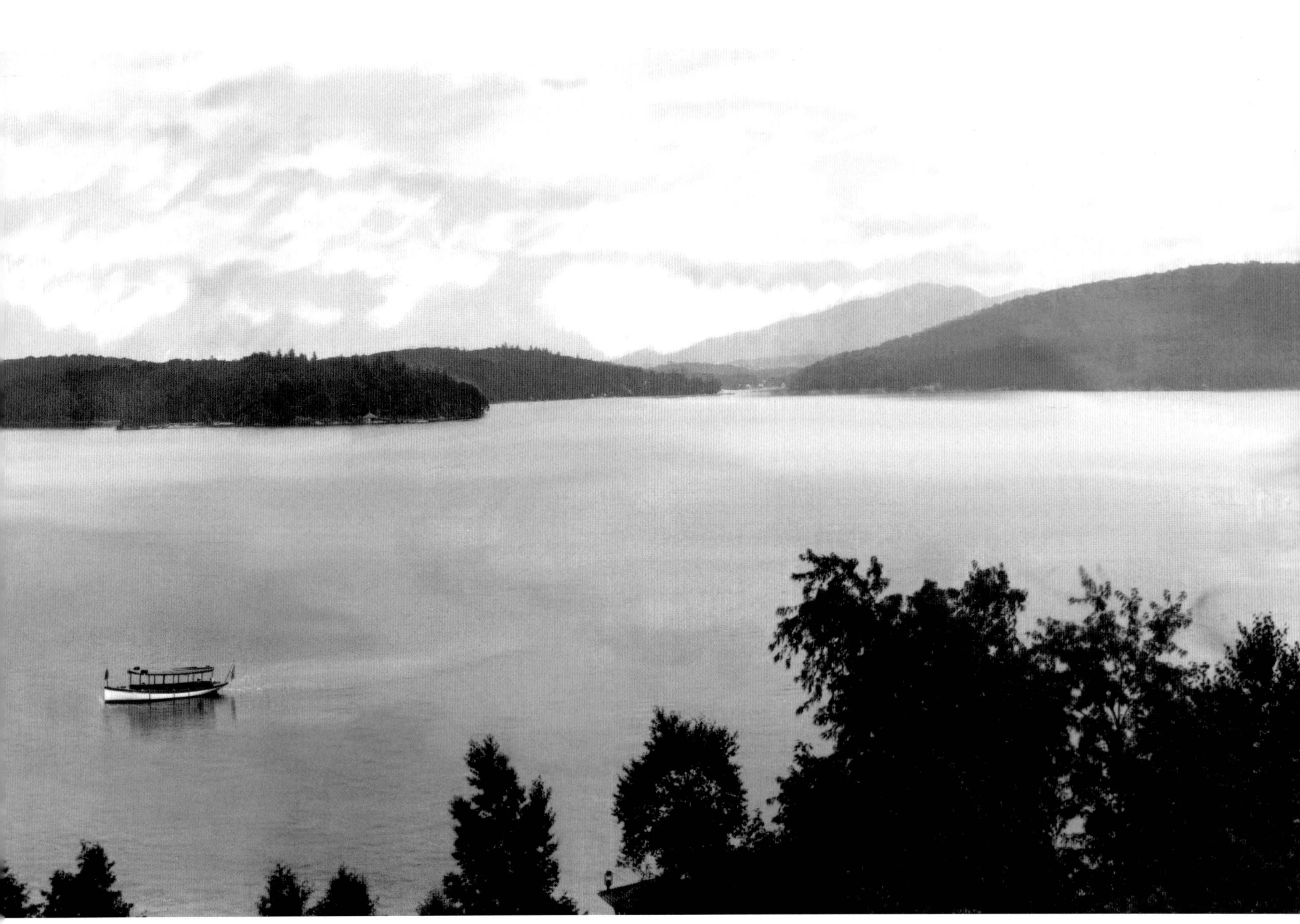

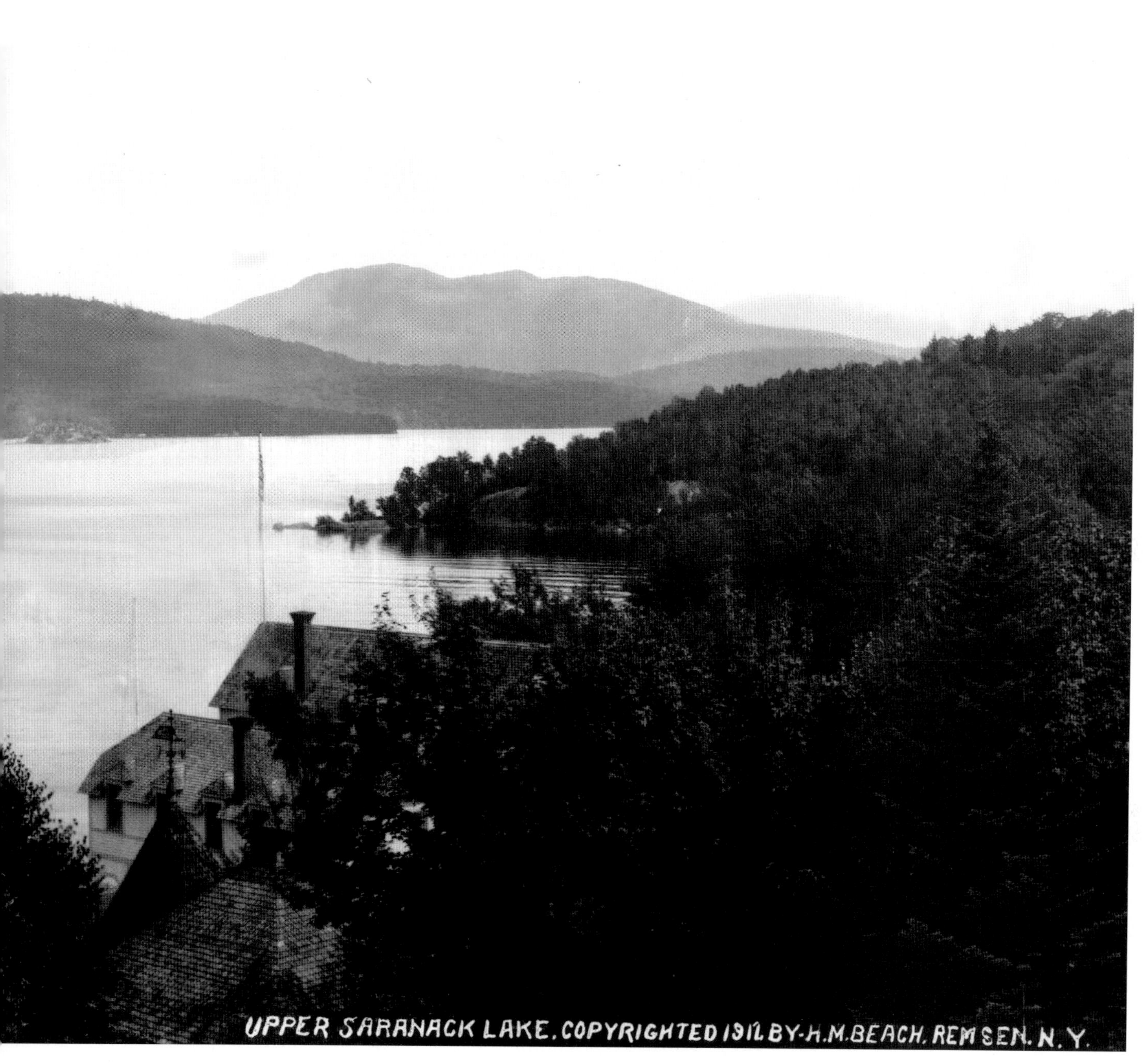
UPPER SARANACK LAKE. COPYRIGHTED 1912 BY-H.M.BEACH. REMSEN. N.Y.

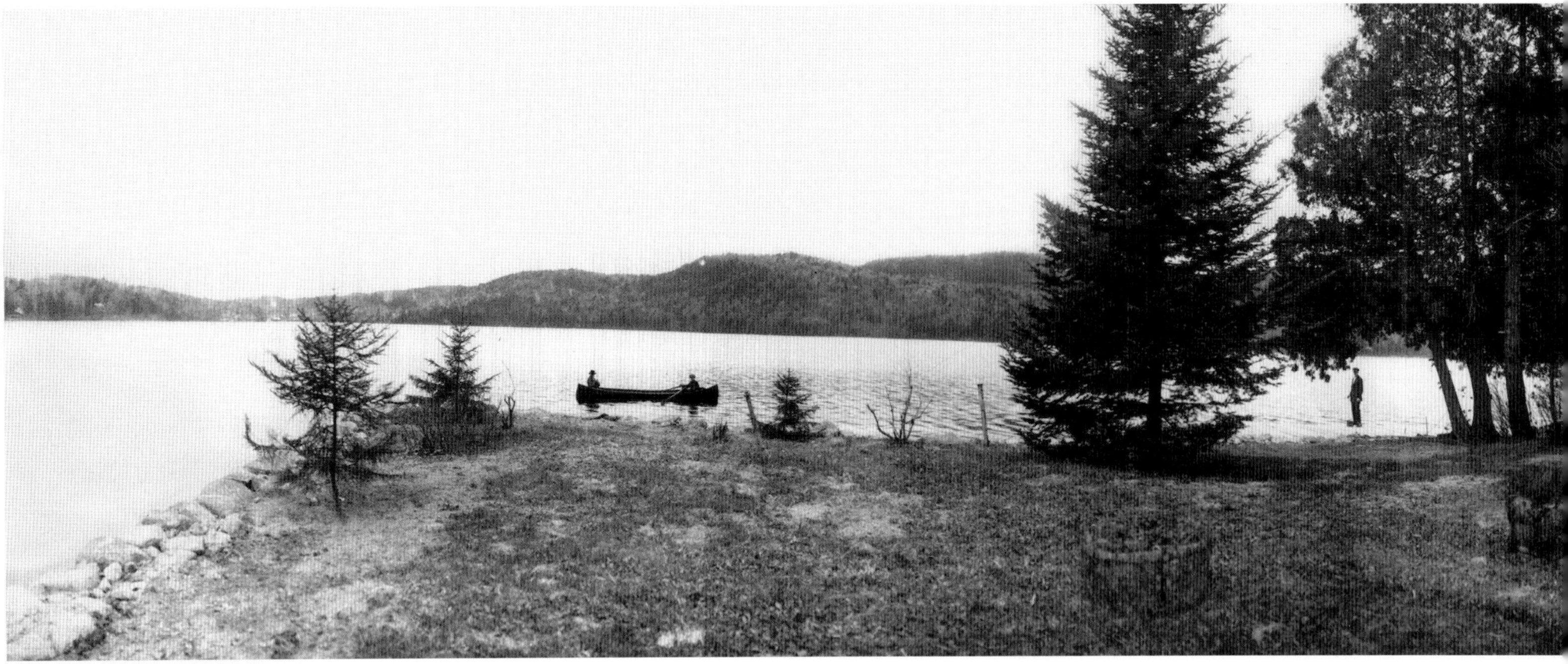

4. Henry Covey and his second wife, Margaret Rose Covey, in front of Camp Crag, Big Moose, N.Y., 1911. Identity of the other couple is unknown. Actual size is 6½ by 32½ in

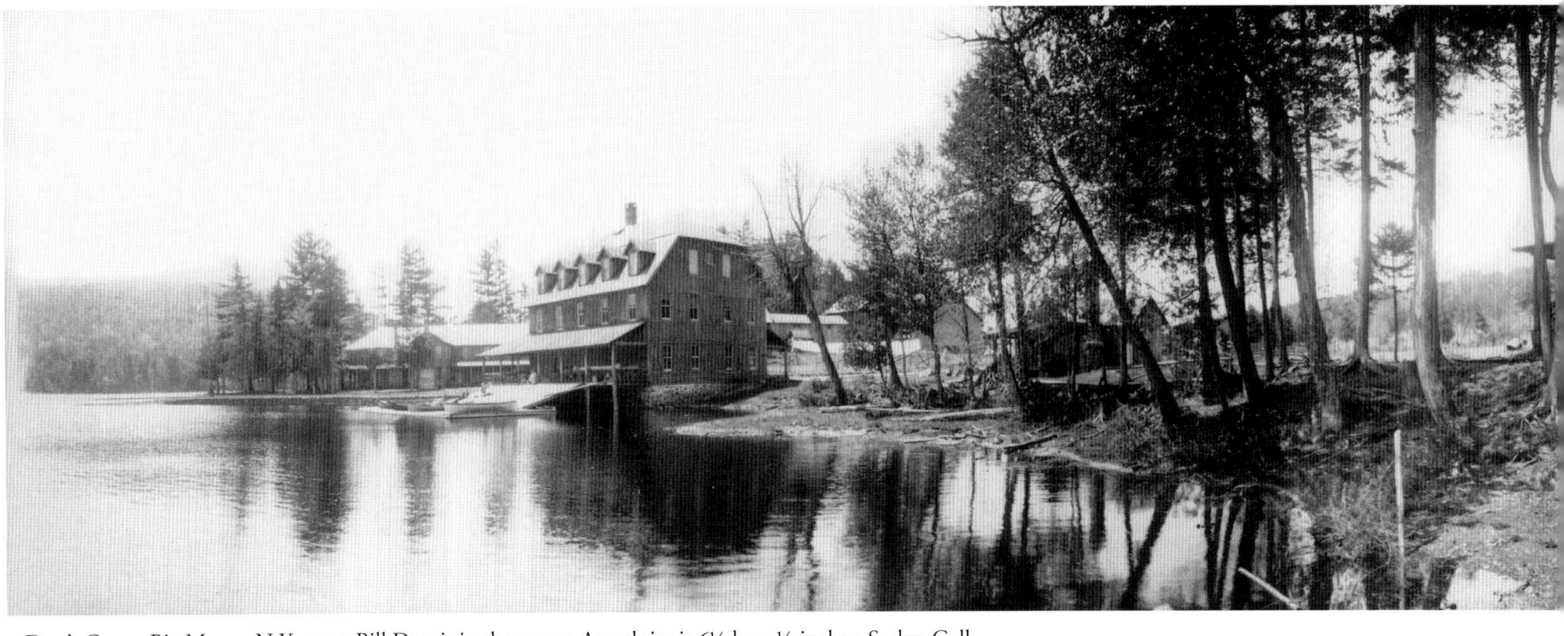

5. Dart's Camp, Big Moose, N.Y., 1914. Bill Dart is in the center. Actual size is 6½ by 35½ inches. Seeber Coll.

3

# How Did You Do Those Pictures, Henry?

## Postcards and Panoramic Photographs

Fifty-pound cameras, negatives five feet long, huge wooden vats filled with developing liquids, glass plates rather than film—Beach's photography was from another era (illus. 3.1). To fully appreciate his work you need to know how he did it. This chapter is about Beach's photography practices. It provides general background, semitechnical information, and particulars about Beach's equipment and techniques.

### The Postcard

During the years Beach was in the postcard business, up to one billion postcards were mailed annually in the United States. That amount was more than ten times the country's population (Blake and Lasansky 1996; Morgan and Brown 1981). This figure represents only a fraction of the cards produced. Postcards' small size made them easy to handle and store—they were much more convenient than other pictures. People passed on cards by hand, enclosed them in envelopes with letters, as well as procured them for their own collections. Travelers bought and sent postcards, and people who stayed at home coveted them as well. Henry Beach embraced the postcard fad early in its trajectory, stuck with it through the mania, and remained loyal to it in the early 1930s while he and it were in decline.

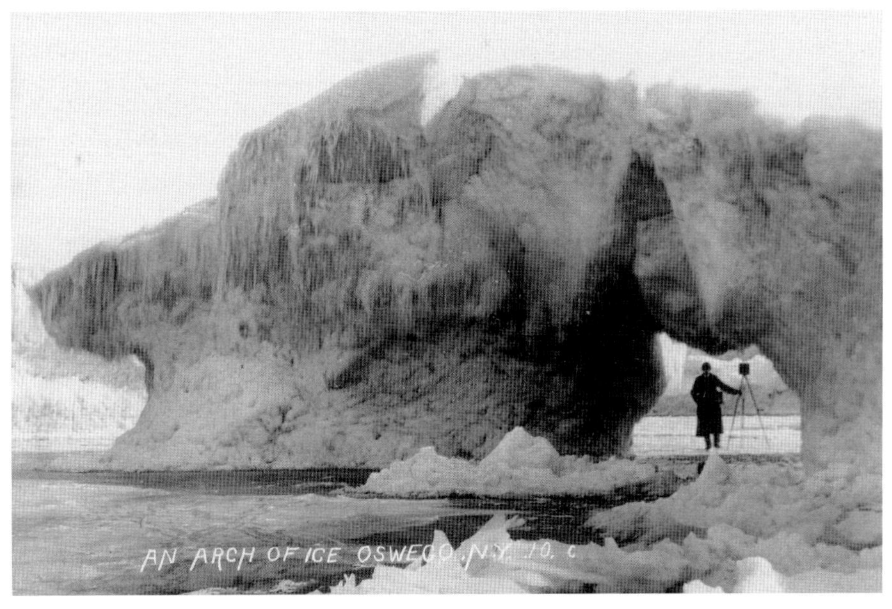


3.1. Beach in an arch of ice, Lake Ontario, Oswego, N.Y., ca. 1912. Courtesy of the Adirondack Museum.

Picture postcards came in two types: printed cards and real photo cards. Printed cards were manufactured using the printing plates and were produced in large lots by major commercial manufacturers on printing presses. Printed cards were most often in color. Real photo cards were actual photographs produced from negatives and printed directly onto postcard stock (heavy photographic paper with preprinted postcard backs). Under a magnifying glass, the picture on the printed card is composed of many small dots, whereas the photo card is continuous. They were produced in smaller runs than printed

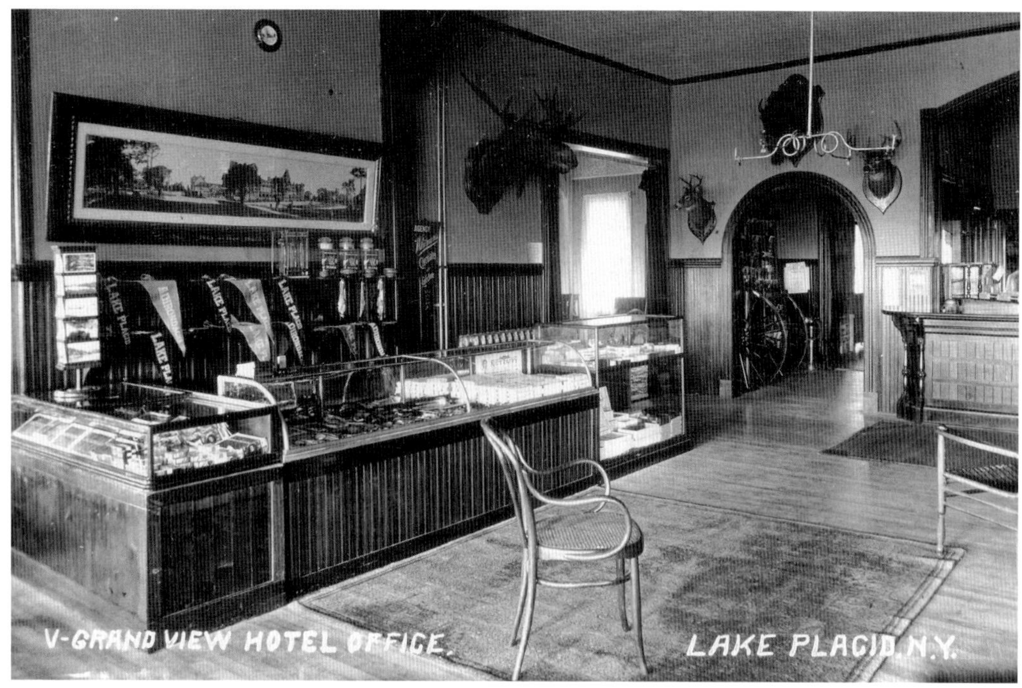


3.2. Grand View Hotel office, Lake Placid, N.Y., ca. 1912. Note the postcard rack on the left. Courtesy of the Adirondack Museum.

cards. Local photographers sold them in their own shops or, like Beach, placed them with local merchants, hotel owners, and roadside businesses (illus. 3.2; see also illustration 1.7).

Printed postcards dominated the urban market, but in rural regions, such as the Adirondacks, photo postcards did quite well. Because they were produced in smaller runs, a larger variety of views customized to a particular locale could be created. The crisp images on photo postcards documented with intense clarity the details of life in rural and small-town America in a way that their printed counterparts could not. Although a few of Beach's photos were pirated and made into printed cards, Henry dealt exclusively in photo postcards. They were the major source of his livelihood.

Compared to other locally based photographers, Beach was a large producer. He took thousands of different views and produced multiple copies of many of them (in one 1910 advertisement he offered to dealers one thousand cards for thirty-five dollars, not less than fifty of any one view). How many he printed from a particular negative varied according to how popular he thought the print would be and how buyers responded. What cards survive is a function not just of how many were made but also of how many were saved. Aggressive spring-cleaners dumped many. Others are available because collectors stored them in shoe boxes or albums. Some Beach views are quite common, whereas others are one of a kind.

Although Beach was prompt in taking up the postcard and some other photographic innovations, he was reluctant to embrace others. For his postcard work he remained devoted to the use of bulky glass dry plates well into the 1920s, long after celluloid film was available. He, like many postcard photographers who came into their own before the turn of the century, chose the higher-quality prints that the glass negative produced over the convenience of rolled film. The fact that Beach's postcards are contact prints made from glass negatives contributes greatly to their clarity. He used a large-view camera mounted on a tripod for his postcard work.

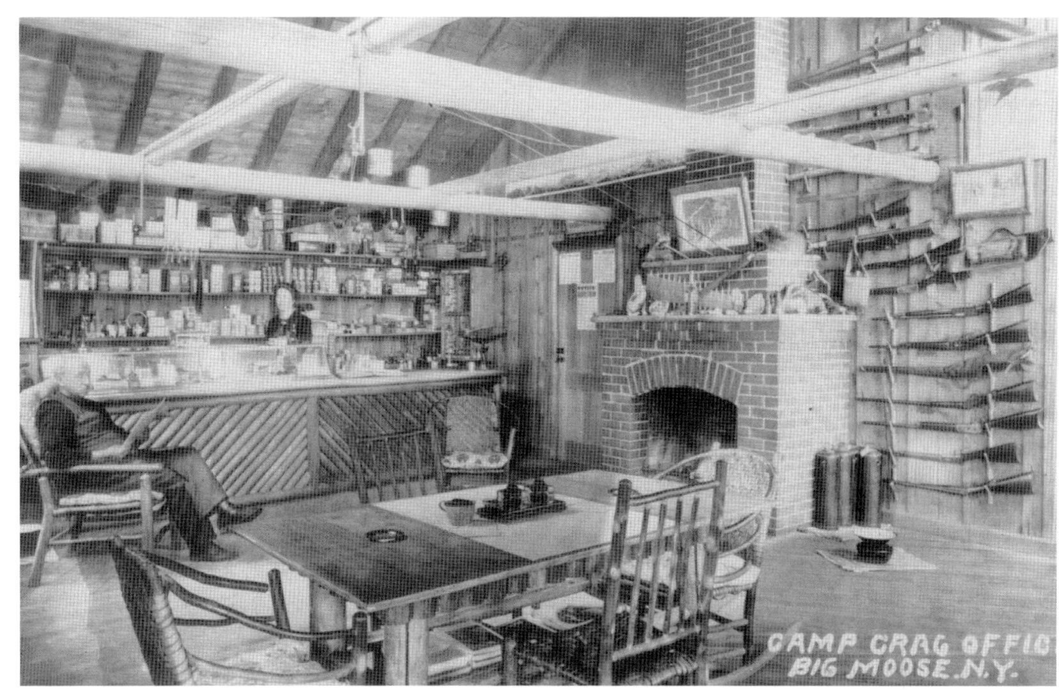


3.3. Camp Crag office with Henry Covey shown fully, ca. 1911. Comstock Coll.

Although the finished product was a contact print, postcard size, the glass negatives he used were larger (5 by 7 inches) than the postcards themselves (approximately 3½ by 5⅜ inches). Beach selected the area of the negative that he wanted on the card. This form of cropping was imprecise and often produced slightly different postcard prints from the same negative. One example is Beach's card of the interior of the office at Camp Crag, Big Moose Lake (illus. 3.3). In some versions one can see the proprietor, Henry Covey, sitting in a chair. In others, only his legs are visible (illus. 3.4). Such disparity is not typical of Beach's cards, however. Apparently, he used a device in some of his printing that simplified making multiple prints and provided consistency in what was printed on the card.

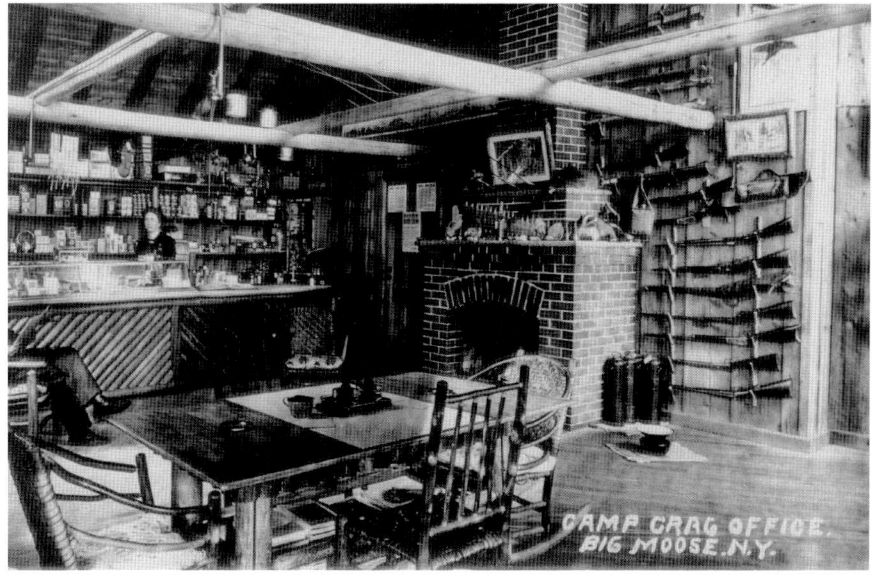


3.4. Camp Crag office, Big Moose, N.Y., with Covey's legs showing, ca. 1911. Gates Coll.

## Identifying Beach Postcards

How can you tell a Beach photo postcard from the ones taken by other photographers? After 1907, Henry printed the majority of his images on photo-paper stock with a characteristic and distinctive graphic design on the back that included his name.

In addition, he often incorporated "Beach" in white printing as part of the caption on the picture side of the card (he did so by writing in black ink on the negatives). The majority of Beach cards have one or the other or both imprints. Many of Beach's post-1907 cards were not printed on distinctive backs. He ordered his postcard paper from major producers. If you ordered in quantity you could get the cards personalized with your design printed on the address side, at no additional charge. But when Beach got busy he ran out of inscribed backs and relied on the standard stock. In addition, when his business was in decline, in the mid- to late 1920s, he stopped using special backs. Many of his postcards do not have his name on the image side either. He was not diligent in marking them.

Even without these obvious markers, the discerning, practiced eye can identify his images by the characteristic handwriting on the captions. But it can get tricky because more than one hand did the lettering. Advanced postcard collectors claim to be able to tell a Beach by its look. Although his style is distinctive, jumping to conclusions about particular images can lead to misidentification.

One difficulty in identifying Beach photograph cards by the backs is that Beach printed other people's negatives as well, or at least he promoted this aspect of his business in advertisements. Part of the text in his logo on some backs is the phrase "made from any photo." We do not know whether others' images were printed on his own distinct stock. Further, it is possible that Henry's son Harry printed from his father's negatives on Beach postcard paper left over when his father died. All of these unknown factors complicate the task of coming up with a definitive answer to the question of whether a particular card is an authentic Beach and even just what "authentic" means.

## Dating Beach Cards from Backs

Identifying Beach cards becomes more complex when we consider his earliest postcard work. Before 1907 Beach did not print his cards on paper stock with a distinctive back. Then, in 1907, postal regulations mandated that the back side of the postcard, the side without the picture, be reserved exclusively for the stamp and the address. No messages! After 1907 the government allowed divided backs. A line down the center split it into two sections—the left for messages, the right for the address.

Predivided-back Beach cards are not as distinctively marked as his later ones. His notation consists of small, plain printed letters—"Photo by Beach, Remsen," "Beach Photo'r," or "Beach, Lowville"—on the bottom of the picture side or on the end of the address side. (Some are accompanied by the phrase "Souvenir Photograph" followed by the name of the town in the picture.)

The backs of Beach's divided cards catch your eye. There are slightly different versions of the basic Beach design that allow you to approximate a date when the card was produced. The back in illustration 3.5 was used from about 1907 until 1911. Note the lettering in the heading and the absence of text in the upper-left corner.

On the back of the card in illustration 3.6, the one he used in 1912 and 1913, the style of the lettering changed slightly, and the text appears in the upper-left corner. (The letters "B. S." refer to "Beach-Series.")

He started using the back we see in illustration 3.7 in 1913. The typeface for "Postcard" in the heading is distinct; "Beach-Series" was dropped and "Beach's Real Photograph" added. Also, the phrase "Beach Quality" replaced the line dividing the message from the address sections. Beach continued to use this back after he left Remsen in 1917.

The three card backs illustrated are by far the most common, but similar designs were produced with only slight variations. For example, one back he used after returning to the Lowville area included "Made at Glenfield, N.Y." as part of the heading. (Beach did not live in Glenfield, but that town was his postal address when he moved back to Watson.) Although the generalizations

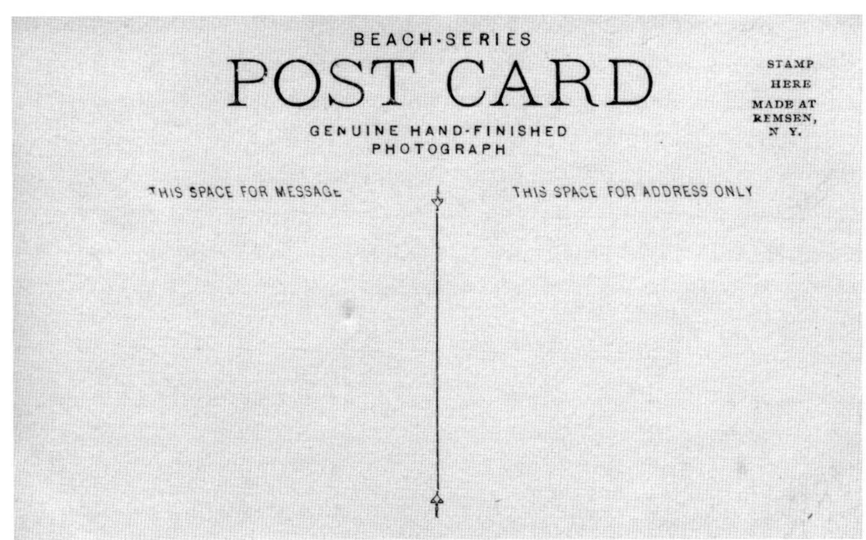


3.5. Beach-Series postcard back, ca. 1909. Author's Coll.

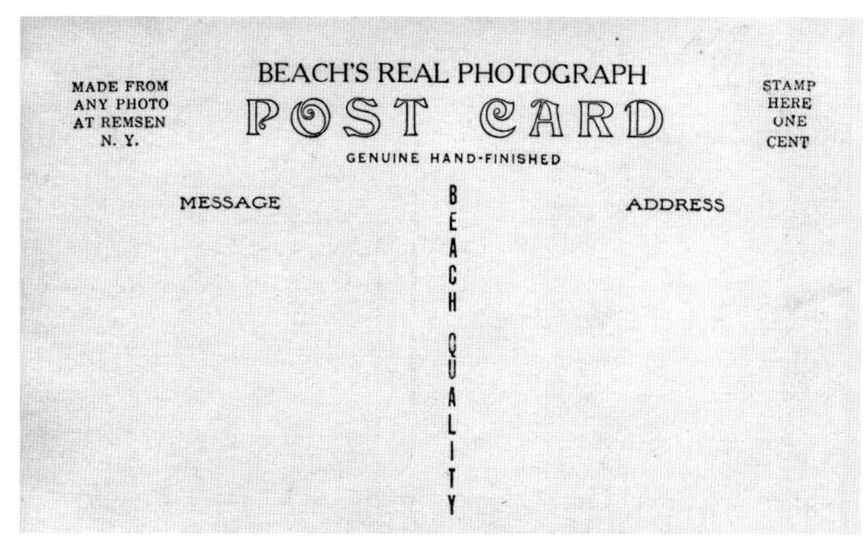


3.7. Back of Beach postcard used after 1913. Author's Coll.

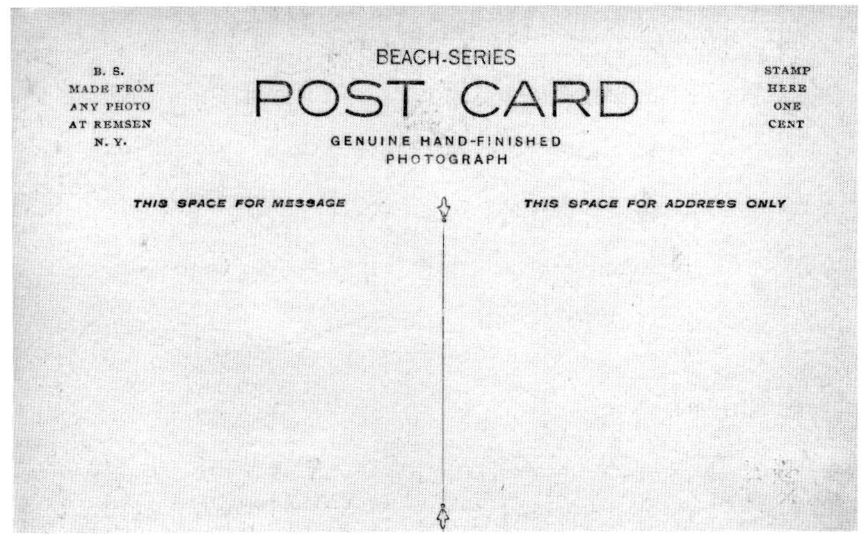


3.6. Back of Beach postcard used in 1912 and 1913. Author's Coll.

regarding dating Beach's cards hold up over many cards, a good deal of overlap occurred in the use of the various backs at different times.[1]

## Captions

Like most postcard and panoramic photographers Beach printed handwritten captions on the majority of his photographs. Many photographers accomplished this task by writing in india ink in reverse on the negative. It was awkward and resulted in backward-letter mistakes on the printed pictures. Although Beach's captions contain many printing and spelling blunders, I have seen only one with backward letters. Although this detail would suggest that he used another captioning method, the captions on the negatives owned by the Adirondack Museum are in india ink. Some Beach cards have captions that are very close to the edge or even cut off, which is the result of the printer not lining the paper up properly on the glass plate.

In part two, as I review Beach's images I will discuss the text in his captions. As you will see, they were part and parcel of the view, not just informational add-ons. They provide insights about Henry's view of the world and of his North Country culture.

## "Beach-Series"

"Beach-Series" is printed on the backs of many cards. Beach photographed specific locations and printed them in groups or in series that he numbered consecutively. It is very difficult to decipher his numbering scheme and to tell what photographs belong to what groups. One cause for confusion is Henry's practice of changing the captions with different printings of the same negative. Another is that he would produce one numbered series of a particular location one year, then go back and produce another numbered series of the same place another time, without acknowledging in the caption that they were from different sets.

He packaged some sequences in envelopes with printed titles (for example, "Herkimer Flood Series") and sold them together. We know very little about this marketing strategy because the envelopes he used were disposable and fragile and only a few survived. Although the sale by series might have been an important part of his business, it did not constrain him from marketing cards individually. Indeed, the sale of single cards in bulk to retailers was his biggest source of income.

Except for the terse, semiliterate captions on individual images, Beach's series were not accompanied by any written text. The total effect of his particular groupings, however, adds up to much more than the sum of the individual shots. Together they tell a story of sorts, albeit fragmented. Beach appears to have had a grasp of the concept of the photo essay in its most rudimentary form.[2] We will see more examples as we examine his work, especially his work on Benson Mines in chapter 10.

## Panoramic Photography

In 1904, just at the time photo postcards were becoming popular, the Cirkut panoramic camera came on the market.[3] The Cirkut defined the meaning of panoramic as it launched another photographic rage: the long picture.[4] Al-

1. This dating scheme is precarious in that it is based on postmark dates on the cards. Postcards can be bought and mailed long after they are produced, so postmarks are not a precise way to tell when a card was produced. Also, there could be a significant time lag between when Beach actually took the picture and when he printed it as a postcard for sale. As we will see, a few of his logging postcards printed after 1907 were likely taken well before the turn of the century.

2. His clusters of numbered photos do not approach photographic essays that began appearing in magazines such as *National Geographic* soon after postcards became popular, or the full-blown versions of photo-documentary essays launched by *Life* magazine in the late 1930s (Edey 1978; Willumson 1992).

3. The Cirkut was patented by William Johnston in 1904 and was first manufactured by the Rochester Panoramic Camera Company that merged with Century Camera Company in 1905. Various companies were involved in the development of the camera's technology, but it was the Eastman Kodak Company that dominated its production.

4. Although extremely popular, and an important source of revenue for commercial photographers, Cirkut panoramics and the photographers who used them are absent in histories of photography. There is very little written about panoramic photography in general (Meehan 1990). Eugene Goldbeck (Burleson and Hickman 1986) was a talented photographer who founded the National Photo Service in San Antonio, Texas, and is the subject of a fine book that reviews not only his life and work, but also the history of the Cirkut camera (Borsavage 1979).

though we do not know exactly when Beach bought his first Cirkut camera and started experimenting with it, he was selling large panoramic prints by 1909.

By *panoramic photograph* I am not referring exclusively to scenery shots taken at a distance, such as might be captured from the top of a mountain. It was the dimensions of the picture rather than the subject matter that made a photograph "panoramic." Compared to their height, they were unusually long. Although their length varied, a common synonym for the panoramic print was "the yard-long photograph." This down-to-earth expression came into use because thirty-two inches was the popular size, but in addition the slang phrase fitted the genre's awkward shape and widespread use.

Scenic panoramics were not the best sellers. All commercial panoramic photographers specialized in pictures of large groups. This point was a matter of business rather than of aesthetics. People bought pictures in which they were included, so the more people in a shot the greater would be the sales. Outings, celebrations, graduations, workers outside their factories, and more were all photo opportunities. Beach photographed all of these groups. The photograph of the Lowville Fish and Game Club shows Beach's vernacular approach as he captures locals assembled at the annual clambake at Number Four near Stillwater (panoramic 1). Taken in 1927, it is one of Beach's later panoramics.

Like his contemporaries, Beach took panoramics of military units. Especially during World War I, when "yard-long" photos were the craze and recruits gathered at training camps, photographers prospered by selling photo mementos to the troops. Beach took many panoramics of Pine Camp (forerunner of the present Fort Drum in St. Lawrence County) before, during, and after World War I. As I mentioned in chapter 2, Beach also traveled to training camps in the South during the war years, taking and selling his yard-long images.

Unlike typical town or urban photographers, Beach took scenery panoramics of the Adirondack landscape. He also took expansive pictures of large Adirondack hotels and other North Country resorts, especially the ones around the Fulton Chain, Big Moose, Saranac Lake, and Lake Placid.

## The Cirkut Camera

The name "Cirkut camera" derives from "circuit," which means to follow a circular path. That basic concept is what was behind the engineering of the camera. The heavy instrument was mounted on a platform that turned on top of a large, sturdy tripod. Spring-powered gears allowed slow rotation. As the camera turned in an arc, the image was projected through the lens (a regular lens, not a wide-angle one), and then through a narrow slit onto the celluloid film (the aperture remained open as the camera swung). The film moved too. It was taken up on a spool that was connected to the large gear on the tripod head. The movement of the camera (with its corresponding projection of the changing image onto the film) was ingeniously synchronized with the film's progress as it was pulled past the light slit. The result was huge exposure.[5]

Cirkut cameras were numbered according to the maximum width of the film each could accommodate. They ranged from a no. 5 to a no. 16. Beach owned a no. 8 and a no. 10. The pictures produced were contact prints that made them the same size as the negative and spectacularly sharp and detailed. Looking at a large group of people in a yard-long picture, you sense that you are there with them and looking each of them in the eye. The majority of Beach's panoramics were six and one-half inches wide printed on ten inch–wide paper (which left a black border around the image). The panoramics ranged in length from about twenty to forty-six inches.

Although the cameras could rotate a full 360 degrees, Beach almost always set the gear to take an arc of less than a half circle. He adjusted how far the camera panned to accommodate the size of the group or the scene being photographed. Pictures taken by a camera rotating too many degrees had an obvious convex distortion. Therefore, smaller arcs were preferred (which is probably the reason for the widespread use of the approximately thirty-two-inch length). I will return to the topic of distortion later.[6]

For readers unfamiliar with the Cirkut, let me try to give a better sense of how it worked and of the nature of the picture it produced. Imagine being in

5. Appearing in the same panoramic photograph twice was a favorite prank of young people. It was possible because of the slow rotating speed of the Cirkut. You could run from one side of the group around the back side of the camera to the other side in time to be panned twice. I have never seen a Beach panoramic illustrating this phenomenon, which is because either it was frowned upon in the North Country or Beach prohibited the trick.

6. The speed of the rotation was also adjustable and allowed for exposure times for any section of the film from one-half to one-twelfth of a second. The lenses supplied with the Cirkut camera were convertible, giving a choice of three focal lengths, depending on whether the front, rear, or both lenses were used. The various adjustments gave the photographer considerable choice in the length and width of the picture, exposure, and angle of view.

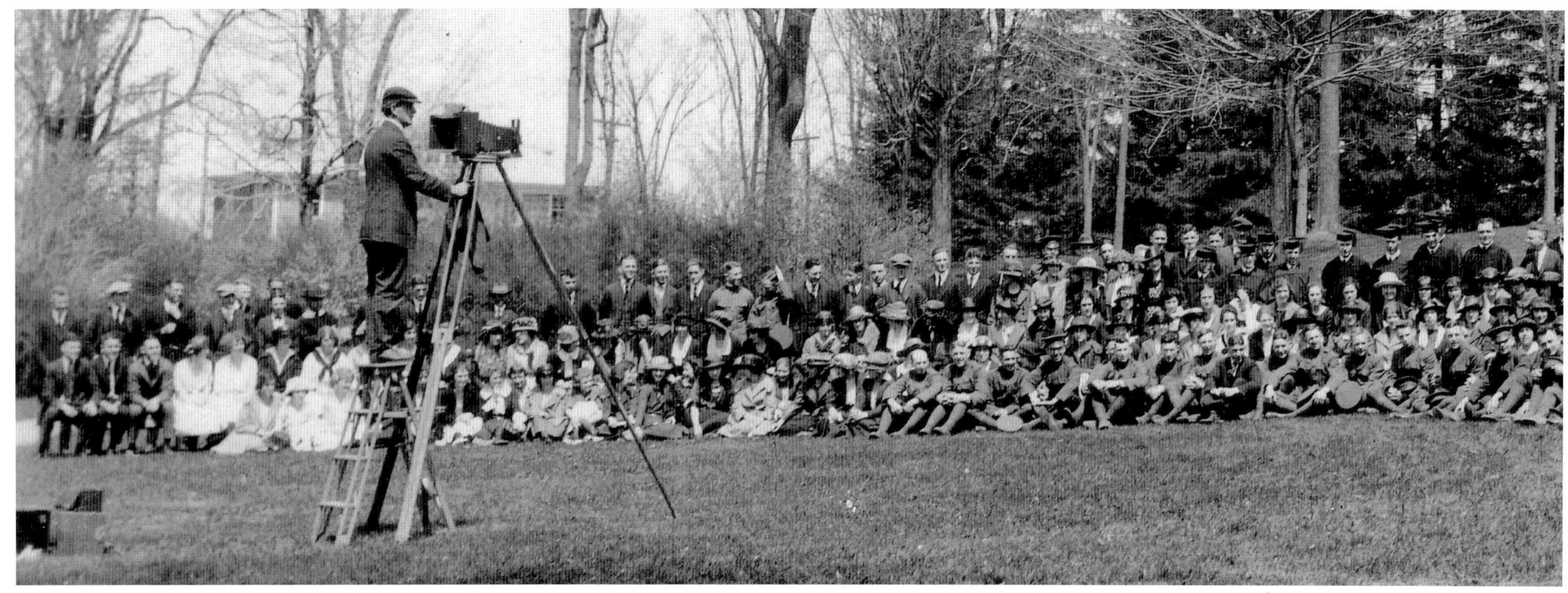

3.8. Panoramic photographer McAllister in the process of taking a group panoramic photograph with a Cirkut camera, ca. 1923. Courtesy of the University of Vermont.

the city and standing in the center of an intersection of two perpendicular streets. With a normal camera you could point it in any direction and take a picture of one or, at most, two of the street corners. With the Cirkut, it was possible to have all four street corners in one picture. Imagine the photographer with a tripod-mounted Cirkut camera standing at equal distance from the four corners ready to take a picture. He or she pushes the button and the camera rotates 360 degrees, stops, and shuts down. The camera would have taken a picture of the circumference of a circle from the center. If you developed the film, printed it, and spread the long photograph on a flat table, you would be looking at a picture of the circumference flattened out. This picture would include the four corners of the intersection but would have a convex visual distortion that would be very disorientating.

Beach took the picture of the porch of the New Hermitage Hotel, Lake Bonaparte, by placing his Cirkut camera in the entryway of the hotel and setting it to rotate 180 degrees (panoramic 2). His picture shows both the scope of what could be included in a panoramic picture and the convex distortion. If you stood in the doorway, where Beach stood, and turned your head to the left to see the seated women, and then to the right to see the man sitting in the chair, you would be simulating the camera's range of movement.[7]

As you can see, there are visual advantages to taking a picture with the Cirkut. What can be included is amazing. The range of activity that is captured

7. By looking at a panoramic from the center of arch made by bending an unframed panoramic, the distortion is minimized.

provides a different view of the scene. The camera creates images that would be impossible to capture by any other means.

Beach created his pictures with the convex effect in mind. In some cases, such as the picture of the porch, he used it for his own purposes. In another shot he used it effectively to exaggerate the length of a train. On a few occasions he experimented with purposeful distortion to create photographs that looked like abstracts. We will see such examples in the second part of the book.

Most often, Beach attempted to mitigate or minimize the effect. One way of doing so in taking group photos was to arrange the subjects in an arc that corresponded to the circumference that the camera would swing through. The corresponding curvature created a picture where the people looked like they were in a straight line.

It was not easy to accomplish a well-executed picture with a large Cirkut camera (illus. 3.8). The Cirkuts and the accompanying equipment were large, cumbersome, and difficult to use, lug to the site, and set up. The no. 10 Cirkut camera weighed fifty pounds. Mounting it on a level tripod was a big job. Then there was the task of arranging the crowd in just the right way with each person positioned so he or she could be seen. Neither getting the camera settings correct nor getting the people to cooperate was easy. Processing the large film and printing the long negatives required special equipment and talent. In addition, the cost of the equipment made panoramic photography a substantial investment. In 1915 the suggested retail price of a no. 10 was $290.

The problems involved with panoramic photography discouraged snapshot amateurs from getting involved. It was a form of picture taking that local commercial photographers could latch on to and in which they would make a profit. Some photographers jumped at the opportunity and made it their specialty, almost to the exclusion of all other forms of work. It was common for people who embraced postcards as a source of revenue to do large-format panoramics as well.

## Identifying Beach Panoramics

The broad black borders (two inches or so) surrounding Beach panoramic photos are characteristic of his work (they have been cropped from the photos used in illustrations in this book). Some photos, however, are occasionally found without the border, though the owner most often removed it to get the photo to fit into a smaller frame. The border frames the pictures, creating a dramatic effect and drawing your eye to the image. Upon examining the borders carefully, one often sees irregularities and other imperfections that clash with the otherwise professional effect of the dark circumference. Beach probably produced the borders by placing the large panoramic negative in the center of a rectangular light box the surface of which was significantly larger than the negative. Thus, when the negative was exposed to light, the border would get a full dose of illumination and the dark border would be created.

The majority of Beach panoramic photographs have his name prominently displayed on the front. It appears as H. M. Beach followed by the location of his studio: H. M. Beach, Lowville, or H. M. Beach, Remsen. Most often, it appears as part of the border and under the caption centered under the picture. Alternatively, it is in the bottom-right corner of the image itself.

Beach practiced a particular writing and design style in many of the panoramic captions that appear on the borders. The lettering is informal, quirky, with squiggly lines and other kooky features that resemble graffiti more than professional script. Be it flamboyant or more conventional, the style of the lettering resembles his postcard captions, only greatly enlarged. Unlike the postcard lettering, the jumbo version often looks crude and uneven, an effect that adds to its homespun quality. That folksy quality is enhanced by traces of erased or corrected letters and whole captions seen when the pictures are examined carefully.

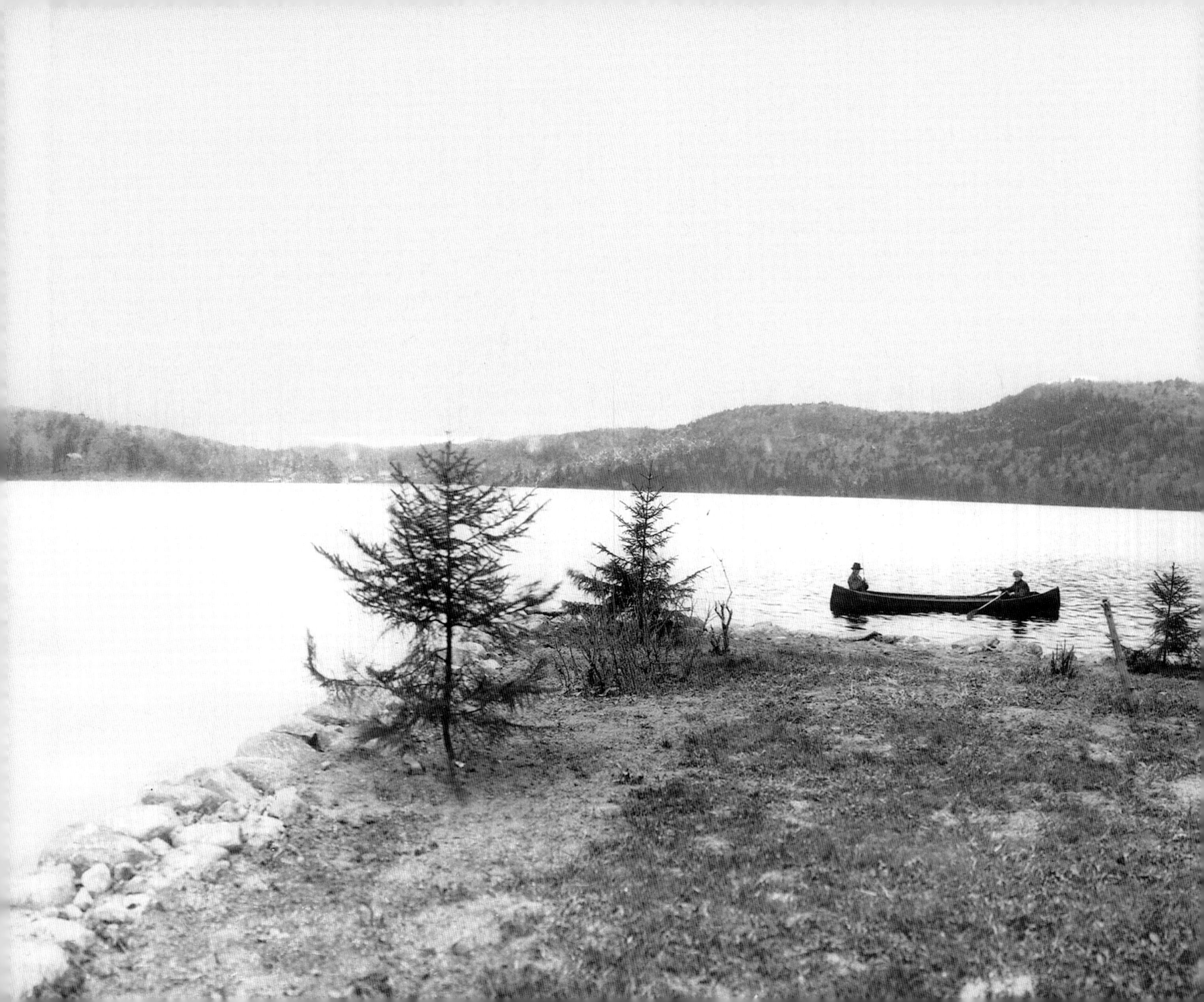

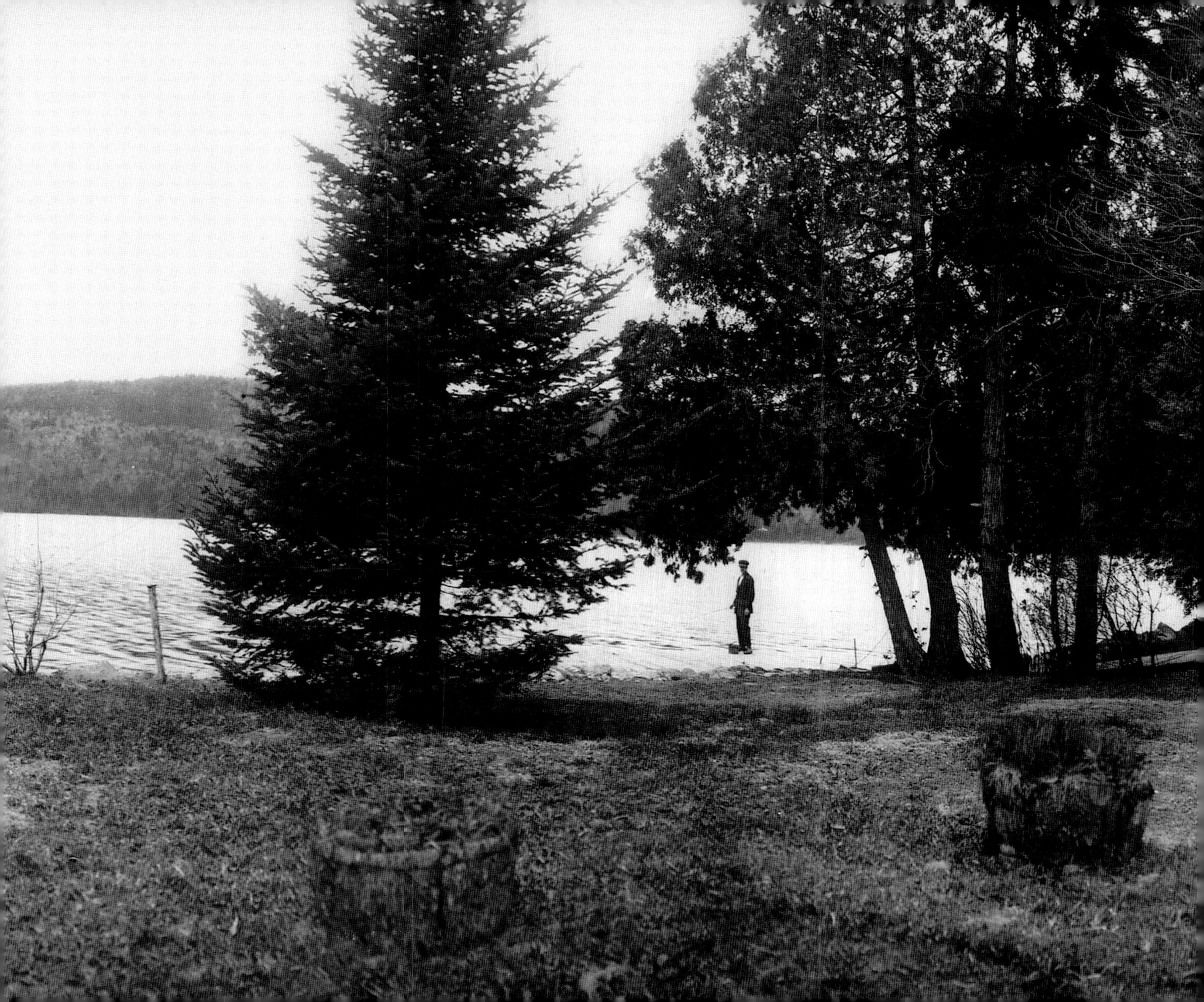

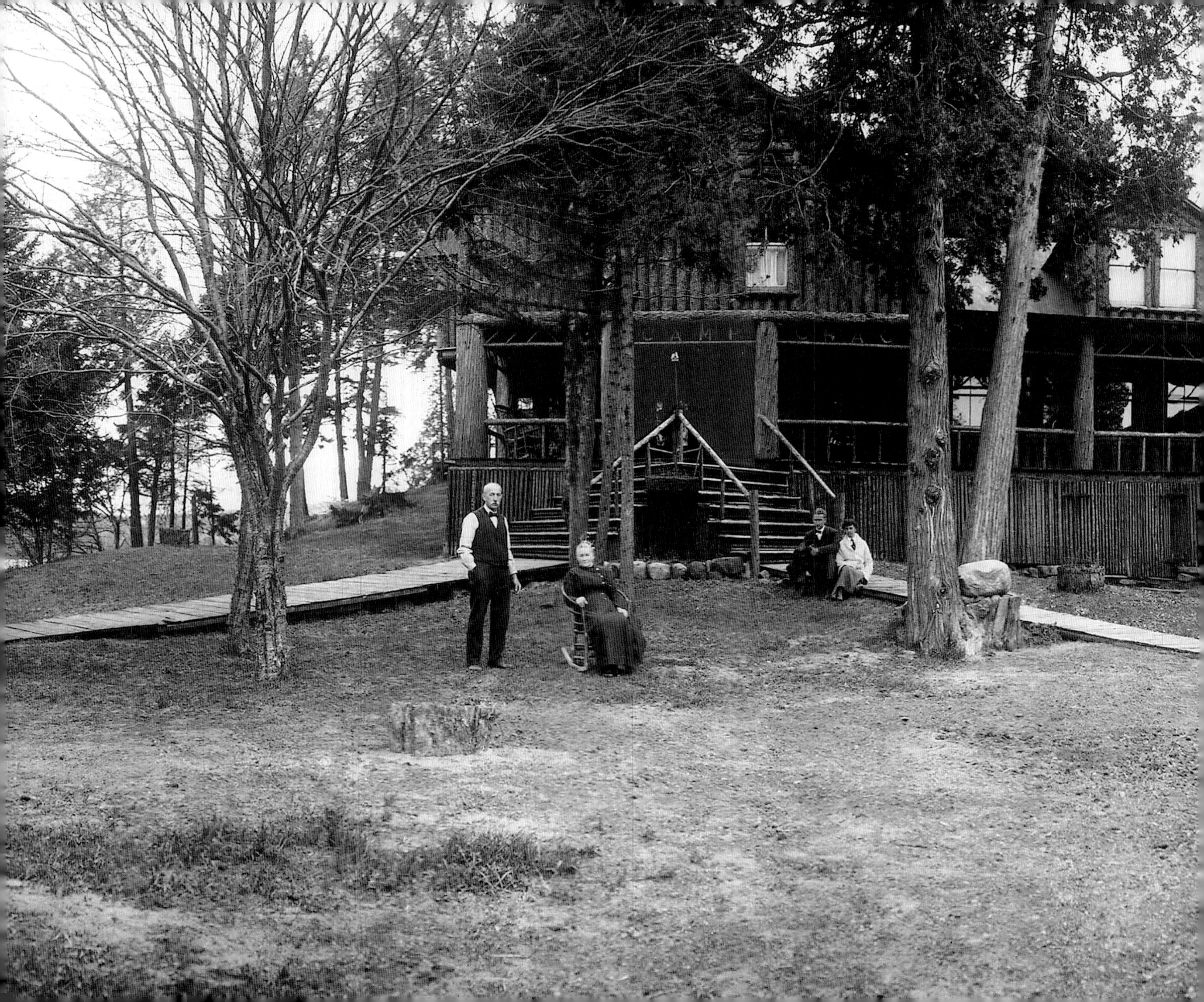

# PART TWO The Photographs

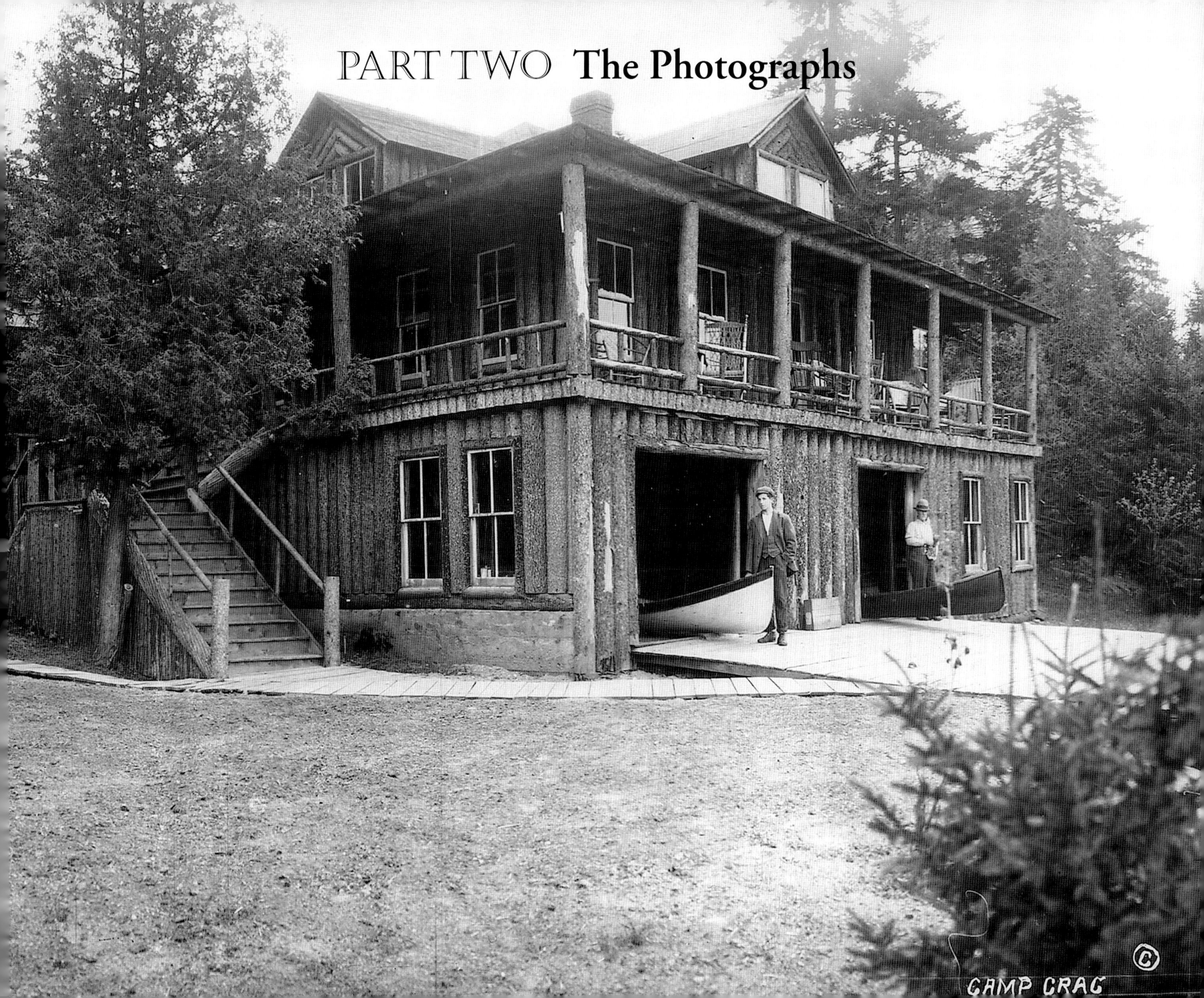

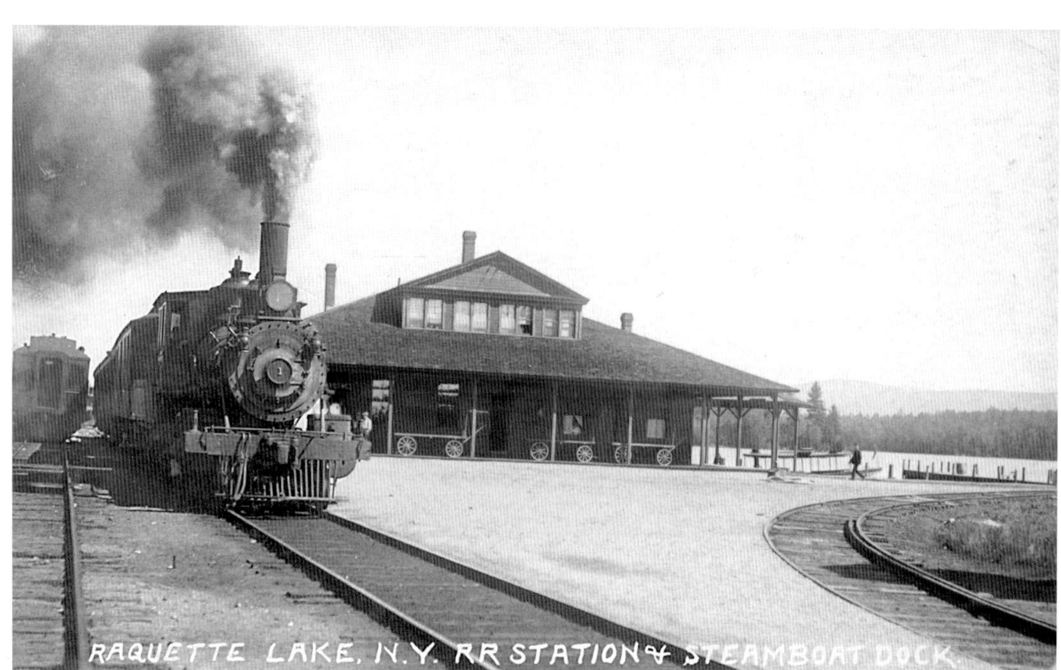


4.1. Raquette Lake, N.Y., railroad station and steamboat dock, ca. 1914. Rollins Coll.

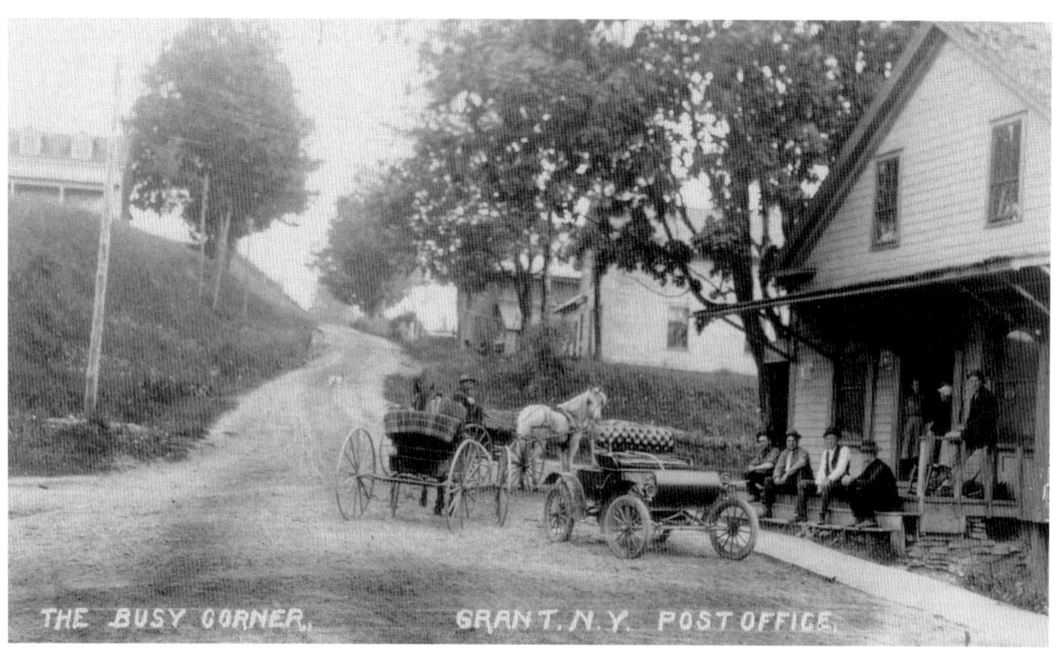


4.2. "The Busy Corner," Grant, N.Y., Post Office, ca. 1907. B. J. Slusarczyk Coll.

# 4

# Hard Traveling
## Buggies, Trains, Boats, and Automobiles

Henry Beach did not consciously produce a collection of transportation photographs, but when I began plucking pictures from his vast inheritance I realized he had.[1] Henry always operated his photography business from a home base, but nevertheless he was a traveling photographer who knew the North Country transportation system firsthand. Travel views appear frequently in his work, regardless of the area of the North Country you study (illus. 4.1).

It was not until after 1906, when Henry and his family moved to Remsen, that automobiles began appearing in his photographs. Prior to that era, gasoline-powered transportation was so uncommon in the region that a horseless carriage turned heads (Hochschild 1962a). By the early 1930s, when Beach was withdrawing from commercial photography, the extensive system of roads that crisscrossed the Adirondacks, serviced by an industry catering to motorists and automobiles, was a regular feature in his views. Although travel by rail and steamer was still important, the North Country had entered the automobile age and horse-drawn transportation was old-fashioned.

1. Part two is organized into topical chapters such as this one on transportation photographs. This method of organizing Beach's photographs skews how Beach thought about most of what he did. His point of reference was most often location (Big Moose, Old Forge, Tupper Lake), not thematic topics. This generalization does not hold in three topical areas: logging, hunting, and fishing. In these areas he produced some generic views that he could sell almost anywhere. But for his other work, he shot, captioned, stored, and marketed his work by towns and by other geographic markers. Beach was a commercial photographer, and most people wanted to buy photographs of their town, their lake, the hotel or resort they stayed in, or some other scene that had personal meaning.

In this chapter I concentrate on the array of pictures Beach took of horse-drawn vehicles, trains, boats, and automobiles as well as the infrastructure (bridges, liveries, train stations, and roadside services) that supported these forms of transport.

### Buggies Meet the Automobile

Beach was caught up in the rapid changes in transportation that surrounded him, but he was mindful of them, too. Several of his photographs demonstrate his awareness. Henry liked pictures where the horse-drawn rig and automobile were juxtaposed. These shots turn up too frequently to be coincidental. If they were, Beach resolutely seized the moment. Likely, some were staged. Henry arranged the scene to construct a moment of the old meeting the new. One example he titled, perhaps tongue in cheek, "The Busy Corner" (illus. 4.2).[2] Notice that the horse seems to be staring at the 1904 curved-dash Oldsmobile. This element, combined with the alignment of the people, makes the car the center of attraction. Its presence, alongside the buggy, is what makes this moment at this rural outpost a "Busy Corner."

"The Belshaw Store" was taken a few years after "The Busy Corner" and in a different location (illus. 4.3). By then cars were common, especially in areas south of the Adirondack region where this photograph was shot. In "The Busy

2. It is one of two postcards he took of the same scene, on the same day, but at slightly different angles.

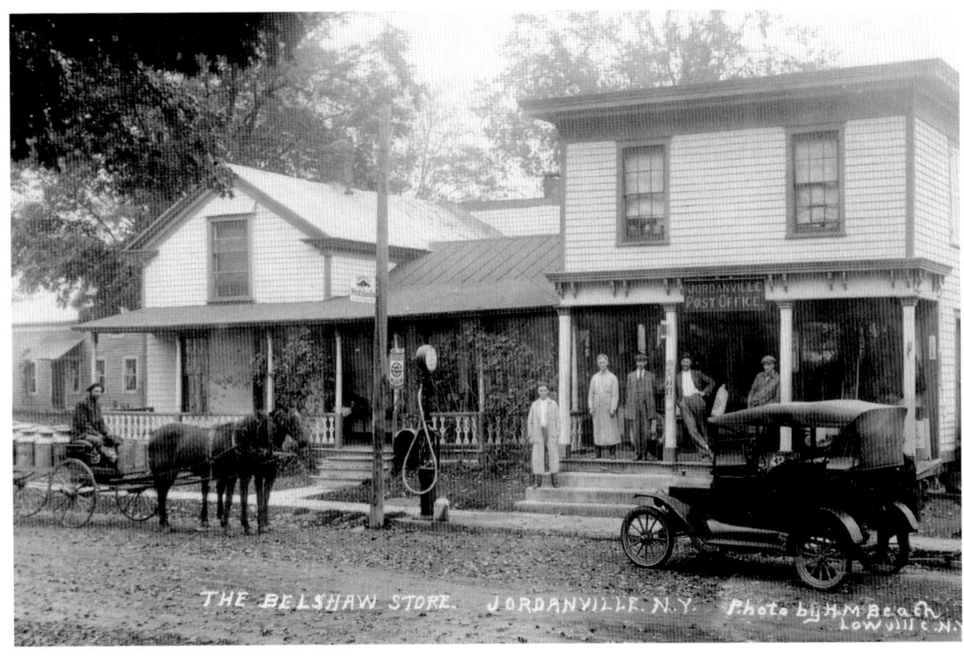


4.3. The Belshaw Store, Jordanville, N.Y., ca. 1918. Courtesy of the Adirondack Museum.

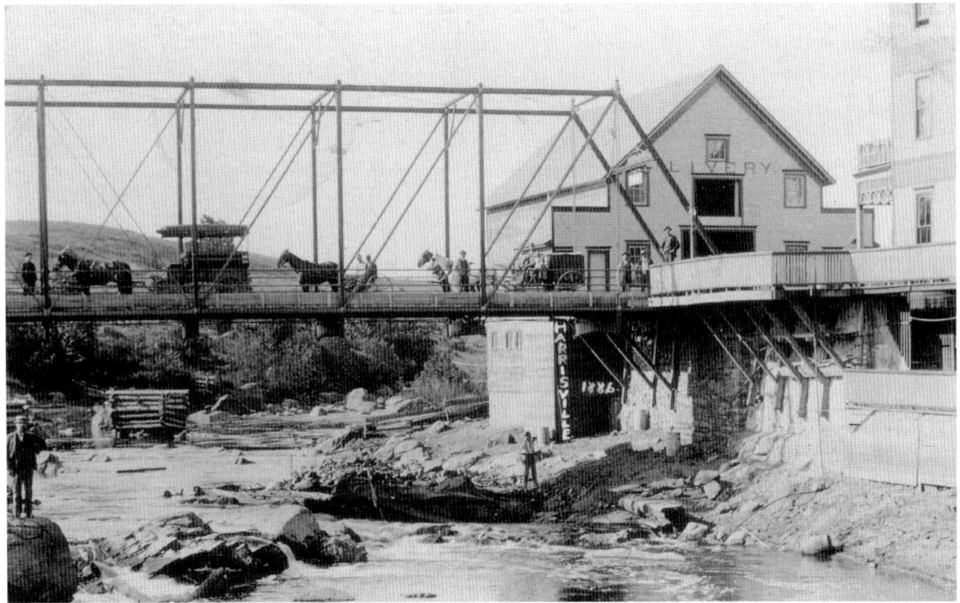


4.4. Harrisville livery, ca. 1912. Author's Coll.

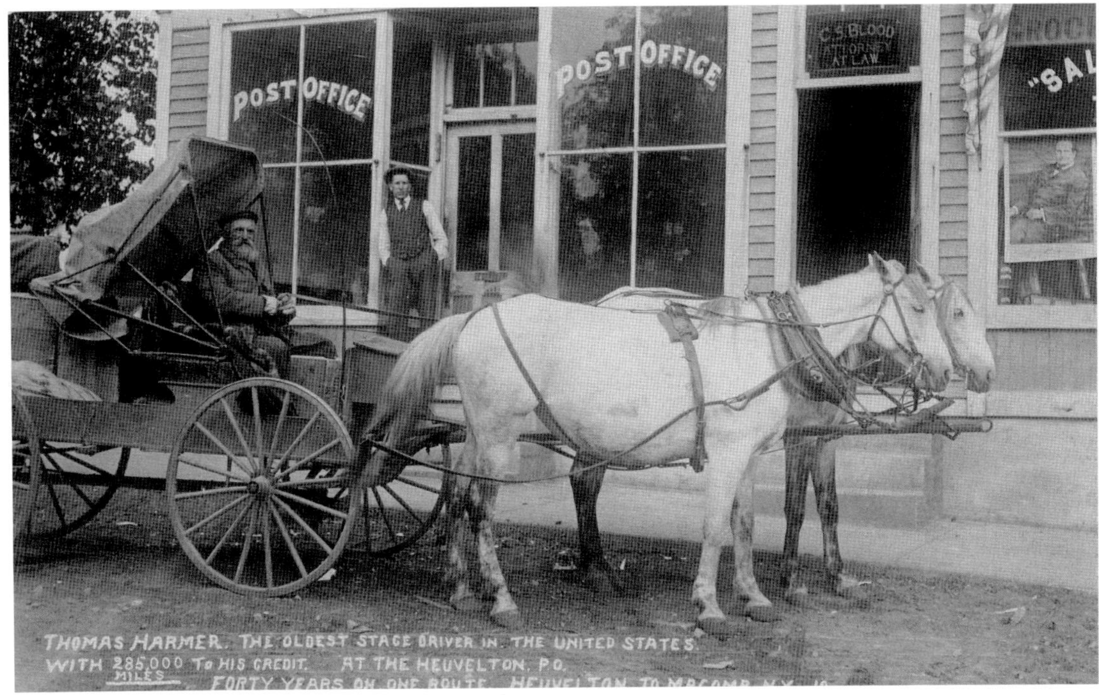


4.5. Thomas Harmer, "the oldest stage driver in the United States, with 285,000 miles to his credit," at the Heuvelton Post Office, ca. 1908. Author's Coll.

Corner," the automobile is the center of attraction because it is out of place, an odd addition to the rural scene. In "The Belshaw Store," the Model-T Ford and the gas pump dominate, and it is the horse-drawn wagon that seems peculiar.

## Bridges and Wagons

It must have involved considerable effort for Beach to get the livery workers and townspeople to pose on the bridge across the west branch of the Oswegatchie River in Harrisville in order to create the uncaptioned picture (Bowen 1970) (illus. 4.4). There is not an automobile in sight.[3] The first rig on the left is the stage that brought patrons to the Riverside House Hotel from the train station. After 1912, about the time this picture was taken, liveries like the one to the right of the bridge either began selling gasoline and evolved into service stations or went out of business.

In his portrait of Thomas Harmer, "The Oldest Stage Driver in the United States," Beach pays homage to a veteran of an occupation about to be displaced (illus. 4.5). Harmer, reins in hand, poses in front of the Heuvelton Post Office in St. Lawrence County. The caption lists Harmer's bragging rights to 225,000 miles and "forty years on one route." Not only does the picture provide the details of the driver and his rig, but in the window on the far right there is also a campaign poster for William Jennings Bryan's 1908 third run for president against William Howard Taft.

Henry honored other chauffeurs by producing posed postcard portraits. For example, in the town of Remsen, the Robert L. James Meat Market was a thriving business when the Beaches were residents. In illustration 4.6, Willard James, who provided country delivery for the market, is pictured (Davis 1976, 94).

3. The year written on the picture, 1886, refers to when the bridge was built, not to when the picture was taken.

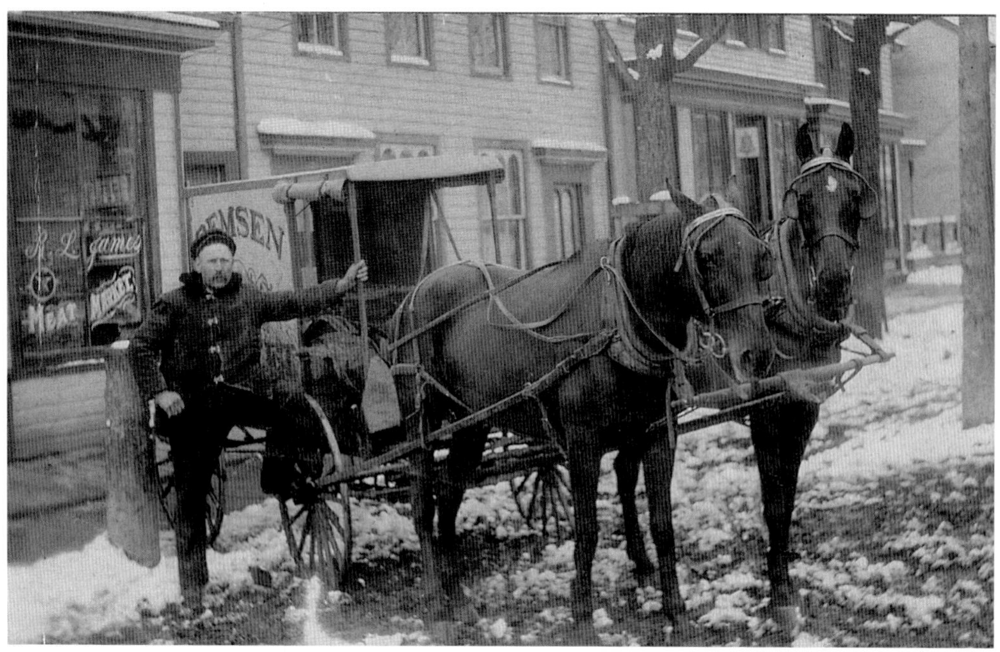


4.6. Willard James with his wagon outside the James Meat Market in Remsen, ca. 1910. G. Jones Coll.

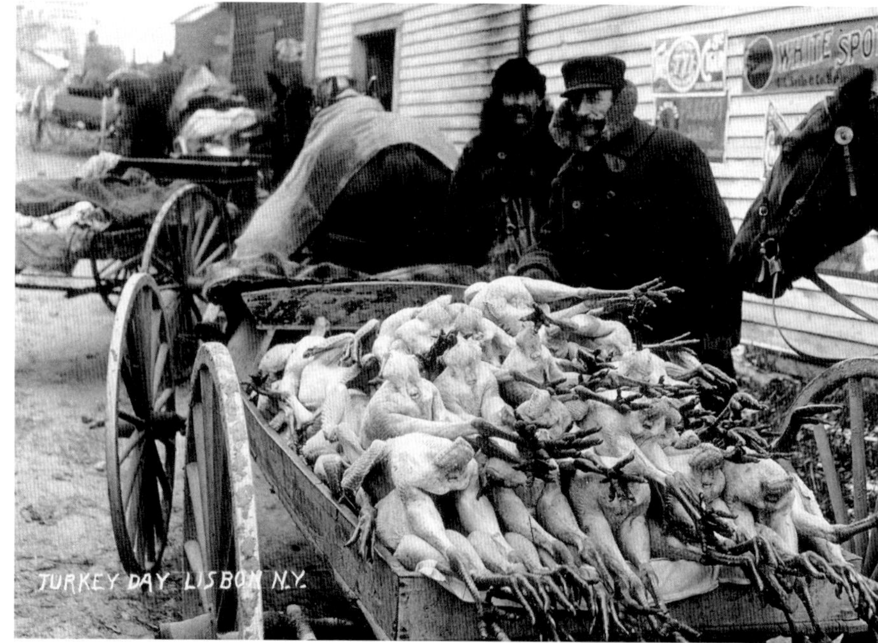


4.7. Turkey day, Lisbon, N.Y., ca. 1912. Courtesy of the Adirondack Museum.

Wagons not only delivered produce to rural residents, but also brought the farm products into town. This fact is illustrated dramatically in Henry's picture of a buckboard loaded with dead turkeys. Towns in the North Country held turkey days in the late fall. They were occasions when farmers delivered poultry to market. "Turkey Day in Lisbon" is an excellent example of Beach's realist approach (illus. 4.7). The signs on the wall on the right, the direct contact between the subjects and the viewer, and the starkly real, down-to-earth subject matter are all hallmarks of the vernacular documentary style that would become fashionable nationally in the 1930s.

## Meeting the Train

When the railroads penetrated the central Adirondacks in the last quarter of the nineteenth century, they replaced stagecoaches as a means to bring summer visitors long distances to the heart of the Adirondacks. But horse-drawn transport was still essential where rails did not reach, for short hauls, and for delivering passengers from the rail stations to their destinations. In "Waiting for the Train," taken at Fulton Chain Station (now Thendara), Beach shows carriages lined up on a deserted street awaiting the arrival of the afternoon train with

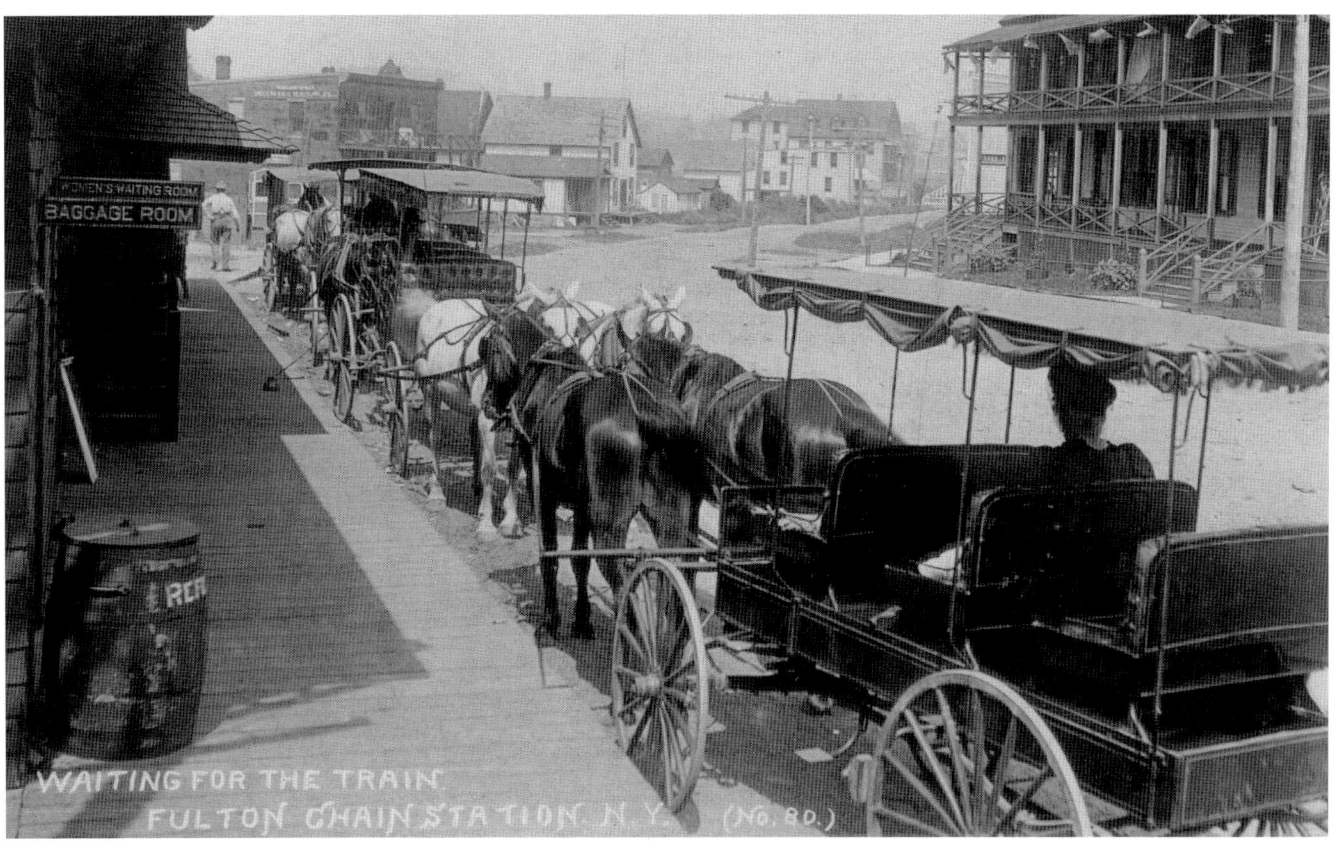


4.8. Waiting for the train at the Fulton Chain Station, N.Y., ca. 1911. Myers Coll.

guests to be shuttled to their hotels or camps (illus. 4.8). Here the composition is more orderly and the scene more tranquil than in "Turkey Day." Beach captures detail, but he also seems concerned with capturing the mood of the hot summer day.

"Birds Eye View from the Mountain, Eagle Bay, N.Y." provides another view of livery wagons waiting for the train to arrive (illus. 4.9). One of the wagons belonged to the Eagle Bay Hotel on Fourth Lake, which is in the background. Although transportation companies were established to deliver tourists to their hotels, many enterprises had their own rigs (illus. 4.10). Not only did they pick up and deliver passengers, but they also drove patrons on excursions.

## Train Stations

Beach photographed trains, stations, and the small businesses that served the passengers up and down the tracks. Remsen Station was his most photographed depot, but he took many pictures of stations to the north, south, east, and west of Remsen (illus. 4.11, 4.12). There are few surprises in his railroad pictures. They are visually tidy scenes that fit well with the set routines of train schedules, people waiting, and trains arriving and departing.

Henry photographed the small eateries that served travelers. A wonderful example is the series of postcards he produced of a family-run restaurant located

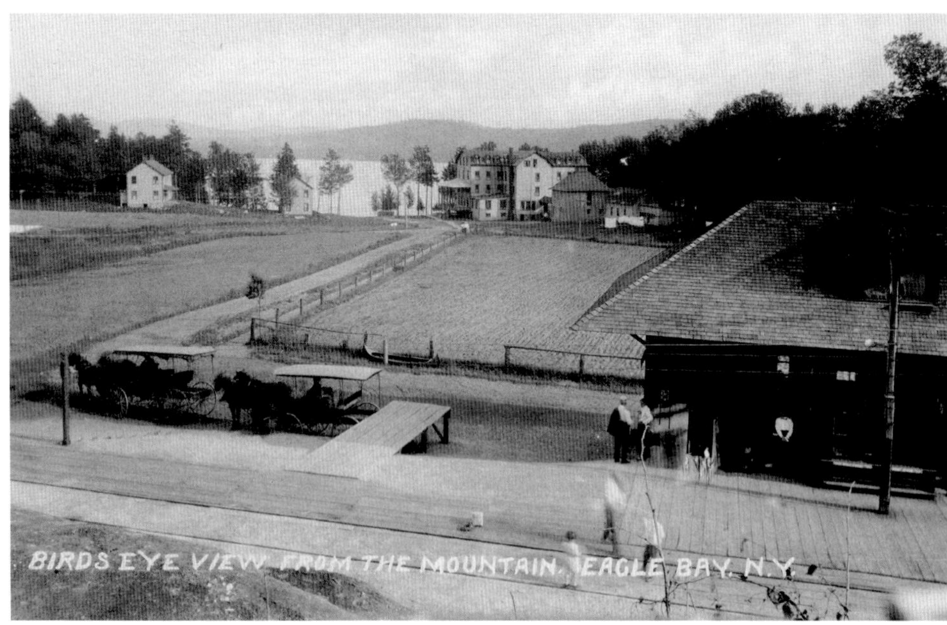


4.9. "Birds Eye View from the Mountain," Eagle Bay, N.Y., ca. 1914. Courtesy of the Adirondack Museum.

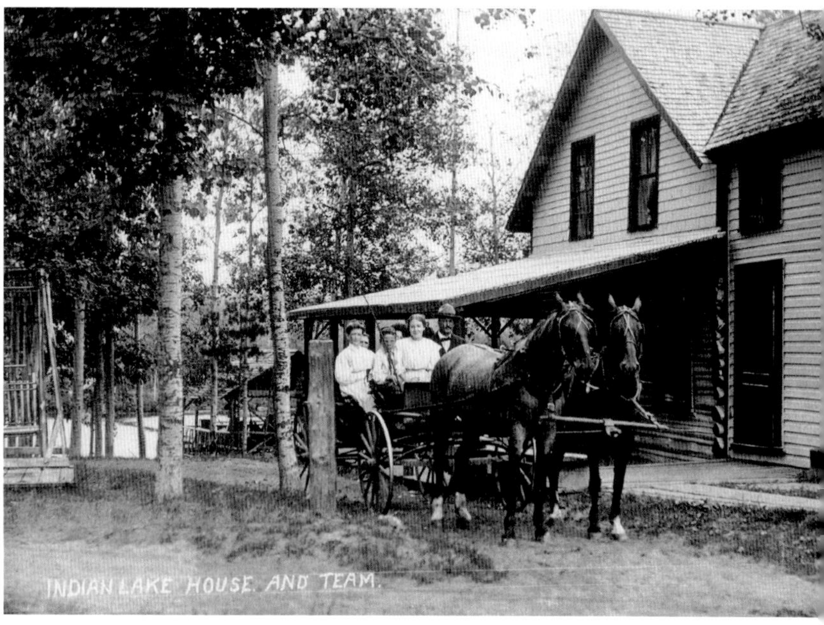


4.10. Indian Lake House and team, Indian Lake, N.Y., ca. 1910. Courtesy of the Adirondack Museum.

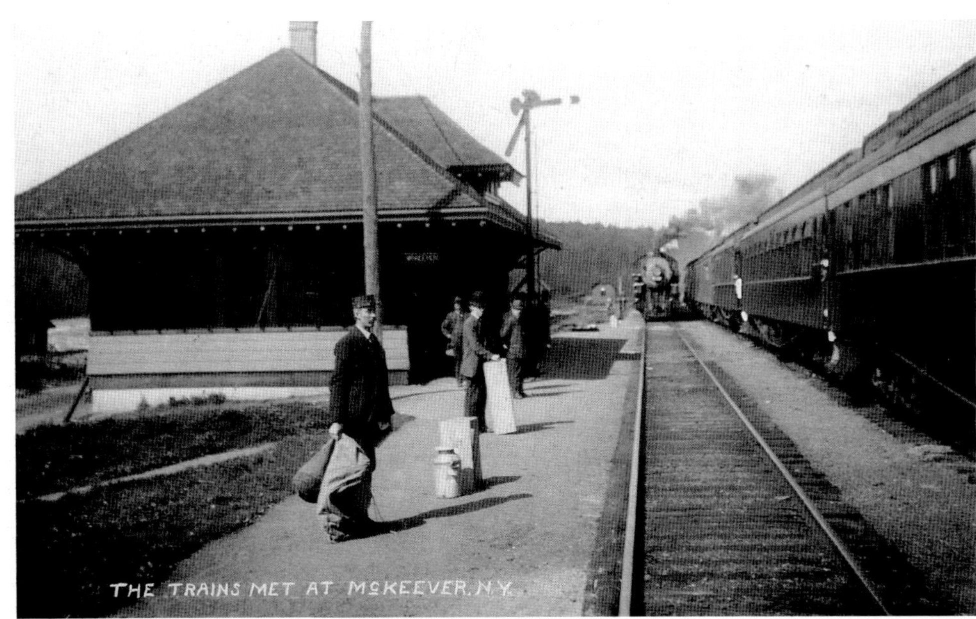


4.11. The McKeever, N.Y., train station, ca. 1911. Author's Coll.

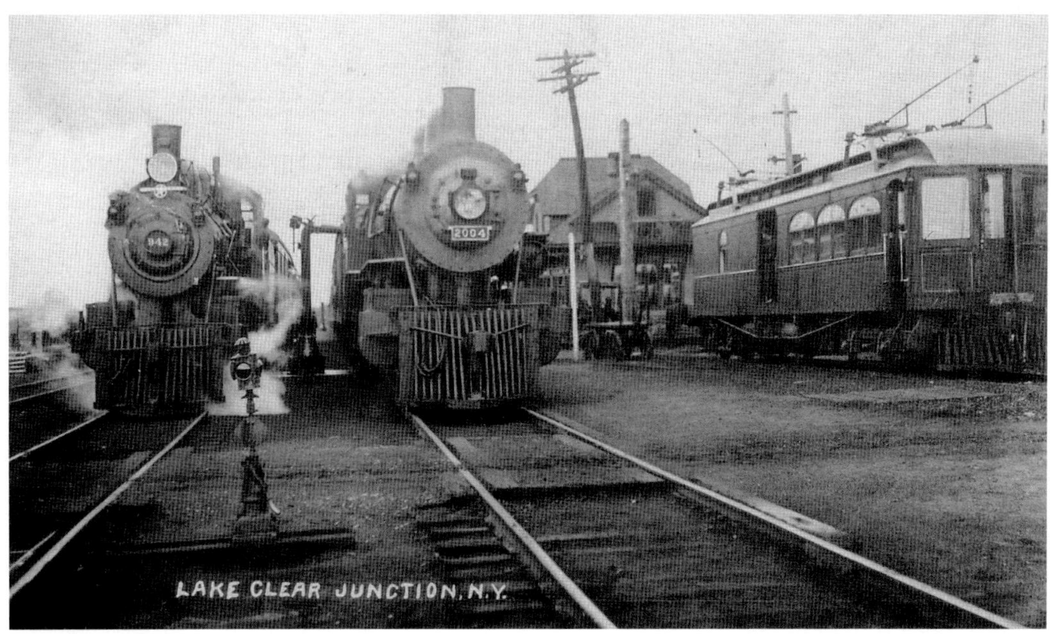


4.12. Lake Clear Junction, N.Y., ca. 1911. E. Pierce Coll.

next to the tracks at Wanakena, the Boardwalk Restaurant (also known as the Morrow Café) (illus. 4.13). Mr. and Mrs. Morrow, the proprietors, stand outside with their young daughter and their employees. Henry takes us inside, too, where, to our surprise, we find an immaculate and fancy dining room filled with Victorian bric-a-brac (illus. 4.14).

The railroad brought summer people and tourists to the region, but it served local needs as well. Mountain View, inside the northern boundary of the Adirondack Park, was such a popular spot for wild blueberries that extra railroad cars were added in August to accommodate the pickers from Malone (Hyde 1970, 65). In "Blue Berry Pickers" the tired gatherers with buckets filled are waiting to return home after a long day in the bush (illus. 4.15).

Henry created a conundrum with his portrait of Mike Shanahan, a blind man with his dog, selling newspapers at the Benson Mines station (Reynolds and DeCrosse 1976) (illus. 4.16). The caption is odd. Henry appears to have inappropriately given all the credit to the "wise dog" for taking Mr. Shanahan to Hot Springs, Arkansas (as if Shanahan had nothing to do with it). This postcard portrait, like the one of Harmer, the oldest stagecoach driver (see illustration 4.5), is an example of Beach photographing from inside North Country culture.

4.13. The Boardwalk Restaurant, Wanakena, N.Y., ca. 1912. Rollins Coll.

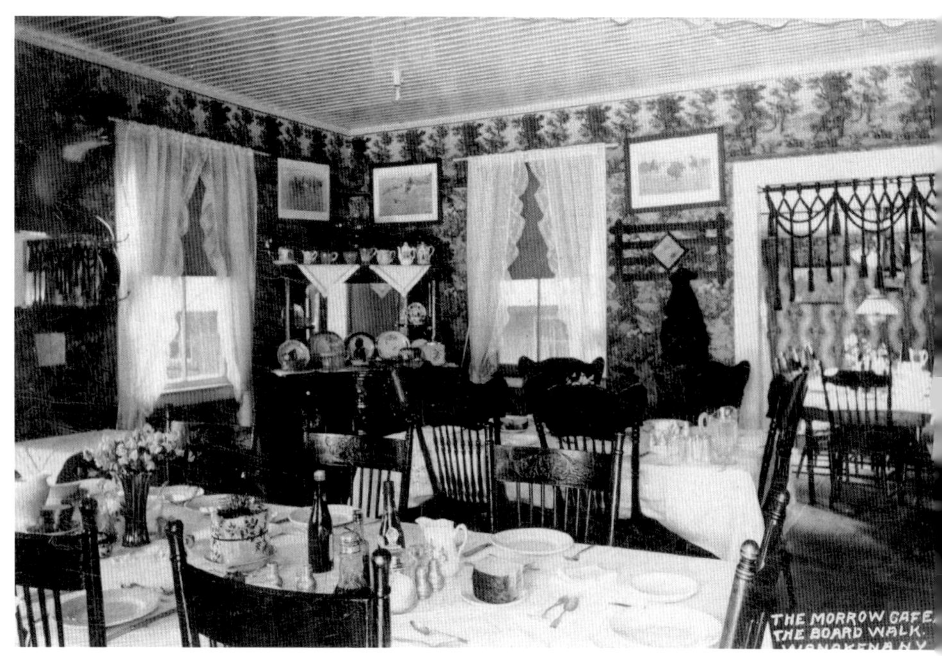


4.14. The Boardwalk, also known as the Morrow Café (interior), Wanakena, N.Y., ca. 1912. Rollins Coll.

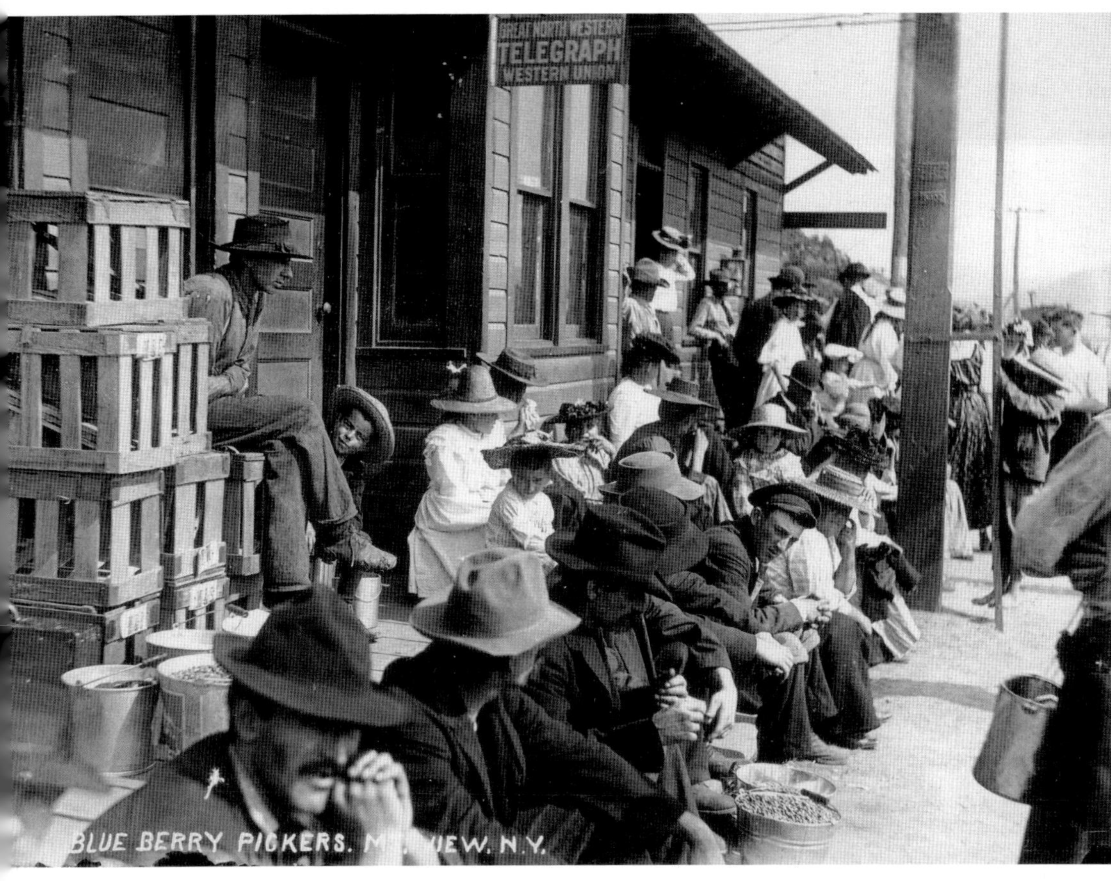


4.15. Blueberry pickers, Mountain View, N.Y., ca. 1912. Courtesy of the Adirondack Museum.

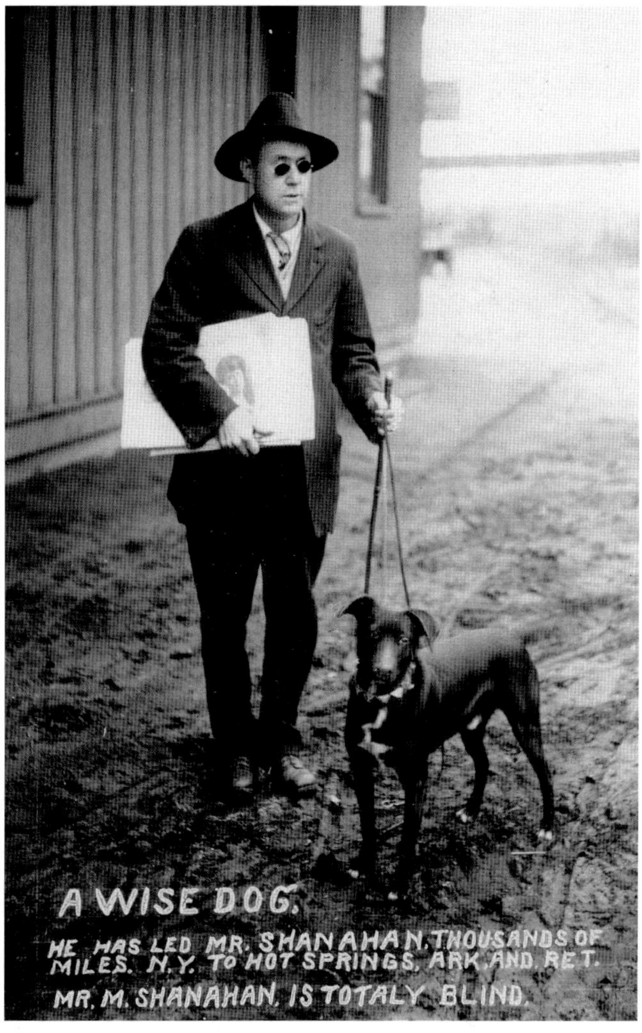


4.16. Mr. Shanahan and his "wise dog," Benson Mines, N.Y., ca. 1911. Courtesy of the Adirondack Museum.

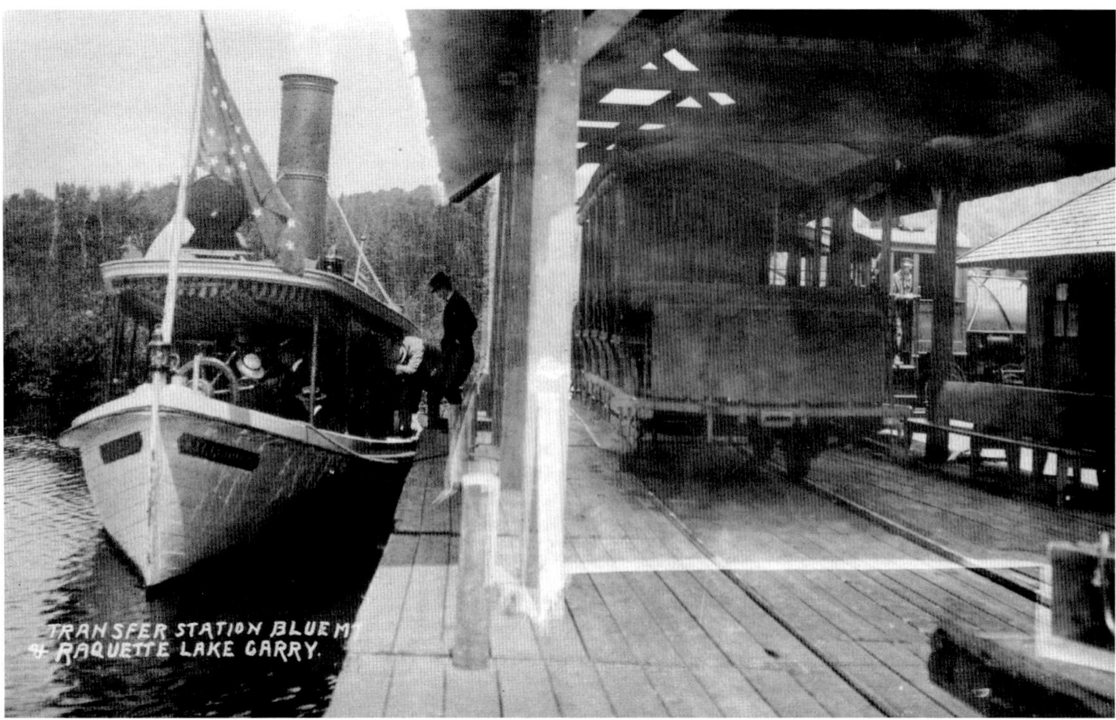


4.17. Transfer station, Blue Mountain and Raquette Lake, ca. 1909. Courtesy of the Adirondack Museum.

Without being privy to an insider's knowledge, the content is confusing and easily misinterpreted. I can only guess at what is going on in the photographs, but both Mr. Shanahan and Harmer were probably well-known, colorful local characters.[4] Although their accomplishments, from a local point of view, might have been worthy of fame, to us they look like oddballs with dubious achievements (though perhaps the captions were done tongue in cheek). Their status in the community is not clarified by the captions. We will see this lack of communication between Beach, the North Country insider, and us, the outsiders, as we survey Henry's work.

4. Michael Shanahan was originally from Watertown but moved to Benson Mines and rode trains around the North Country selling newspapers. Before losing his eyesight in a work-related dynamite accident, he was construction supervisor for the Gouverneur and Oswegatchie Railroad. He died in 1937.

### Boats

At some railroad stations passengers made connections with steamers and, later in the century, motorized craft that took them to hotels, camps, and other outlying locations not directly accessible by rail (illus. 4.17). Beach photographed the large steamboats that traversed the bigger lakes such as Fourth Lake and the Saranac lakes, as well as the smaller vessels that served hotels and camps on smaller bodies of water. The Fulton Chain steamer *Clearwater* was a favorite subject (illus. 4.18).

The Big Moose Transportation Company operated a steamer that delivered passengers to and from the dock at the Glennmore Hotel to the resorts and camps around Big Moose Lake (illus. 4.19). As we will see in the next chapter, Big Moose was a favorite stomping ground for Henry. In the illustration shown

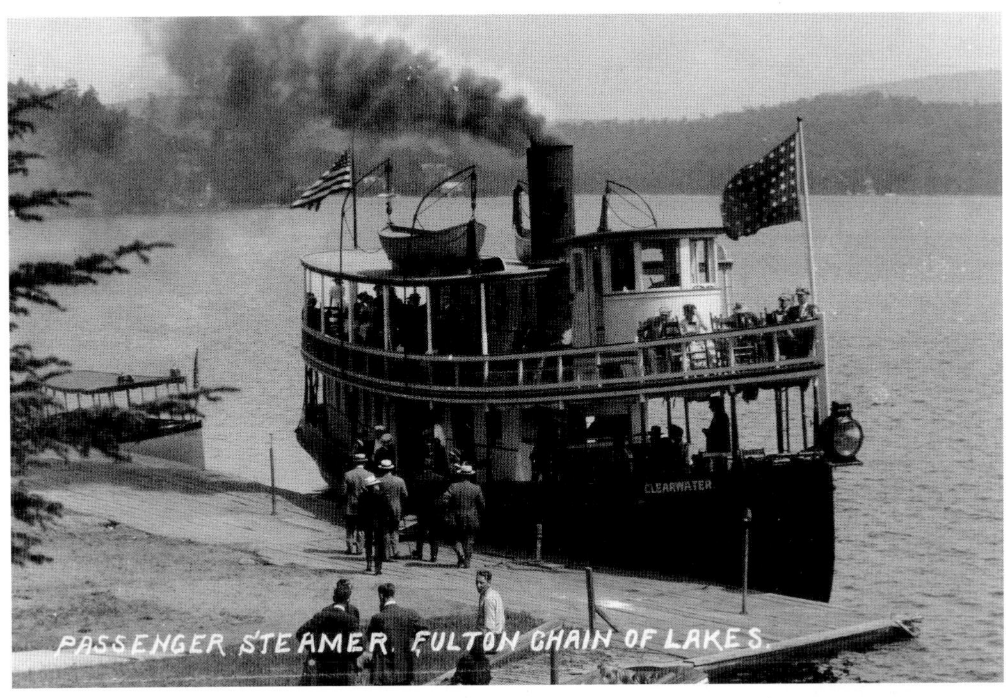


4.18. Passenger steamer, Fulton Chain of Lakes, ca. 1913. Courtesy of the Adirondack Museum.

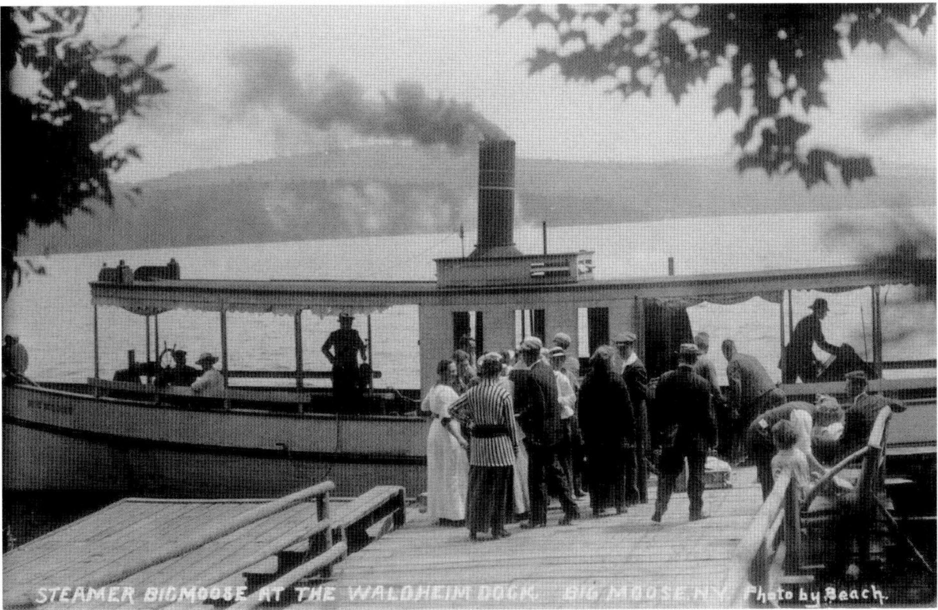


4.19. Steamer *Big Moose* at the Waldheim Dock, Big Moose, N.Y., ca. 1912. Winter Coll.

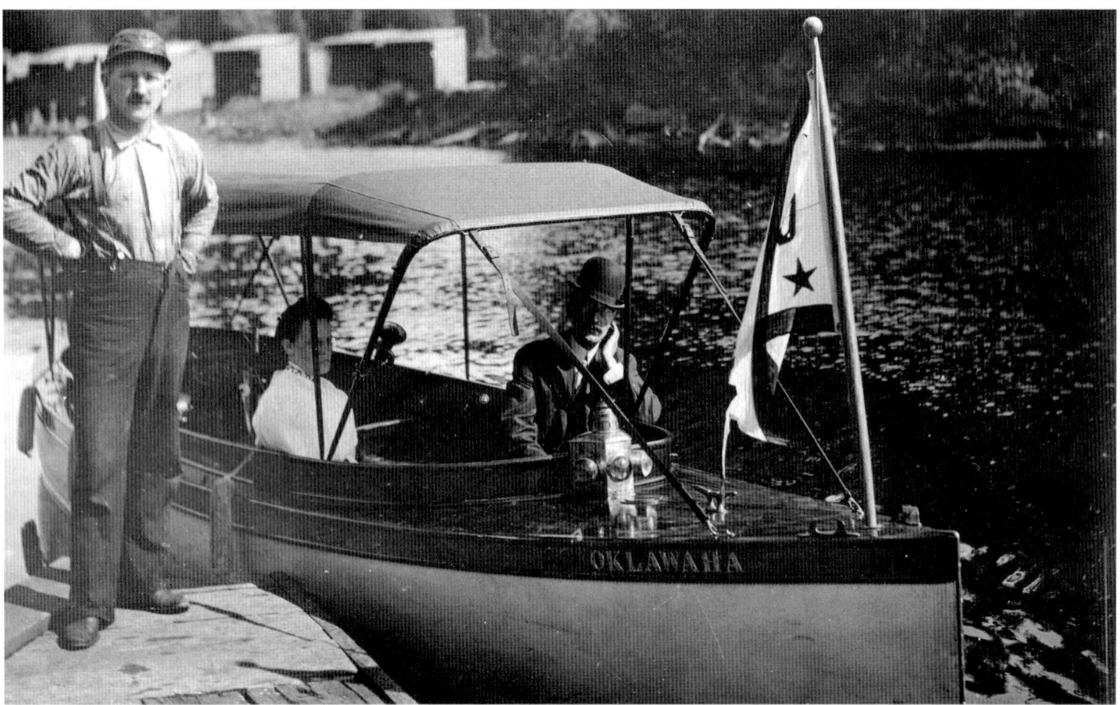


4.20. Motorboat at Cranberry Lake, ca. 1912. Smeby Coll.

here, the steamer is at the Waldheim, a rustic Adirondack hostel that still hosts guests much in the same way as it did when this picture was taken (Scheffler and Carey 2000). On the dock, on the right, bending toward the bench, is Edward Martin, the builder and proprietor of the Waldheim.

As Beach's postcard career took off, the gasoline-powered launch ascended into popularity (Bond 1995). Beach seemed taken with this new form of transportation and featured it in a number of pictures, including illustration 4.20, taken at Cranberry Lake (see also illustration 1.3).[5]

5. In the chapters that follow you will see many pictures that include guide boats and other nonmotorized vessels. It seemed more appropriate to include them in the chapters on resorts, hotels, and outdoor life.

## Motorized Ground Transportation

When motor vans replaced horse-drawn carriages, Beach photographed them as well. Like an earlier illustration in this chapter in which horse-drawn wagons waited for passengers (illus. 4.9), the vehicles are parked for quick loading in Beach's scene of Thendara Station (illus. 4.21).

The horse-drawn rigs that carried train passengers from the Big Moose Train Station to the dock at the Glennmore were replaced by an open van. That vehicle is shown in the illustration captioned "At the Steamer Landing" (illus. 4.22). Illustration 4.23 is a close-up of the same bus. Given the posture of the passengers, we can surmise that it is a posed shot. Probably, Beach scooped the vehicle's maiden voyage. If not on its first run, the auto is certainly a spanking-new addition to the resort's services, an add-on worthy of a postcard.

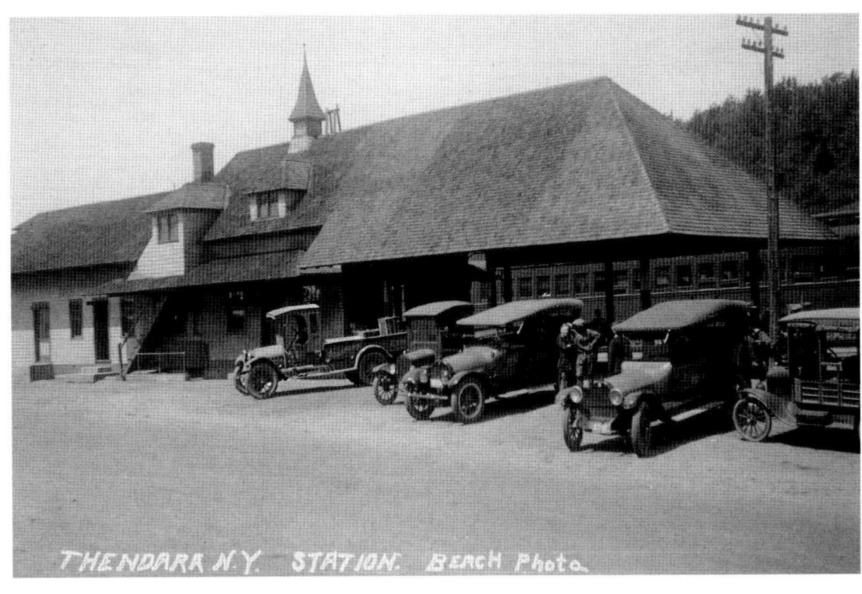


4.21. Thendara, N.Y., station, ca. 1920. Courtesy of the Adirondack Museum.

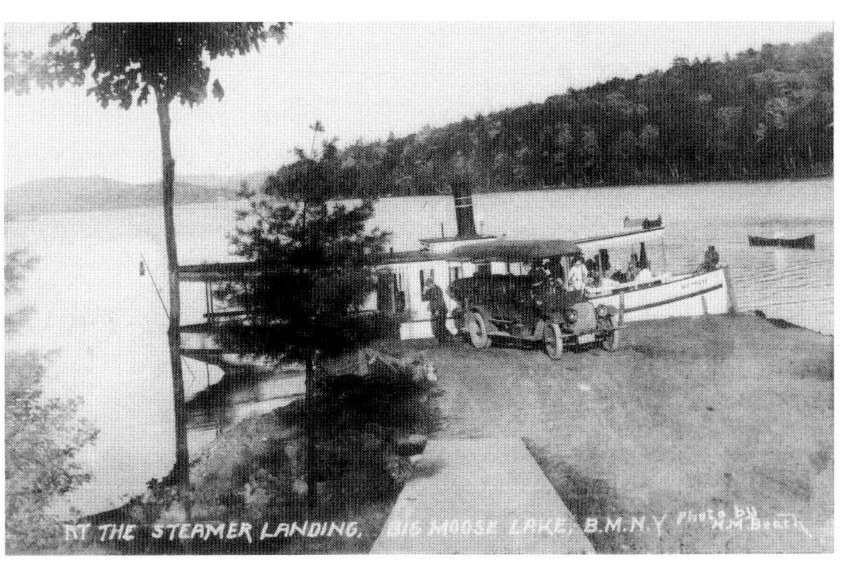


4.22. Steamer landing at Big Moose Lake, N.Y., ca. 1915. Martin Coll.

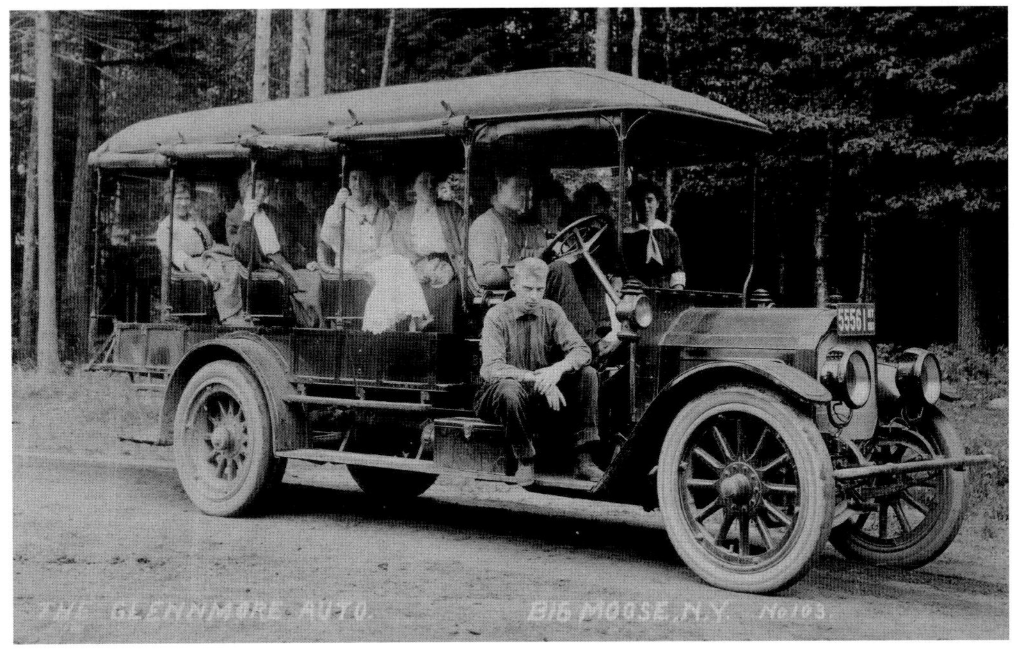


4.23. The Glennmore auto, Big Moose, N.Y., ca. 1914. Author's Coll.

## Roadside Services

As automobiles made their way into the North Country, general stores and livery stables accommodated the new traffic until there were gas stations and small restaurants up and down the improved roads. In the beginning, the infrastructure consisted of modest stops such as the Otter Creek Store. Beach printed two different views of the primitive gas station, one with the school in the background (illus. 4.24) and another with the proud proprietor standing out front (illus. 4.25).

Henry's 1919 picture with the title "New Garage" confirms the impression that the automobile had taken over (illus. 4.26). The details in the photograph include advertisements for a full line of automotive products and services. The angular, steep grade of the road, combined with the early-morning shadow, makes for an interesting image. Uncharacteristic of other examples of his work, Henry chose to date this view, suggesting that he wanted to make note of that time in history.

Socony gasoline, Goodrich tires—in "New Garage," the arrival of brand-name automotive products is evident, but clearly Dickins Garage in a locally owned and operated small business. So is Turners Garage, the subject of illustration 4.27. On the one hand, the converted colonial-style home with Mr. Turner out front wearing his mechanic outfit shows how the automobile was integrated into traditional small-town life and architecture. On the other hand, the prominently displayed Texaco sign warns of the coming of the uniformly corporate franchised gas station that was not far behind.

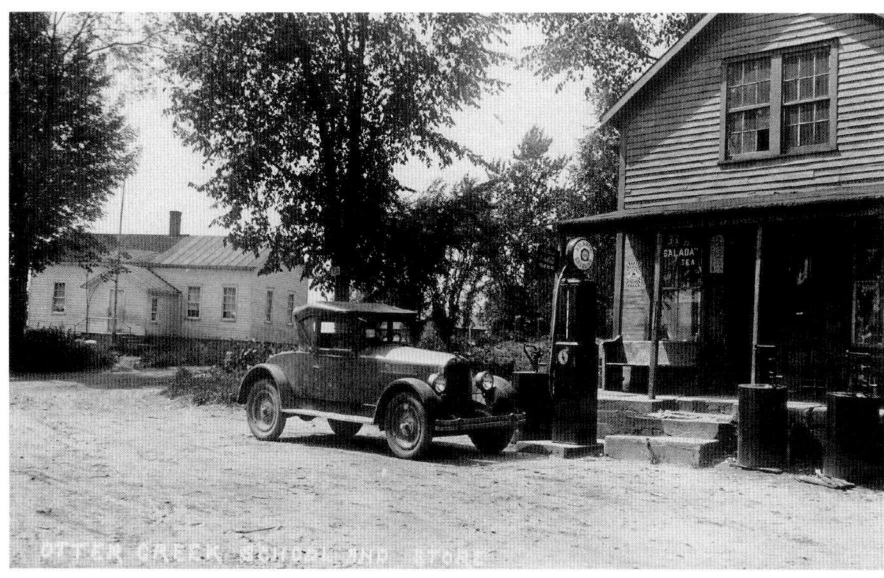


4.24. Otter Creek School and store, ca. 1925. Author's Coll.

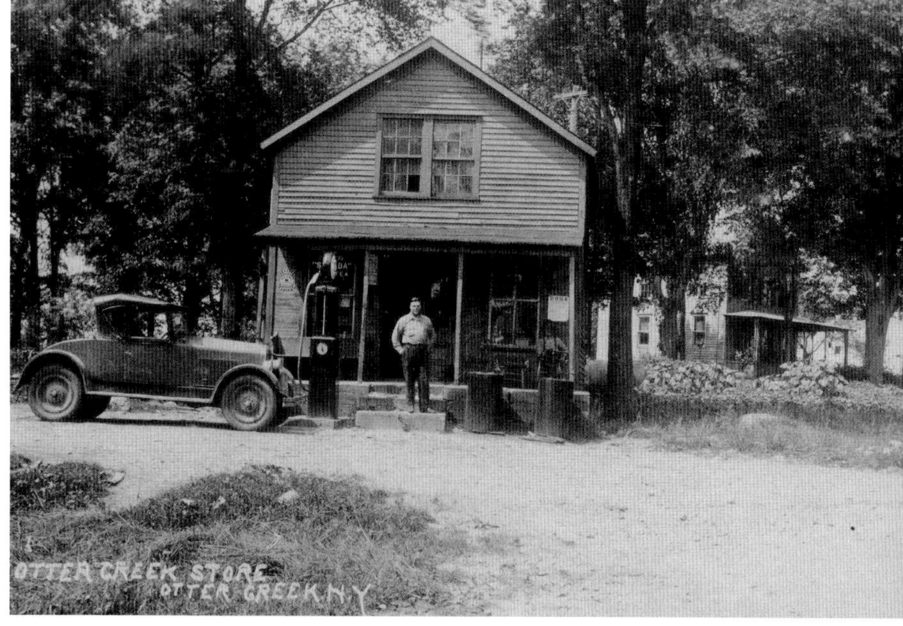


4.25. Otter Creek store, ca. 1925. Author's Coll.

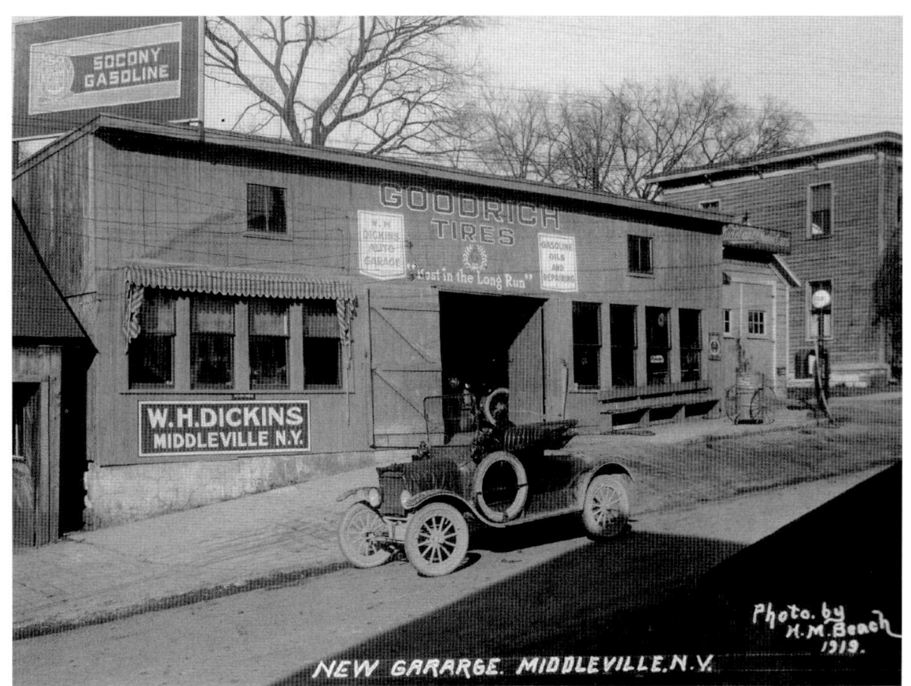


4.26. "New Garage," Middleville, N.Y., ca. 1917. Courtesy of the Adirondack Museum.

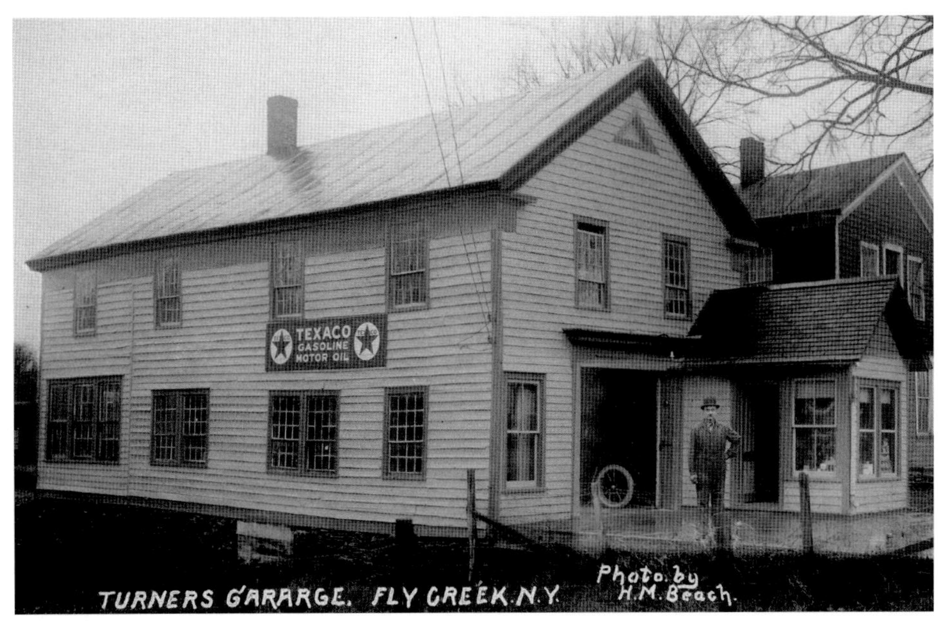


4.27. Turners Garage, Fly Creek, N.Y., ca. 1922. Courtesy of the Adirondack Museum.

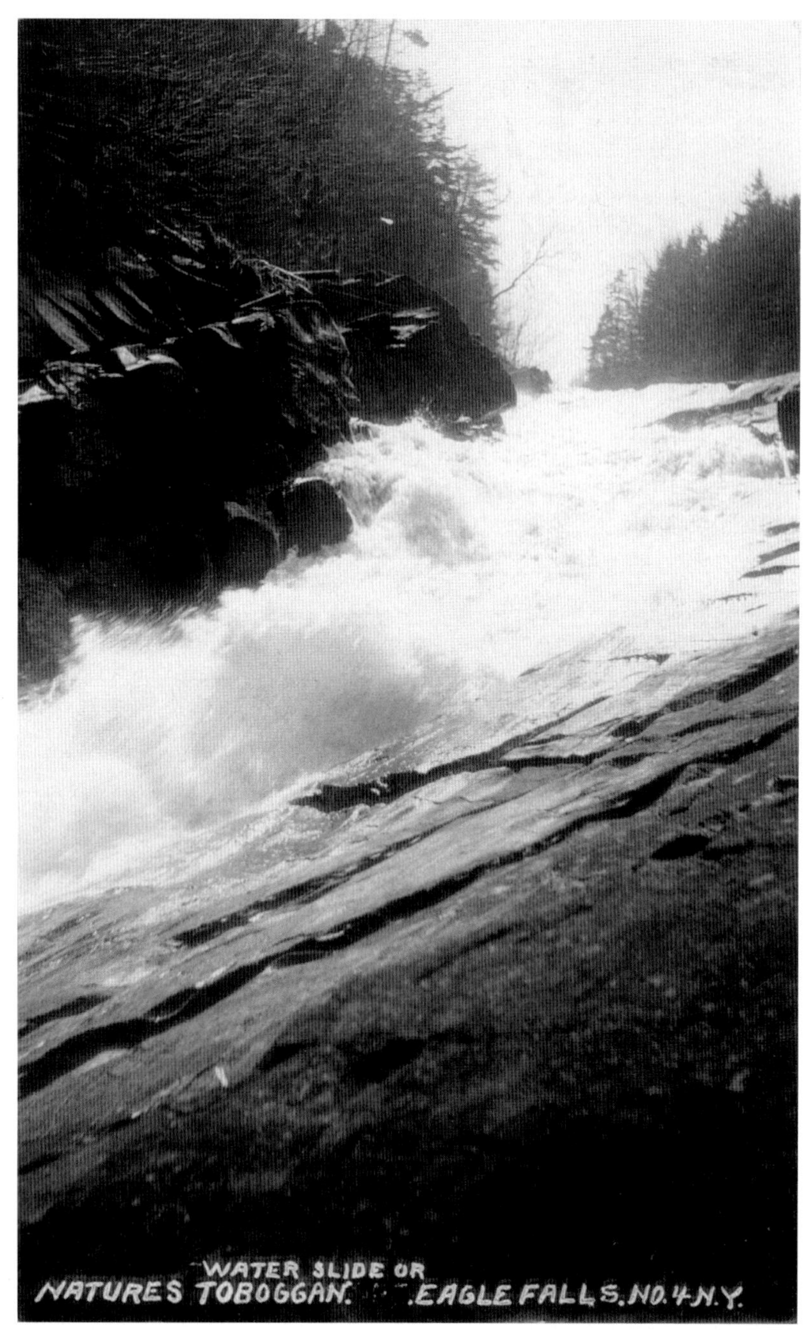


5.1. "Water Slide or Nature's Toboggan," Eagle Falls, Number Four, N.Y., ca. 1910. Davis Coll.

# 5

# Scenic Views

## Woods and Waters

When we think "postcard," we think picturesque renditions of valleys and mountains, lakes and rivers, and sunrises and sunsets. Although most early printed postcards (factory-produced color cards) fitted that description nicely, photo postcards did not. The relative absence of scenic views in photo-postcard photographers' stock was not by choice. Limited by black-and-white film, the absence of good filters to create cloud contrast, and the small format, most attempts at pretty pictures on photo postcards failed.

In spite of these difficulties, Beach did produce some pleasing scenic postcards, and his work with the Cirkut camera resulted in notable views. Here I concentrate on his successes and explain how he dealt with the problems of producing and marketing what we would call "scenics."

### Panoramic Landscapes

General Cirkut landscapes were a tough sell for Beach. But in spite of the financial disincentive, he climbed mountains and took about twenty expansive bird's-eye views of bodies of water such as Big Moose Lake, Fulton Chain, Lake Placid, and Saranac Lake.[1] Once you set your eyes on the breadth of these lake and mountain shots you can see why Henry might have been drawn to them. They are overwhelming, more than the eye can take in at one time. When viewing them you have to pan the surface to get their entire content.

1. In relation to his total output, twenty is a small number. They are hard to find on the antique photograph market, which leads me to the conclusion that Beach did not sell many.

His panoramic of Upper Saranac Lake is one example of the genre (he misspelled *Saranac* as *Saranack*) (panoramic 3). The wide body of water, with the mountains in the background and the trees in the foreground, the coves and islands, the small steamer in the center, and the buildings to the right all add up to a pleasing composition. The picture would be much less attractive if it were not for the delicate cirrus clouds. I have seen the negative for this print, so I speak with authority when I say that Beach tampered with the heavens. Using one of the earliest versions of "Photoshop" technique known in the business, he brushed the clouds onto the negative before printing. (He did it often in his panoramics and occasionally in his postcards.)

Beach did much better selling panoramics that contained mountains and lakes when they showed specific and identifiable hotels, camps, and resort grounds. Although Henry did not caption the panoramic just discussed as being taken at the Wawbeek Hotel, the buildings on the right are part of that complex, as is the steamer.[2] Likely, the picture was sold at the hotel. What you and I might see as a general scenery landscape was in Beach's time probably consumed as a resort picture.

### Waterfalls

The waterfalls he photographed were of different sizes, shapes, and types. He took them close-up, from a distance, from their bases, and from their tops. He was

2. More pictures and text about the Wawbeek is found in chapter 7.

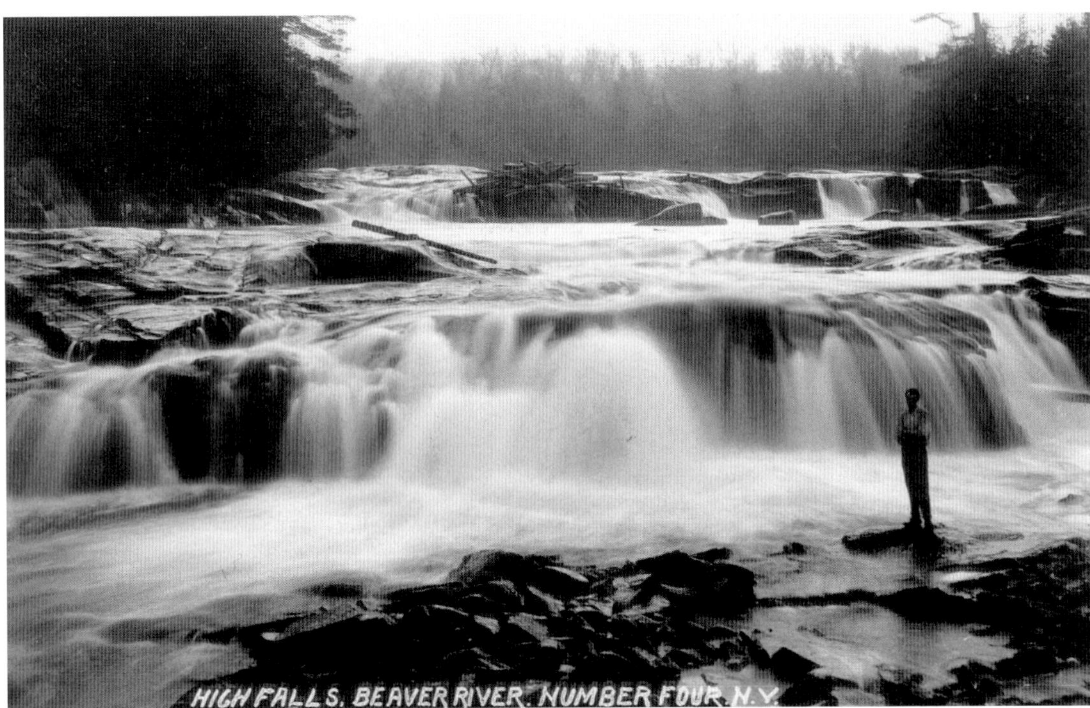


5.2. High Falls, Beaver River, Number Four, N.Y., ca. 1910. Davis Coll.

attracted to natural settings where the rushing water had raced over smooth rock and crashed into deep trout pools for thousands of years. He loved to locate his camera close enough to feel the mist, but far enough away to not get wet. Many of his pictures carry the viewer to a cool spot next to powerful flowing water where the sound of the turbulence could be heard. Sometimes he paid homage to nature in his captions. An example of what I have been describing is "Water Slide or Nature's Toboggan," a picture Henry took at Eagle Falls, near Number Four, an area he visited regularly (illus. 5.1).

Some of the natural falls he photographed were less dramatic than Eagle Falls, with the deluge spread out and cascading down less steep inclines. It was typical of Henry to include a human figure in a waterfall scene. The person provided depth as well as a gauge for the viewer to judge the height of the falls.

Although in some ways an exemplar of Henry's waterfall work, his image of High Falls on the Beaver River does not seem quite right (illus. 5.2). It is otherworldly, almost too postcard perfect to believe. The water coming off the bottom level of the falls seems unnaturally effervescent. Henry probably simply used a long exposure speed to improve on Mother Nature.

In "High Falls, Talcottville," Beach included a man standing behind a camera that is mounted on a tripod (illus. 5.3). Although the waterfall is shot from a distance, the person pulls our eye toward the rock precipice because he is focusing on a section of the swash close-up. The shack on the shore, at the top of the falls on the left, interrupts the notion of "postcard perfect" but adds to the vernacular appeal of the scene. Careful inspection of the man in the view confirms that it is not Henry Beach.

The waterfall shown in illustration 5.4 is an example of a more domesticated flow, a picture of water spilling over a human-made dam. Hundreds of such

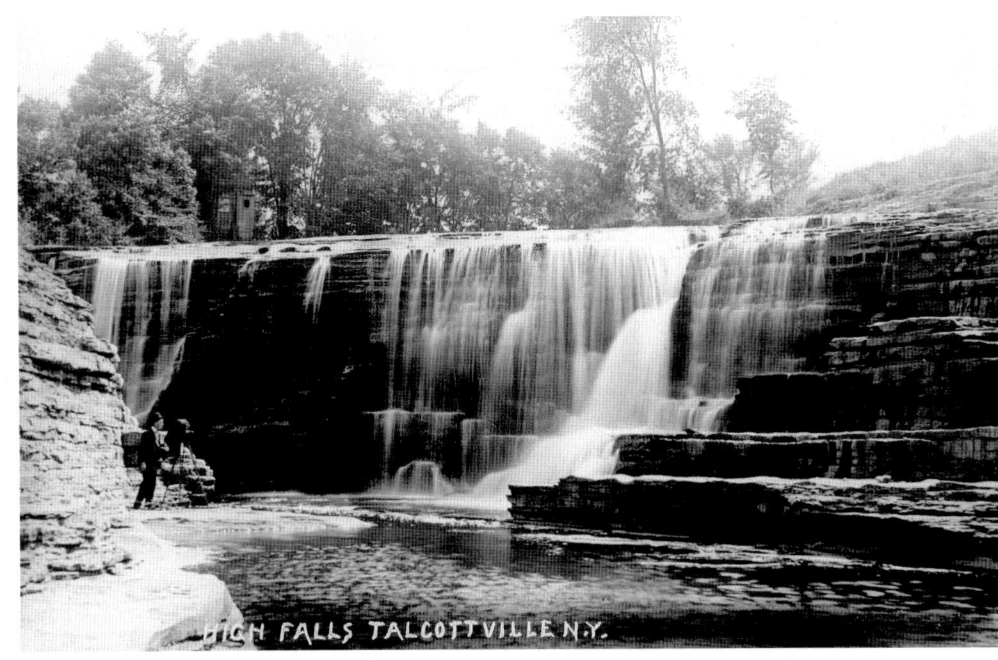


5.3. High Falls, Talcottville, N.Y., ca. 1912. Myers Coll.

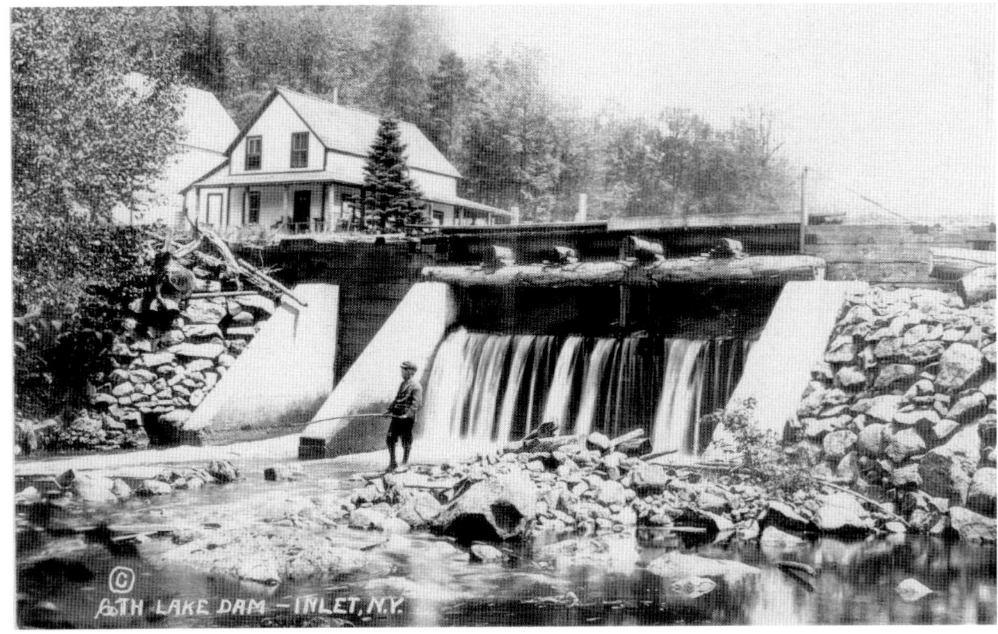


5.4. Sixth Lake Dam, Inlet, N.Y., ca. 1912. Gates Coll.

structures were built in the North County to harness energy, aid transportation, control floods, and create recreational areas. The pictures Beach took of these rural landmarks are often romantic renditions of the bucolic life. Some, like the view of the Sixth Lake Dam, include Tom Sawyer–like figures. As we shall see, there were other dams, structures more massive and industrial. Beach photographed them as well.

## Silhouettes

What was very effective for Beach's black-and-white film and for his equipment were scenery shots with dark foregrounds and light backgrounds—human figures against water, trees against sky: in other words, silhouettes. "Sand Beach and Bathing" at Lake Brantingham is an example of this type (illus. 5.5; see also illustration 1.6). The women with their full-length dresses, some with their hands on their hips, standing along the shore, set a calm tone to this attractive composition. The activity on the lake adds an upbeat tempo. The trees frame the view and compensate for the fact that the sky is an undifferentiated light blotch.

His springtime picture "A View from the Lake from L.V.L." at Big Moose Lake, with the trees profiled against the lake and sky, is another charming shot but one whose significance can easily be missed if you are not familiar with North Country weather (illus. 5.6). We are looking at a picture of "the ice going out," a North Country expression for when a frozen lake becomes liquid again. The phrase and the event mark the end of winter.

## Hotel Scenics

Notice that in the caption of the last illustration Beach refers to the picture as a view of the lake from L.V.L. The initials stand for a specific resort, Lake View Lodge. As I suggested earlier, many of Beach's pictures that I would classify as

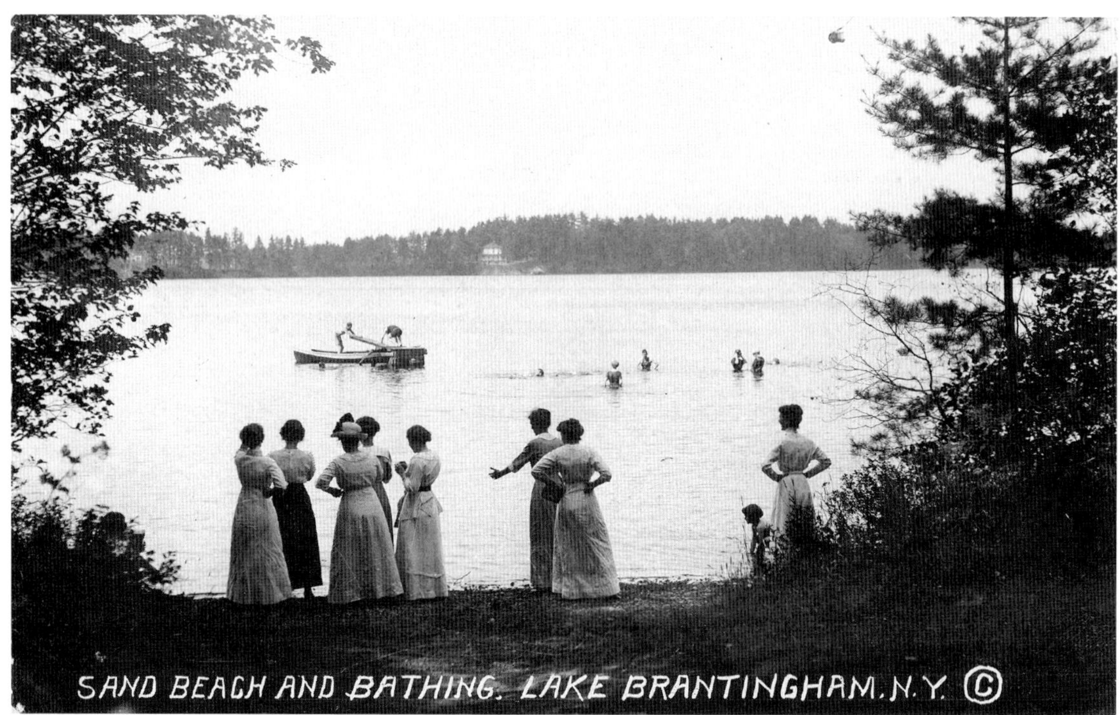


5.5. Sandy beach and swimmers, Lake Brantingham, N.Y., ca. 1917. Author's Coll.

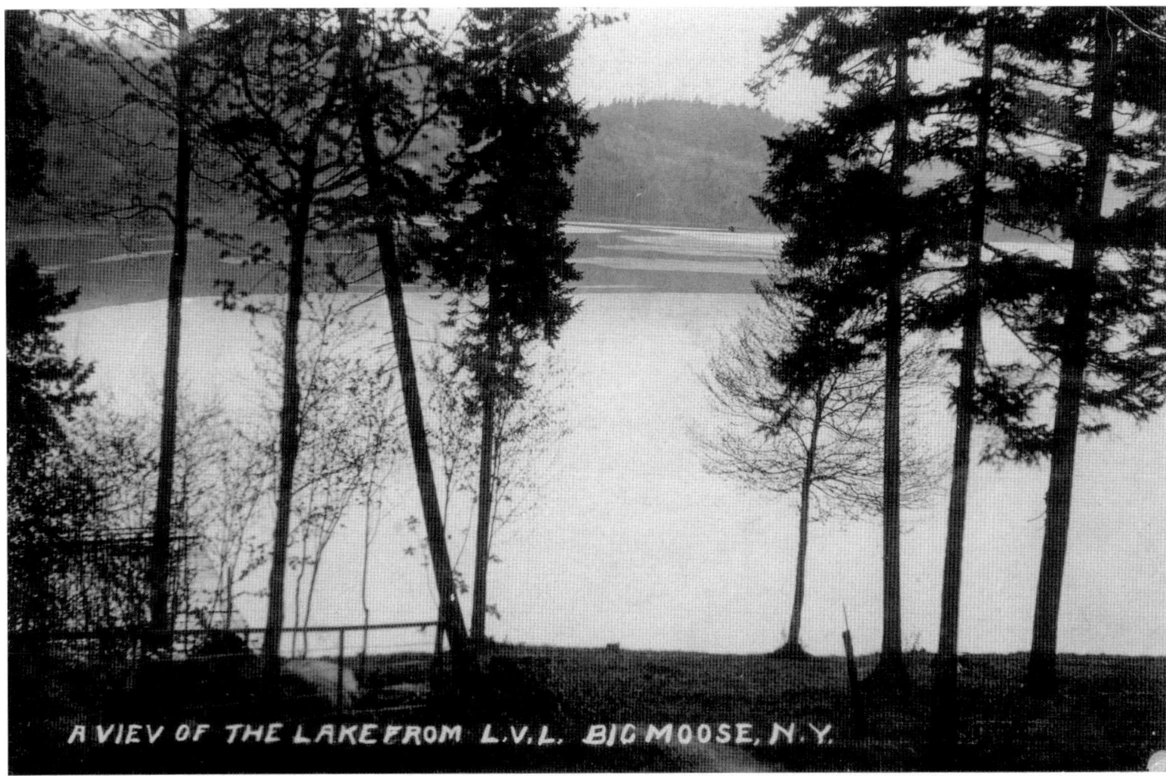


5.6. A view of the lake from the Lake View Lodge, Big Moose, N.Y., ca. 1913. Author's Coll.

scenic views were taken at specific resorts and are captioned to be sold to patrons of those facilities. In other words, "scenic views" were probably not how Beach and his customers thought of them; rather, they were lumped with pictures of that location.

Some of these pretty resort scenes are like the silhouette views already discussed. Take, for example, his picture of the boathouses at Brantingham Lake (illus. 5.7). On the other hand, other resort scenics are more layered and contain more detail in the foreground. In his picture of the pavilions and porches at the Arrowhead Hotel on Fourth Lake, we see another characteristic of Beach's work: the blending of natural elements, in this case trees, with the buildings, pavilions, and porches (illus. 5.8).

In some of his pictures, though (for example, his picture of the bridge at Long Lake), he emphasized the sharp angles on bridges, but here the vertical iron girders are softened by and integrated into the trees (illus. 5.9). Likewise, in his postcard of the waterside gazebo on Third Lake the silhouetting is toned down by the exposure and de-emphasized by the reflection (illus. 5.10).

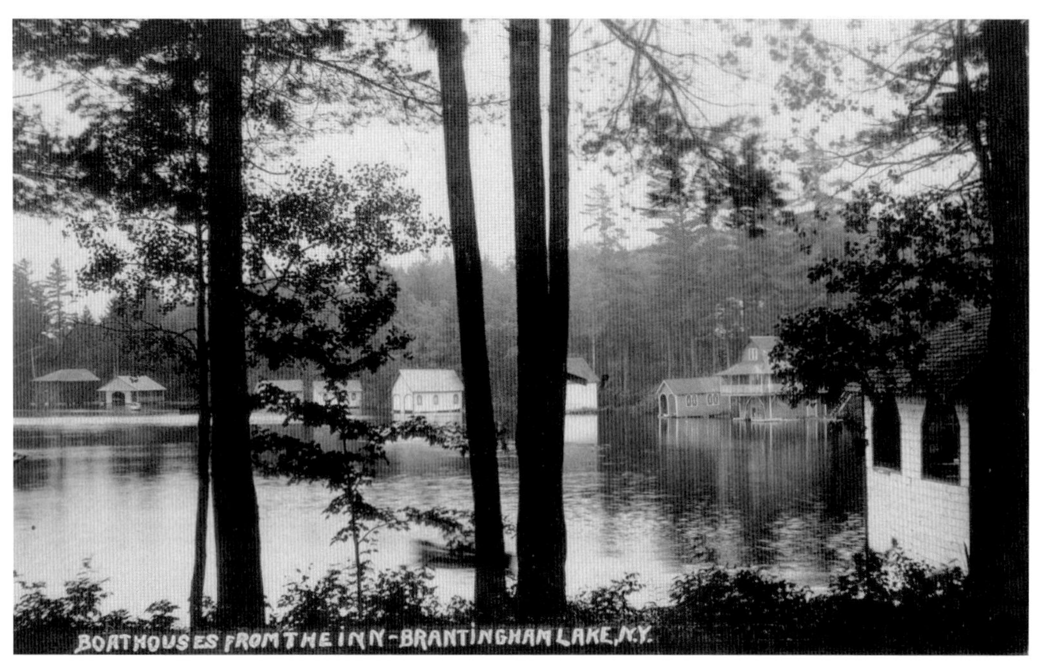


5.7. Boathouses viewed from the inn, Brantingham Lake, N.Y., ca. 1914. Myers Coll.

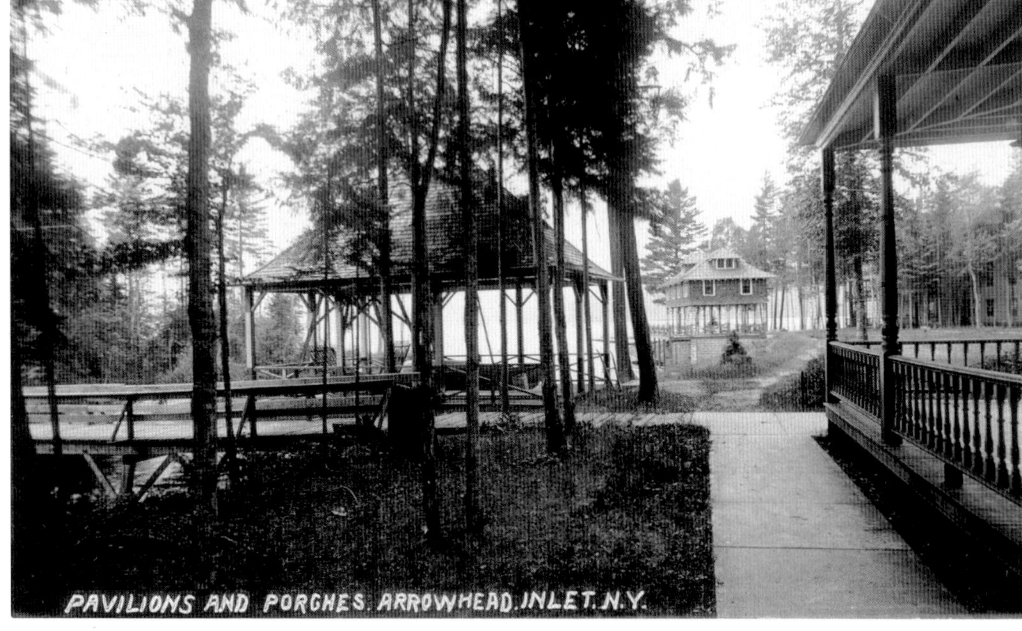


5.8. Pavilions and porches, Arrowhead, Inlet, N.Y., ca. 1912. Myers Coll.

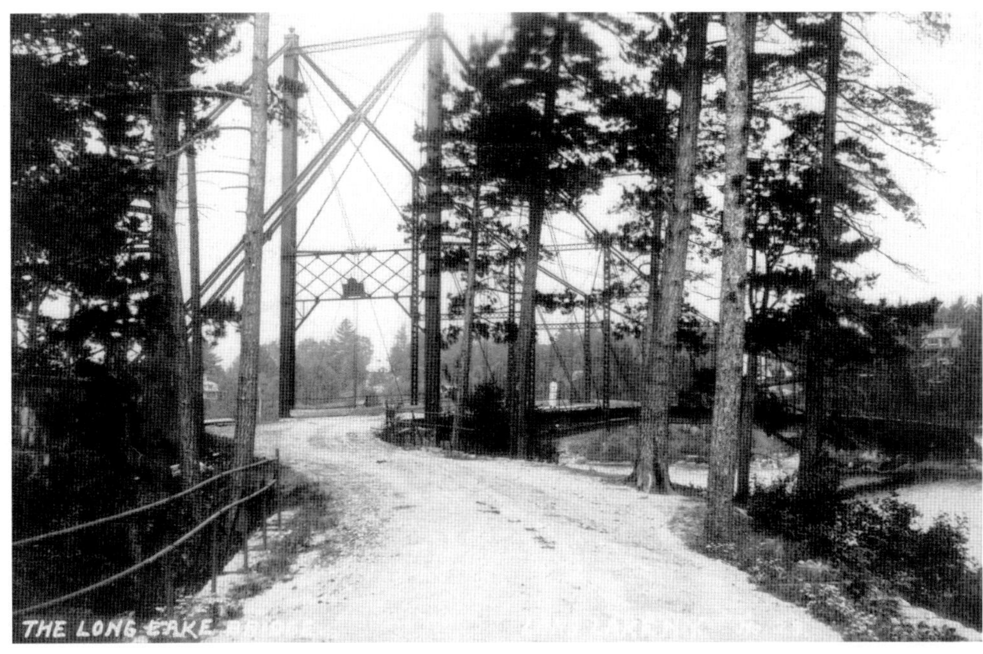


5.9. The Long Lake bridge, Long Lake, N.Y., ca. 1914. Davis Coll.

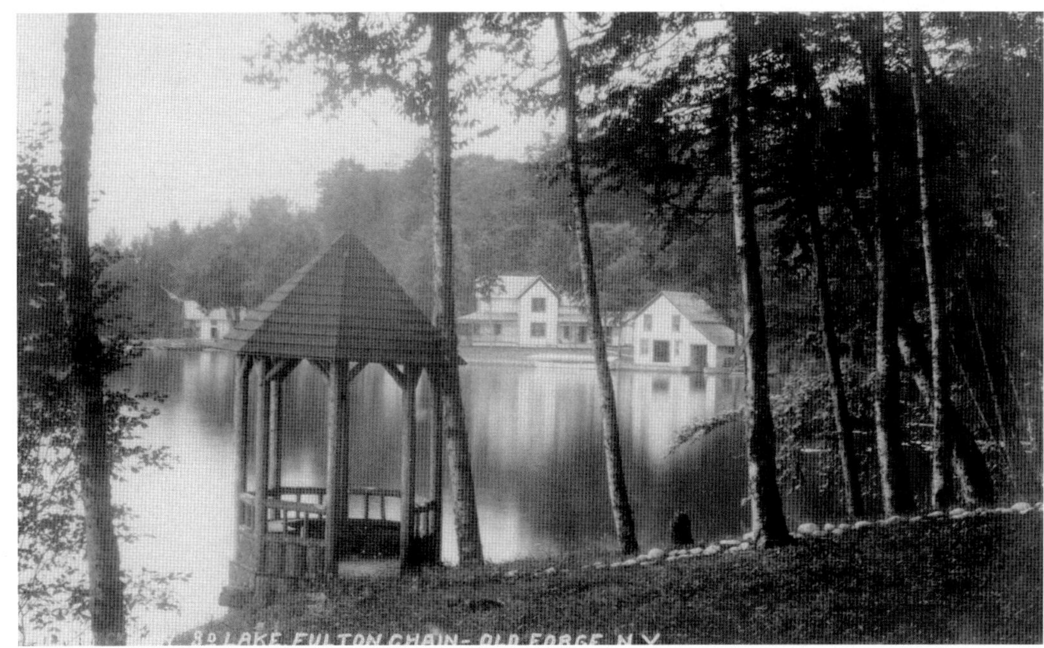


5.10. Third Lake, Fulton Chain, Old Forge, N.Y., ca. 1913. H. Slusarczyk Coll.

## Reflections

Henry's fondness for reflections on water shows up in many of his views (see also illustration 1.5). His postcard of Fisher's Cottage at Number Four is a wonderful example of reflection as the central element in the picture (illus. 5.11). Although the picture is captioned "Fisher's Cottage," the camp is a minor element. With the structure hidden by the trees and upstaged by the reflection, the picture turns into a nature study rather than a photograph of a building. In a different use of reflection, Beach treats the shadows on the river in the card captioned "F. W. Smith's Landing" as just one of many elements of a more complex scenery view (illus. 5.12).

## This Land Is Their Land

The scenic pictures I have shown are almost exclusively water views. That emphasis is consistent with the contents of Beach's portfolio, but Henry photographed mountains and woods, too. Most of this work is ordinary, not warranting special recognition. But there are two pictures I end this chapter with that provide insight into how Beach thought about the land he was photographing.

The first picture of a woodland path is not unusual (illus. 5.13). It is a pleasant picture containing the details of forest vegetation in the foreground with sunlight streaming through the trees at the end of the path. But there is a conspicuous sign, "Private Property," nailed to the large tree. "Private Property"

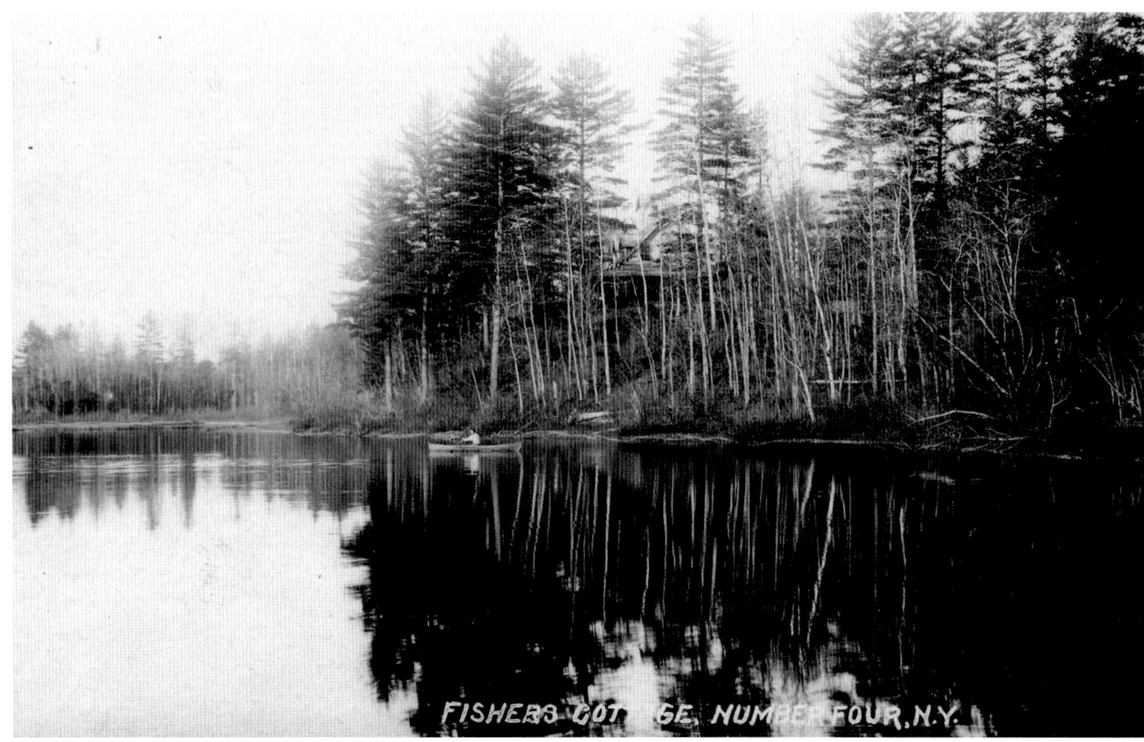

5.11. Fisher's Cottage, Number Four, N.Y., ca. 1914. Author's Coll.

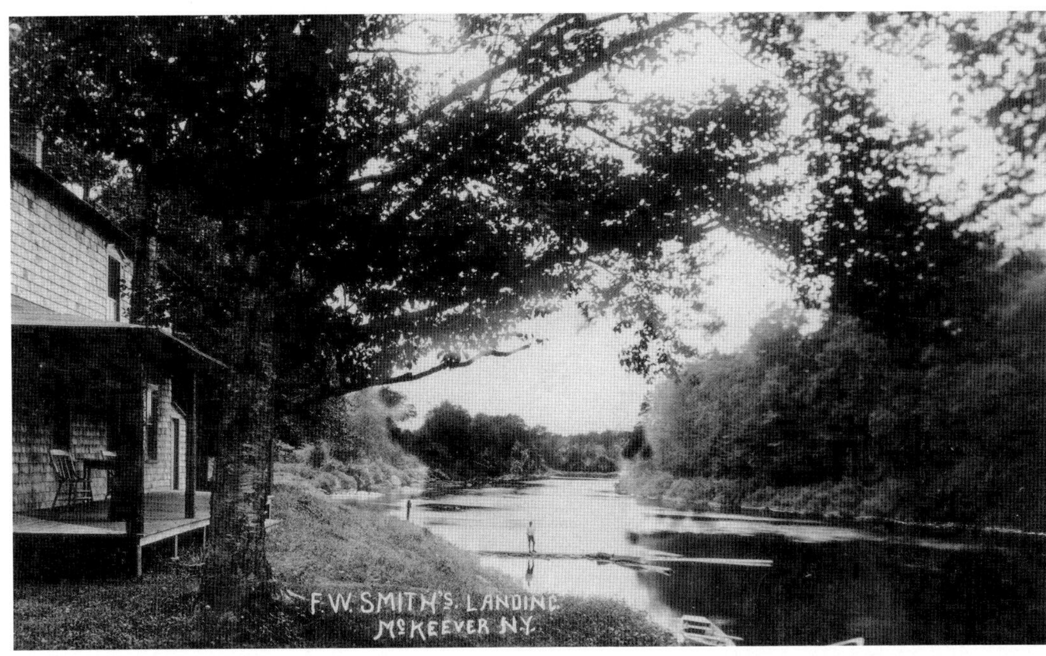


5.12. F. W. Smith's landing, McKeever, N.Y., ca. 1915. Holstein Coll.

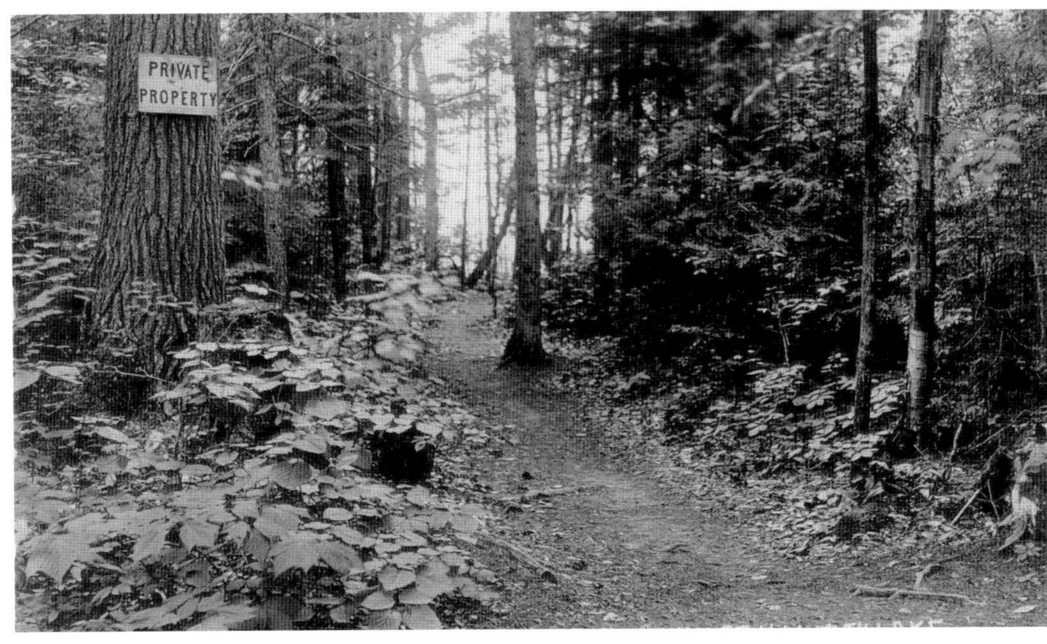


5.13. A woodland path, Fourth Lake, Inlet, N.Y., ca. 1915.
G. Jones Coll.

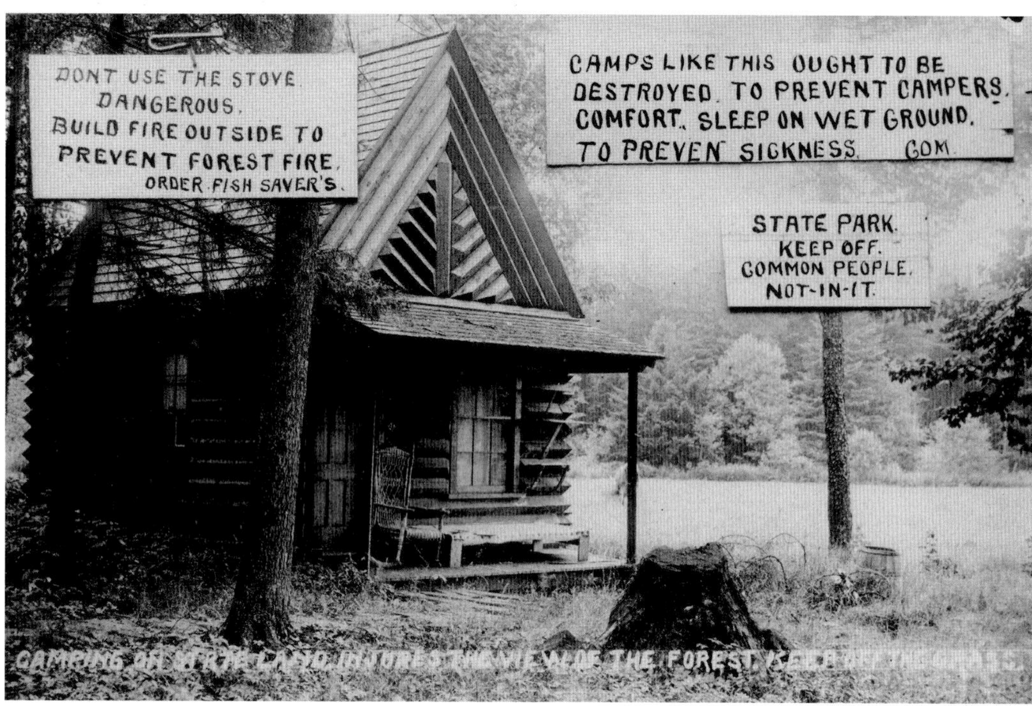


5.14. "Keep Off the Grass," ca. 1910. Courtesy of the Adirondack Museum.

and "No Trespassing" signs pop up in Henry's wood scenes too often not to suspect that they are not there just by chance. Did he purposely take views with such signs in them? If so, why? One possible explanation is that he was critical of landowners who restricted the use of their land. For decades outsiders had been buying property and posting it for their exclusive use. Adirondackers, who had free access to the land before, resented such actions.

Illustration 5.14 might fit the category of an ugly, as opposed to scenic, view. I include it because it provides more information about Beach's relationship to the land and the changes that were occurring while he was a photographer. This unusual view consists of a cabin with superimposed signs containing Beach's editorial comments. The garbled message is difficult to interpret. An interesting part of the puzzle to me is that Beach likely knew what he wanted to convey and was probably successful in communicating with his neighbors. It is we, the modern-day viewers, who are at a loss. The text seems to be critical of New York State's use of the land that it was acquiring to expand the Adirondack Forest Preserve. The sign "State Park, Keep Off, Common People Not-in-It" suggests that Beach thought that state policy about land use favored outsiders rather than Adirondackers and that he was not happy with the state's intervention.[3] Although his message may leave us confused, one lesson to be learned is that postcard views have political as well as aesthetic, and personal, dimensions.

3. Beach made another version of the card without the superimposed commentary. In this version the caption reads, "The Cottage at the Norridgewock, Beaver River, N.Y." Perhaps this card was made before the state began acquiring the land around Beaver River for the expansion of the reservoir.

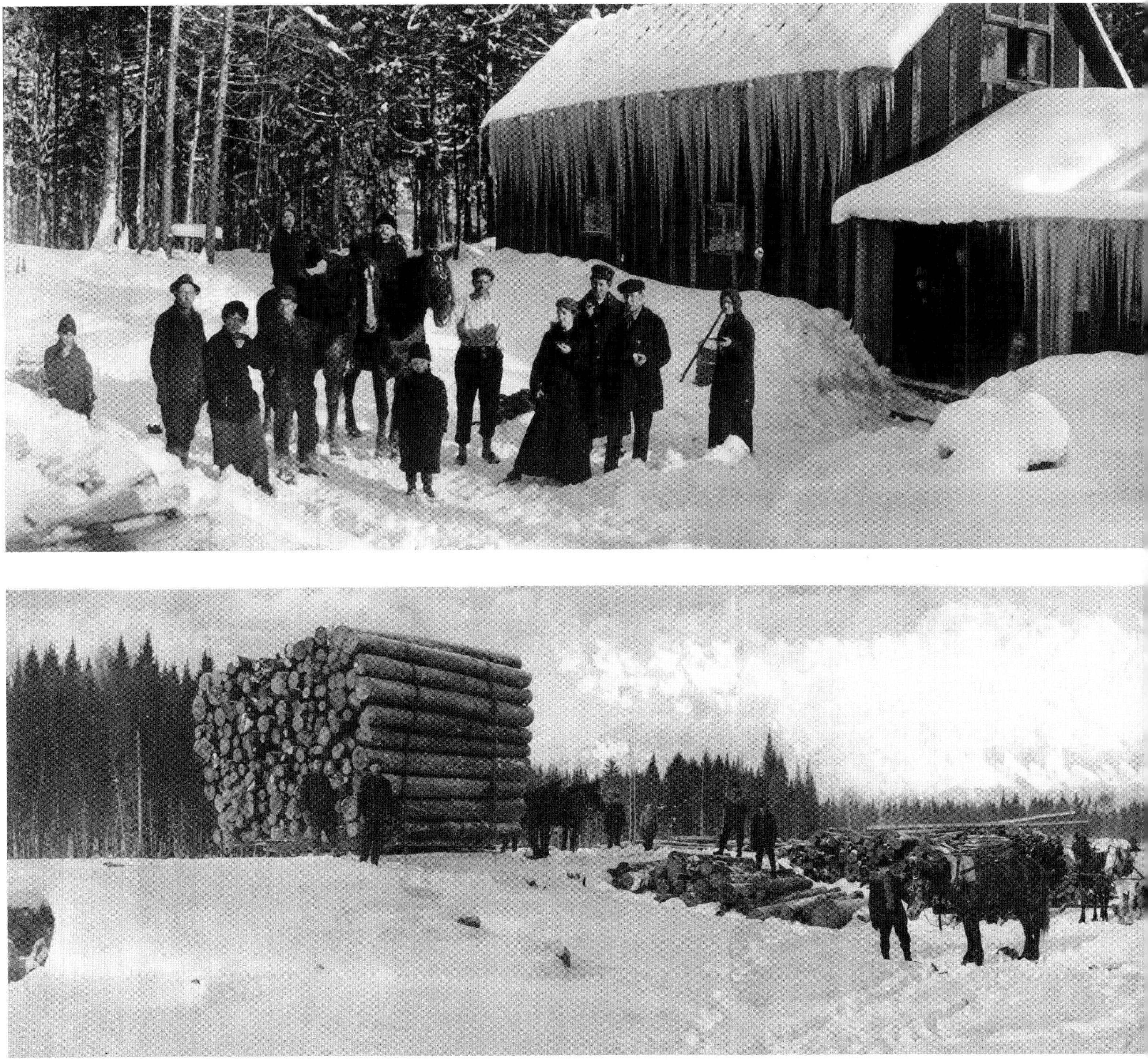

10. Horses and teamsters at Carlson's Landing, Brandreth Lake, N.Y., ca. 1916. Actual size is 6½ by 30 inches. Courtesy of the Adirondack Museum.

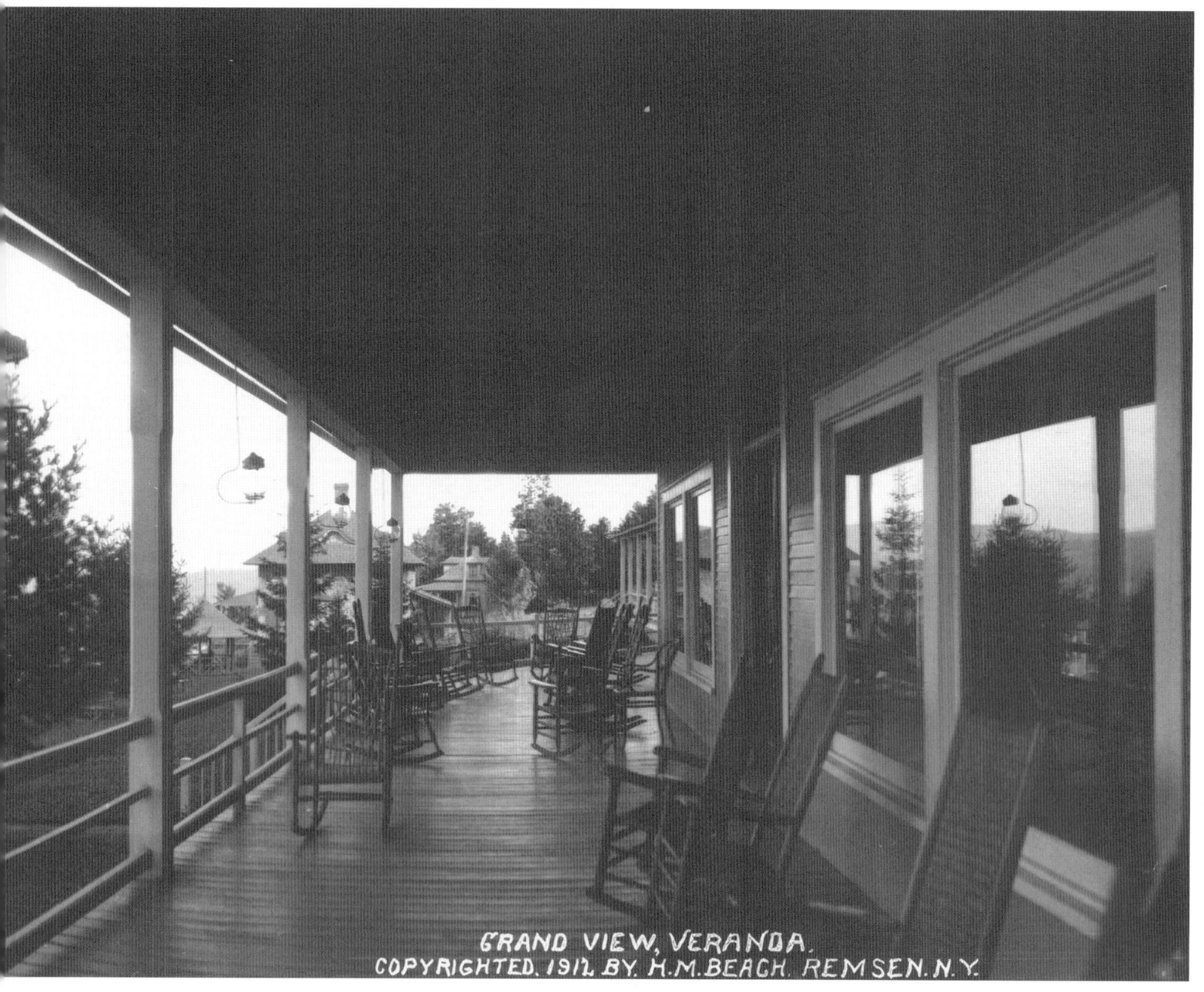
GRAND VIEW, VERANDA.
COPYRIGHTED. 1912 BY. H.M.BEACH. REMSEN. N.Y.

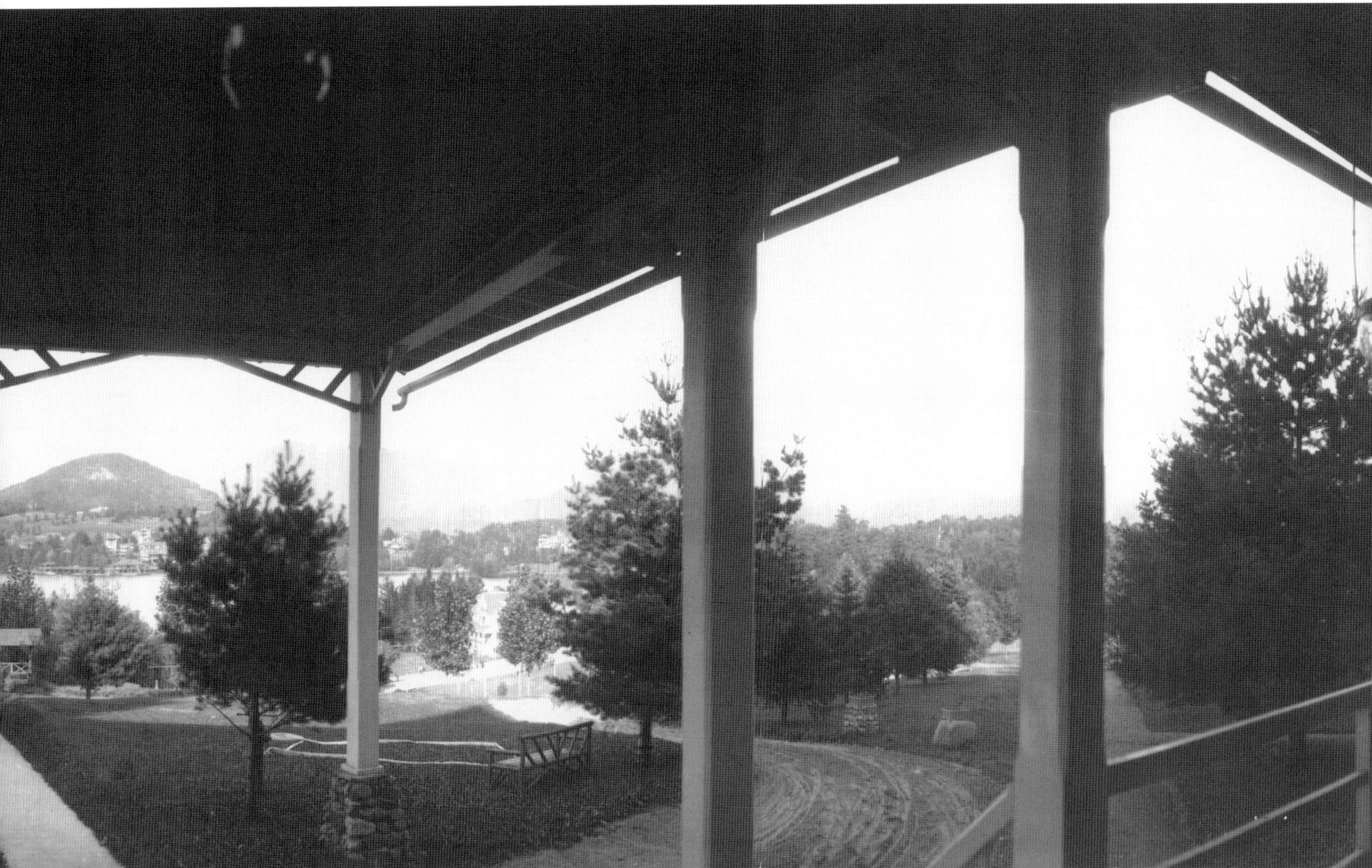

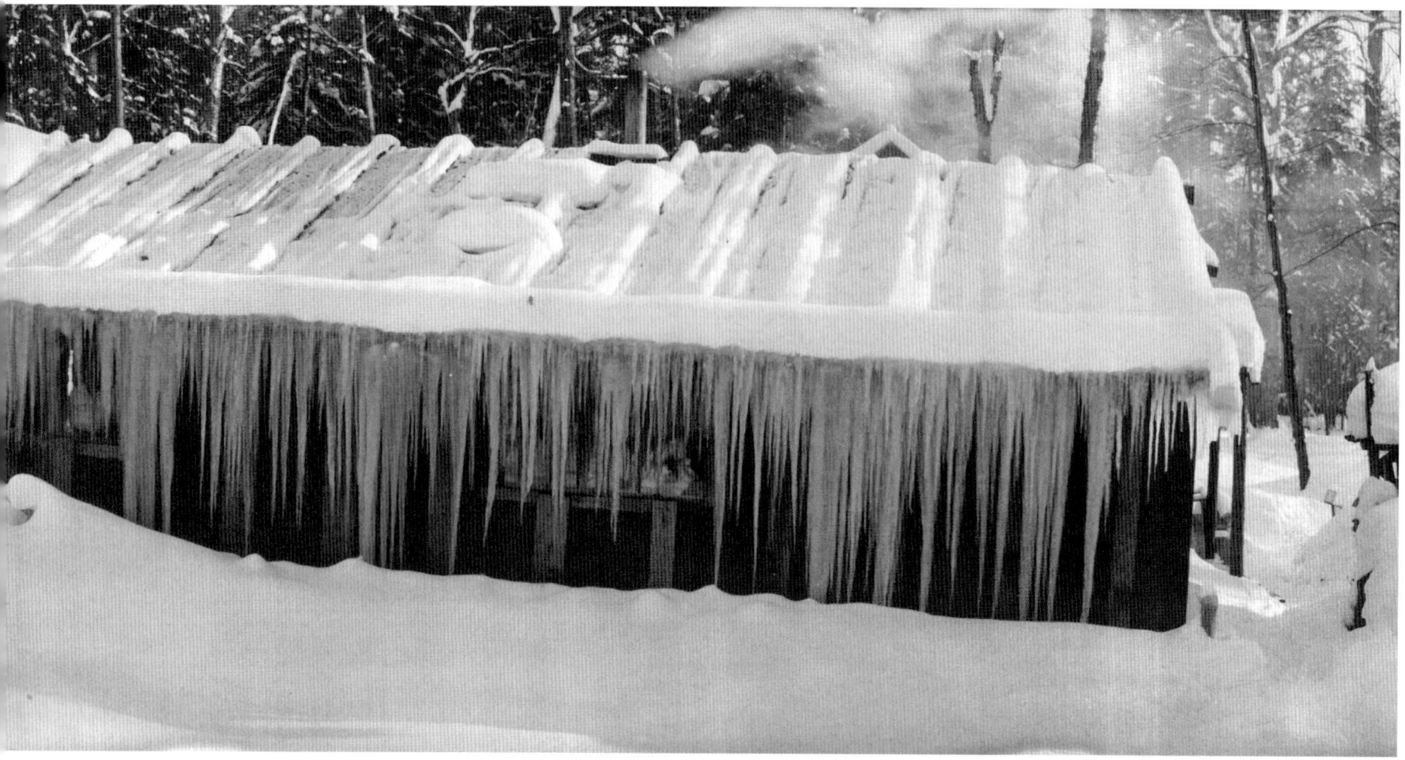

9. Carlson's Camp, Mac-A-Mac Corporation, Brandreth Lake, N.Y., ca. 1916. Actual size is 6½ by 26 inches. Courtesy of the Adirondack Museum.

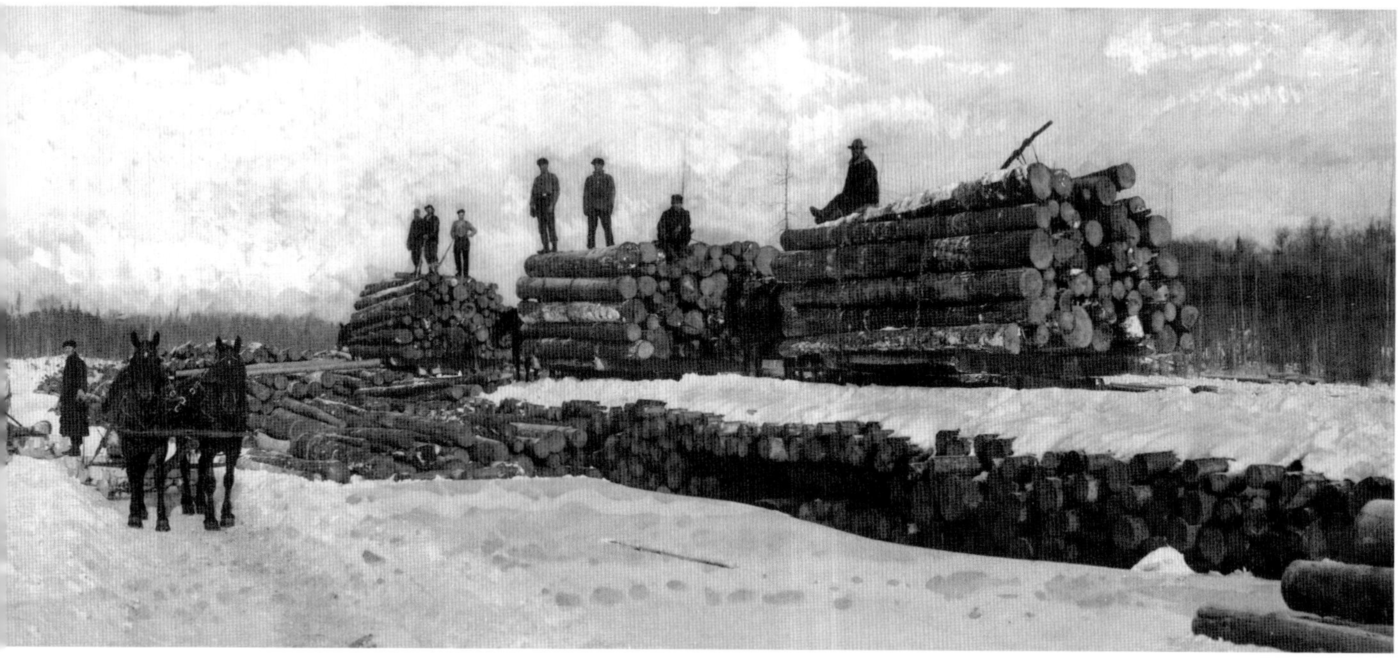

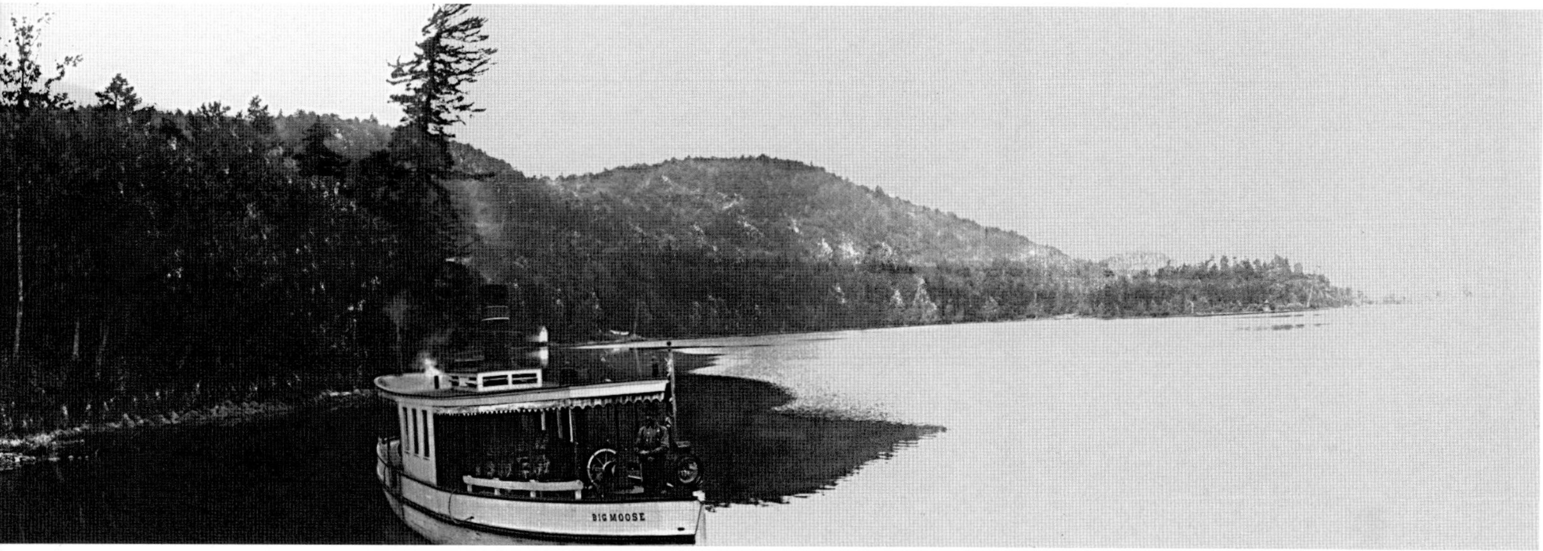

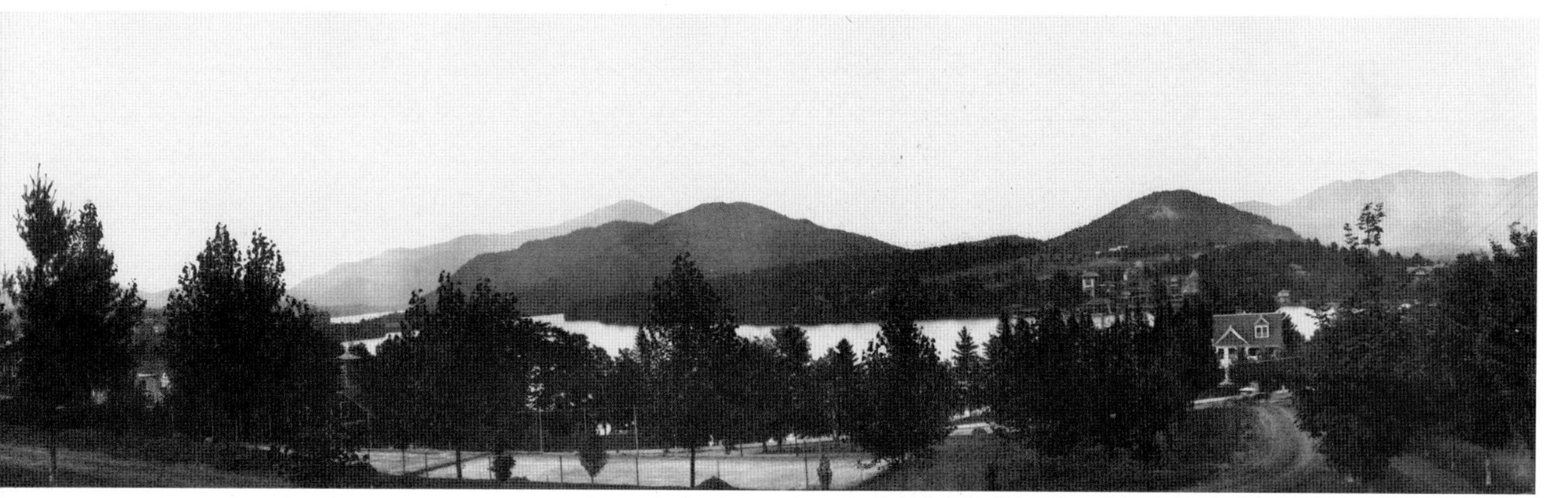

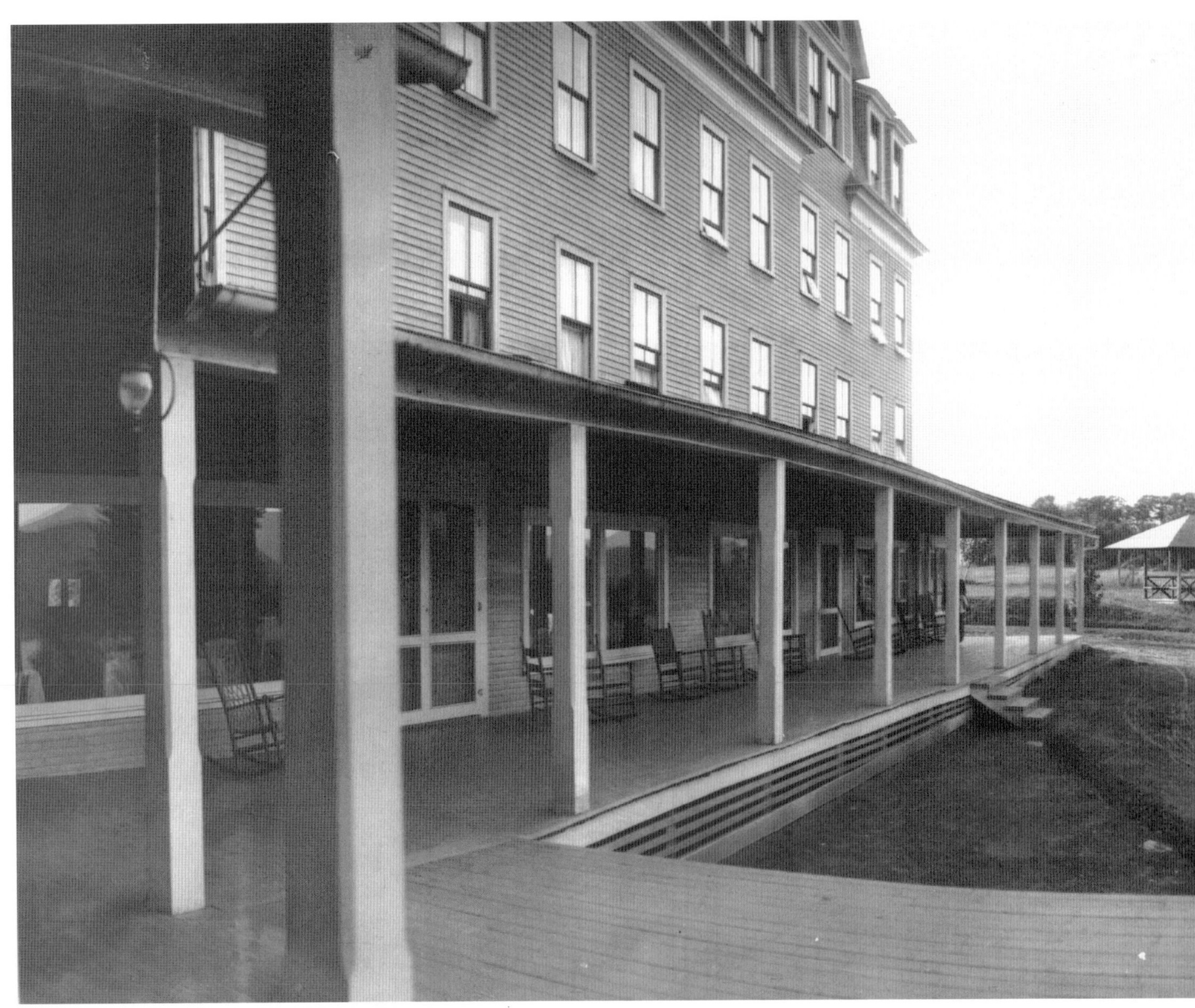

8. Grand View Hotel, veranda, ca. 1912. Actual size is 6½ by 36½ inches. Seeber Coll.

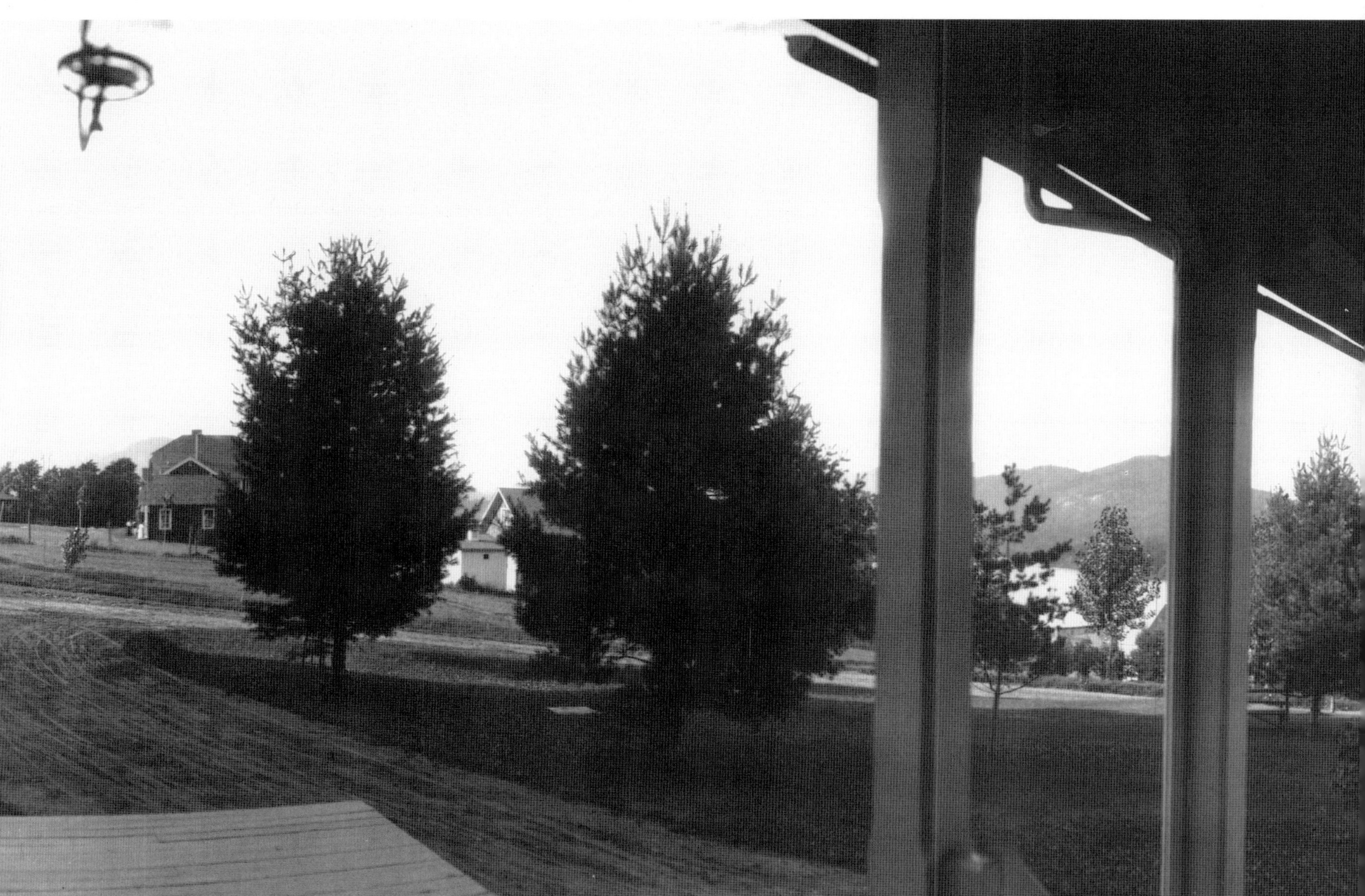

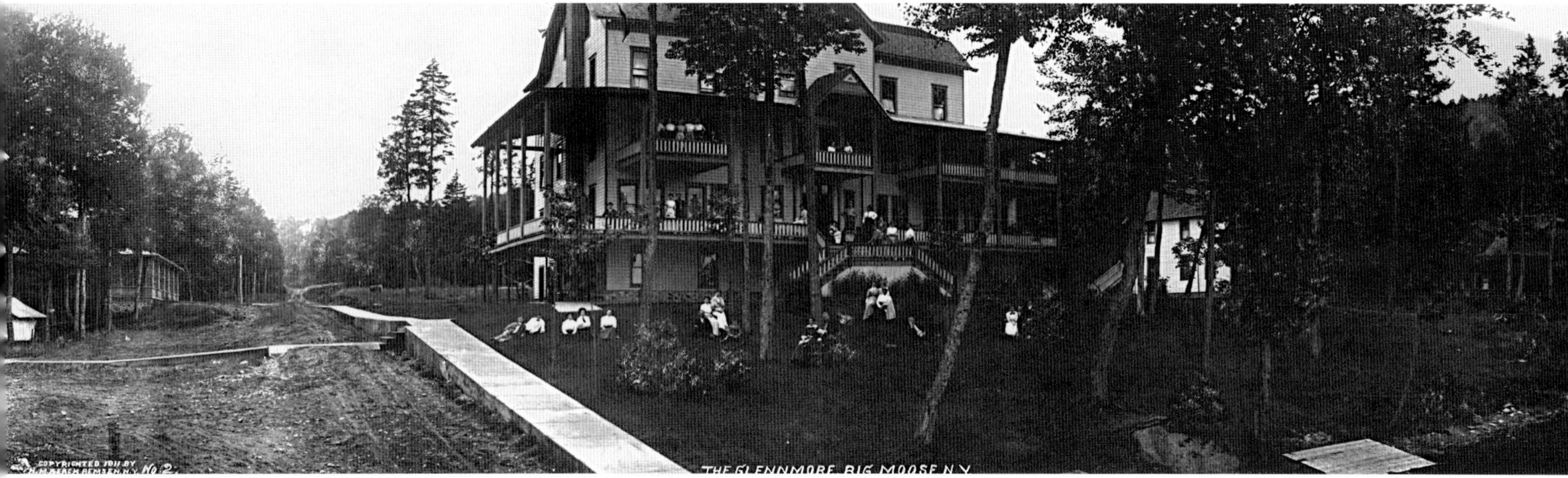

6. The Glennmore, Big Moose, N.Y., 1911. Actual size is 6½ by 40 inches. Seeber Coll.

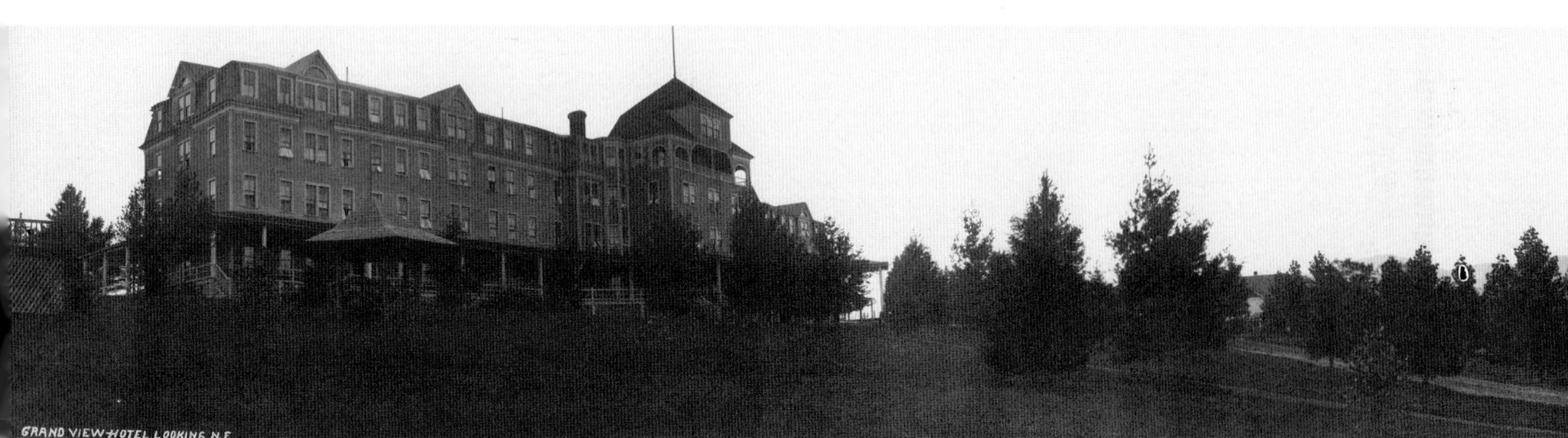


7. Grand View Hotel looking northeast, showing pines and lawn, Lake Placid, N.Y., ca. 1912. Actual size is 6 by 41 inches. Seeber Coll.

6

# Vacation Retreats
## Family-Run Camps and Modest Hotels

The seasonal visitors to the vacation areas of the Adirondack region were the backbone of Beach's business during his Remsen years (illus. 6.1). They stayed at the hundreds of tourist homes, camps, hotels, and cabins of every size and description disbursed throughout the North Country.[1] The proprietors of these establishments were Henry's best customers.

Beach sold his postcards and panoramics to the innkeepers, and they in turn marked them up and sold them to their guests. They were mostly interested in pictures of their own establishments. In some tourist locations Henry took just a few views, but in places where he had good customers, the selection was extensive. The assortment included shots of the buildings (inside and out), the grounds, adjacent sites, adjoining bodies of water, and the transportation that took guests there and about. Beach photographed details that would be lost on all but the most astute observer. There were bird's-eye views of entire resorts as well as close-ups of such fine points as the fireplaces in cabins and boardwalks around the grounds. In many cases, Henry returned year after year to improve and update the offerings.

1. *Camp* is a widely used term in the North Country that refers to almost any human-made structure used as a vacation retreat (Gilborn 2000). *Resort* was not a favored term in the early part of the nineteenth century, but it is what many of the places I refer to as camps would be called today.

2. Many of them began as primitive cabins thrown together by guides.

### The Family-Run Camps

Beginning in about 1885 a number of small- to medium-size unpretentious room-and-board establishments that were started by families who had taken in hunting and fishing parties began to emerge as the core of a special type of family-oriented summer vacation industry in the North Country.[2] The railroad that was built in the early 1890s directly through what is now the western part of the Adirondack Park made many of these early vacation retreats easily accessible, and they prospered. Many were secluded, far from the noise of the stylish large hotels that were located in more trendy spots. Hardy, plain meals were served family style, and the owners treated repeat guests (mostly families) like friends.[3] Big Moose, Beaver River, and the Fulton Chain had a large concentration of these homegrown hotels and camps (Grady 1933; Scheffler and Carey 2000). The industrious owners, who were skilled builders and managers,

3. Although there are books about the great camps, the famous clubs, and other aspects of Adirondack life, aside from a few books of reminiscences (Covey 1964; Grady 1933; Higby 1974) these small family-run hotels and resorts have not had their share of coverage in the literature (see Gilborn 2000). From the turn of the century, they were at the heart of many people's Adirondack experience, and some carry on the tradition of family resort today. Fortuitously, they were essential to Beach's postcard and panoramic business. More Beach photographs exist of these resorts than of any other subject.

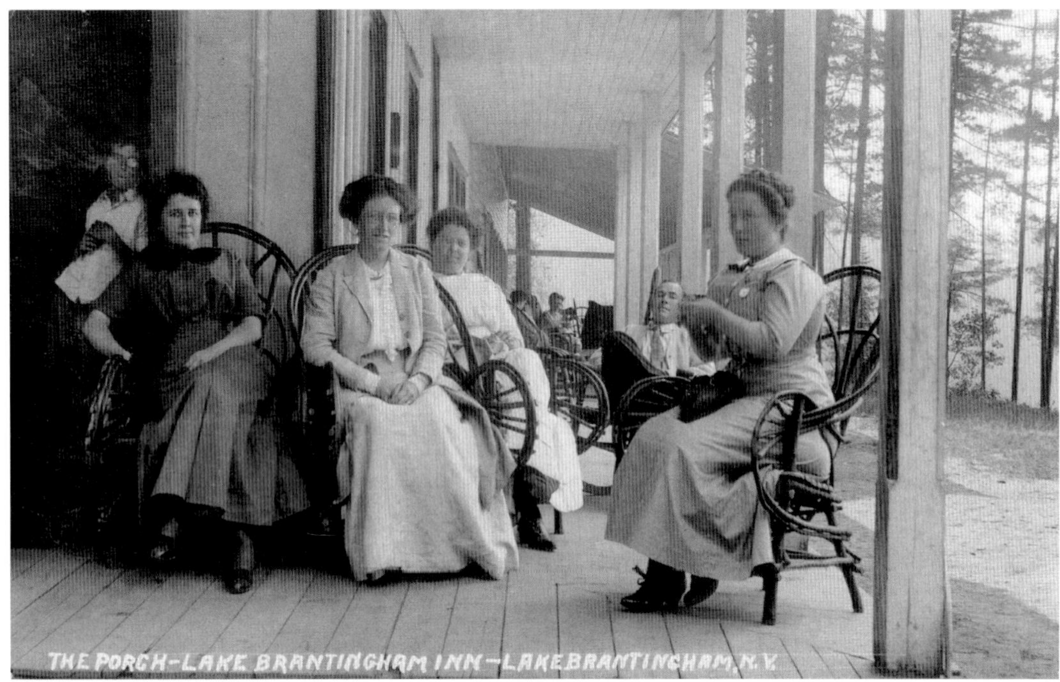


6.1. Porch at the Lake Brantingham Inn, Lake Brantingham, N.Y., ca. 1908. Brantingham Lake was one of the resort areas closest to Henry's Watson home. Teal Coll.

assembled their businesses with their own labor. Proprietors, some of whom became Adirondack legends, shared camaraderie and pride about their vocation. They were proud of the good-natured, personal service they provided their guests (Covey 1964; Grady 1933; Higby 1974).[4]

Many of these resort pioneers had migrated from the Lowville area, and Henry Beach knew them and their families personally. Walking through Beach's Bridge Cemetery in Watson, one sees Beach gravestones interspersed with ones of the Higby, Covey, Puffer, Wood, Glenn, and other families whose names are closely linked with Big Moose and the Fulton Chain area.[5] Although Beach covered the entire Fulton Chain as well as points north and east, the Big Moose Lake area was his favorite spot.

4. Not all potential guests were welcome. Some resort brochures stated that "Hebrews and consumptives" were not allowed.

5. See references in note 3 in this chapter. See also Pilcher 1992.

You cannot separate Beach's photographs of the area from his lifelong connection with the inhabitants. As we shall see, he took pictures not only of the facilities, but also of the resort pioneers, their staff, and the guests. Even their dogs were his subjects.

## Big Moose Lake and Vicinity

### *Higby Camp*

Beach photographed James Higby's place many times. Jim (1842–1914) came to Big Moose toward the end of the Civil War as a surveyor and later returned as a guide, hunter, and trapper.[6] In his youth, this energetic man drove a stagecoach route from Boonville to Moose River and hunted deer for market.

6. The information about the resort owners and their establishments comes mainly from Covey 1964; Grady 1933; and Higby 1974.

Jim and his wife, Francena, started the famous Higby resort at Big Moose. Both were from Watson. Francena's father's sawmill was down the road from the Beach homestead. There, as a child, she lost the lower half of her right arm. She had been a schoolteacher in Watson before she moved to Big Moose in the late 1870s, so it is possible that she taught Henry.

Jim Higby built one of the first hunting and fishing camps on Big Moose Lake in the mid-1870s. In addition to being the carpenter, he was the guide as well as the steward. Slowly, the clientele grew, and rooms and then whole sections were added. The first dwellings were built entirely from rough hand-hewed logs because the site was without access to a sawmill. By the turn of the century, Jim had built the lodge that he called "the largest rustic building in the Adirondacks." It was four stories high and ninety feet long. It had about thirty guest rooms, and Jim boasted that it had the first flush toilets in Big Moose.[7] Henry took dozens of views of Jim's place that included details of the main building from many different angles and distances (illus. 6.2, 6.3).

Family-run camps like the Higbys' supplied jobs for a special breed of older workers, people who were flamboyantly independent and who avoided nine-to-five domestic life at all costs. Many were quirky characters. Gardeners and maintenance workers often fitted this description, as did the hunting and fishing guides who were frequently affiliated with specific resorts. Characters contributed to the informal atmosphere. Though forgotten by other photographers, these unconventional Adirondackers were included in Beach's views.

In spite of the fact that the Higby Camp's chief gardener, Mr. Batty (first name unknown), tipped the bottle, Jim Higby, who abstained from smoke and drink, kept him on staff for years (Higby 1974) (illus. 6.4). Batty was bearded and toothless. He regaled guests with tales of the days he had allegedly spent with the Pony Express in the old Wild West fighting grizzly bears and other creatures. The gardener was skilled enough to work Higby's five-acre plot to produce a substantial amount of food for the guests and staff. He specialized in strawberries and honey. Batty's unsuccessful schemes for keeping deer out of the vegetable garden were the sources of many camp jokes (Higby 1974, 106).

7. Jim's son, Roy, was born in 1893 at Big Moose without the help of a doctor, nurse, or midwife. Roy went on to be a camp builder and successful resort proprietor, and achieved some fame as well (Higby 1974).

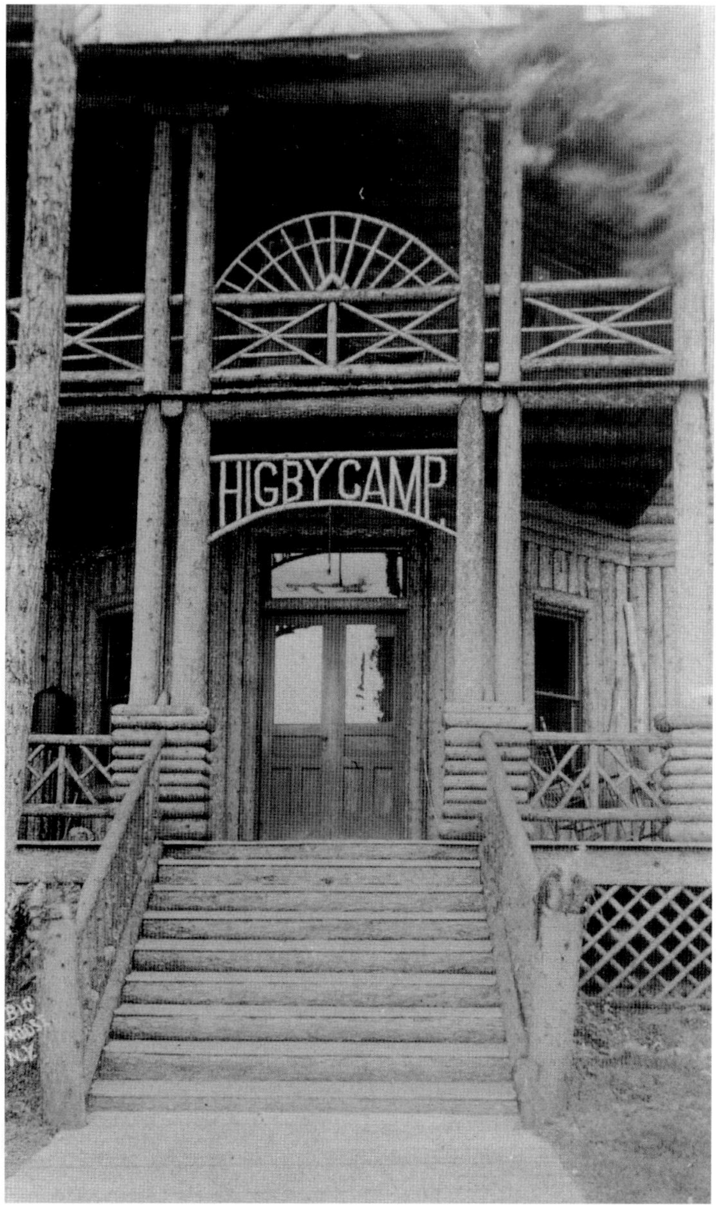


6.2. Entrance to Higby Camp, Big Moose, N.Y., ca. 1908. Scheffler Coll.

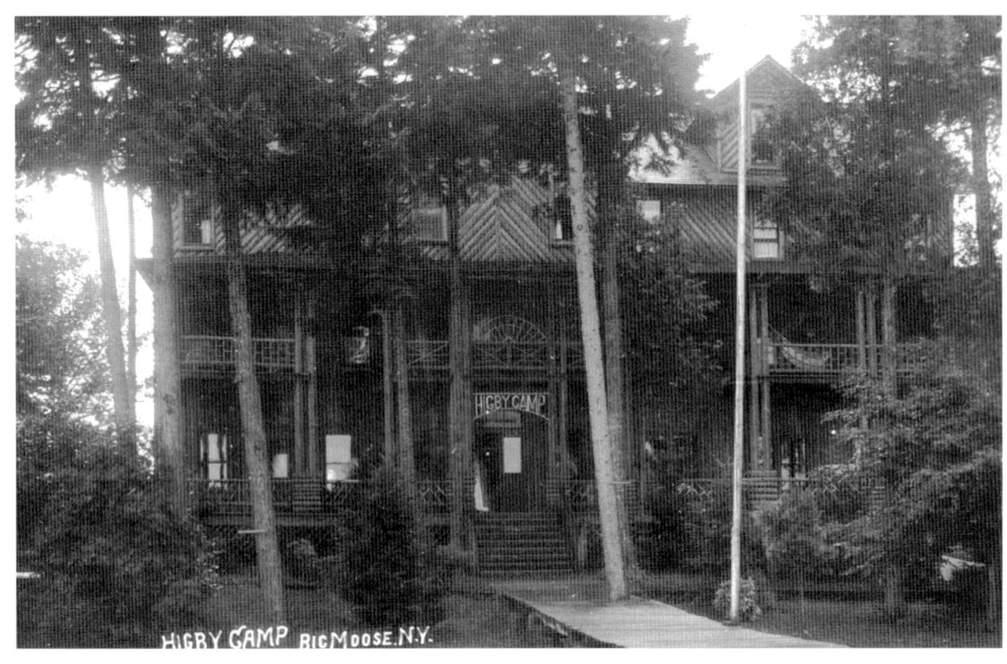


6.3. Higby Camp, Big Moose, N.Y., ca. 1908. Scheffler Coll.

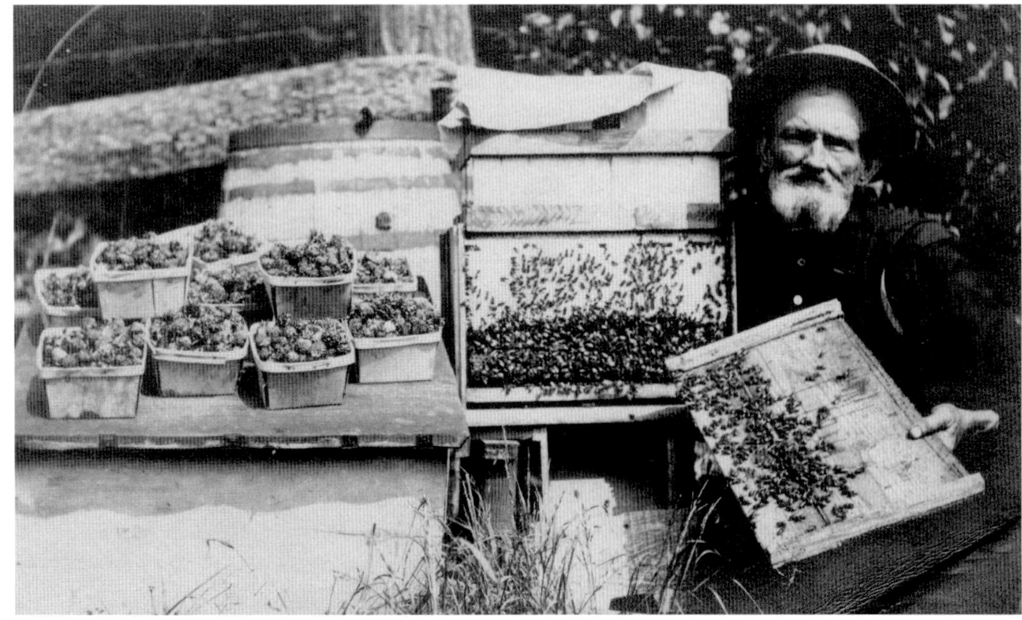

6.4. Higby gardener with bees and strawberries, Big Moose, N.Y., ca. 1912. Author's Coll.

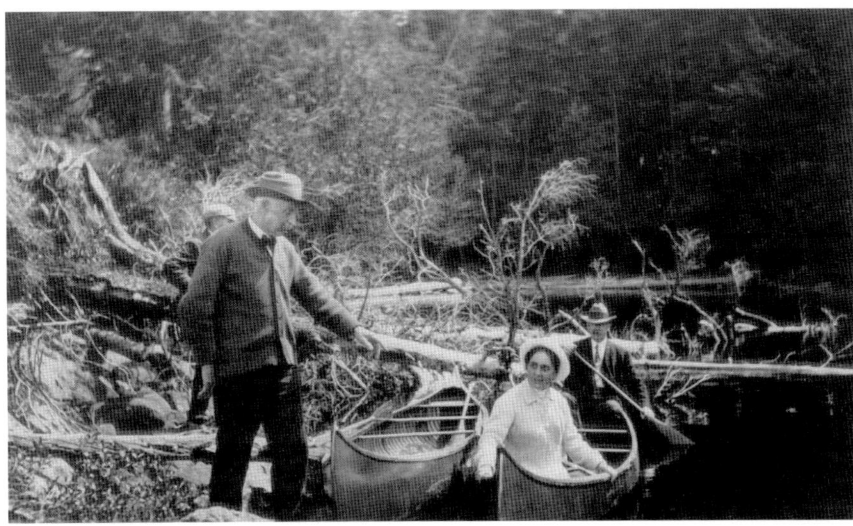

6.5. Jim Higby on the shore of Big Moose Lake with unidentified canoeists, ca. 1908. Author's Coll.

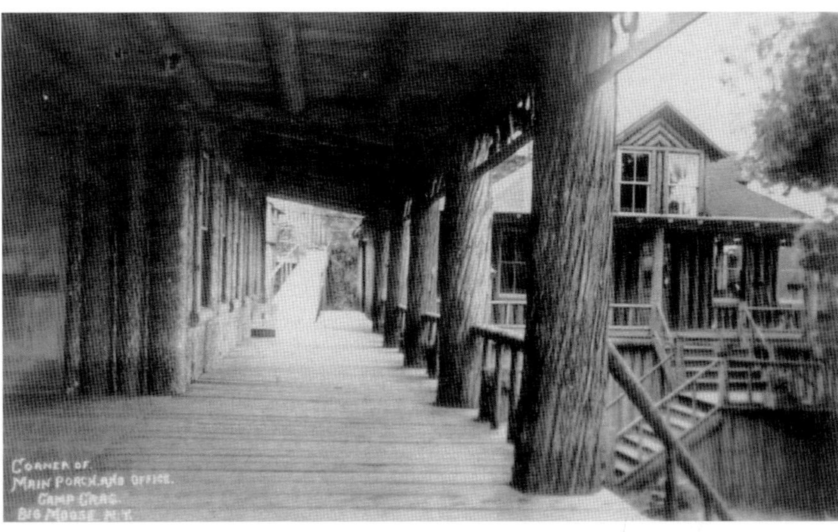


6.6. Corner of main porch and office, Camp Crag, Big Moose, N.Y., ca. 1911. Scheffler Coll.

As Jim Higby got older he remained at the resort, but his son, Roy, became the manager. When Beach got around to photographing the Higby, Jim was an old-timer.[8] Jim died at Big Moose in 1914. His son kept Mr. Batty on staff. In 1921 the original main building burned to the ground. Beach's pictures of Jim and his camp are historic treasures as well as fine examples of his portrait and architectural photography (illus. 6.5).

### *Camp Crag*

Jim Higby recruited Henry Covey to Big Moose as a carpenter to help install doors and windows in cabins he was building in the 1880s. Covey was also from the area of Beach's birth. So was Covey's first wife, Emma Chase, who was a member of the Chase family of Chase's Lake, the body of water just up the road from the Beach family home in Watson (Covey 1964).

A woodsman by background, Henry Covey took a liking to Big Moose and stayed to build another famous resort, Camp Crag (panoramic 4). The central building in this resort complex grew out of the original structure that was constructed in the late 1880s.

Covey favored a type of construction in which the logs were cut lengthwise and stood on end, with the bark side facing out (Gilborn 2000) (illus. 6.6). Although the styles of Big Moose Lake buildings vary considerably, this form of dwelling became a hallmark of the area.

Camp Crag consisted of a main house and a number of smaller cabins all connected by boardwalks. Beach photographed every nook and cranny, each rental cabin, both inside and out (illus. 6.7, 6.8).

Henry Covey sold Camp Crag in 1922. Two years later he died at Big Moose Lake.

8. Jim Higby resembled Henry Covey. A number of people who have seen his picture in a prepublication version of the manuscript have asked me if I was sure that the man in the picture is Higby. Handwriting on the backs of two copies of this picture identifies the person as Higby. In illustration 6.5 the man is dressed in the same hat and sweater as in another picture that I identified as Higby in *Exposing the Wilderness* (1999). That picture was taken in front of the main building of Higby's camp and was identified on the back as being Jim Higby.

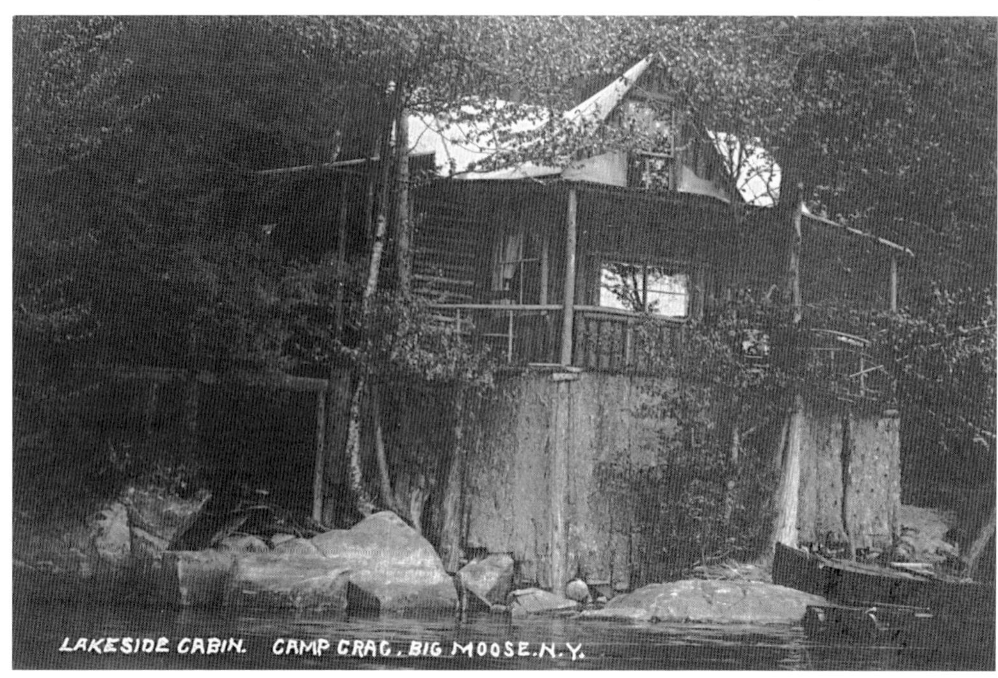


6.7. Lakeside cabin, Camp Crag, Big Moose, N.Y., ca. 1911. Scheffler Coll.

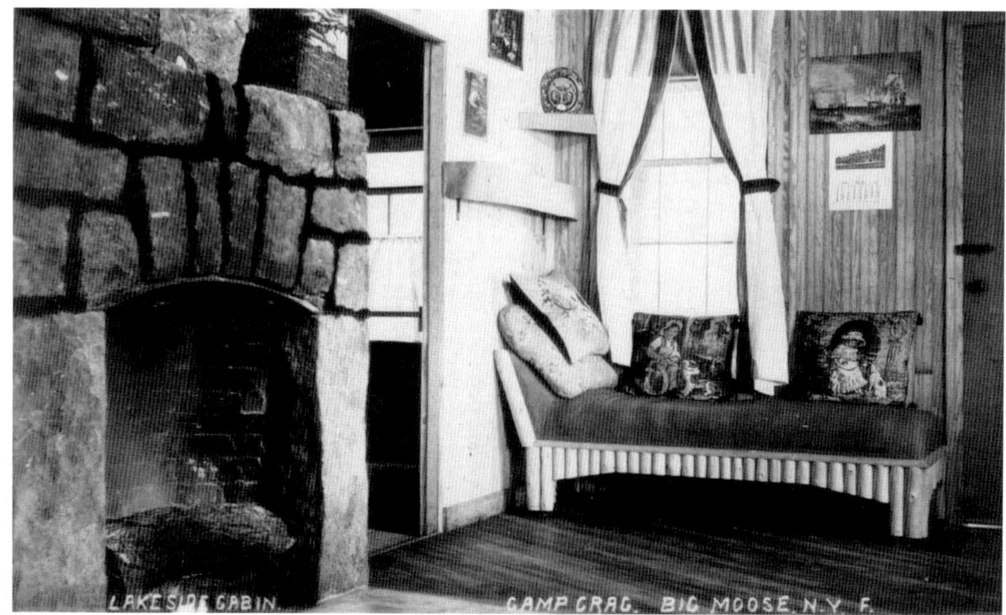


6.8. Interior of lakeside cabin, Camp Crag, Big Moose Lake, N.Y., ca. 1911. Scheffler Coll.

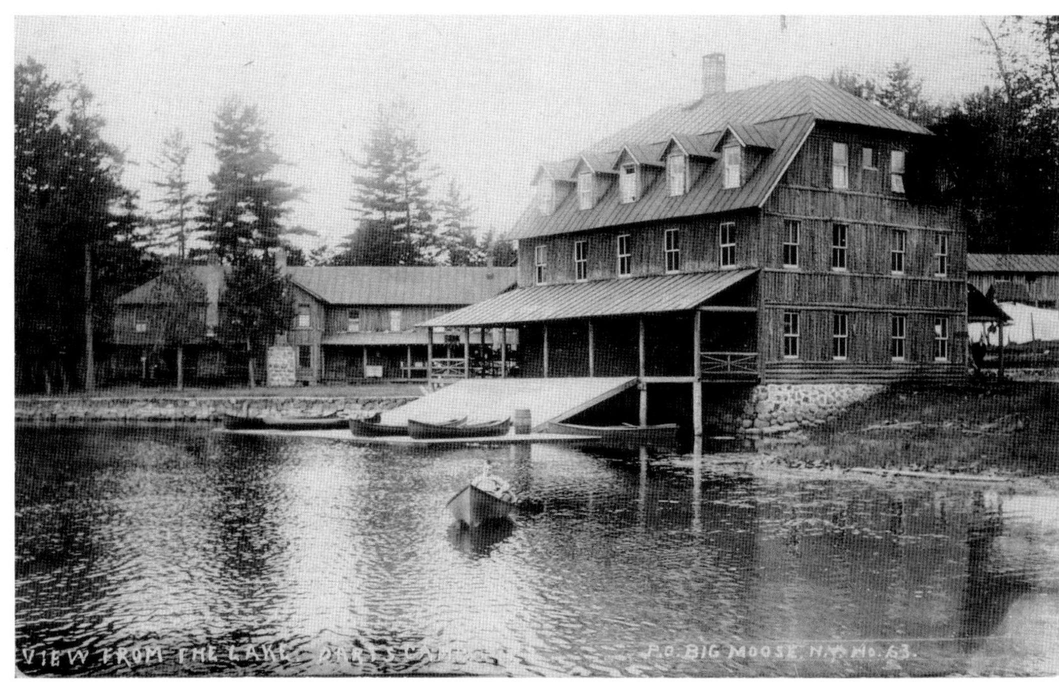


6.9. View of Dart's Camp from the lake, Big Moose, N.Y., ca. 1914. Author's Coll.

### *Dart's*

Covey built Camp Crag with the help of a neighbor, William Dart. By then, Bill had established a resort of his own on a lake only a few miles from Big Moose. Dart, like Higby and Covey, was the prototype of the colorful, self-reliant, multitalented woodsman turned entrepreneur of the old Adirondack school.

Dart first came to the central Adirondack region as a young man in 1876 with a party of trappers. He became a partner in a log cabin that served city people who came to hunt and fish on what was then known as Second Lake.[9] As Bill Dart's reputation as a host and guide spread, he added rustic cabins one by one to form a colony that became the nucleus of his summer resort. In 1888 Dart married Mary Krohnmiller of White Lake, and together they managed the business: she ran the kitchen and dining room, and Bill tended to the maintenance, the boathouse, guiding, and construction. Eventually, they created one of the most picturesque family camps in the Adirondacks (illus. 6.9).[10]

Beach photographed Dart's place many times, but during the summer of 1914 he focused on Bill and Mary to produce a number of memorable photographs of the aging couple, sometimes with their cat and dog, Sancho (illus. 6.10).

9. It was actually the second upstream widening of the north branch of the Moose River. In 1901, the Darts successfully petitioned the state conservation commission to rename Second Lake Dart's Lake. The old resort is now called Camp Gorham, and is a summer camp for children run by the Rochester YMCA.

10. Like many early camp builders, Bill began his business as a squatter. After the railroad came to the area in 1892, he purchased the entire lakeshore from Dr. Webb. Like all of the successful old-timers, he was a good businessperson and a hard worker.

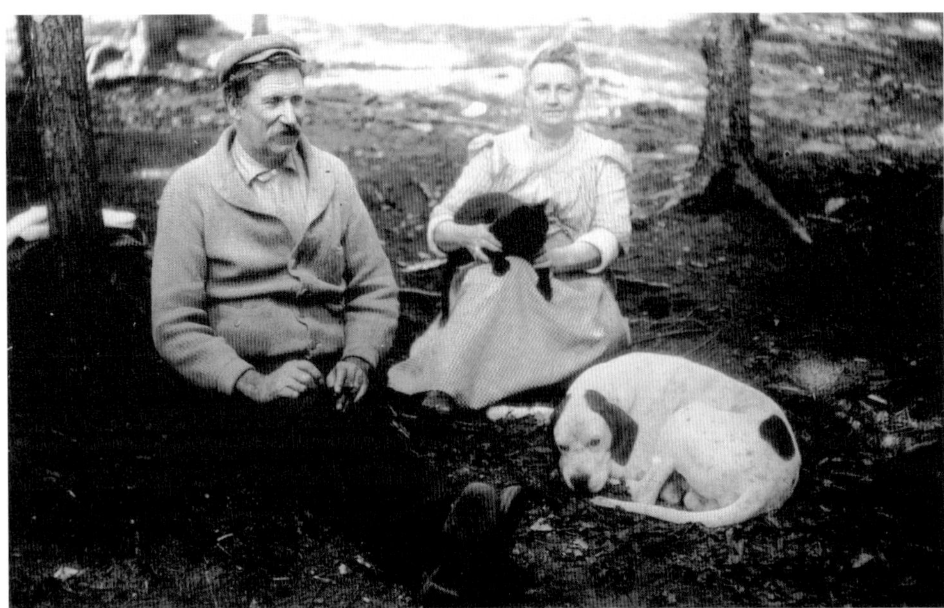

6.10. Bill and Mary Dart, Big Moose, N.Y., ca. 1914. Davis Coll.

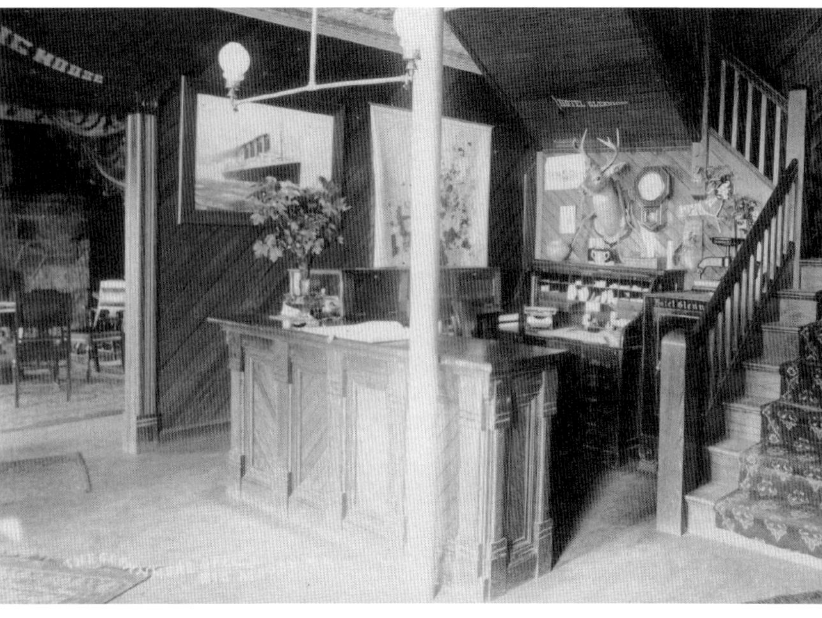

6.11. The Glennmore office, Big Moose, N.Y., ca. 1914. Author's Coll.

During that summer, Beach took at least two large panoramic photographs of the Dart establishment. Both include Bill standing in the midst of his buildings. The capacity of the Cirkut camera to pan large sections of the shoreline and Henry's ability to work with the equipment are vividly demonstrated in panoramic 5.

As sharp in business and camp construction as he was in hunting and fishing, Bill Dart was successful enough to spend his later years comfortably in Avon, Florida, among other retired Adirondack businesspeople. He died there in 1934.

### *The Glennmore*

The Glennmore was one the earliest and largest of the Big Moose clapboard hotels. Its name is derived from the Glenn family who came to Big Moose from Lowville. It was built around 1896 and stood at the entrance to the lake in West Bay. The road from Big Moose Station ended at the public dock at the Glennmore, making it a transportation hub and central to lake life (Grady 1933; Scheffler and Carey 2000).

Dwight Sperry, a Watson native and Jim Higby's brother-in-law (Higby 1974), built and, for a time, managed the Glennmore. D. B., as Sperry was called, was unkempt, loud, and aggressive, a real character (Higby 1974, 105). Industrious in hotel management and construction, he had his hand in transportation, ice, and electricity as well. In addition to the Glennmore, he built and owned the Eagle Bay Hotel on Fourth Lake.[11]

11. In 1908, Dwight Sperry brought the first automobile to Old Forge, by train.

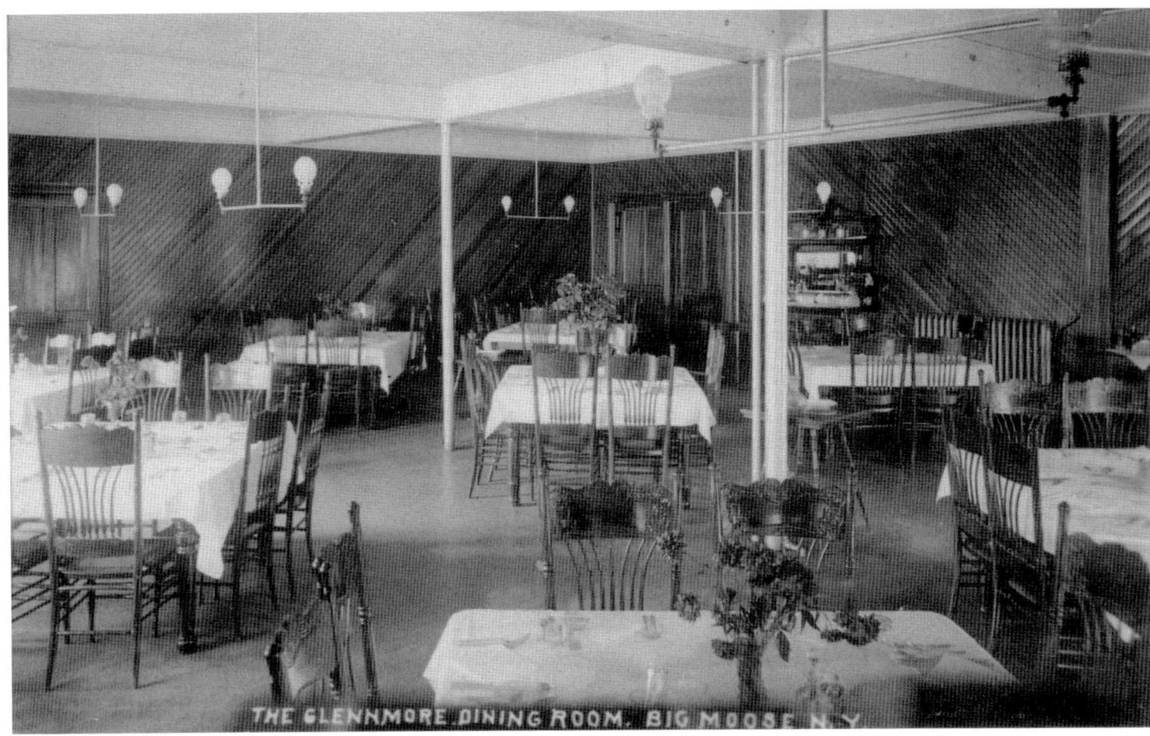


6.12. The Glennmore dining room, Big Moose, N.Y., ca. 1914. Author's Coll.

Henry took two panoramics of the Glennmore in 1911. The one shown in this book as panoramic 6 includes the guests assembled before the main building and the Big Moose steamer. Henry sent an original print of this panoramic to the Library of Congress to register the copyright.

In addition to the panoramics, Beach produced an extensive series of postcards of the Glennmore. His inside views provide incredible detail about the layout and functioning of the hotel when it was in its prime. In the pictures of the office, Beach gives us a sense of what it was like to check in at the front desk (illus. 6.11). We can see the decorative woodwork on the counter, the cut flowers, the gas lighting fixture, the stuffed deer head, and other decorations. The sitting room with the fireplace is on the left.

The building was not rough-cut, but it was simple with rustic touches. Even the formal dining room had natural wood walls and plain wood floors (illus. 6.12). The ample porches were decked out with rustic furniture made locally (Gilborn 1987) (illus. 6.13). In addition to the main house, the Glennmore had seven waterfront guest cottages that could be reached by boardwalks with rustic railings (illus. 6.14).

### *Burdick's Camp*

As machine-cut lumber became available after 1900, clapboard and wood-frame structures, like the Glennmore, provided an alternative to the earlier construction techniques. But they did not eliminate old-time construction and rustic

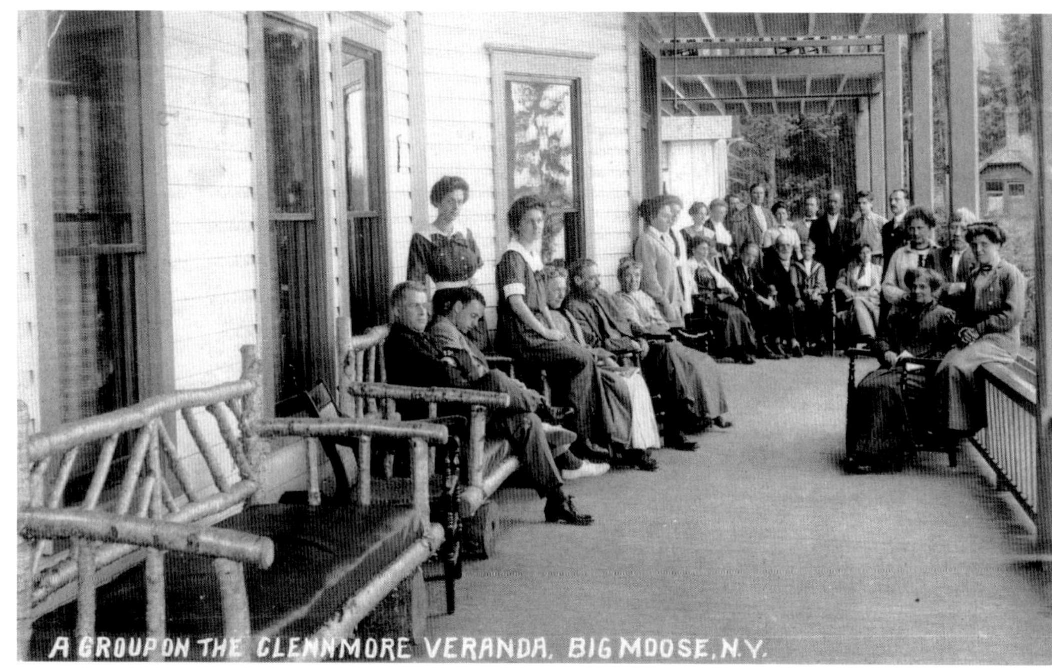


6.13. A group on the Glennmore veranda, Big Moose, N.Y., ca. 1914. Keebler Coll.

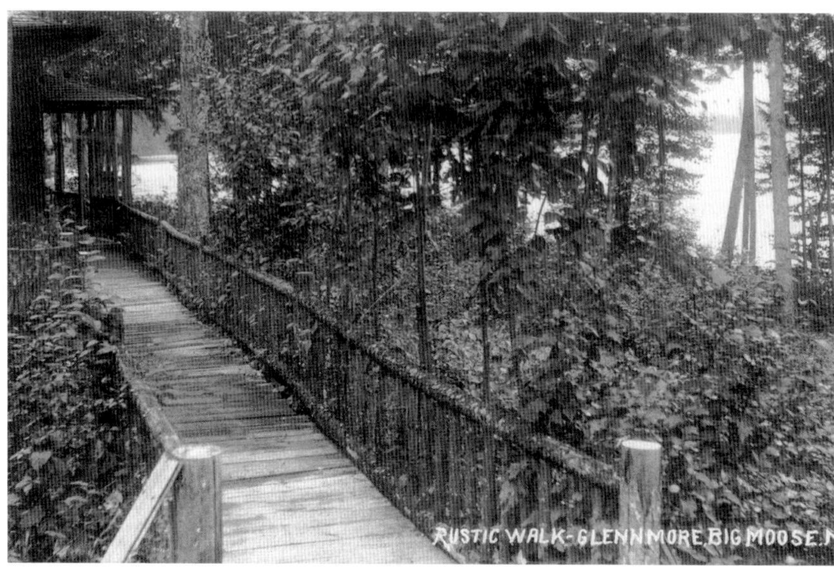


6.14. Rustic walk at the Glennmore, Big Moose, N.Y., ca. 1914. Scheffler Coll.

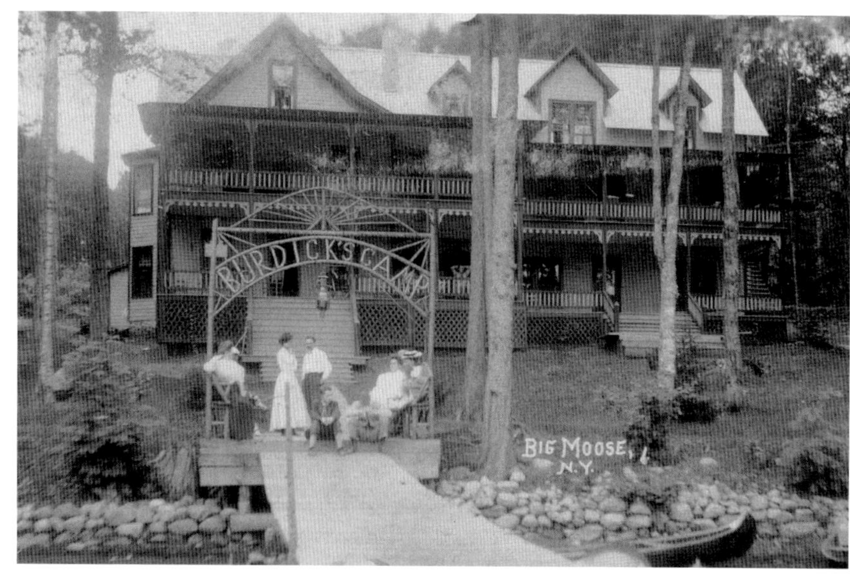


6.15. Burdick's camp, Big Moose, N.Y., ca. 1908. Davis Coll.

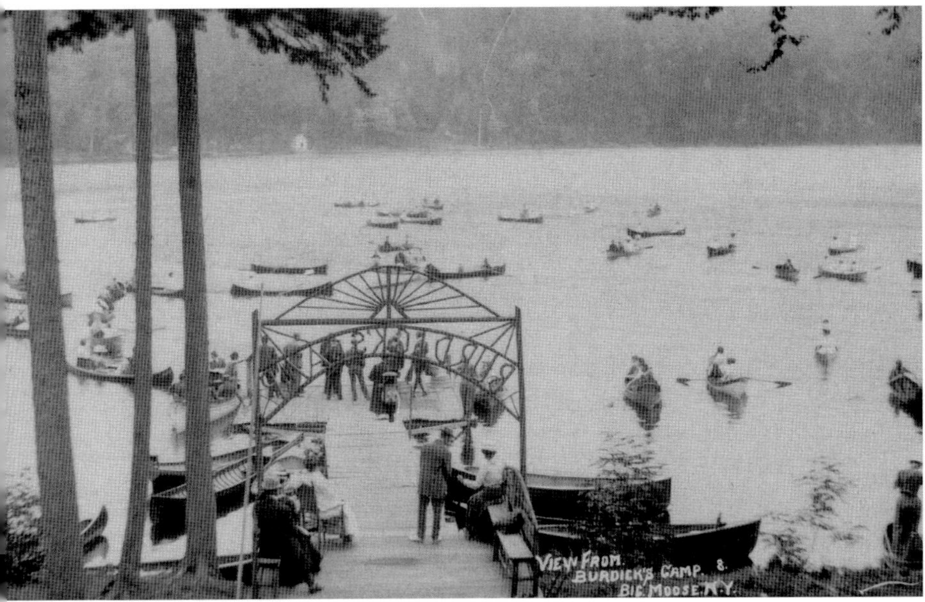


6.16. View from Burdick's camp, Big Moose, N.Y., ca. 1907. Martin Coll.

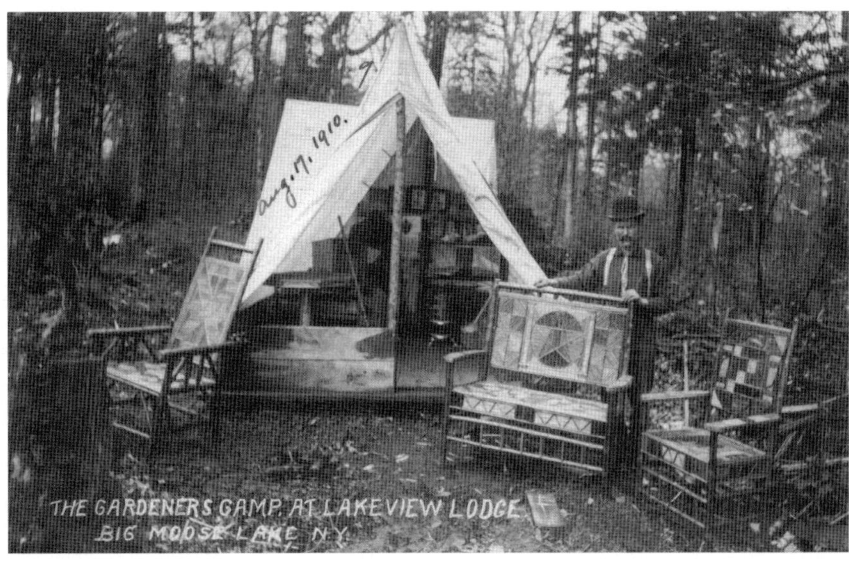


6.17. The gardener's camp at Lakeview Lodge, Big Moose Lake, N.Y., ca. 1910. Carey Coll.

style. Even in clapboard structures, like the main building at Burdick's, many woodsy elements remained. Fireplaces, for example, were often made of irregular hand-cut stone. As is evident in Beach's pictures of Burdick's, decorative arches were often of twig construction (illus. 6.15). Outbuildings, including the detached guest cottages, continued to be built in the old style. Builders located their structures among the trees; clear-cutting to get expansive views was not their approach.

Wide, roomy porches with views of the lake's trees silhouetted in the foreground were characteristic of camp and hotel architecture. This feature is emphasized in Beach's picture of the Burdick dock from the veranda, entitled "View from Burdick's Camp" (illus. 6.16). Burdick's was the main site of the area's annual regatta day, and is the location of the Beach photograph featured at the beginning of chapter 1.

The furniture inside turn-of-the-century resort hotels tended to be factory made and formal. But the interior design of the rough-cut cabins and older structures included mosaic twig household furnishings. Almost nothing is known about the early practitioners of this craft (Gilborn 1987, 189). Fortunately, Henry took a picture of George Wilson, an exceptional furniture maker who worked as the gardener at Lake View Lodge on Big Moose Lake (illus. 6.17).[12] Handmade rustic furniture was his sideline (O'Leary 1998). Henry's photograph is only one of two surviving images of the man and his handiwork (Gilborn 1987, 197, 327).

### Beaver River

Beaver River was a few stops by rail north of Big Moose. An isolated hunter's and angler's paradise, no permanent community existed there until the depot was built in 1893 (Bowes 1965). When Beach began photographing the area around 1906, it served family summer tourists but maintained some of its

12. Gilborn reports that he was the gardener at Sagamore in 1910 and that by 1916–1917 he was employed at Kamp Kill Kare (1987, 190).

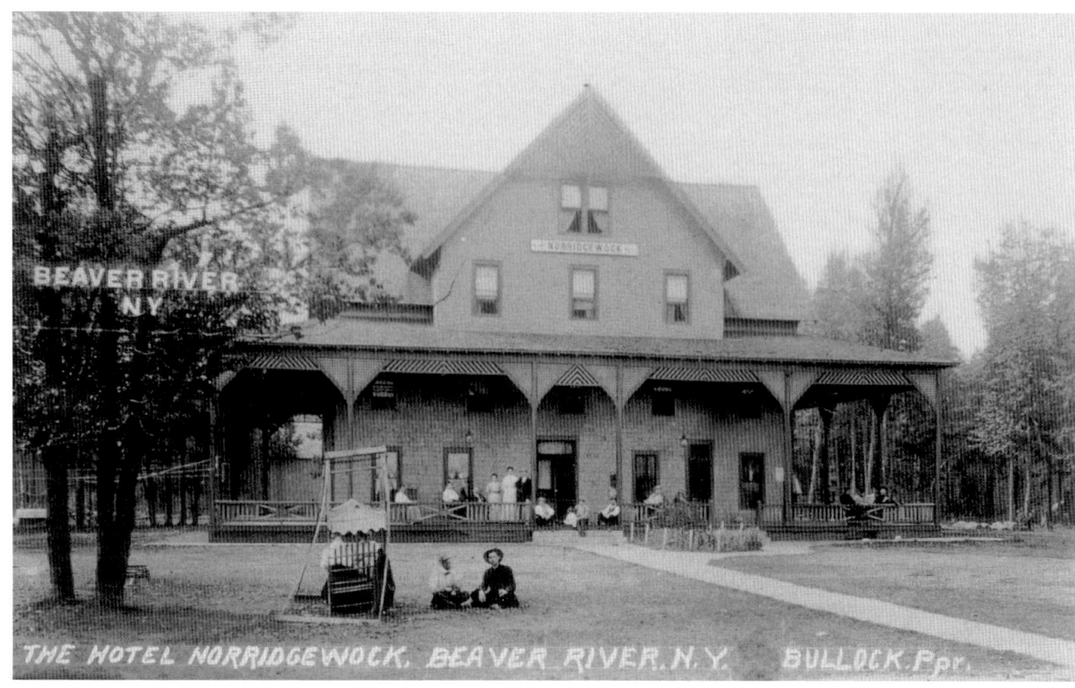


6.18. The Hotel Norridgewock, Beaver River, N.Y., ca. 1908. Davis Coll.

frontier character. The core of Beaver River was six-tenths of one square mile of private land surrounded by state forest preserve.

### *Norridgewock Hotel*

The Norridgewock Hotel, a large Victorian building close to the station, was the center of the enclave (Thompson 2000) (illus. 6.18). Bert Bullock owned it when Beach visited in 1909, but Henry's brother Lou was the manager. This fact probably accounts for Henry's frequent visits and his large number of photos of the area.[13] The wraparound veranda was a feature that Henry was fond of photographing (illus. 6.19).[14]

13. Note the typed caption on the left. It is uncommon in Beach's work, but there are a few Beaver River views by Beach with that style of lettering.

14. The first Norridgewock burned in 1914. A series of replacements followed. Train service was dropped in the early 1960s, leaving the area to revert to its previous isolated state, inaccessible by road.

### *Elliot's Camp*

There were also a few modest hotels in Beaver River. One infamous place was Elliot's Camp, an establishment run by "Wild Jess." Elliot was an attractive, flamboyant woman who wore masculine garb and packed a pistol. Undoubtedly, the tales of her free-spirited sexual behavior are exaggerated, if not completely fabricated (Donnelly n.d.). There are certainly no hints of her eccentricities in Henry's photographs of Elliot's Camp (illus. 6.20). The assembled look ordinary and subdued. If Jesse is in the picture, she is difficult to spot from her description.

When she was in her seventies, did Jesse really freeze to death? Did her dogs eat her iced dead body (Donnelly n.d.)? Is this story just a part of Adirondack lore? When we look at Henry's photograph of Elliot's Camp, is there something there that we do not see?[15]

15. See illustration 8.15 in the chapter on hunting and fishing for a picture of Conkey's camp at Beaver River.

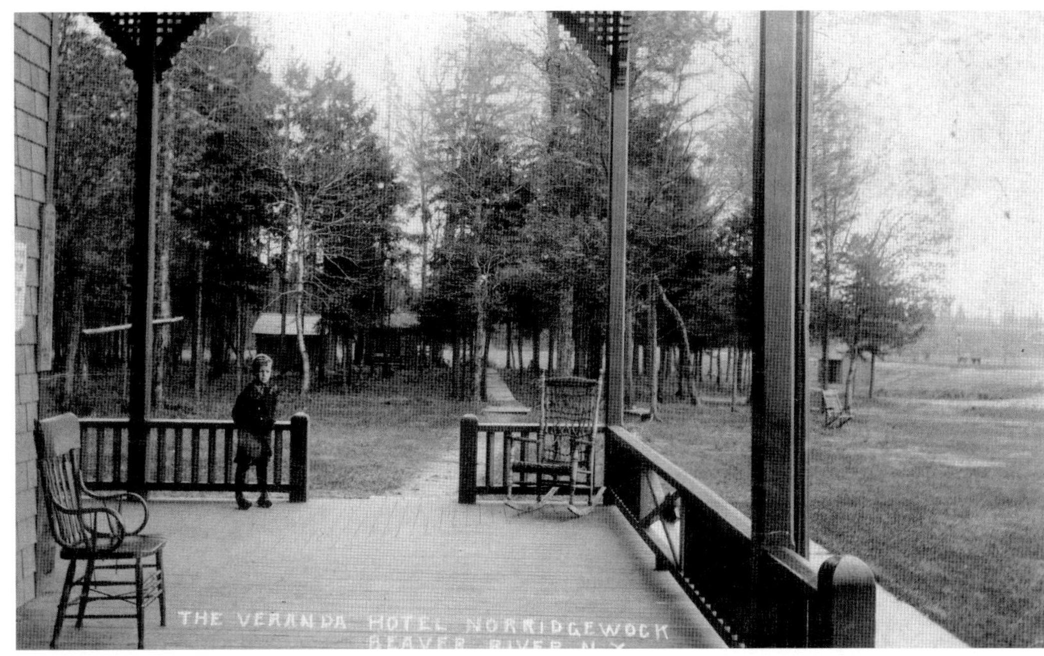


6.19. The veranda at the Norridgewock Hotel, Beaver River, N.Y., ca. 1908. Author's Coll.

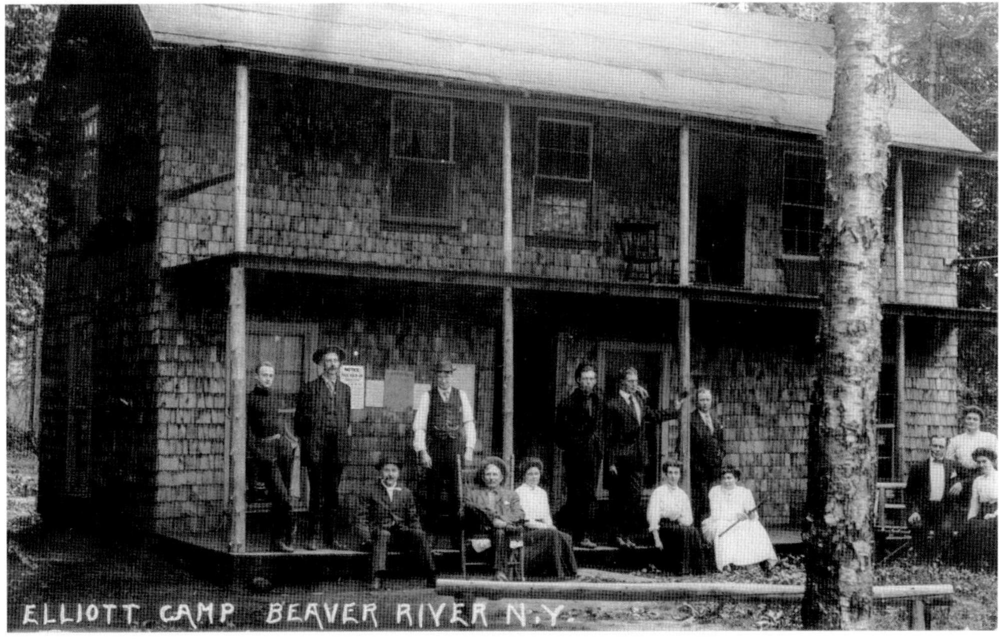


6.20. Elliot's Camp, Beaver River, N.Y., ca. 1908. Myers Coll.

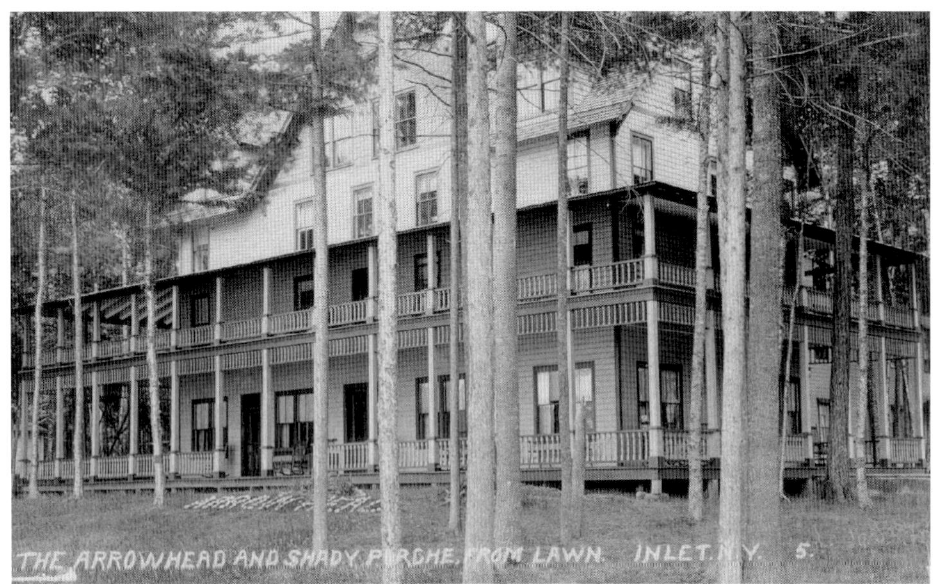


6.21. "The Arrowhead and Shady Porch," Inlet, N.Y., ca. 1915. Davis Coll.

## Fulton Chain

By the time Beach got around to being a serious postcard photographer, the hotels and resorts around the Fulton Chain were plentiful and well established. The Fulton Chain consists of eight lakes (First Lake to Eighth Lake) extending approximately twenty miles northeast from Old Forge. The first four lakes provided a waterway to transport building materials, settlers, and tourists into the area and were the main sites for the early hotels and camps on the chain. Although many of the resorts were family built, owned, and managed, they were often larger and had a higher landlord turnover than the ones at Big Moose. Nonetheless, early hotel and resort landholders had much in common with the Big Moose pioneers, and they had direct connections to them.

For example, Fred Hess was a good friend of Jim Higby, Bill Dart, and Henry Covey. Another Adirondack woodsman with roots in the Lowville area, Hess had the reputation of being a superior carpenter and builder. He built large, plain, symmetrical hotels around Fourth Lake that were important to the growth of the area's tourist industry. Hess even tried to be a hotel manager.

Fred Hess was large, strong, and kind. His talent as a builder far exceeded his aptitude as a resort manager. His first resort project was the rustic Cedar Island Camp that he built in the 1870s. After operating it at a loss for a few years, he sold it in 1892 (Grady 1933).

In 1895 he tried again and built the Hess Inn, later renamed the Arrowhead, on Fourth Lake.[16] He planned to be its proprietor. Beach's photographs of the main building nestled in the trees by the lake point to Fred's construction skills as well as his knack for locating buildings in natural settings (illus. 6.21, 6.22; see also illustration 5.8).

Like most early Adirondack builders, Hess was not trained as an engineer or architect, but that fact did not keep him from building sturdy structures that were simple and handsome, inside and out (illus. 6.23; see also illustration 5.7).

16. This one was the original Arrowhead that burned to the ground in the 1920s. An important institution in its own right, the Arrowhead deserves a special footnote for being the hotel that Chester Gillette stayed in after he murdered Grace Brown. The tragedy was the inspiration for Theodore Dreiser's fictional account *An American Tragedy* (1925). The Higbys were also players in the murder case. Roy, Jim Higby's son, found Grace Brown's body floating in Big Moose Lake (Brandon 1986).

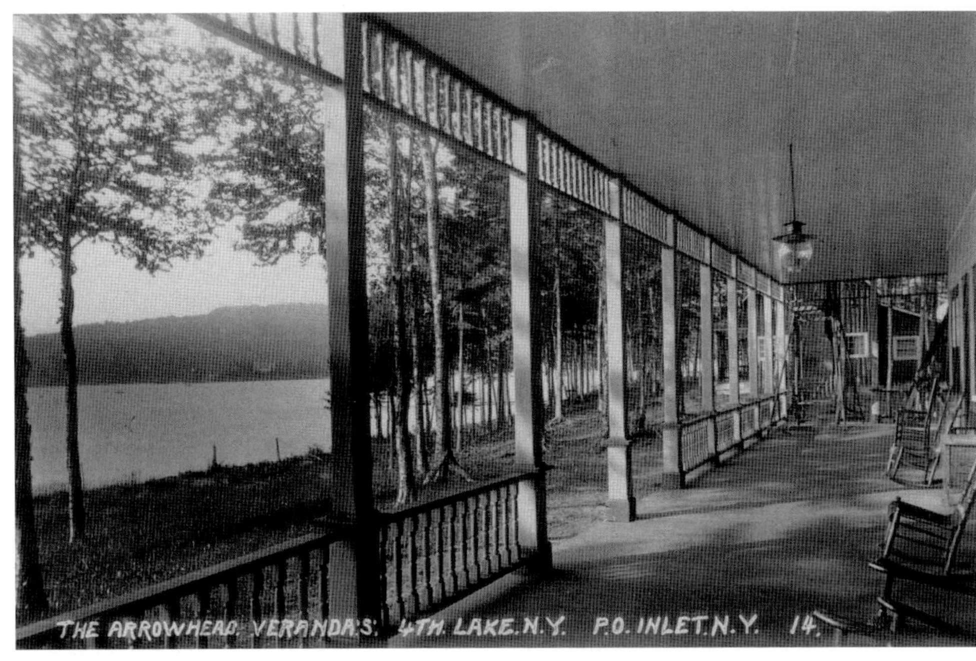


6.22. The Arrowhead veranda, Fourth Lake, Inlet, N.Y., ca. 1912. Davis Coll.

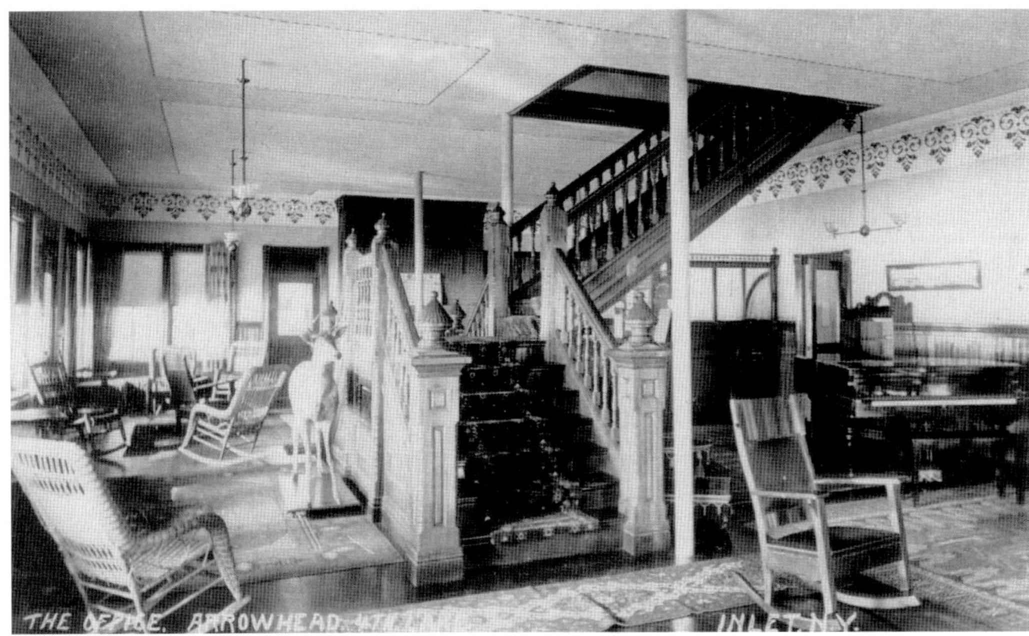


6.23. The office at Arrowhead, Fourth Lake, Inlet, N.Y., ca. 1912. Notice what is likely a Beach panoramic on the wall to the right. D. Jones Coll.

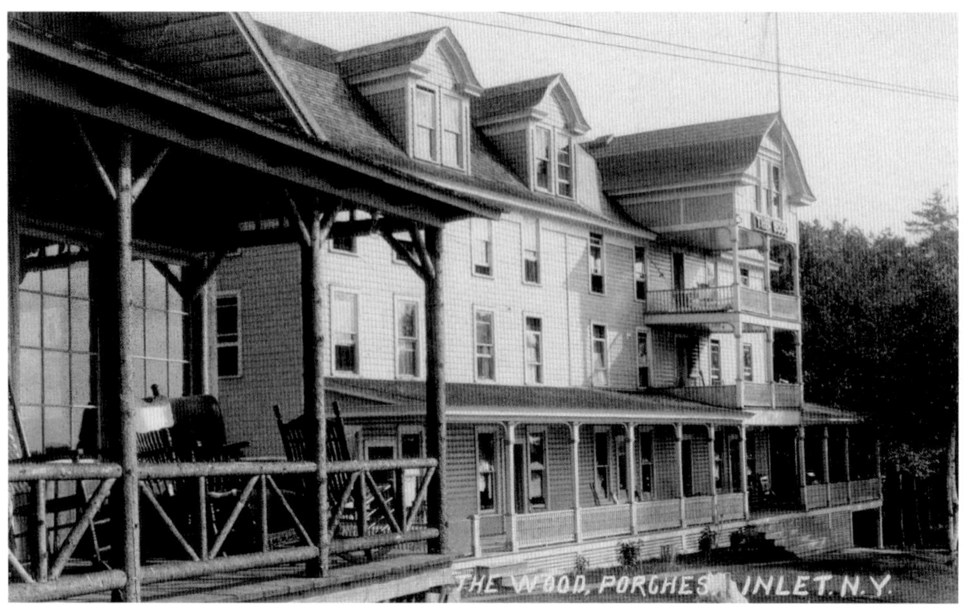


6.24. The Wood, porches, Inlet, N.Y., ca. 1915. Gates Coll.

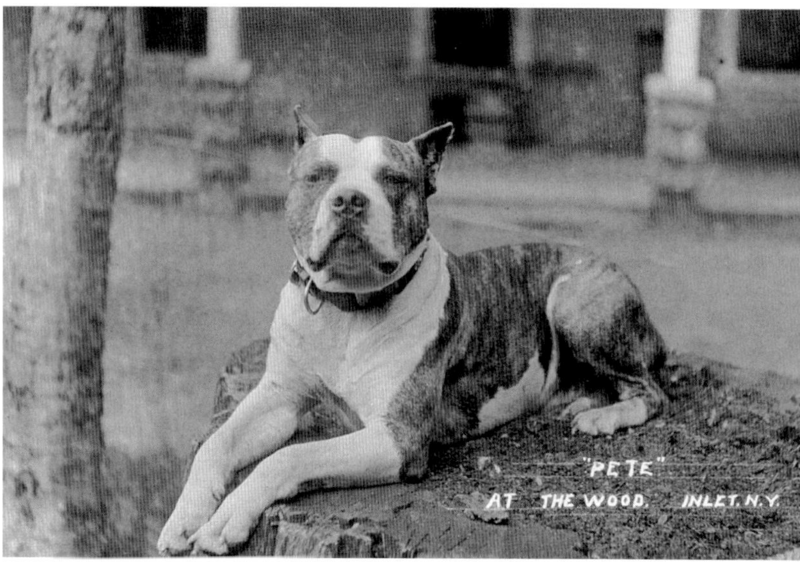


6.25. "Pete" at the Wood, Inlet, N.Y., ca. 1915. Author's Coll.

Unfortunately, Hess failed at management again and was forced to sell. His failure did not stop him from constructing yet another establishment, originally named the Hess Camp. Again, he could not operate it at a profit and was forced to sell to Philo Wood, who renamed it the Wood. Beach photographed that Fulton Chain establishment often.[17] Illustration 6.24 is interesting because of the juxtaposition of the rustic with the more formal porches.

Many of the small resorts and hotels had mascots. Although sometimes cats, horses, and even oxen fitted the category, proprietors' dogs were the favored attractions. Canines were a feature so often taken for granted that most postcard photographers overlooked them. Beach's understanding of the pet's place in resort life, plus his love of dogs, led to his frequent dog portraits. In illustration 6.25 we see Pete, from the Wood, sitting in front of his hotel. Henry took formally posed pictures of other canine mascots, including Dart's Sancho and the mutt that hung around the Lake View Lodge on Big Moose.[18]

There are many more resorts and medium-size hotels on the Fulton Chain and other parts of the central Adirondacks that Henry photographed. I have only presented his work and sketched the context. Before we move on, let me share a few more of his views.

Beach produced some splendid views of the Seventh Lake House, including a panoramic. From the pictures of the main structure to the guests gathered on the porch, Beach provides a sense of what it might have been like to be there on a midsummer's afternoon (illus. 6.26, 6.27). Neither did Henry forget the cottages with the decorative log exteriors dispersed on the Seventh Lake House grounds and other such resorts (illus. 6.28).

17. The Wood was a medium-size hotel that accommodated one hundred guests and commanded a beautiful view of Fourth Lake and the surrounding mountains.

18. Henry also took a picture of Pete swimming in the lake that he sold as a postcard.

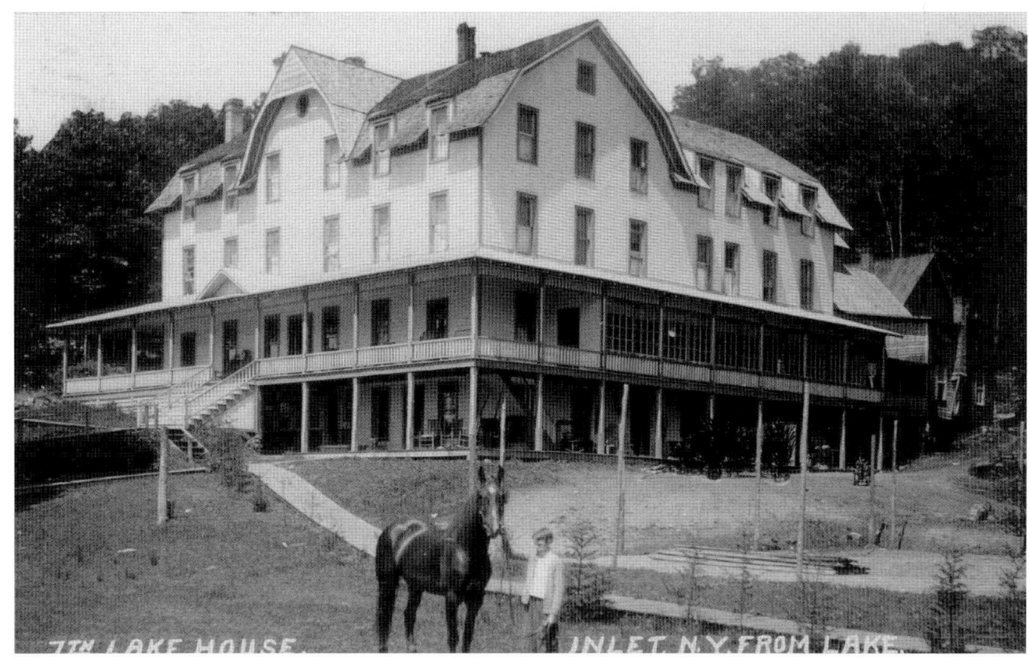


6.26. Seventh Lake House from Lake, Inlet, N.Y., ca. 1913. Gates Coll.

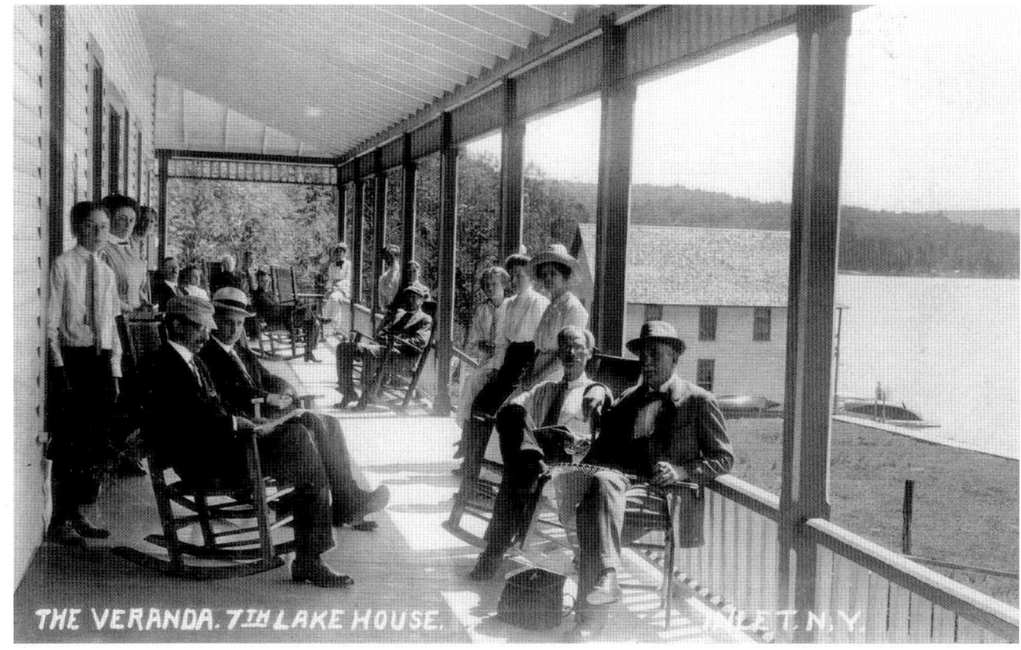


6.27. The veranda at the Seventh Lake House, Inlet, N.Y., ca. 1910. Davis Coll.

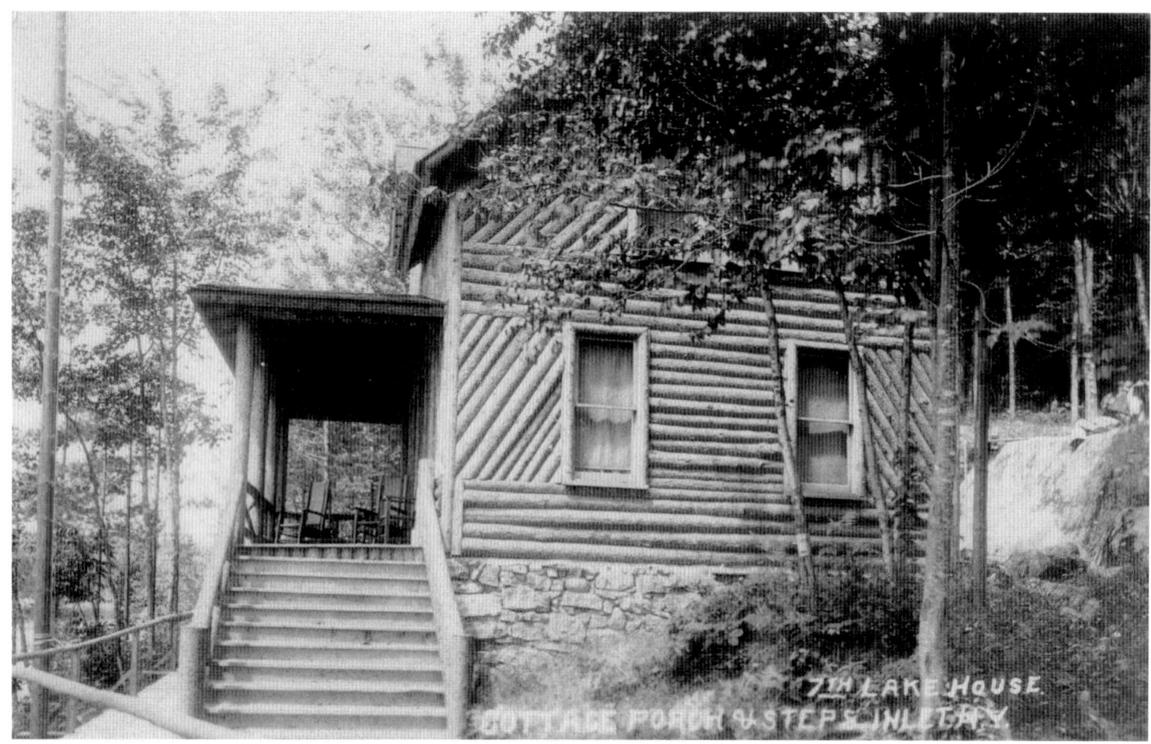


6.28. Cottage porch and steps at the Seventh Lake House, Inlet, N.Y., ca. 1912. Davis Coll.

Hotels and cottages at Eagle Bay on Fourth Lake were constructed on steep slopes. Henry was fond of photographing them from a boat, creating pictures with human-made structures in layers and people busy along the shore (illus. 6.29). His pictures are interesting because of his skill but also because there were so many visually exciting locations to photograph.

Henry also exaggerated the steepness of the slopes of some resorts by photographing at severe angles. In illustration 6.30, a small rustic structure dominates the picture. It is of a hand pump for water. Such architectural detail was characteristic of many of the small hotels, and Henry included them in his series.

On the grounds of most resorts was at least one "open camp," or lean-to. These primitively constructed, rustic-style lodges, which were open at one end, were, at one time, necessary shelters (Gilborn 2000). In the world of the small resort, they served a symbolic function, reminding and providing tourists with a vicarious experience of the old days. For every resort Beach photographed, there is at least one open-camp view. As shown in illustration 6.31, open camps became less primitive and more "Adirondack style" as they migrated into the resort milieu.

Henry's hotel interior views are some of my favorites. One of the reasons "A Glimpse of the Office from the Hall" is so appealing to me is the sense of depth Beach achieves (see illustration 2.4). The effect of looking in the mirror (under the moose) and seeing the reflection of the stairs increases the sense of distance. The rectangular passageway contributes to the depth by dividing the scene into two main sections: the hall and the office. The proprietor at the desk and the window behind him further elongate the interior.

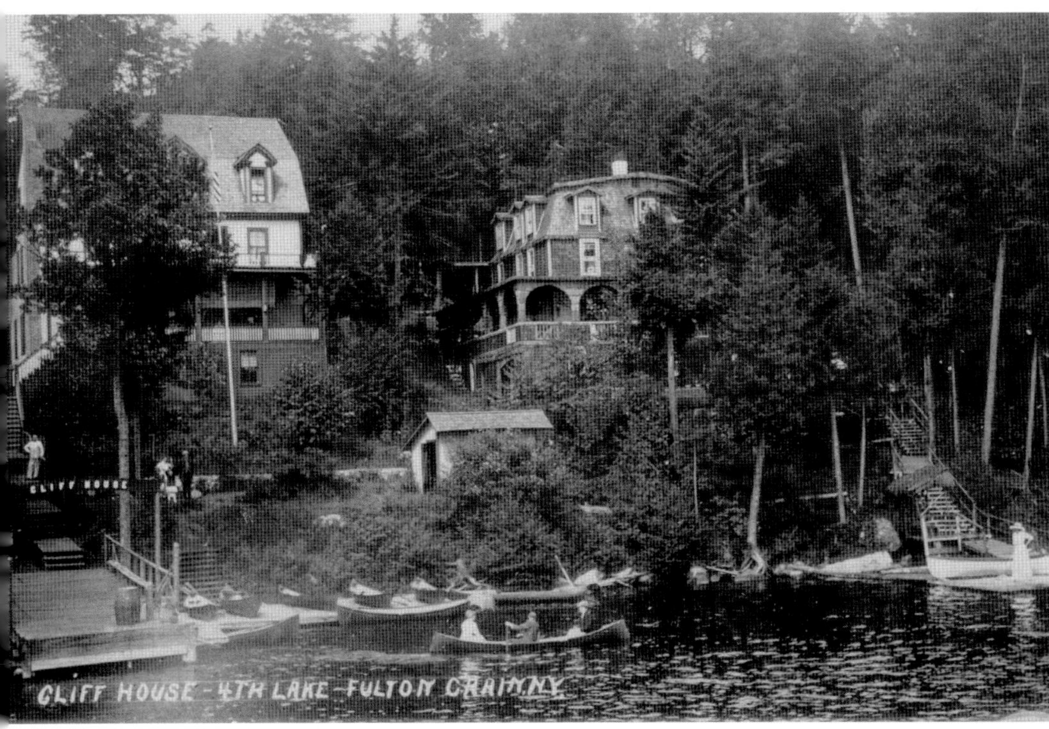


6.29. Cliff House, Fourth Lake, Fulton Chain, N.Y., ca. 1914. B. J. Slusarczyk Coll.

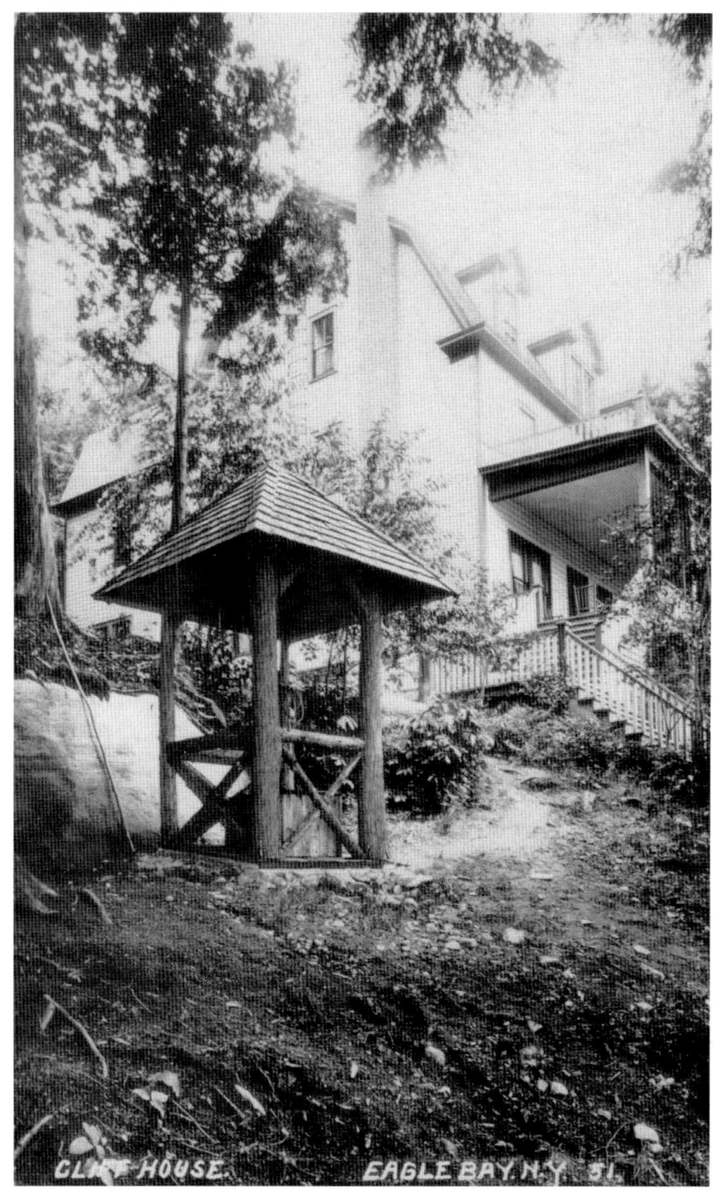


6.30. Cliff House, Eagle Bay, N.Y., ca. 1914. D. Jones Coll.

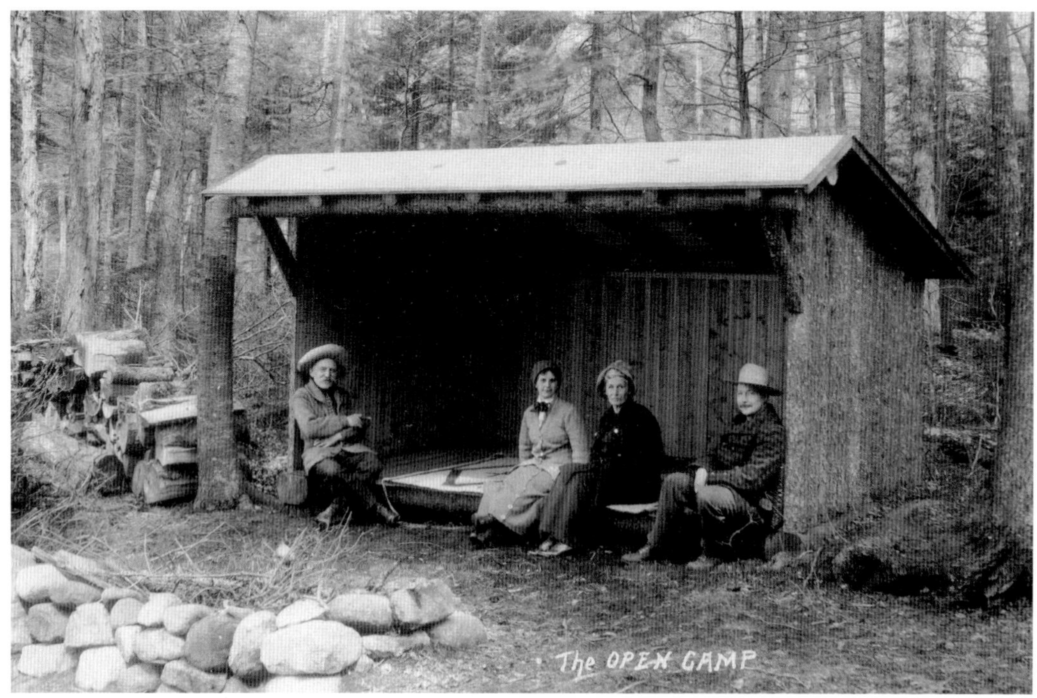


6.31. An open camp, ca. 1915. The location of this rare photograph is not known, but it looks like one at Camp Crag. Courtesy of the Adirondack Museum.

As with illustration 2.4, the picture with the moose head mounted on the wall taken at the Rocky Point Inn on the Fulton Chain,[19] many of Henry's interior pictures are adorned with stuffed animals and other remnants of things that were once wild. Looking into the dining room at the same Rocky Point Inn, the mounted heads seem quite appropriate, taken for granted, a natural part of an Adirondack indoor scene (illus. 6.32). But in a series he did of the interior of Edwin and Annie McAlpin's private lodge at Brandreth Lake, Camp Comfort (renamed Trophy Lodge in 1943), the exhibition is overwhelming (illus. 6.33).[20] General Edwin McAlpin, who shot most of the trophies on display, married into the Brandreth family (Gilborn 2000, 125; McMartin 1994, 212). His wealth allowed him to hunt all over North America and abroad. His conspicuous display of hunting trophies was not the style of Adirondackers; it was the way of outsiders. Interestingly, pictures from this series are some of the most often published Beach photographs (Gilborn 2000, 125; O'Leary 1998, 158; Schneider 1997, 267; Terrie 1997, 124).

19. Until their recent reappearance, the moose vanished from the North Country by the end of the Civil War (Schneider 1997). Nevertheless, the moose emerged as an early emblem of the Adirondacks. It is doubtful that the moose head hanging on the wall in illustration 2.4 is a leftover from the pre–Civil War days. It is more likely a Canadian import.

20. There are four different views in the series. Each contains the type of display of stuffed animals shown in illustration 6.33.

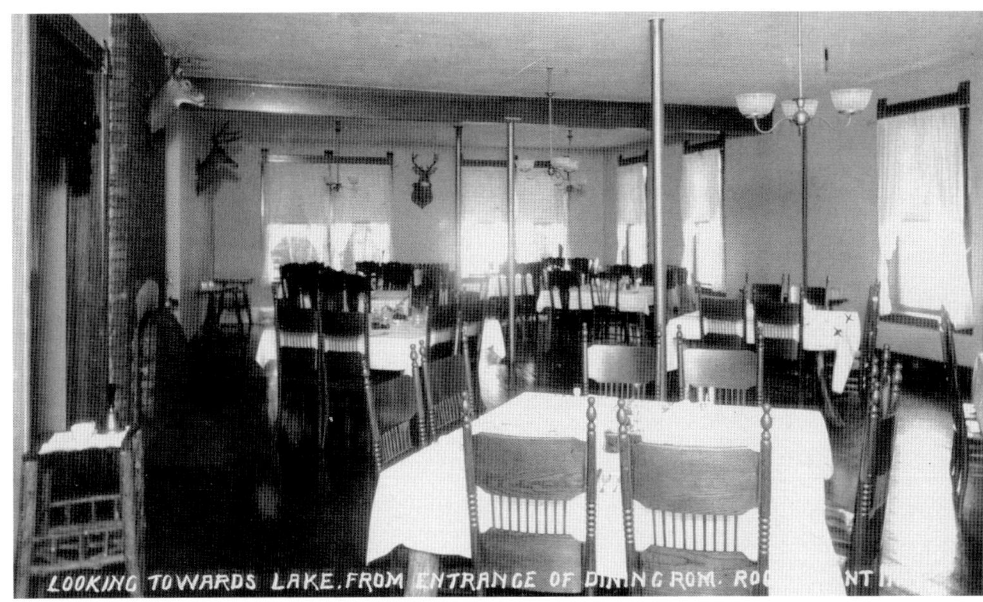


6.32. Looking toward lake from entrance to dining room at the Rocky Point Inn, Inlet, N.Y., ca. 1912. D. Jones Coll.

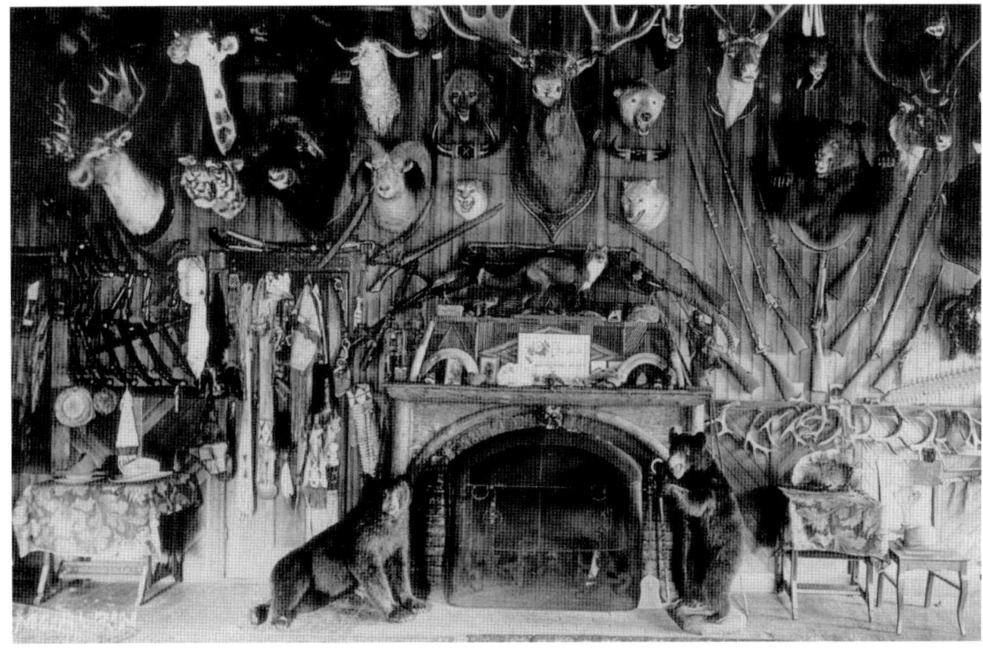

6.33. Interior of McAlpin's lodge, Brandreth Lake, N.Y., ca. 1917. Davis Coll.

Not all hotels were sited in the forests next to lakes. Beach reminds us of this fact with his picture of the Adirondack Hotel in the town of Old Forge (illus. 6.34). This gem was larger than it appears in the picture. Miss Ella Hughes, the manager and owner, probably sitting on the porch in the picture, boasted accommodations for seventy.

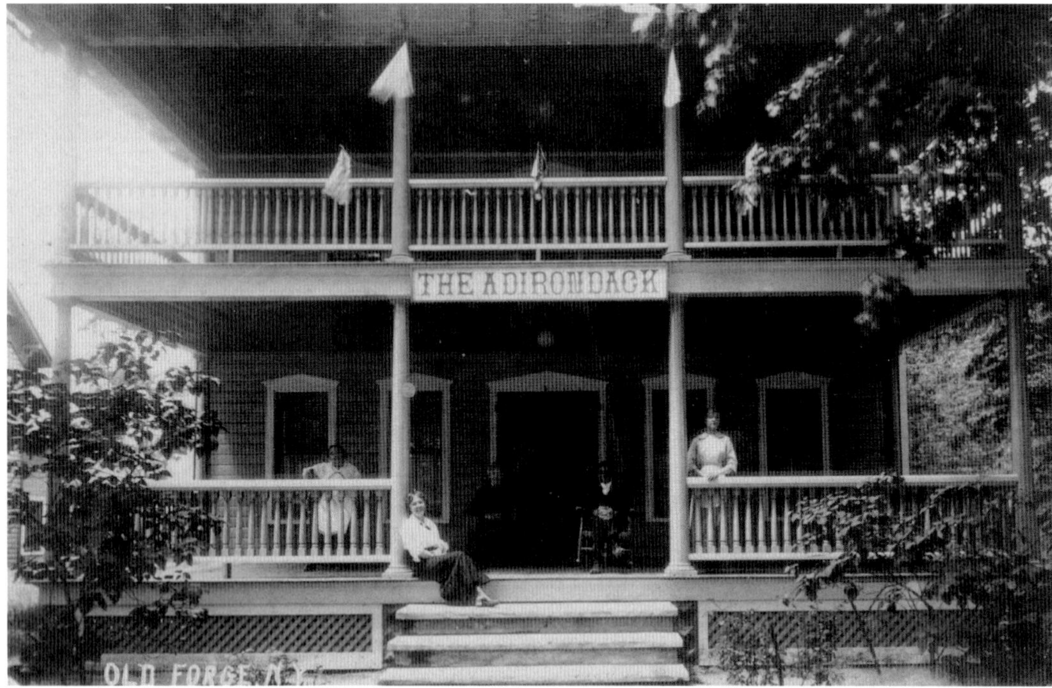


6.34. The Adirondack, Old Forge, N.Y., ca. 1916. D. Jones Coll.

7

# Vacation Retreats
## Grand Hotels and Clubs

The heyday of the grand hotel was the last quarter of the nineteenth century, but as the North Country moved into the twentieth century, some of them remained. They served the well-to-do, people whose tastes were more elegant than home style. Their patrons wanted to look out upon the wilderness from the comfort of a veranda that was part of a proper hotel or to take in the scenic views from the putting green or the tennis court.

The viability of grand hotels diminished as Americans changed their vacation tastes and took to the road in automobiles. Such travelers sought short-term accommodations. The trend toward private camp ownership and clubs did not bode well for the big hotel, either. Its large size and tremendous overhead made survival impossible when reservations started to slip. Maintenance was high and the season short. The last word in grand hotels, the Prospect House at Blue Mountain Lake, was razed and sold for scrap in 1915, though it had closed more than ten years earlier. Beach photographed a few of the grand hotels in their declining elegance.

### The Wawbeek

Seneca Ray Stoddard's Adirondack guidebook for 1889 announced the opening of a new hotel on the shores of Upper Saranac Lake, the Wawbeek (Duquette 1991). The stately structure was built in the shape of a Greek cross. When Beach photographed it in 1912, the main building plus cottages accommodated more than three hundred guests (illus. 7.1).

Visitors arrived by the hotel's steamer from the village of Saranac Lake, where they had arrived by fancy sleeper trains from New York City and Boston. Among the luxuries were a nine-hole golf course, croquet lawns, tennis courts, a children's playroom, and billiard rooms. The wide-ranging grounds were well tended, with prim gardens and formal boardwalks. In some of his images, Beach seemed more intent on capturing the geometric pattern than the location itself (illus. 7.2).

The dominant features of the main building were the surrounding tiers of wide verandas that offered breathtaking views of Upper Saranac Lake (illus. 7.3). The panoramic photograph of Upper Saranac Lake discussed in chapter 5, panoramic 3, was taken near the main house, so it shows the view that guests enjoyed. The porch was Beach's photographic obsession and his most-photographed aspect of this particular location.

The Wawbeek advertised "first-class cuisine" and formal dining rather than food that was plentiful and served family style (illus. 7.4). It, like other establishments of its class, had an experienced professional overseer schooled in the art of hotel management who supervised an efficient and genteel trained staff. No mom-and-pop service there.

The interiors of the grand hotels were more formal than the ones in the smaller places (illus. 7.5). The woodwork was fine and often more elaborate. Beach's pictures capture all of the detail. But in places like the Wawbeek, there was always room for the rustic look. Note the woodwork and stone fireplace in the picture Henry took of a section of the office (illus. 7.6).

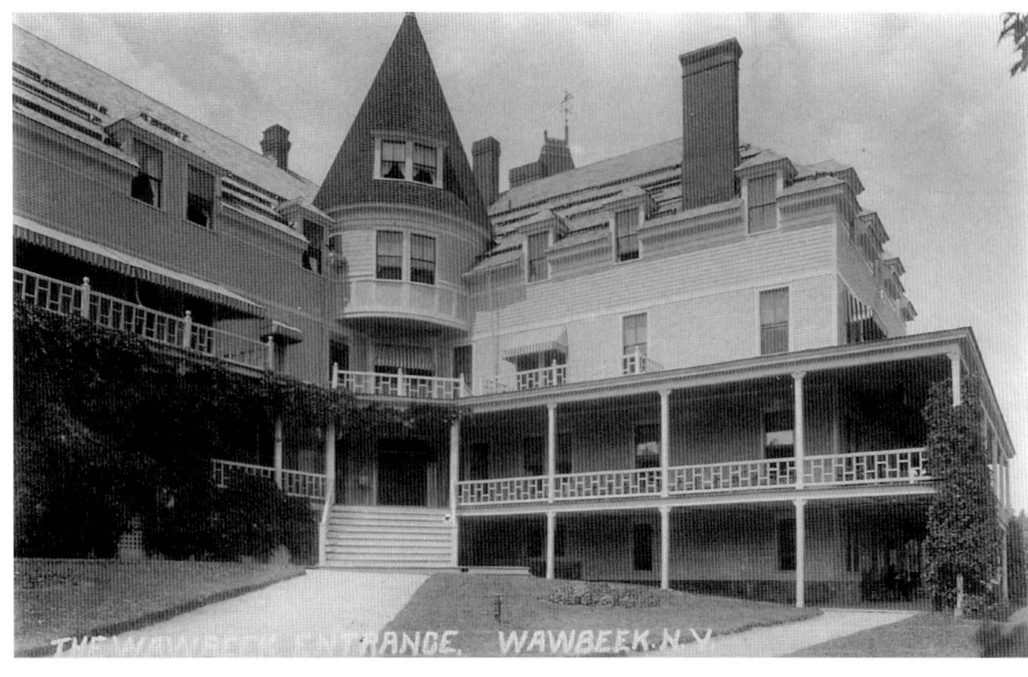


7.1. The Wawbeek entrance, Wawbeek, N.Y., ca. 1912. Author's Coll.

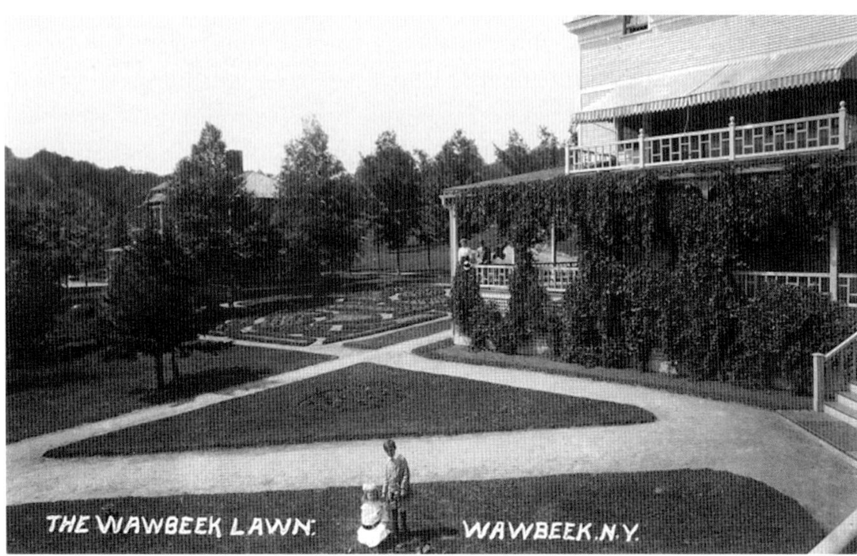


7.2. The Wawbeek lawn, Wawbeek, N.Y., ca. 1912. Author's Coll.

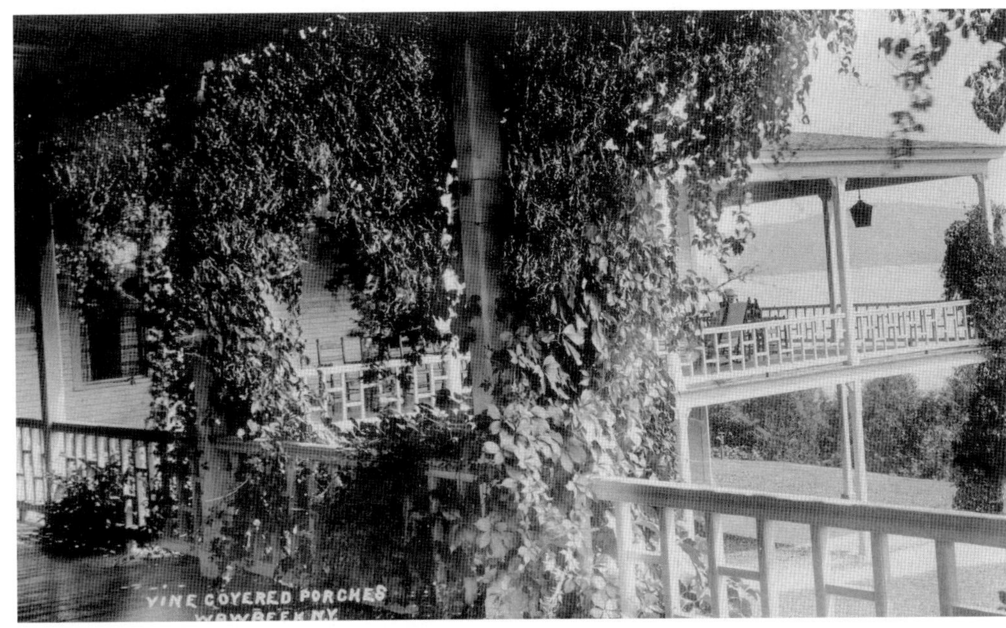


7.3. Vine-covered porches, Wawbeek, N.Y., ca. 1912. Author's Coll.

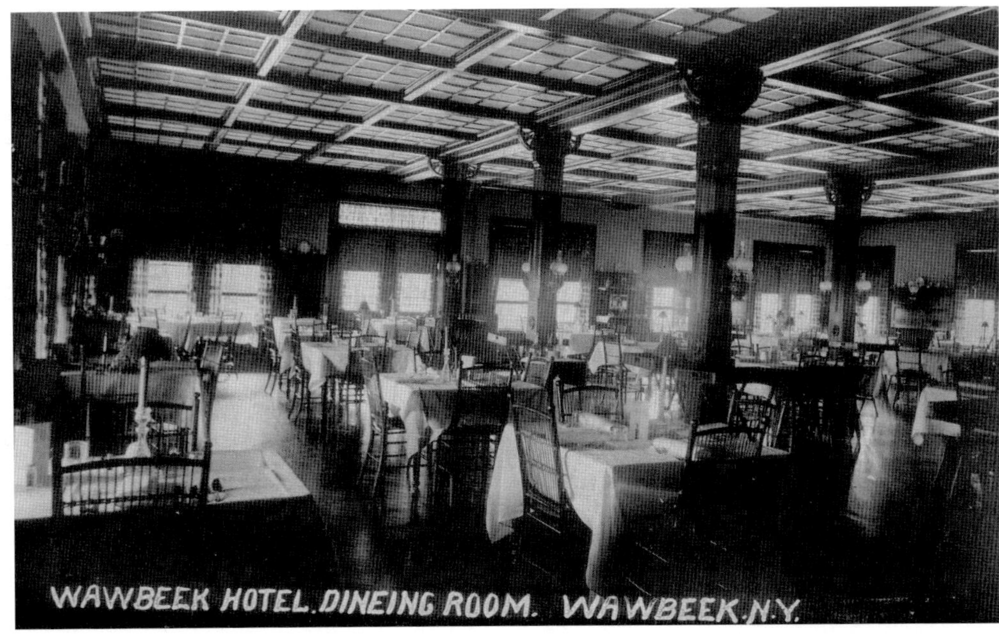


7.4. Wawbeek Hotel dining room, Wawbeek, N.Y., ca. 1912. Author's Coll.

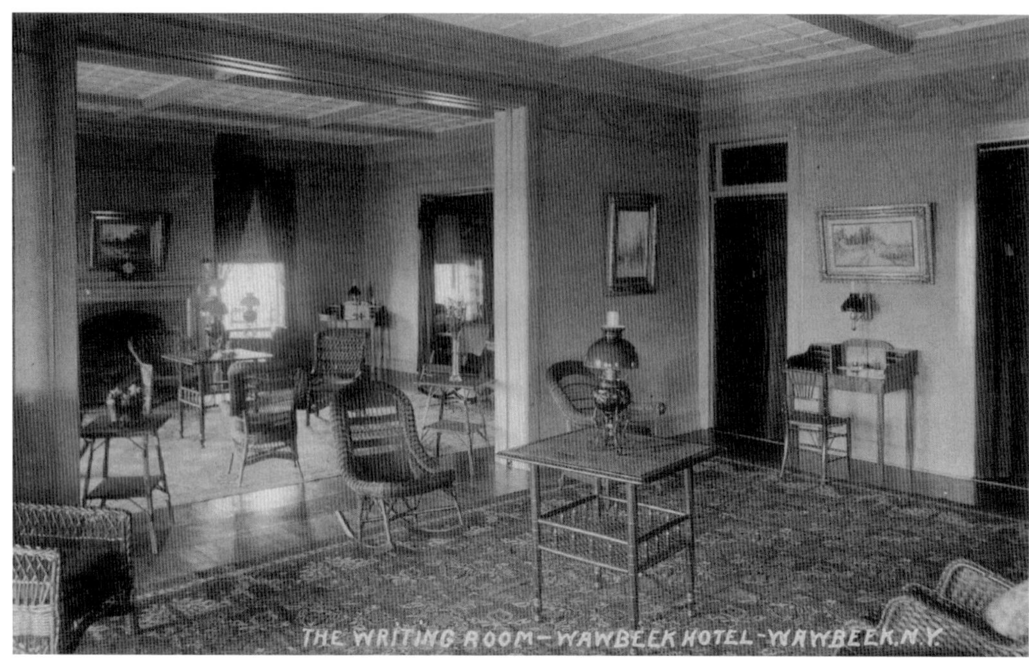


7.5. Writing room at the Wawbeek Hotel, Wawbeek, N.Y., ca. 1912. Author's Coll.

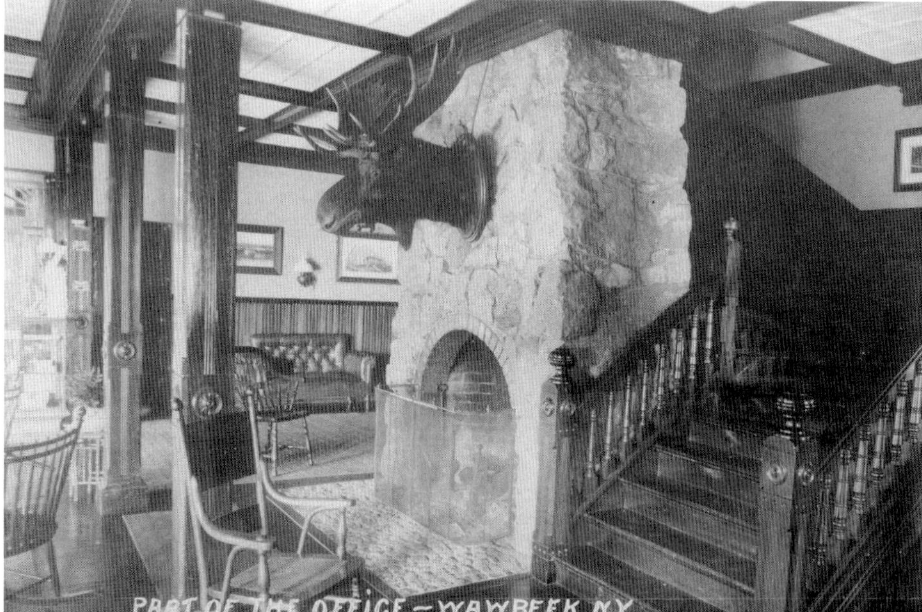


7.6. Part of the office at the Wawbeek Hotel, Wawbeek, N.Y., ca. 1912. Author's Coll.

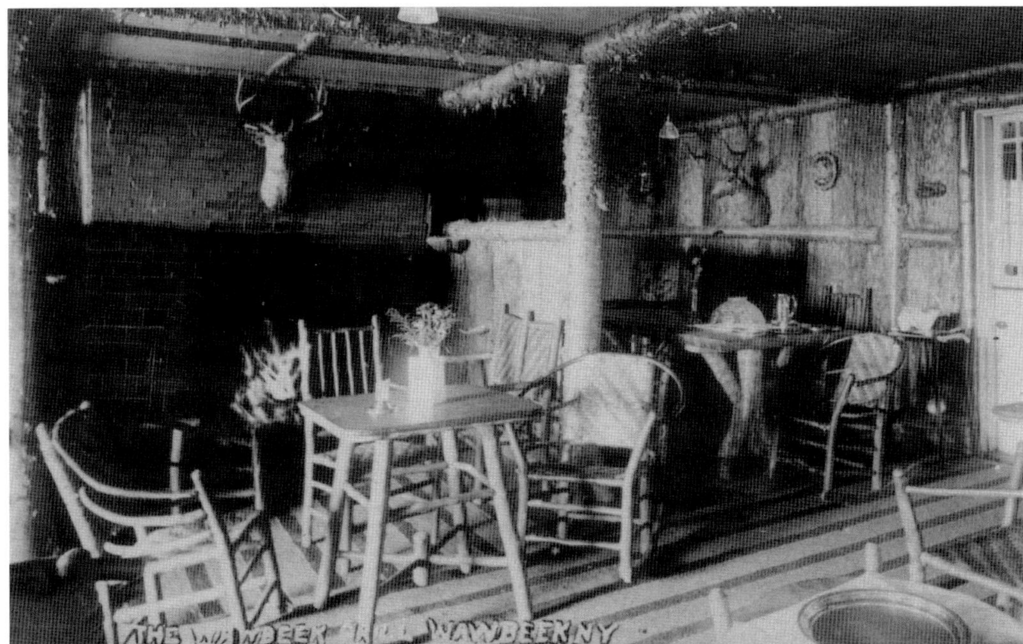


7.7. The Wawbeek Grill, Wawbeek, N.Y., ca. 1912. Author's Coll.

In the out-of-the-way Grill Room, a favorite spot for men, the rustic aspect was even more pronounced (illus. 7.7). The chairs were old hickory and the walls and beams covered with bark. Great detail, preserved for us by Henry Beach.

Not long after Beach visited the Wawbeek it closed. In 1914 the buildings were torn down for salvage.

## The Grand View Hotel

One of the great late-nineteenth-century hotels, the Grand View, was built on Lake Placid. Located at the summit of a hill sloping toward the lake it commanded a sweeping view of the lake as well as of the entire circle of the surrounding mountains, including Whiteface, Marcy, McIntyre, and Colden.

Beach produced a series of engaging postcards of the Grand View, many of which capture the beauty and character of the place. But to fully appreciate the setting as well as the power of the Cirkut camera in capturing a location, one has to study Beach's Cirkut panoramic pictures. He took three of the Grand View that we know of. Two show the hotel perched on high on the hill overlooking the lake with the mountains in the background. Panoramic 7 includes the tennis courts and driveway all labeled on the print.

The third panoramic was taken from the veranda looking out upon the mountains (panoramic 8). Here the convex distortion produces a slightly disorienting picture but one that is visually enticing. The veranda is exaggerated. The mountains and lake in the background pull the viewer out of the covered space into the sunlight, much in the same way that someone sitting on the porch might experience it. It is a study of geometry. In so many of Beach's

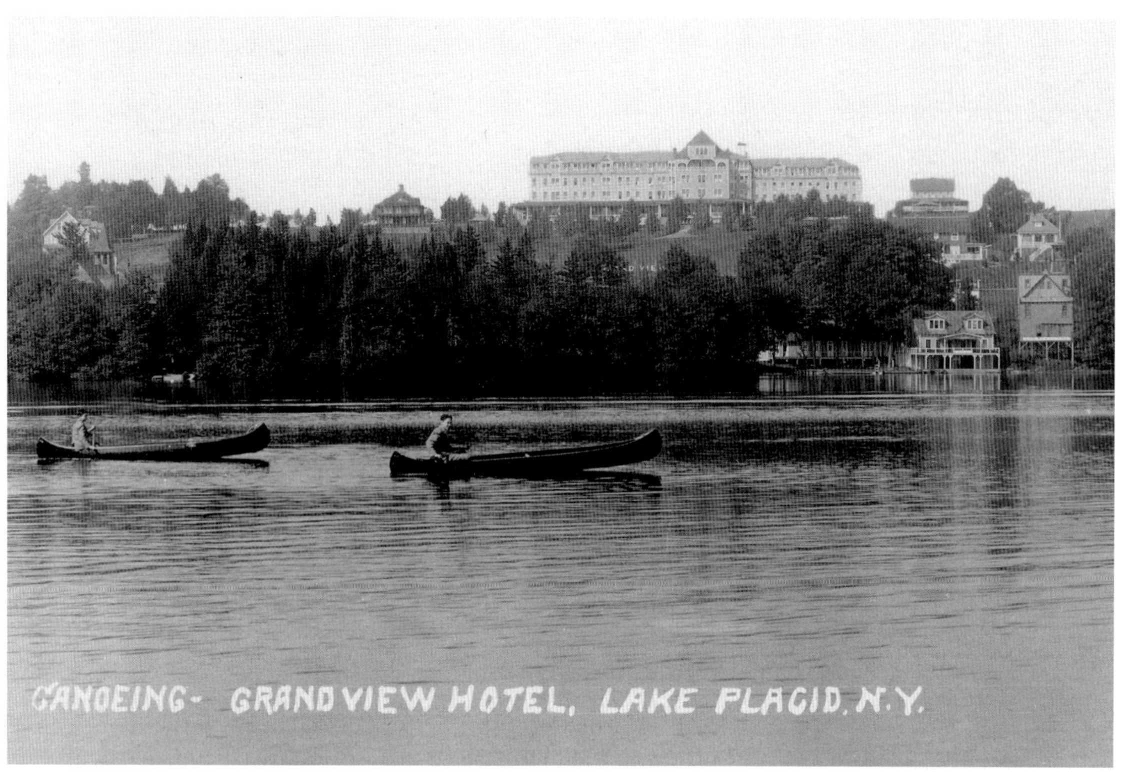


7.8. Canoeing at the Grand View Hotel, Lake Placid, N.Y., ca. 1912. Courtesy of the Adirondack Museum.

photographs the natural setting dominates, but here human structure rules. The decorative trees are incorporated into the building rather than vice versa.

An interesting contrast to the panoramic views is a postcard Beach produced of the Grand View taken from a boat on Lake Placid. Of the postcards I found of the hotel, illustration 7.8 is the only one in which people are present. The hotel, looming large on the crest of the hill, dwarfs the canoe and the paddlers.

Though not huge by standards of the day, the Grand View had accommodations for three hundred guests. It was located in a mountain wilderness setting, but guests hardly roughed it. There were fireplaces in the guest rooms and other comforts of the pampered, including dancing every evening in the ballroom. Henry captured some of the elegance with his interior views, such as the reception desk where his postcards were displayed (see the introduction and illustration 3.2). Another shows the spacious and light-filled dining room (illus. 7.9).

Apparently, fancy hotels were not Henry's mainstays. He left only a few pictures of places other than the Wawbeek and Grand View, nothing like the comprehensive survey he provided of the camps and hotels of the central Adirondacks.[1]

1. Although I have not seen any postcards of Steven's House at Lake Placid or the Saranac Inn, Beach sent panoramics of them to the Library of Congress.

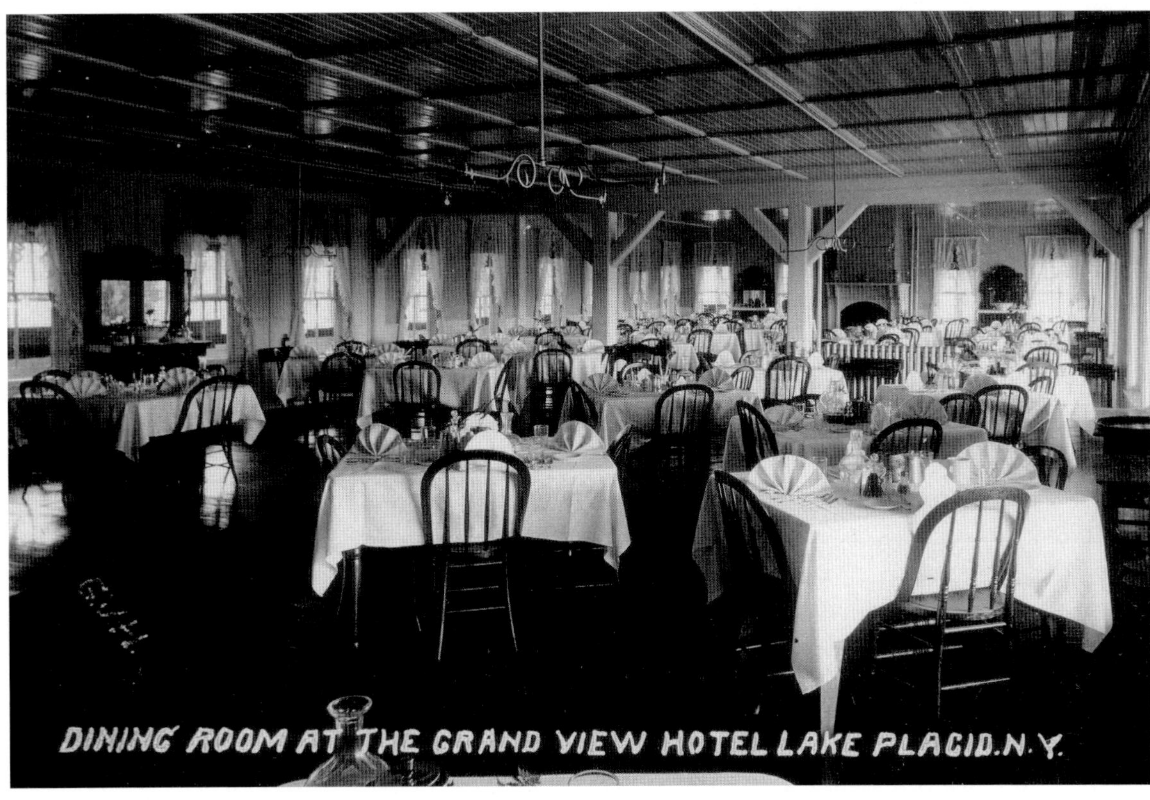


7.9. Dining room at the Grand View Hotel, Lake Placid, N.Y., ca. 1912. Courtesy of the Adirondack Museum.

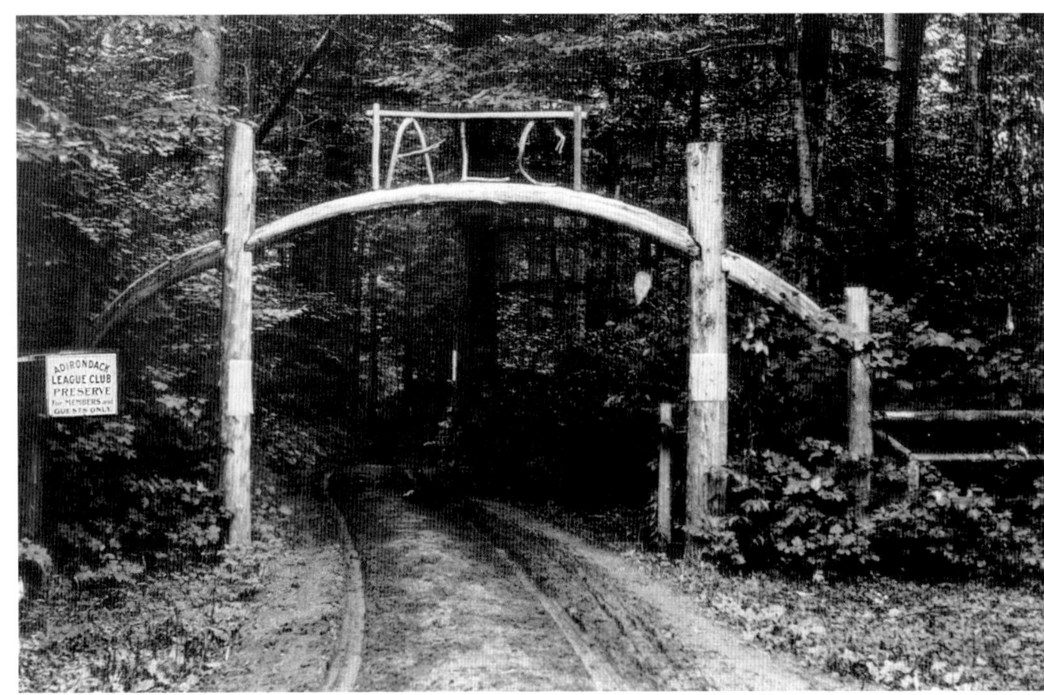


7.10. Adirondack League Club entrance, Mountain Lodge, N.Y., ca. 1914. Comstock Coll.

## Adirondack League Club

Henry was a simple man whose modest ways and provincial background did not include many relationships with well-to-do visitors such as the members of the Adirondack League Club near Old Forge. He was not a regular at such establishments, as he was at Higby's, Camp Crag, or Dart's.[2]

The Adirondack League Club was founded in 1890 and controlled close to two hundred thousand acres of nearly pristine land. The club board managed the holdings with the philosophy that members could enjoy the use of natural resources while preserving them at the same time. Many members owned camps on the property, but social activities centered around three locations on separate lakes. Each had a lodge for room, board, entertaining, socializing, and other indoor activities. The Mountain Lodge was the largest and grandest.

2. In addition to the Adirondack League Club, he took pictures at the Lake Placid Club, which was more of a country club than an estate.

In 1913, the Mountain Lodge burned to the ground. I assume that someone affiliated with the Adirondack League Club recognized Henry's photographic talent and hired him to photograph the new Mountain Lodge that was built on the original site in 1914. He photographed other buildings at the complex as well (Gilborn 2000, 249; Haynes 1990).

Club buildings were "rustic," a stylized version of the primitive vernacular style used by people such as Higby, Covey, Martin, Ainsworth, and Dart. But the club buildings did not just emerge helter-skelter, or piece by piece, as they did at the local resorts. Professional architects designed them. In the case of the new Mountain Lodge, it was Augustus D. Shepard. He used natural materials, adhered to Arts and Crafts movement notions of simplicity, and emphasized comfortable interior design.

Henry must have felt a little uncomfortable visiting the Adirondack League Club. We can almost feel it in his picture of the rustic-design gate that guarded the main entrance to the premises from outside intruders (illus. 7.10). The sign

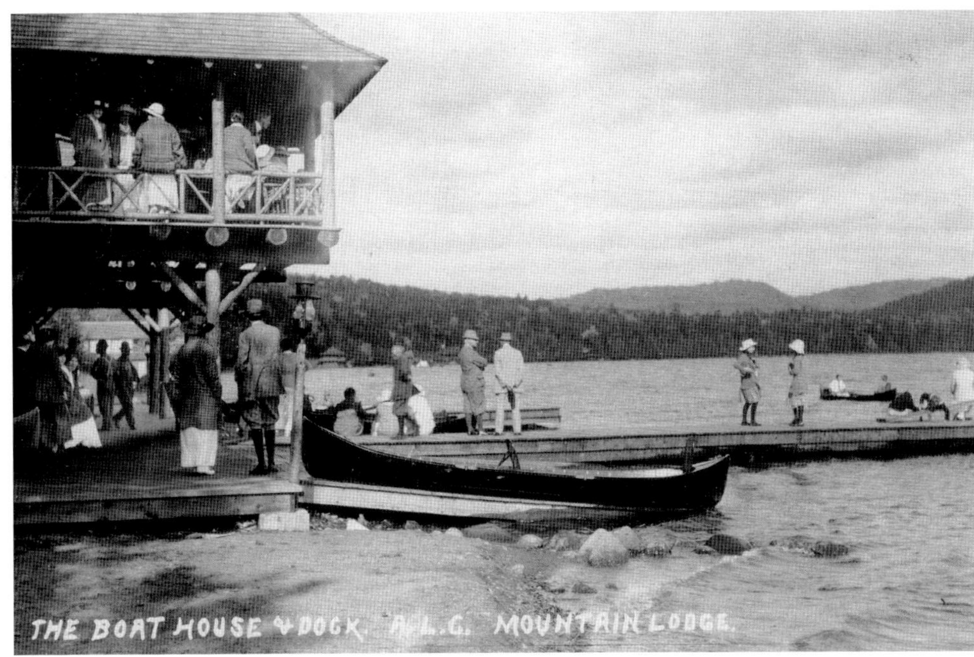


7.11. The boathouse and dock, Adirondack League Club, Mountain Lodge, N.Y., ca. 1914. Courtesy of the Adirondack Museum.

on the left reads, "Adirondack League Club Preserve, for Members and Guests Only."

Henry produced approximately thirty postcard views of the club and three panoramic photographs. He took some of the boathouse at Mountain Lodge, a structure that Shepard had designed in 1912 and one that had survived the fire (illus. 7.11). One of the days Henry photographed at the club there was a regatta, which accounts for the crowd in some of the views. Note the faint clouds in illustration 7.11. Uncharacteristic of most of Henry's scenic postcard views, there is some contrast in the sky. The clouds are Beach clouds, the brushed-in variety found in his panoramics.

Henry also took tranquil boathouse views, including one on the upper-level deck of the veranda, the level that was so crowded in illustration 7.11 (illus. 7.12). He stepped down to the next level and went inside to the boathouse storage area to take the picture of canoes and guide boats in racks (illus. 7.13).

The formal opening of the new Mountain Lodge was July 18, 1914. Although it was close to completion by that date, many details and furnishings had yet to be tended to. Beach took the picture of the entrance and office in its prepolished state (illus. 7.14). When Shepard designed the building, he attempted to emulate the massiveness of the great western national park lodges he had studied, and probably overdid the size of the ceiling joists, a feature that is exaggerated by the angle of illustration 7.14 and the short height of the ceiling.

If we overlook the joists in the office area, the building achieved the architect's dream in many ways, especially in the interior. It was spacious and cozy, rustic and elegant, open yet had much private space. The new Mountain Lodge had a family-friendly atmosphere with a children's room (illus. 7.15). Look carefully at the flames in the cozy fireplace—more tampering by Beach.

The dining room was a grand achievement (illus. 7.16). The combination of mission-style furniture by Stickley, the massive peeled log beams, and the well-crafted natural stone fireplace created an aura of luxurious-primitive. Unfortunately, in the 1960s, when the dining room wing was in need of extensive repair, and funds were low, it was partially demolished (Haynes 1990, 242).

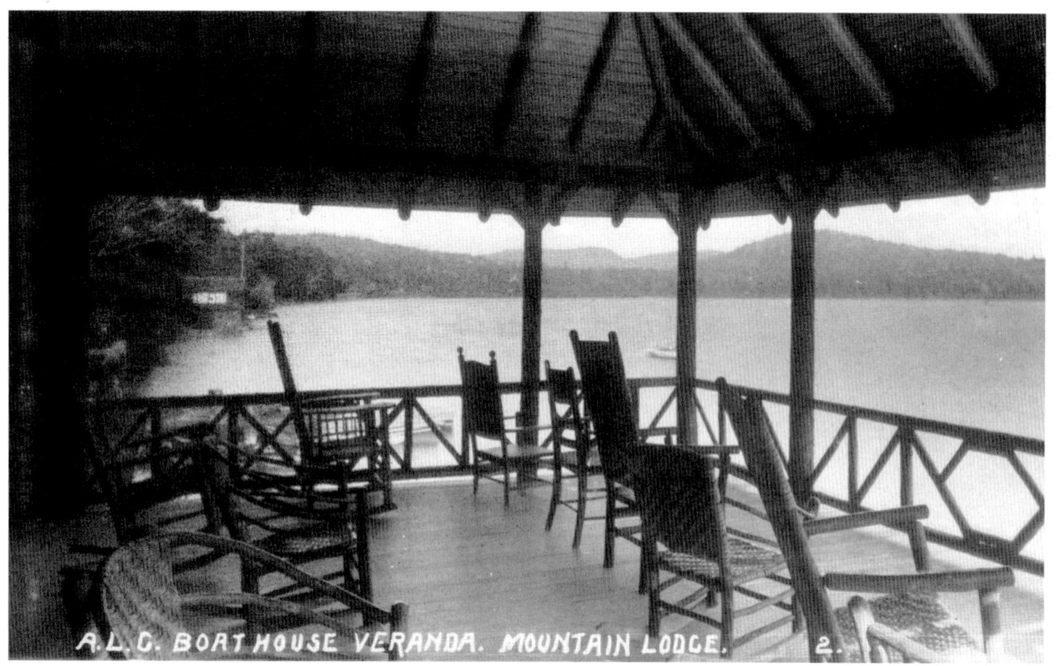


7.12. Adirondack League Club boathouse veranda, Mountain Lodge, N.Y., ca. 1914. ALC Coll.

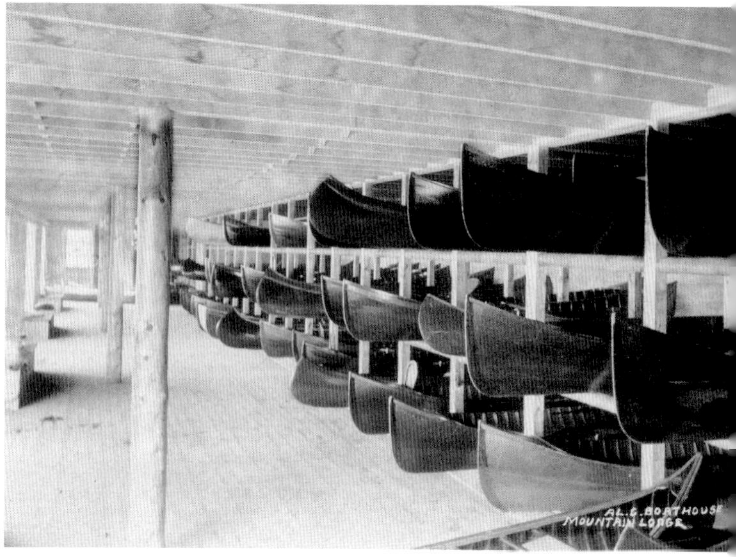

7.13. Adirondack League Club boathouse (interior), Mountain Lodge, N.Y., ca. 1914. Courtesy of the Adirondack Museum.

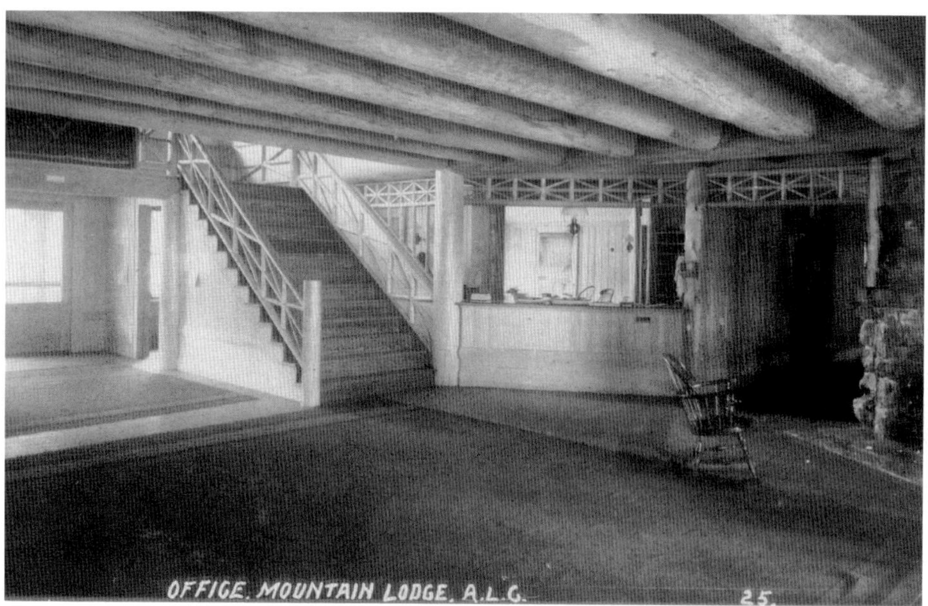


7.14. Adirondack League Club office, Mountain Lodge, N.Y., ca. 1914. ALC Coll.

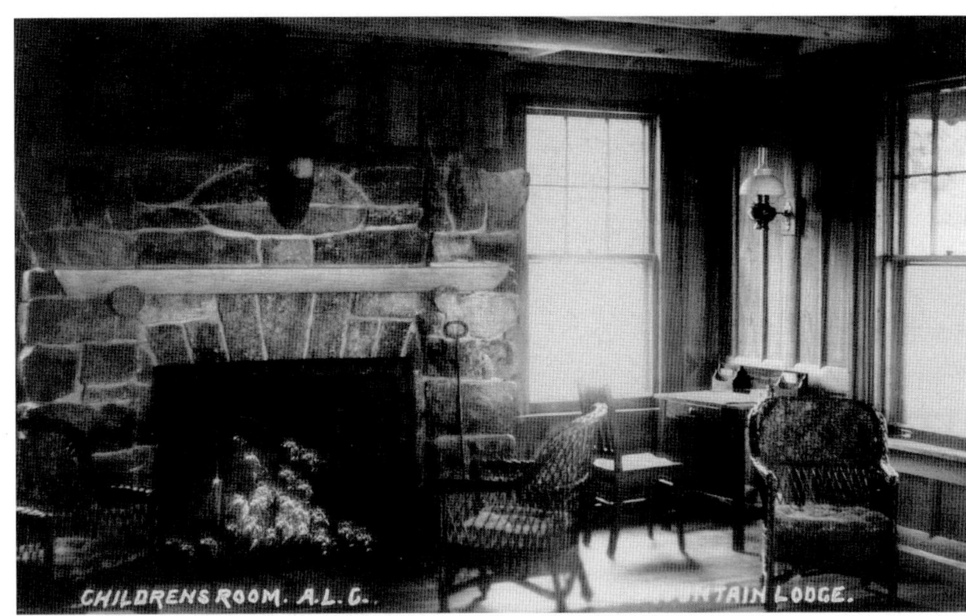


7.15. Children's room at the Adirondack League Club, Mountain Lodge, N.Y., 1914. Author's Coll.

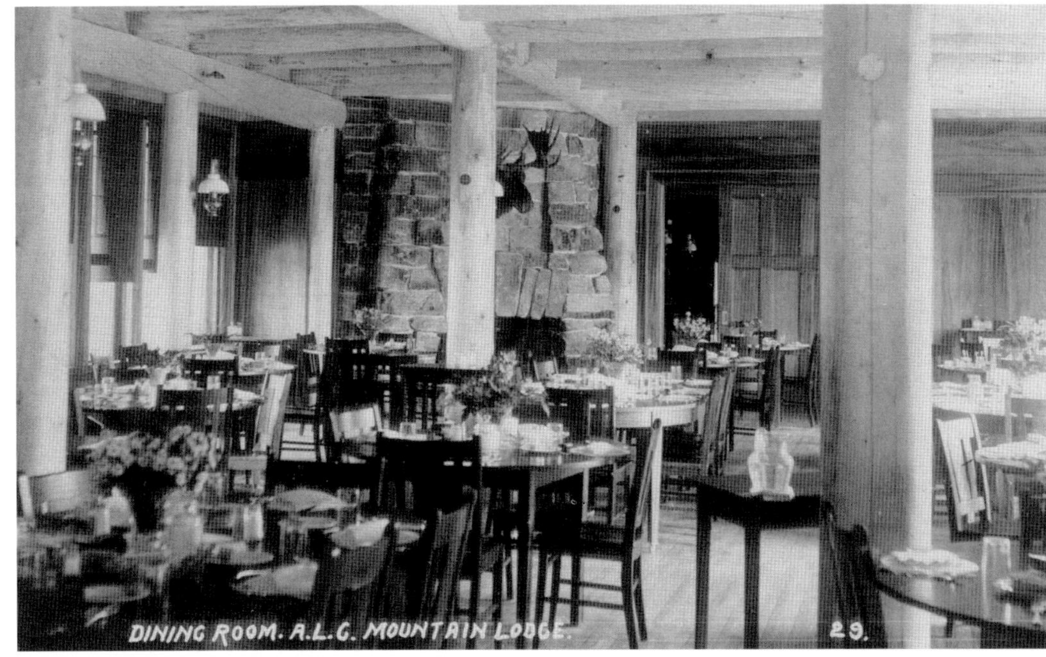


7.16. Dining room at the Adirondack League Club, Mountain Lodge, N.Y., ca. 1914. Author's Coll.

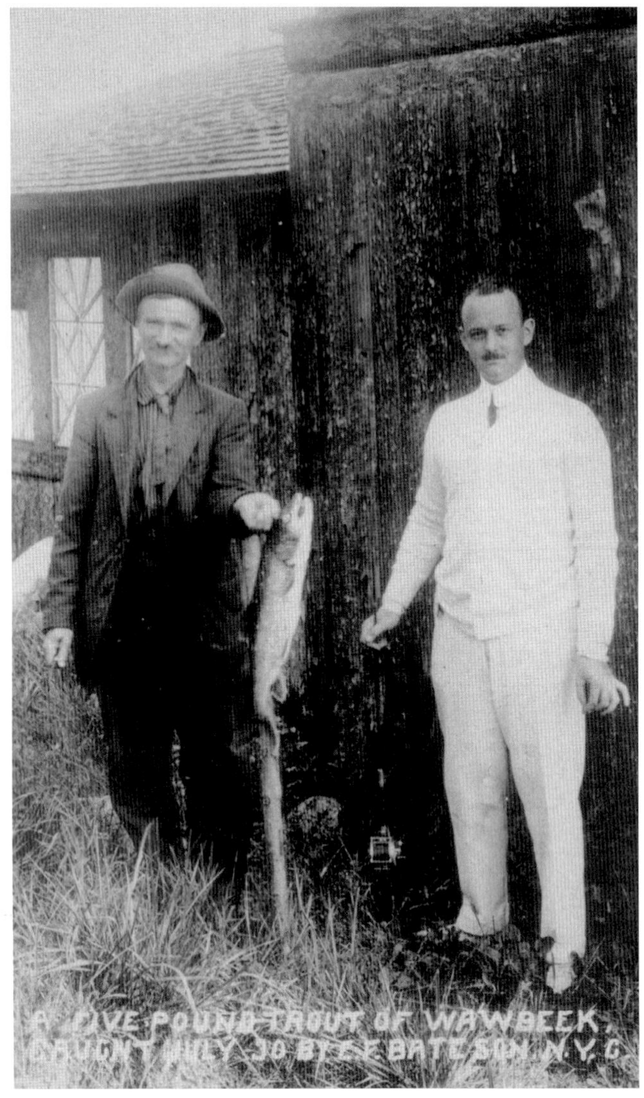


8.1. Five-pound trout, Wawbeek, N.Y., ca. 1911. Caught by E. F. Bateson of New York City. Gates Coll.

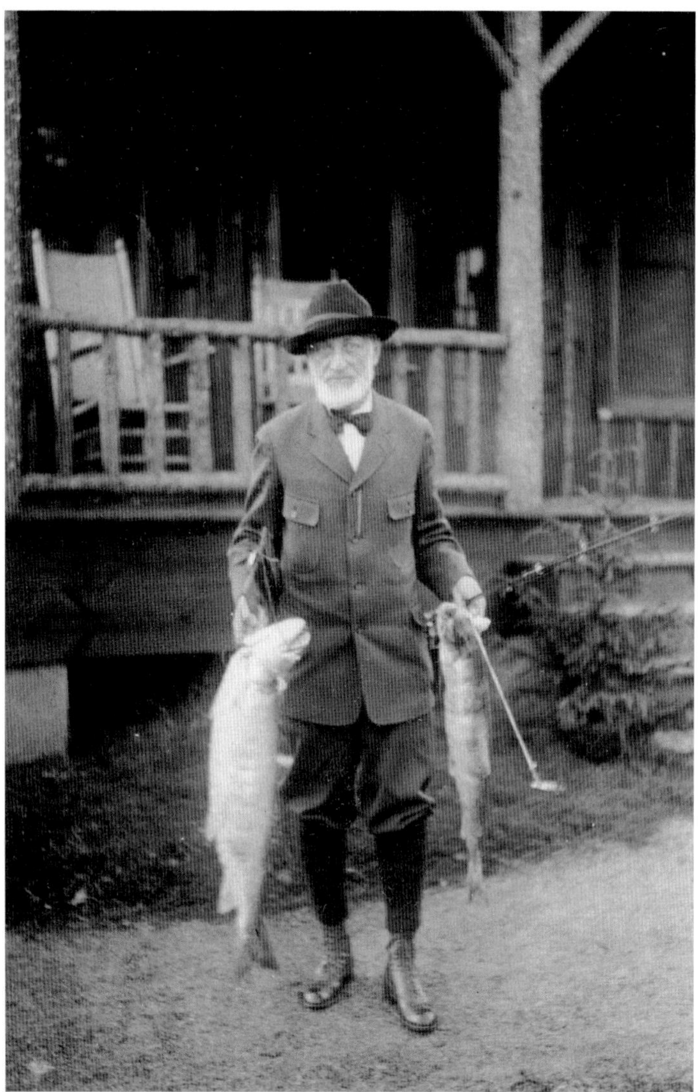

8.2. Man in knickers holding fish. Taken at the Adirondack League Club, Mountain Lodge, N.Y., ca. 1912. Comstock Coll.

8

# Outdoor Life
## Hunting, Fishing, and Camping

Lurking within the topic of outdoor life is a division that goes to the heart of the sociology of the Adirondacks: the differences between outsiders and locals. Leaving the futility of precisely defining the two categories aside for now, one broad generalization that holds is that whereas for visitors outdoor life was recreation, for locals it was about making ends meet, feeding themselves and the family—work (Terrie 1997, 40). Not that locals did not enjoy hunting, fishing, and romping through the forest—most did—but their underlying motivation was different from the intermittent visitor's.

Venison, trout, and other game were relied upon as a regular part of the Adirondackers' diets. In addition, many locals made part of their livelihood as guides, commercial hunters, trappers, anglers, and innkeepers. Some received payment from the "sports," the term locals used to refer to nonlocal hunters and anglers, for providing room and board.[1] The difference in orientation led to tension between the two groups. It found expression in the jokes they told about each other. Adirondack lore is full of humor pointing out the sports' incompetence in the woods. Although sports appreciated the skills of many Adirondackers, they joked about their provincialism.

1. As I stated in chapter 7, the hotel and resort economy began in response to the demands of urban sportsmen, and that industry remained dependent on them well after the core business shifted to the family summer recreation seekers.

### Sports and Locals

Henry understood the uneasiness between the Adirondackers and the "sports," and the uneasiness shows up in his pictures. Take his postcard portrait of Mr. Bateson and a man I presume to be his guide, holding a five-pound trout (illus. 8.1). At the time of the photo, Bateson was probably a guest at the Wawbeek Hotel (see chapter 7). Their placement in the picture as well as the fact that the guide is holding Mr. Bateson's trout punctuate the status difference between the two men. The guide appears relaxed, whereas Bateson's fingers and hands divulge discomfort. Notice, the guide is not named in the caption! Henry wrote in the text that Mr. Bateson was from New York City, a dead giveaway to derided outsider status among Adirondackers. Mr. Bateson's white city-slicker suit catches the light, making him glow like an alien against the rough-cut vertical log-wall backdrop.

Although no caption is offered in illustration 8.2 of a proud angler, the man in knickers and bow tie at the Adirondack League Club is definitely a sport. There were no regulations barring locals from joining such exclusive associations as the League Club. A few wealthy people who were permanent residents of the Old Forge area were members. But dues were well beyond what most Adirondackers could afford, and the members too urbane for local people to feel comfortable. Such clubs helped to create and reinforce the local mentality of "us and them," "Adirondacker and sport."

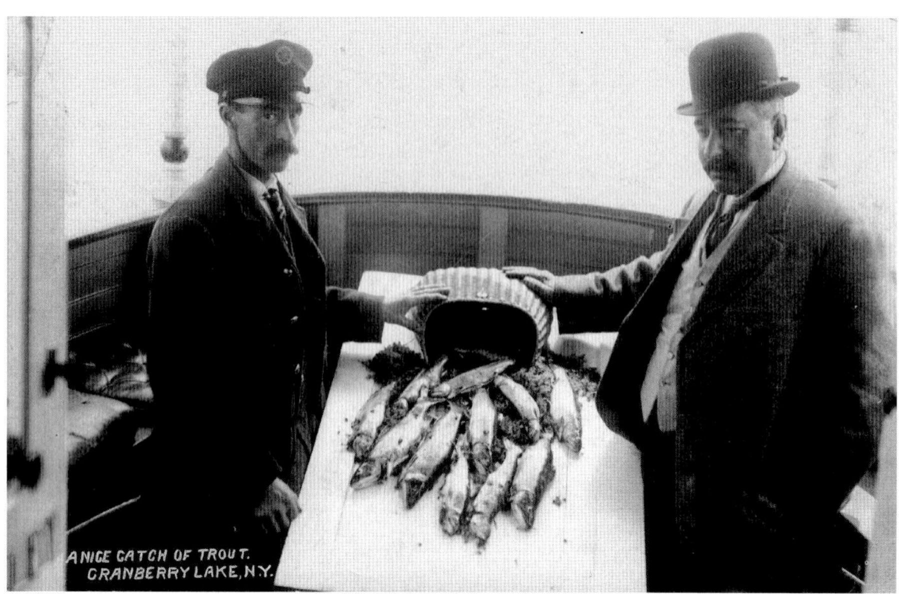


8.3. "A Nice Catch of Trout," Cranberry Lake, N.Y., ca. 1911.
Courtesy of the Adirondack Museum.

The photograph "A Nice Catch of Trout" taken on the steamer at Cranberry Lake is a little harder to decode using the insider and outsider categories (illus. 8.3). But is there any doubt that the man on the right in the bowler is a sport? But what about the other person? Is he the boat's captain? Is he admiring the man's catch, or is he indifferent? The look on his face suggests he might be a reluctant participant.

Beach's portraits of locals include illustration 8.4, a wonderful postcard of a trapper holding his rifle and standing beside his hound with a couple dozen fox and raccoon pelts as part of the background. This one is not of a man at play; it is of a man at work. It, like the portrait of the Adirondack League Club sport, is not captioned. Often, an uncaptioned photo meant that it was produced for private, not general, sale. The picture is visually interesting, with hunter and dog and the weather-beaten building with the foundation and windows in need of repair.

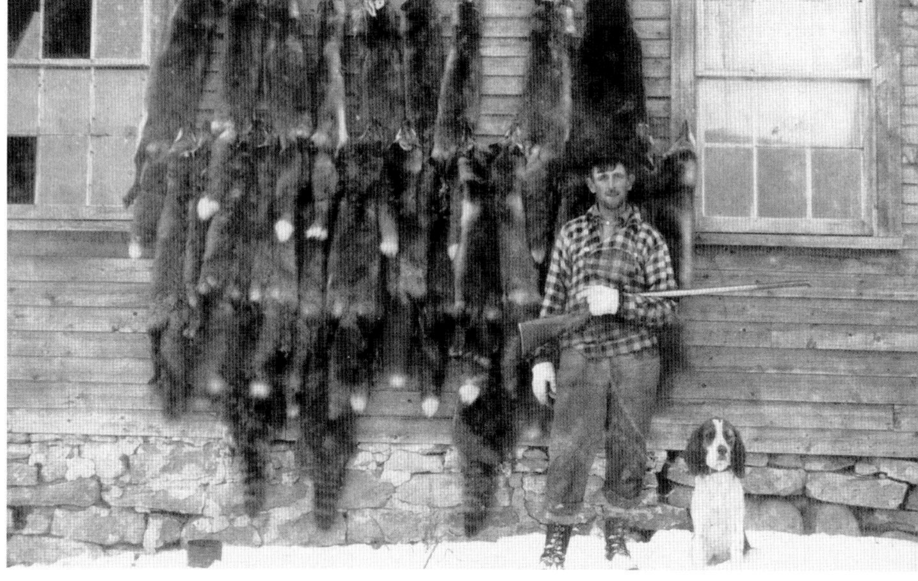

8.4. Fur trapper with hound, ca. 1912. G. Jones Coll.

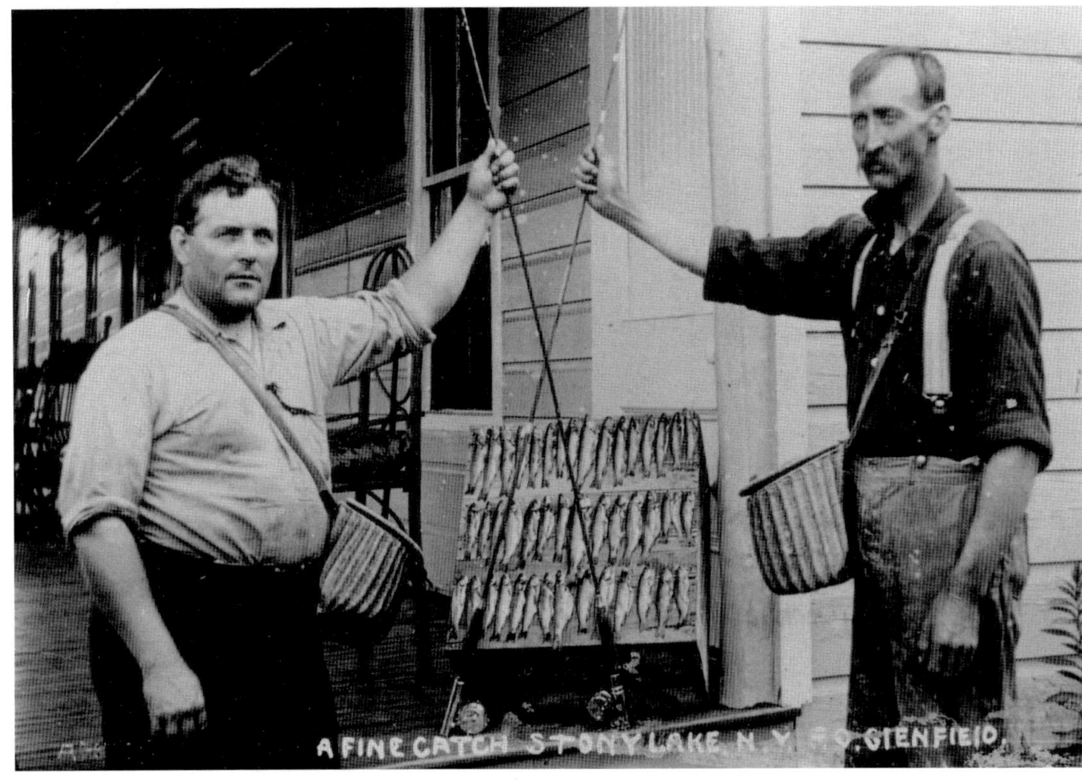


8.5. "A Fine Catch," Stony Lake, N.Y., ca. 1916. Davis Coll.

## Townies

Whereas knowing the distinction between sports and Adirondackers can be helpful in reading Henry's pictures, such broad generalizations often break down. There were many people who lived in communities in and around the region who had complex identities. Although some had regular jobs or full-time trades in town, they hunted and fished for food as well as sport. Some even belonged to local fish and game clubs that owned hunting shacks in the woods.[2] Others maintained inexpensive woods "camps" an easy drive from their homes that they used for hunting and fishing. People who grew up in the region, but settled elsewhere, regularly returned home to hunt and fish. Some of Henry's photographs capture the two worlds of insider and outsider; others call for a rethinking of the simplistic classification system.

In "A Fine Catch, Stony Lake, N.Y." we get support for the notion that although town locals look different from outsiders, both enjoy displaying the catch (illus. 8.5). Stony Lake was deep in the Adirondack forest, a settlement too small to have even a post office. It was near Watson, and Henry frequented the spot throughout his life. The caption in the second picture in the series, the close-up of the catch, identifies one of the anglers as a Beach, a relative of the photographer (illus. 8.6). The two men in the picture were likely Henry's fishing buddies.

2. Henry probably belonged to the Lowville Fish and Game Club. This group owned a hunting camp at Number Four near the Stillwater Reservoir in what is now the Adirondack Park. Henry took panoramic pictures of the members a number of times, including at their annual clambake in 1927 at their facility.

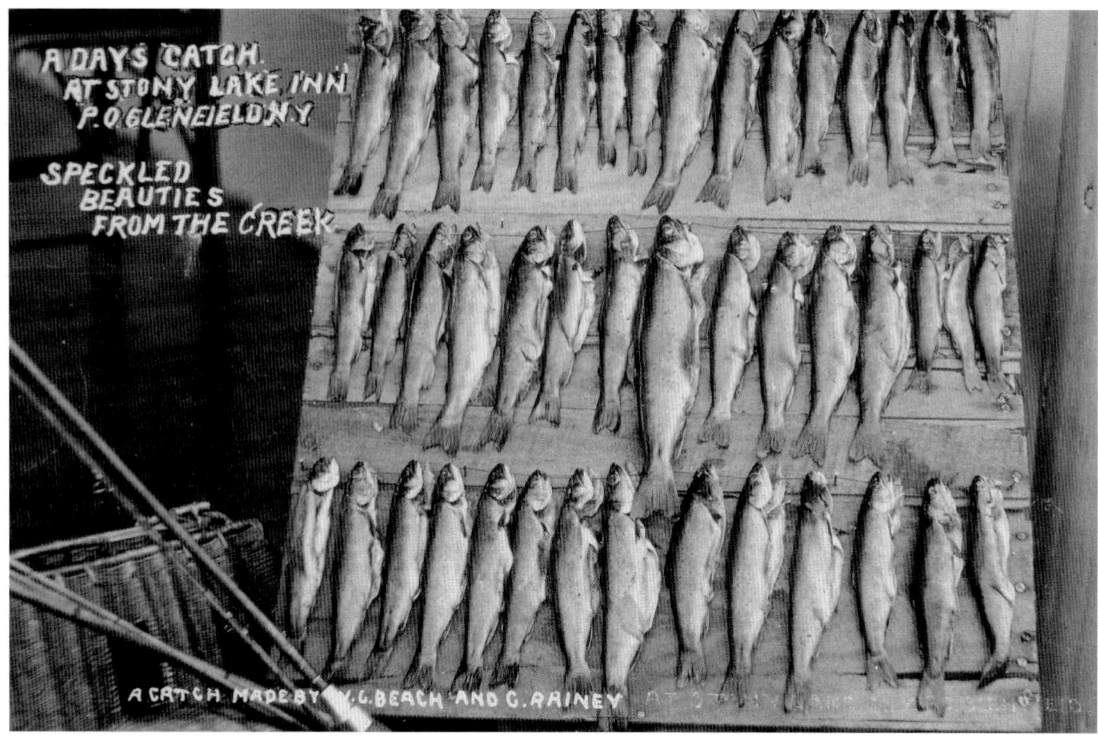


8.6. A day's catch at Stony Lake Inn, ca. 1916. Speckled beauties from the creek. Courtesy of the Adirondack Museum.

The picture of the catch is a still-life. The fish were carefully arranged on the display surface, but the entire display is propped haphazardly and askew against a door to the cottage. Although the fishing rods and creel have been placed in the composition, the set is not burdened with a strong feeling of having been arranged.

In illustration 8.7, a picture of hunters and their catch, it is difficult to figure out the status of the people in the group. Their dress seems local, not the outfit of authentic sports! Perhaps they were hunters from a nearby town out on an excursion at the camp that they jointly owned. Or maybe they were supplying meat for a lumber camp. Part of the picture's appeal is that it conveys a feeling of authenticity. We think we are seeing people engaging in an activity that is part of their culture. The two children in the picture belong; they are not just placed there for effect. The section of the deer carcass on the man's shoulders and the hare with antlers add bona fide local color. Interestingly, its generic caption, "Hunting Season, Adirondacks," indicates that it may have been marketed widely.

Another picture that is difficult to figure out is the unusual shot of hunters with a piebald buck (illus. 8.8). Considering how they are dressed, the group seems to be a mix of sports and guides. The picture contains some of the symbols of the Adirondacks—the rustic woven backpacks—but they fit naturally into the scene, and are not self-consciously on display. The hindquarter of the corpse has been skinned out and placed in the basket to facilitate the carry from the woods where the animal was shot back to camp.

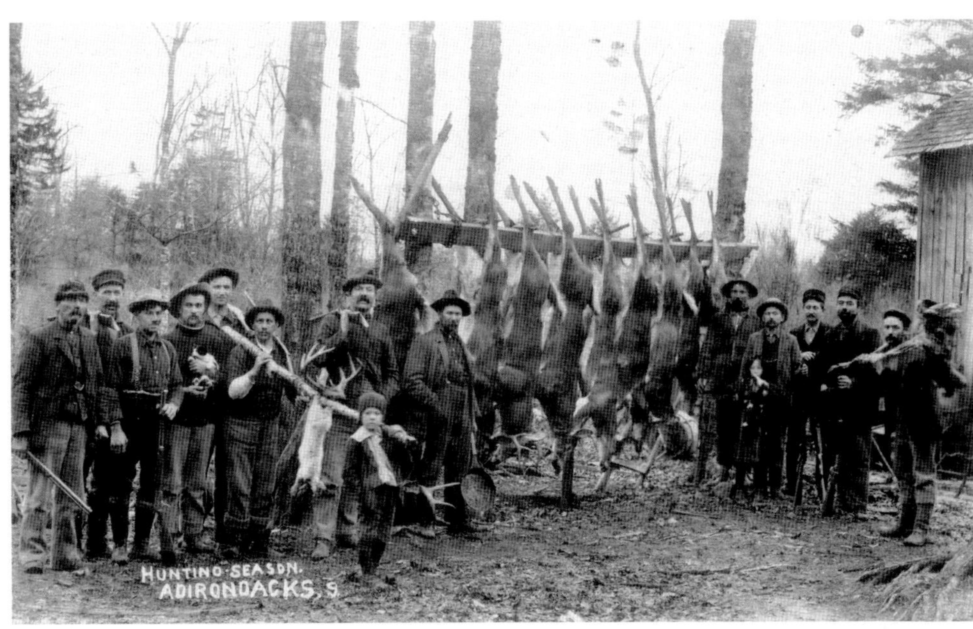


8.7. Hunting season, Adirondacks, ca. 1907. Burhans Coll.

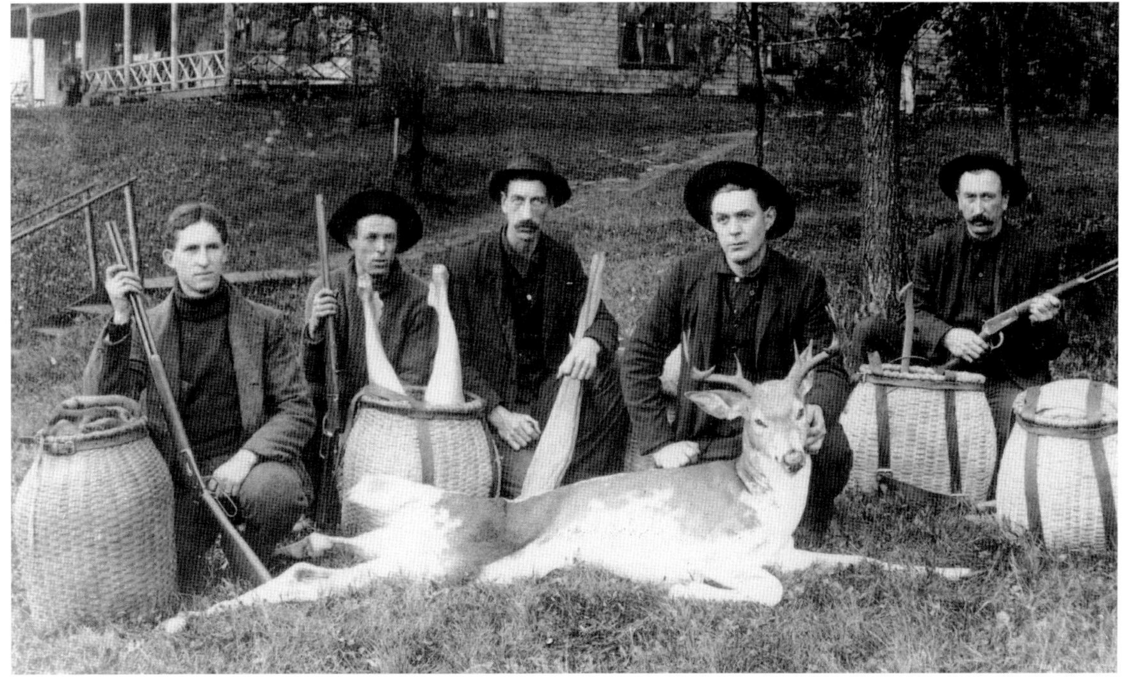

8.8. Hunters with piebald buck, ca. 1911. Comstock Coll.

One more dead-deer photograph before we move on. Illustration 8.9 includes the carcass of a black bear hanging alongside two bucks from the railing of the American Hotel in Grant, New York. Again, because it does not have a caption I would guess that it was not sold in stores but produced for the people in the picture. What is particularly appealing is the expression on the face of the young man sitting on the stairs. Dressed in a shirt, tie and jacket, and dress shoes, he could be a young sport on his first hunting trip to the Adirondacks. Part of the interest of many Beach hunting photographs is that they almost invite viewers to make up their own stories about the scene.

## Guides

Henry was local enough that when he hunted and fished he did not pay a guide for services. That fact does not mean he did not know woodsmen and even go out hunting and fishing with guides. His brother Louis was a guide, and he grew up among people who made their living hunting and fishing.

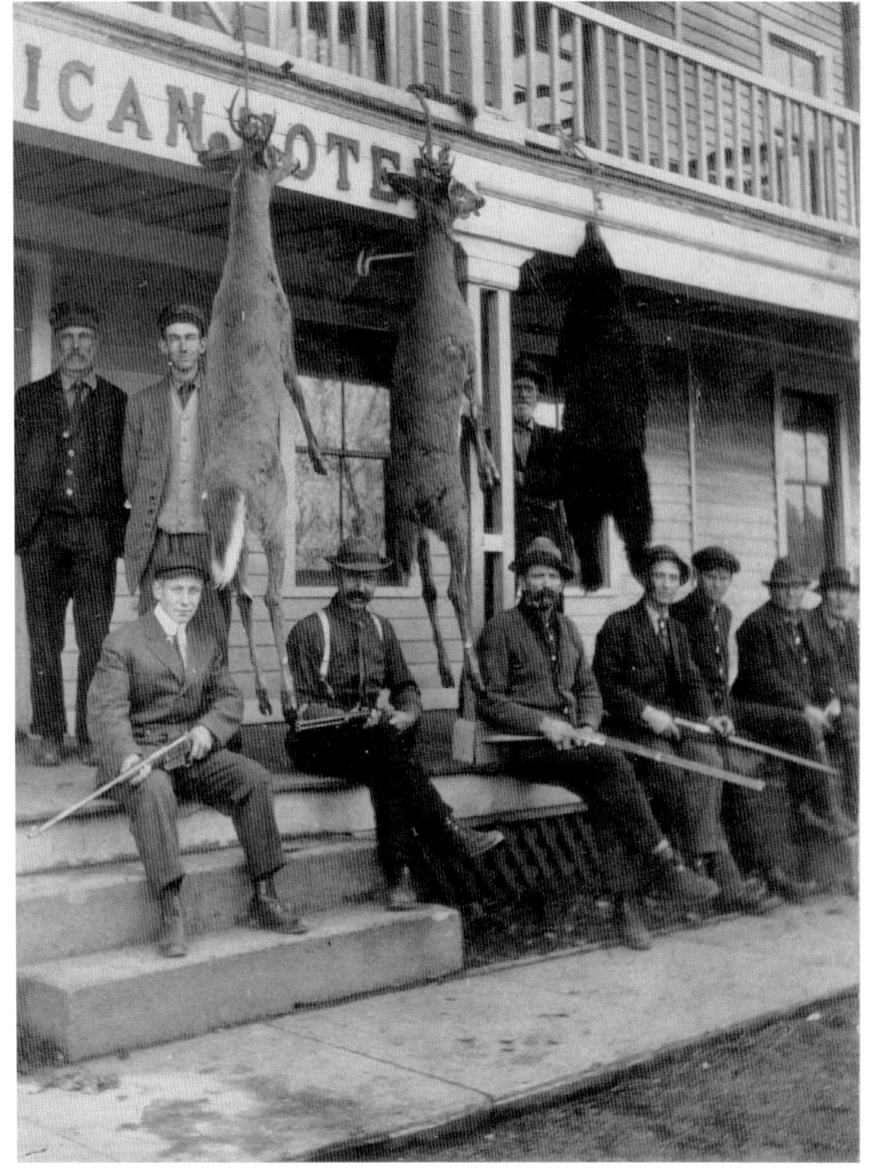


8.9. Hunters at the American Hotel, Grant, N.Y., ca. 1908. Gates Coll.

The Puffers were a family from Watson with a long affiliation with the outdoors who often worked as guides. There are connections between the Beaches, the Higbys, and the Puffers that go far back into the nineteenth century (Pilcher 1992, 88–89). Henry was probably a friend of Gill Puffer, the subject of "Fishing Season" (illus. 8.10). Beach took a number of engaging pictures of this Big Moose Lake guide. At the time he photographed him here rowing his guide boat, Gill was working out of the Lake View Lodge on Big Moose Lake and ready to start a new fishing season.

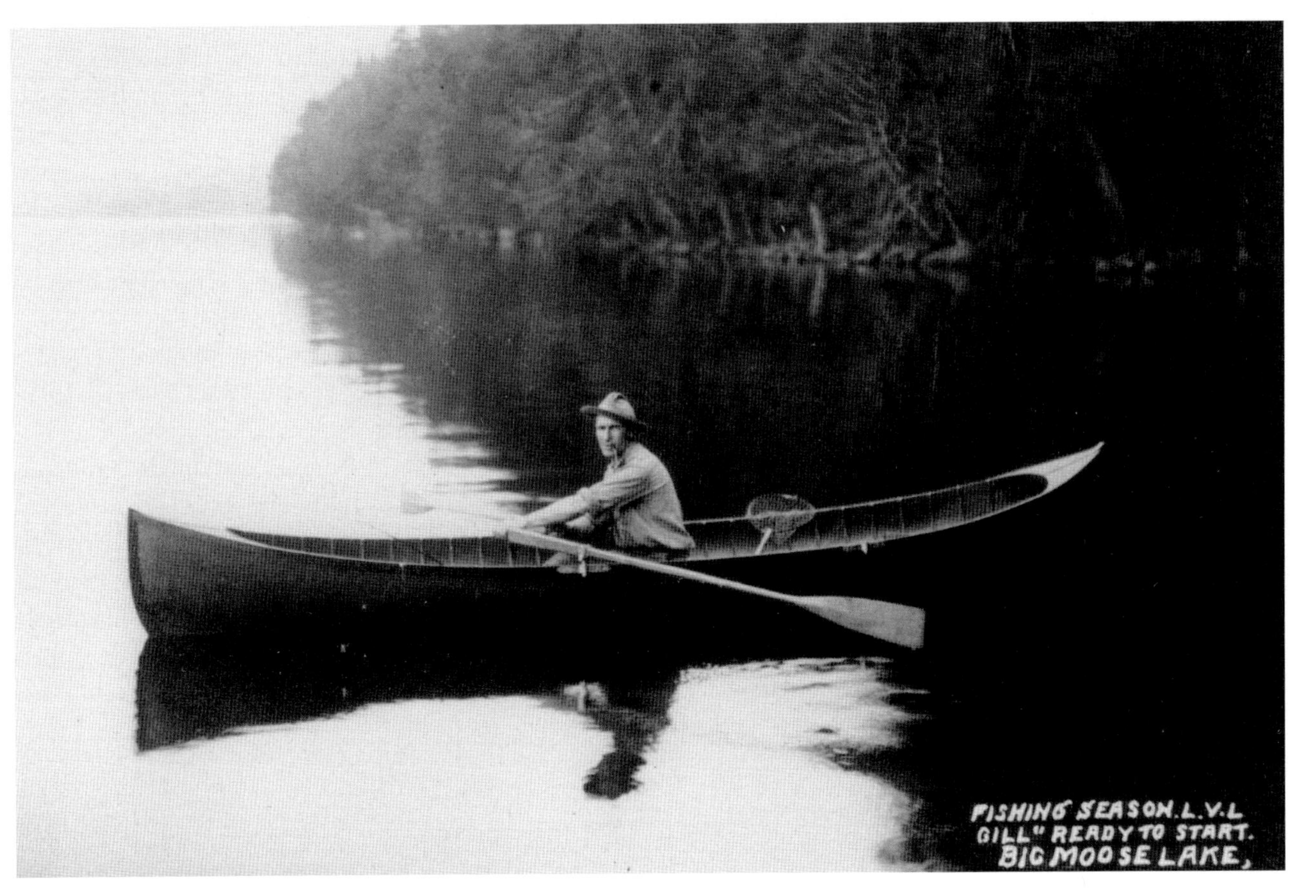


8.10. Gill, a fishing guide on Big Moose Lake, ready to start the fishing season at Lake View Lodge, ca. 1908. Gates Coll.

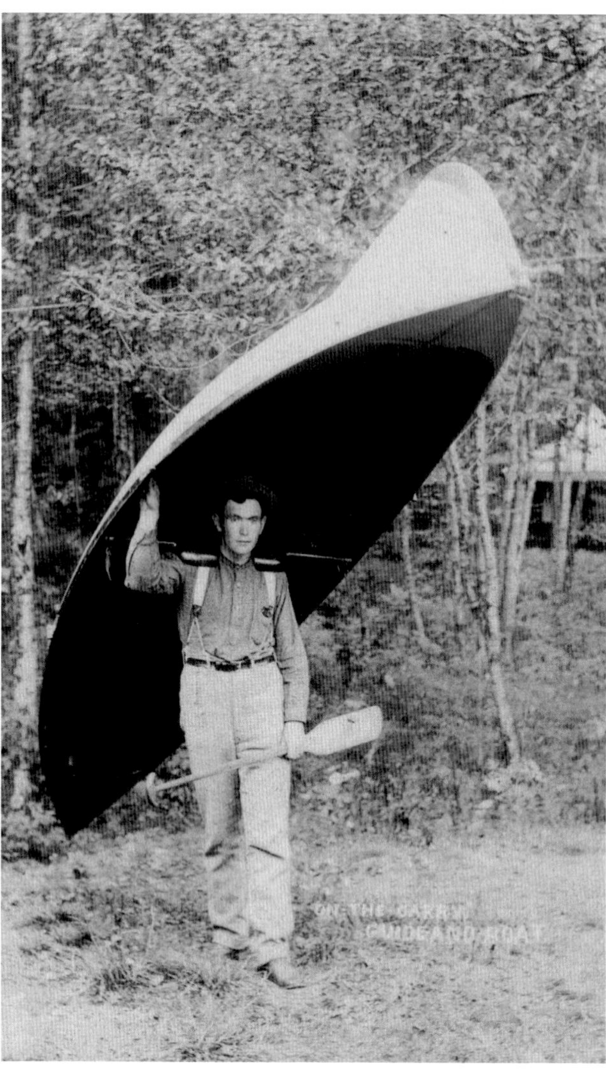

8.11. "The Carry, Guide and Boat," ca. 1911. Gates Coll.

"The Carry, Guide and Boat" is a classic Adirondack guide portrait (illus. 8.11). It, like the previous one, features the region's famous Adirondack guide boat. Unlike most of Beach's pictures, the caption does not name the location the guide is from or any specific information about the scene. Manufactured for sale across the region, Beach created it to appeal to a wide range of customers. He wanted to sell a lot of cards.

Hunting and fishing were not just for men. Women partook, too, but they are missing from the ranks of old-time guides. Lottie Tuttle, whom Beach photographed in action dressed in a full-length skirt, was the first on record (illus. 8.12). She moved to Old Forge in 1906 where she and her husband built the Bay View Hotel on Fourth Lake. They catered to anglers in the spring and hunters in the fall, and tolerated summer guests in-between (Brumley 1994, 165). Lottie became a registered guide in 1912. Talented in many realms, she marketed her husband's Devil Bug fishing lure to national prominence. Her daughter, born in 1903, took up her mother's occupation and became a licensed guide in the 1930s (Cunningham 2000).

Among the early hotels catering to sports was William J. McAleese's Hunters and Fishers Resort at Grasse River (the post office address was Cranberry Lake) (illus. 8.13; see also illus. 2.3). Mac, as the owner was called, arrived from Ireland as a boy and began his life in the North Country working in the woods for the Canton Lumber Company. Mac's skill as a hunter and angler made him a popular guide. In Beach's picture Mac stands on the far left with his rifle over his shoulder. His wife and children are part of the group on the right. In most pictures, hunters are shown with their kill. Perhaps no game was immediately available for this picture, so, as a substitute, and to add levity to the card, a mounted buck head was positioned in the back seat.

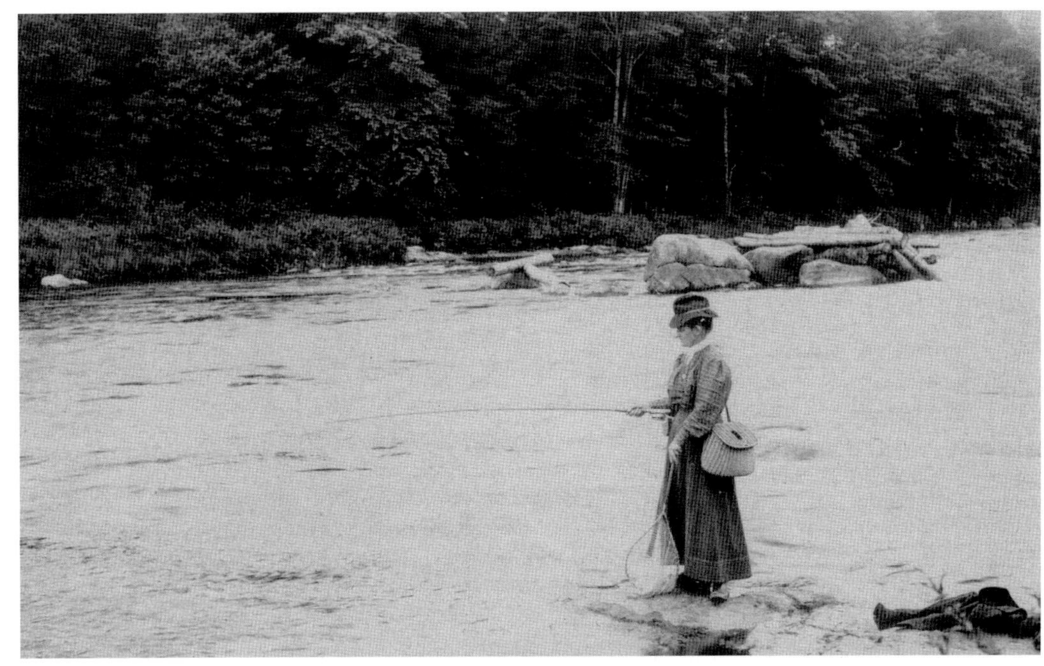

8.12. Lottie Tuttle fly-fishing, ca. 1914. Gates Coll.

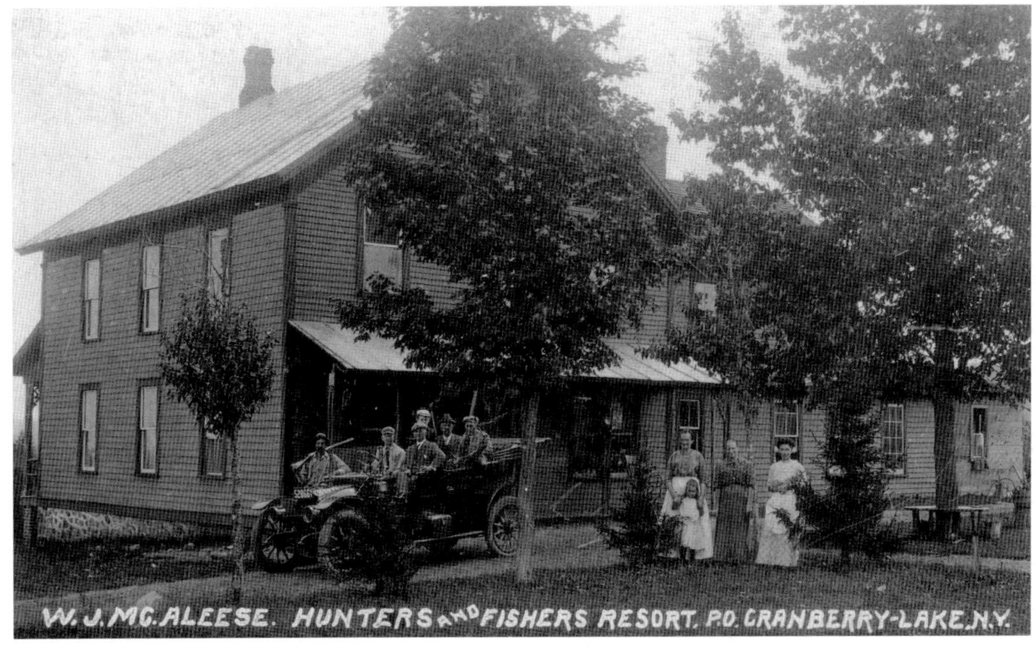


8.13. W. J. McAleese's Hunters and Fishers Resort, Cranberry Lake, N.Y., ca. 1910. Smeby Coll.

Beaver River was a spot where hunting and fishing was a way of life. Dave Conkey, who grew up in Lewis County and worked as a guide and laborer for Jim Higby, settled in the Beaver River area around 1908. The uncaptioned picture shown here as illustration 8.14 is one of a half-dozen pictures Beach took of the Conkey camp with Dave out front. It is the only one that pictures his wife, Mabel, with him. Dave is dressed in his ranger uniform. In 1911 Conkey became the first forest ranger appointed to the area by the New York State Conservation Department. His duties included work as a game warden. As was the case with many of the locals who became state game-law enforcers, Dave was not aggressive in pursuing local violators who used meat for their own tables. Venison from out-of-season hunts was referred to euphemistically as "mountain lamb." The ranger's job was seasonal, so for six months Dave was free to guide. During Prohibition Dave supplemented his income by making home brew (Donnelly n.d.).

## Camping

Not all people experienced outdoor life as hunters and anglers. Many recreation seekers took up trekking up mountains and roughing it. Rather than staying in tourist homes, resorts, or hotels, they slept in tents. Resort owners provided tents on their own property at reduced rates, but as the century moved forward, many people began to camp on state land.

Although not a common topic for Beach, there are a few pictures showing early-century camping, such as "The Summer Camp" (illus. 8.15). I include this picture because it is such a nice composition and provides a sense of a broader range of outdoor experience than is present in his hunting and fishing images.

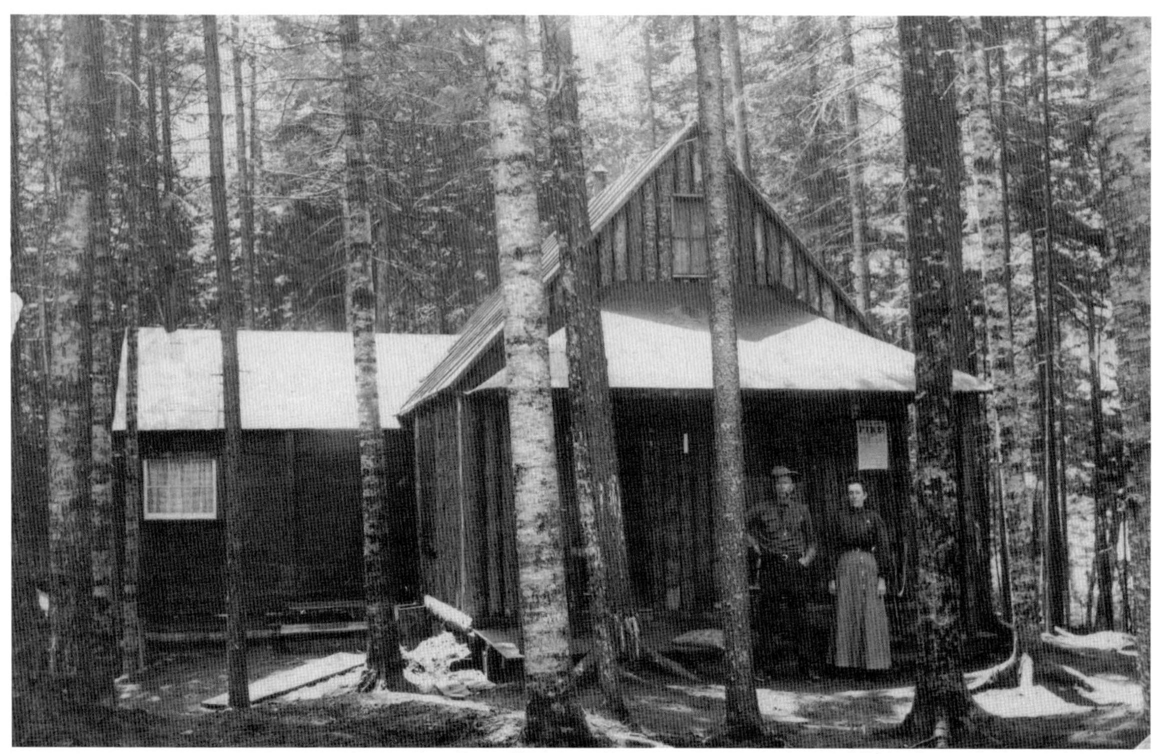

8.14. Dave Conkey and his wife, Mabel, in front of their cabin at Beaver River, N.Y., ca. 1916. Carey Coll.

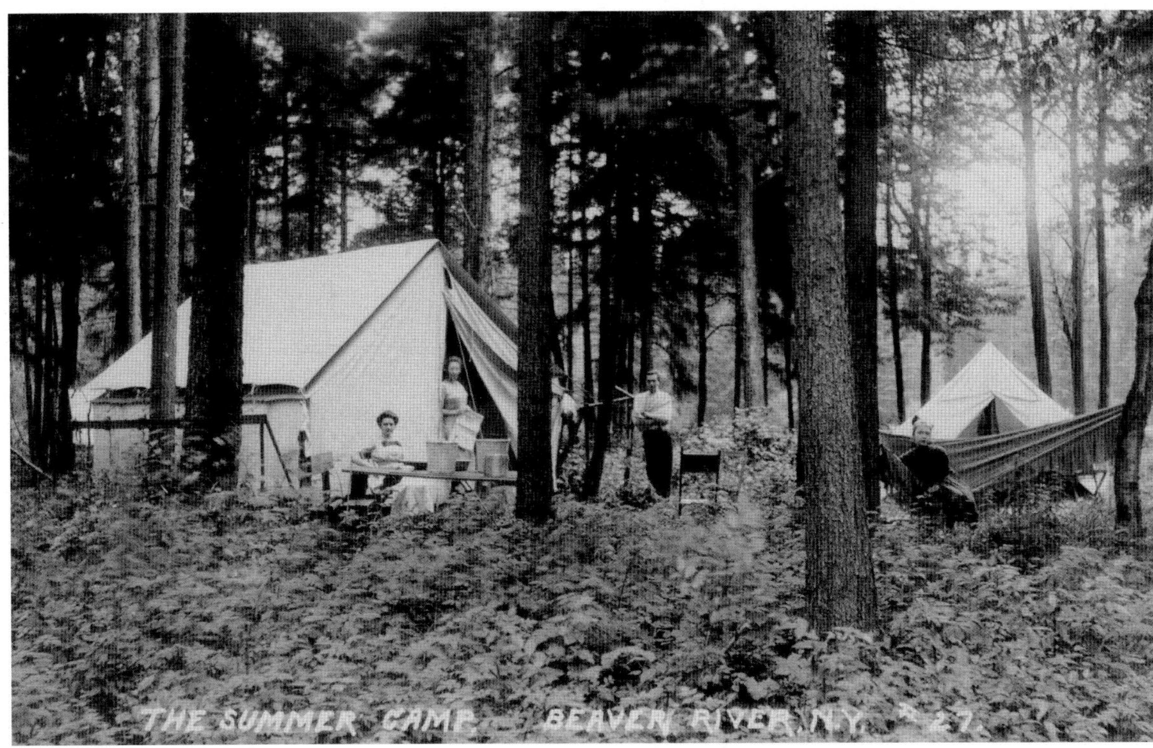


8.15. “The Summer Camp,” Beaver River, N.Y., ca. 1912. Gates Coll.

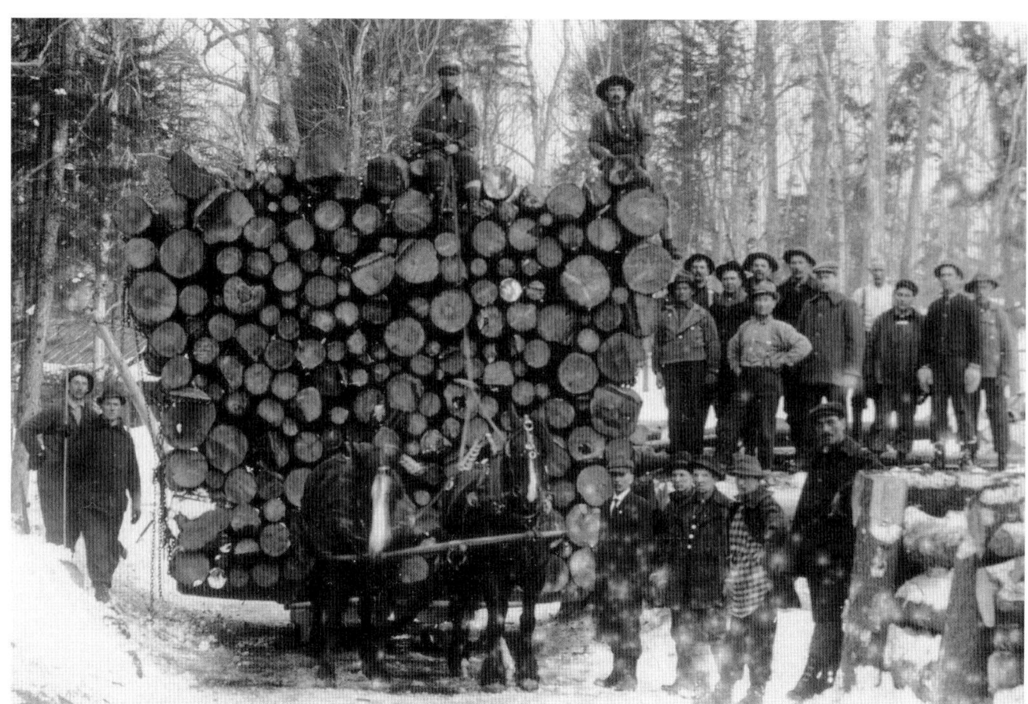

9.1. Champion load from Carlson's Mac-A-Mac job, Brandreth Lake, N.Y., ca. 1914. Courtesy of the Adirondack Museum.

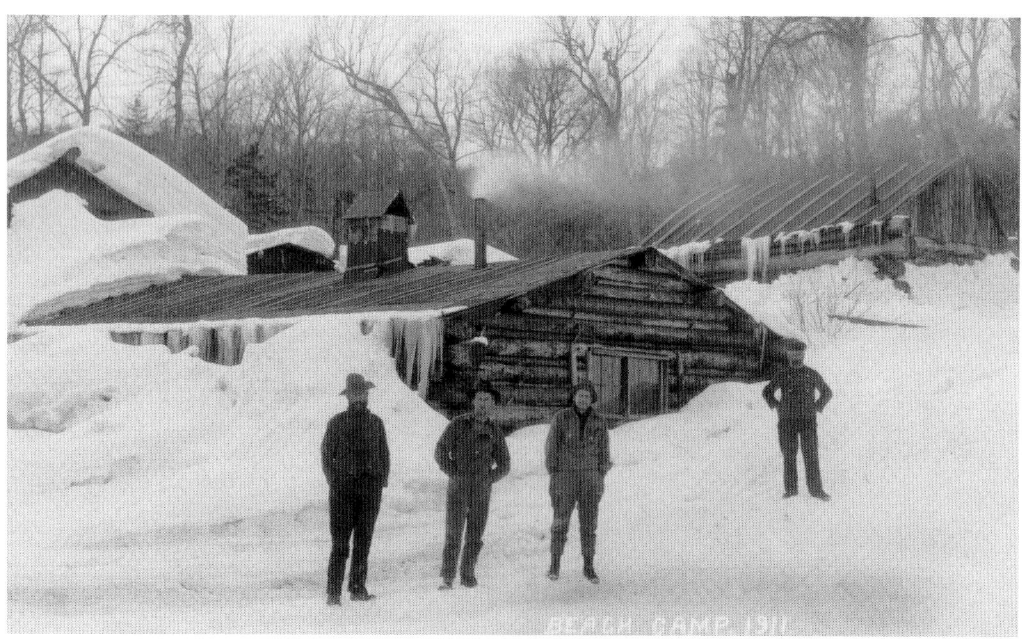


9.2. Beach loggers camp, ca. 1911. Gates Coll.

9

# Logging and the Wood-Product Industry

Adirondack memorabilia collectors have a weakness for logging photographs. Treasured images are nostalgic scenes such as illustration 9.1, showing men posing with a huge load of logs that are about to be taken to the banking grounds.[1] Over his career, Beach photographed hundreds of such scenes, capturing a rustic and romantic version of men working in the woods. But as we shall see, he also recorded a more troubling view, a portrait of mechanization and ruin. His documentary of logging covers a longer period and a wider range of sites than any Adirondack photographer. In addition to his extensive postcard coverage, he is the only photographer who took large-format panoramic photographs of lumbering.

## Twentieth-Century Logging

Toward the end of the nineteenth century, the center of the Adirondack logging industry moved west from the Lake Champlain and Hudson River watersheds to Henry's photographic territory, the St. Lawrence and Black River watersheds.[2] At the same time, paper products replaced lumber production as the backbone of the wood industry (Welsh 1995). Eventually, pulpwood (the logs for paper production) became king. In 1912 New York led the nation in the production of pulpwood. Other changes occurred as Adirondack logging moved west and into the new century. The favored method of getting logs to the mills began to change from river drives to hauling by train and, later, by trucks.[3] Heavy equipment began replacing the logging crews, and small locally owned and operated lumber and paper mills began to be bought and consolidated into large companies.

Henry was in the right place at the right time and had the right family connections to be in a position to chronicle western North Country logging. As noted, he was born and raised among loggers. His kin originally provided entry for him and his camera into the loggers' woods. He dabbled in logging images in the 1880s when he was a fledgling picture taker. While in Remsen he still had relatives active in the business. His brother Louis was a logger and a camp cook. One of his cousins was a jobber, and from notations on postcard captions we know that Henry visited his camp to take pictures.[4] Henry not only had easy access, but he was at home with loggers and they were comfortable with him as well. He was not born too late to miss the old-time logging or too early to have been there when the new machinery arrived and the paper mills redefined the harvest (illus. 9.2).

1. For descriptions of logging operations, see Hochschild 1962c, McMartin 1994; and Welsh 1995. For information about the Tupper Lake–Cranberry Lake logging operations see Hyde 1974; and Reynolds and DeCrosse 1976. I have relied on these authors throughout this chapter.

2. The St. Lawrence and Black River watersheds include such rivers as the Independence, Black, Moose, Beaver, Grasse Oswegatchie, Raquette, and St. Regis (Welsh 1995; McMartin 1994).

3. In 1918 the Santa Clara Lumber Company of Tupper Lake was among the first to use trucks to haul lumber. By the 1930s, the gasoline engine was the horsepower of choice to transport pulpwood from the woods to the mills as well as getting lumberjacks to the job sites.

4. A jobber was someone who put together crews to harvest logs under contract with companies that owned the mills. Some companies had their own crews.

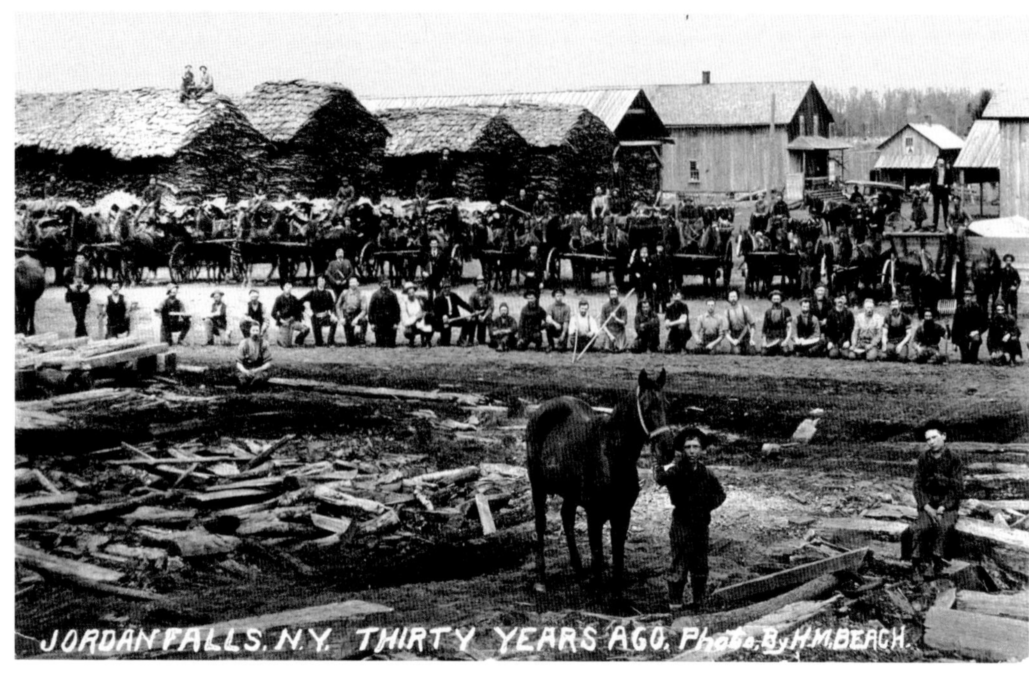


9.3. Jordan Falls, N.Y., thirty years ago, ca. 1914. Author's Coll.

## Logging Postcards

Beach photographed the logging camps that either were owned by or supplied such companies as St. Regis, Santa Clara, Rich, International Paper, Gould, and Emporium with their raw materials. For some postcard series he might have even been under contract with firms to produce photographs.[5]

Although we know some of the logging operations he photographed, it is not easy to sort his photos by geographic location, date, jobbers, or receiver companies. With his logging work, he captioned many cards with general titles such as "Logging in the Adirondacks" rather than identifying specific locations.

Dating his logging cards can also pose problems. When Beach went into postcard production in a serious way, he resurrected some glass-plate negatives he had produced in the nineteenth century and printed them on postcard stock. Occasionally, he stated in the caption that the view was from another era, but most have no such notation. It is not always easy to spot one of his nineteenth-century images when recycled as a twentieth-century postcard.

Henry printed "Jordan Falls" from an old glass negative on postcard stock and marked it clearly as such (illus. 9.3). It is a remarkable view of the gathering of hemlock bark at the Jordan Falls Tannery in Lewis County near the western border of what is now the Adirondack Park (McMartin 1992, 288; McMartin 1994, 31).[6] Because tanneries were on the way out in the region by the turn of the century, tannery photos are rare. The one pictured in illustration 9.3 was in its prime in the 1880s. Given the notation on the card, "Thirty Years Ago," we can assume it was taken then. The postcard version was produced around 1914.

5. Beach took a series of pictures of Emporium operations under contract with that firm. He seems to have had some special relationship with the Mac-A-Mac Corporation, a group that supplied a number of western Adirondack companies.

6. The town was renamed around the turn of the century, which accounts for the disparity in the name of the tannery and the caption on the postcard.

## Logging Camps

Logging camps were short-term settlements, crudely constructed deep in the forest to serve as the base for the lumberjacks' work. (Beach used *wood camp* and *lumber camp* interchangeably with *logging camp* in his captions.) The camps were where the equipment was kept, where the horses bedded, and where the workers slept, ate, and spent the little leisure time they had. One hundred and fifty lumber camps, employing seven to eight thousand lumberjacks, operated in the Adirondacks in 1915 (McMartin 1994).

Beach's postcard captioned "A Model Lumber Camp in the Adirondacks" provides an overview of a large operation during a particularly hard winter (illus. 9.4). Notice that the caption does not specify the camp's location or owner. Beach must have produced this card to educate outsiders. He took the time to label the heavy equipment as well as the main structures, office, stable, outside cellar, men's camp, and cook camp on the negative.

Although Henry's postcards provide wonderful glimpses of "wood camp" life, they cannot approach the capacity of his large panoramic photographs to bring you back to these places. Aside from the kitchen staff and the wives of a few teamsters and other upper-level staff, logging camps were supposed to be rough and tough male bastions. The women and children present in panoramic 9, "Carlson's Camp," contradict that assumption. What we are viewing is probably a holiday visit at the main camp building. There is no contradiction to the theme of male dominance in the image of Carlson's Landing, the banking grounds for the Mac-A-Mac Corporation at Brandreth (panoramic 10). The caption on this panoramic, which has been cropped out in this reproduction, brags that the load on the left is the "Largest Load of Pulp," 298 logs, 16 feet high by 16 feet wide, for a total of 21⅜ cords.

Some of Henry's best work takes us inside the buildings. "In the Cook Camp" provides a rare glimpse at dinner preparation in the kitchen of a large lumber camp (illus. 9.5). The print is so clear and detailed that you can make

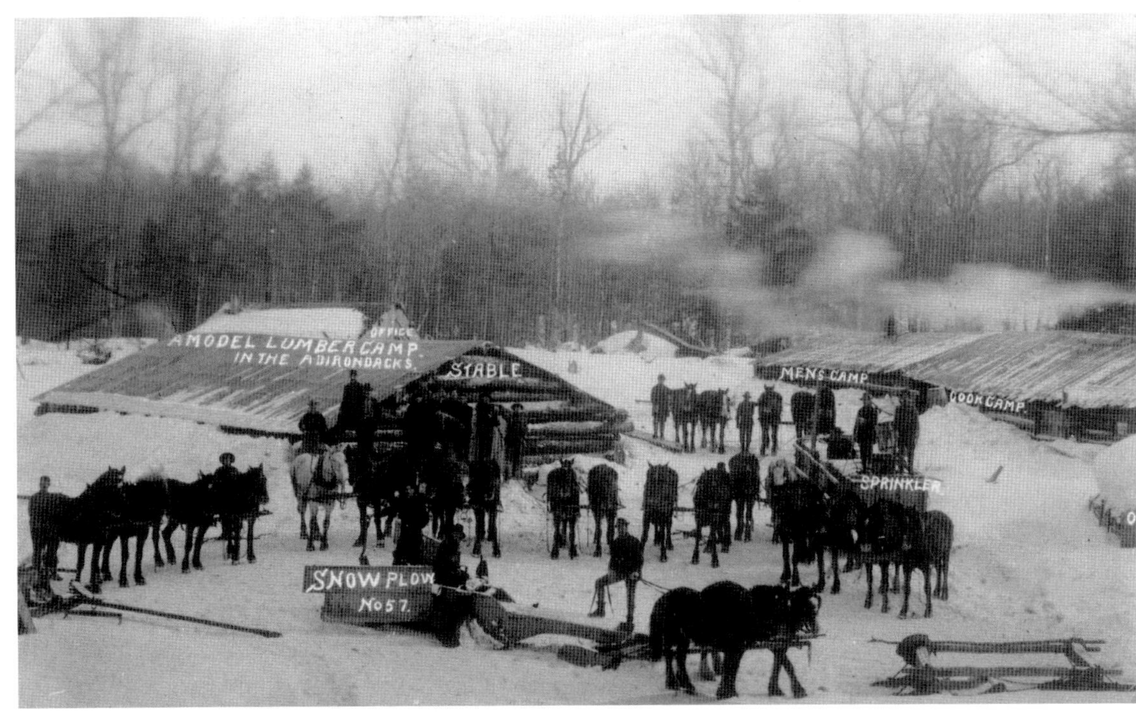


9.4. Lumber camp in the Adirondacks, ca. 1913. Davis Coll.

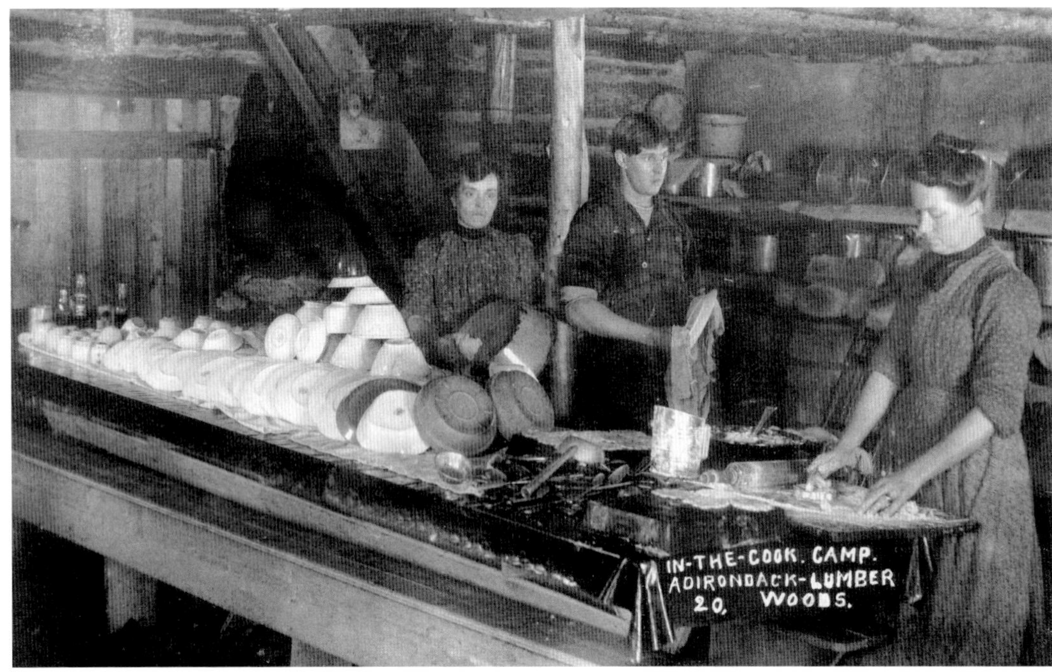


9.5. In the cook camp, Adirondack lumber woods, ca. 1910. Author's Coll.

out what the women on the right are preparing, biscuits. It must have been one of those rare bright, sunny days in the North Woods; otherwise, the light from the open door on the right (out of sight in the picture) would not have been sufficient to produce such a fine exposure.

In "Dining Room at Lumber Camp," we can glimpse the eating area of the cook camp with the long tables being set for the nightly lumberjack dinner where it is alleged that mountains of food were consumed in a few minutes (illus. 9.6). The indistinct female figure at the left adds an impressionist touch to an otherwise orderly, no-frills scene.

The final example of a lumber-camp interior view is of the sleeping quarters at the Emporium Lumber Company at Conifer (illus. 9.7). In 1910 the Emporium Lumber Company of Pennsylvania purchased a small locally owned sawmill located in Conifer (west of Tupper Lake) and transformed it into a modern plant equipped with its own small company town with dwellings for fifty families (Welsh 1995, 46). Beach took this picture as part of a long-term assignment he carried out for the Emporium's owner, W. L. Sykes, who wanted to document the improvements he made to the facilities (Welsh 1995). Although the bedding and slumber facilities do look ample and up-to-date, in assessing the desirability of the accommodations you need to factor in that men slept two to a bed (note the two pillows on each) and that bedbugs were plentiful.

## The Harvest

Beach took clear, graphic shots of all the stages and aspects of the timber harvest. Horses were indispensable to logging through the first two decades of the twentieth century (see panoramic 10). They provided the basic transportation for delivery of equipment, supplies, and personnel into the forest as well as for

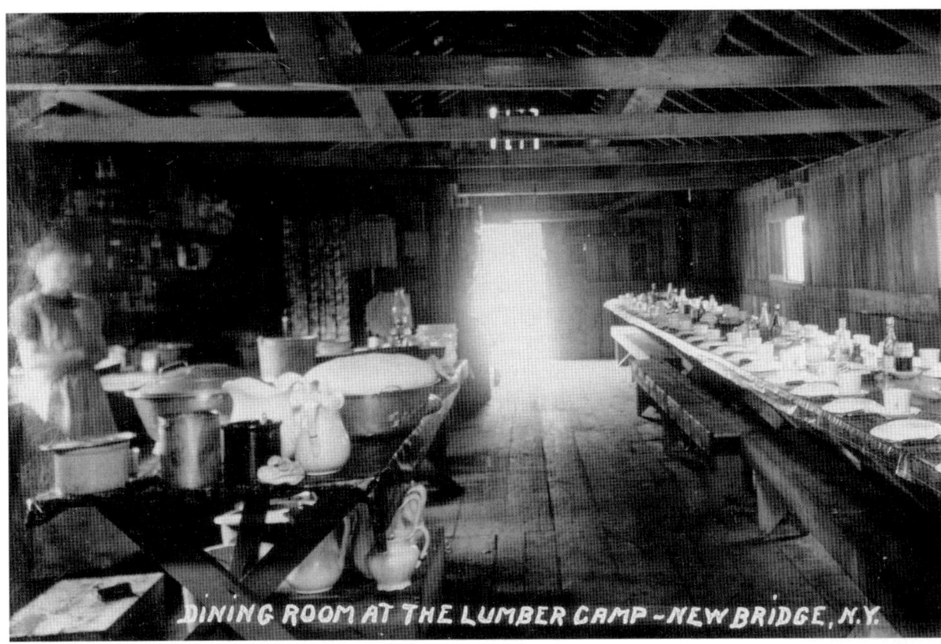


9.6. Dining room at the lumber camp, New Bridge, N.Y., ca. 1910. Courtesy of the Adirondack Museum.

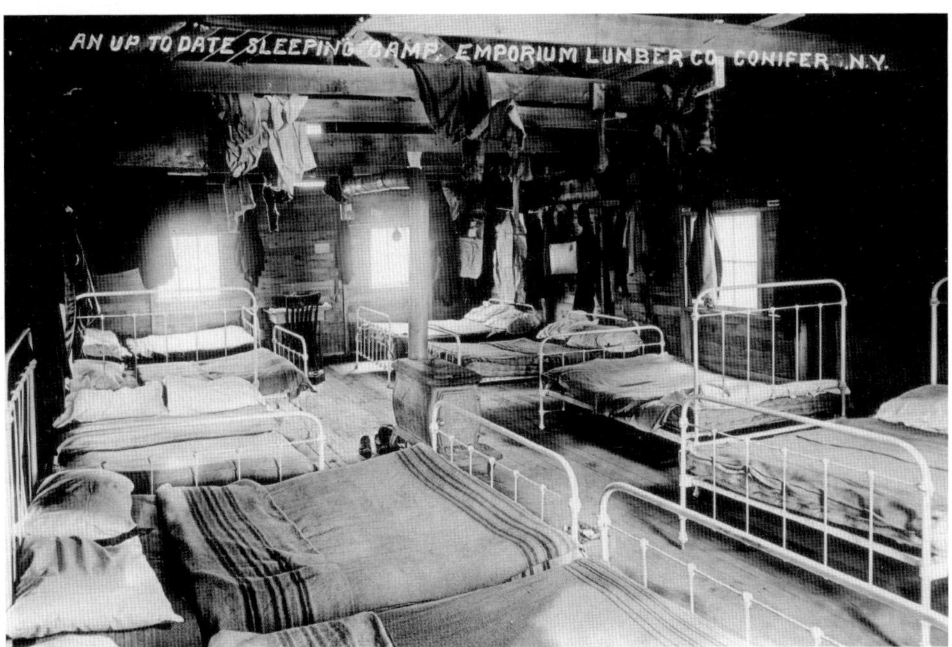


9.7. An up-to-date sleeping camp, Emporium Lumber Company, Conifer, N.Y., ca. 1911. Courtesy of the Adirondack Museum.

moving them to the exact cutting locations and much more (illus. 9.8). After the timbers had been cut and trimmed, horses equipped with chains, guided by skilled woodsmen, dragged the logs to terrain that was accessible by crude roads. There the logs were stacked on "skidways," roughly built loading platforms under which horse-drawn sleds could be parked so the timbers could be loaded (illus. 9.9). The stacks of logs that accumulated at these sites were sometimes enormous. The men who took the logs from the pile onto the sleds were always in danger of being crushed by logs flipping in unexpected ways or by the support structure failing.

The great pile that Beach chose to photograph at Brandreth Lake seems precariously held in place by two vertical logs that do not seem suited to the task. The force of gravity on the load, created by the steep hill, is directed toward the men on the sled who work under its threat. The logs, covered with newly fallen snow, combined with the bright sunlight, add to the feeling of wonder one gets when contemplating the whole operation.

Although the loading of the sleds at the skidways was not always a competitive game, at certain sites, among particular lumbermen, teams vied with each other to see who could get the most on a sled. For Henry, these big loads were one of his favorite logging subjects.

Beach had the large crew pose proudly on and about their exceptionally large load in illustration 9.1. Although this picture is not captioned with the particulars, another postcard of the same load gives the name of the three men who were responsible for loading the sled, and of J. LaPont, perched up top, the teamster who drove it to the banking grounds.

The cards Beach produced of winners must have sold well both among people in the logging trade and to Adirondack visitors because they remain common today on the antique postcard market. In another example titled "The Best Load This Year," Henry jam-packed the photo with the load, making the point that we are looking at a mighty load of timber (illus. 9.10). He came close to decapitating the logger riding highest on the load in making the point.

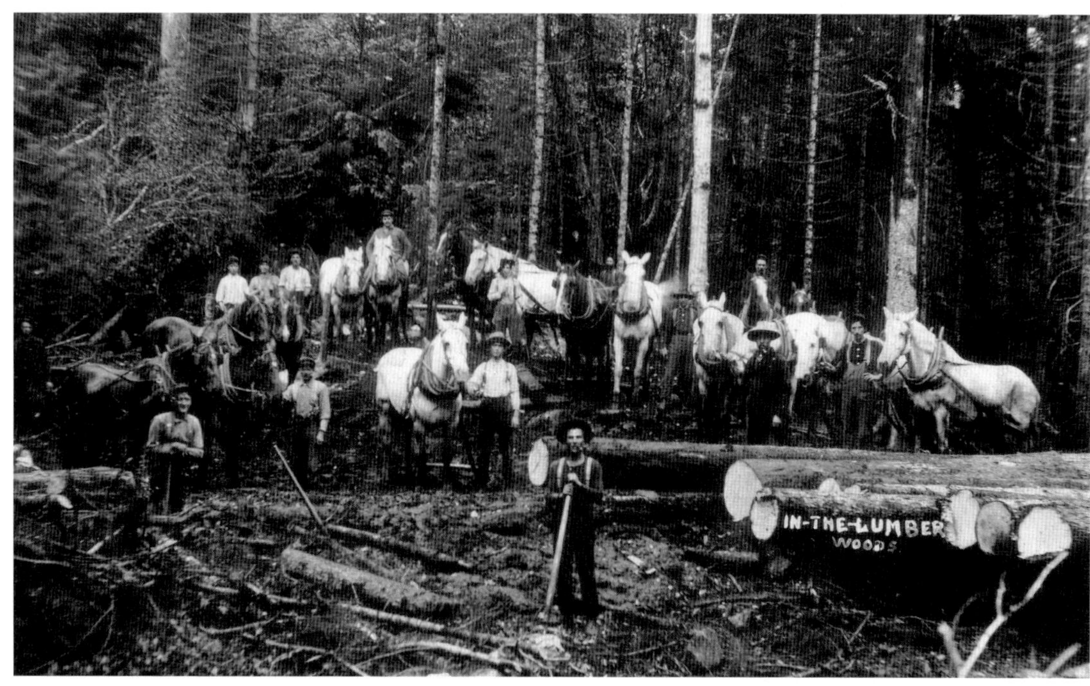


9.8. In the lumber woods, ca. 1910. Teal Coll.

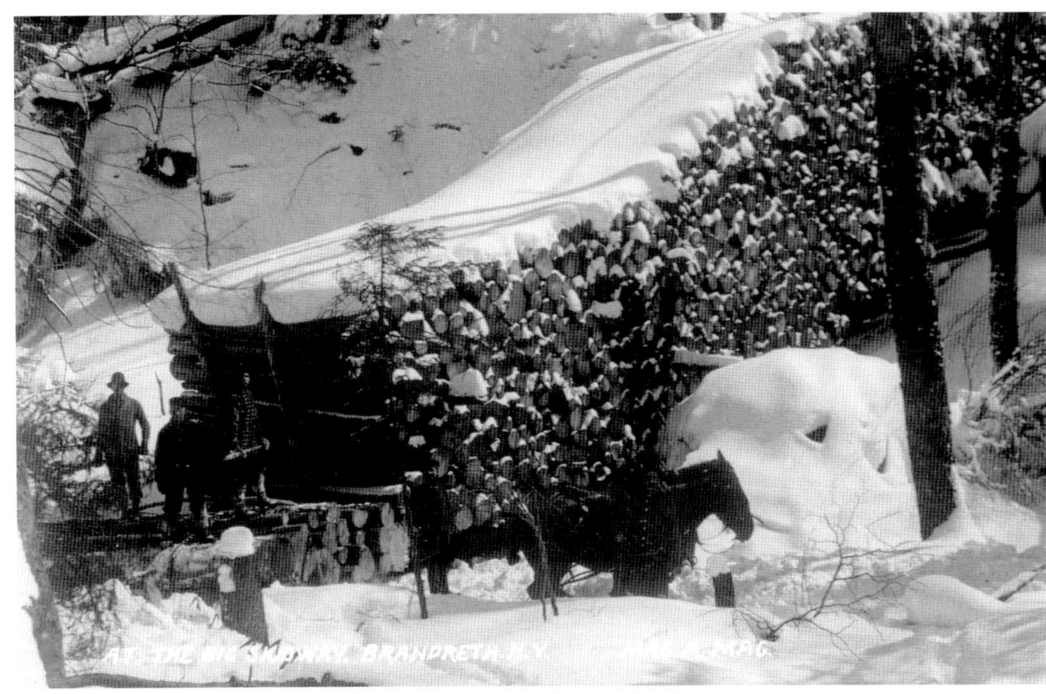


9.9. A large skidway, Brandreth, N.Y., ca. 1916. Courtesy of the Adirondack Museum.

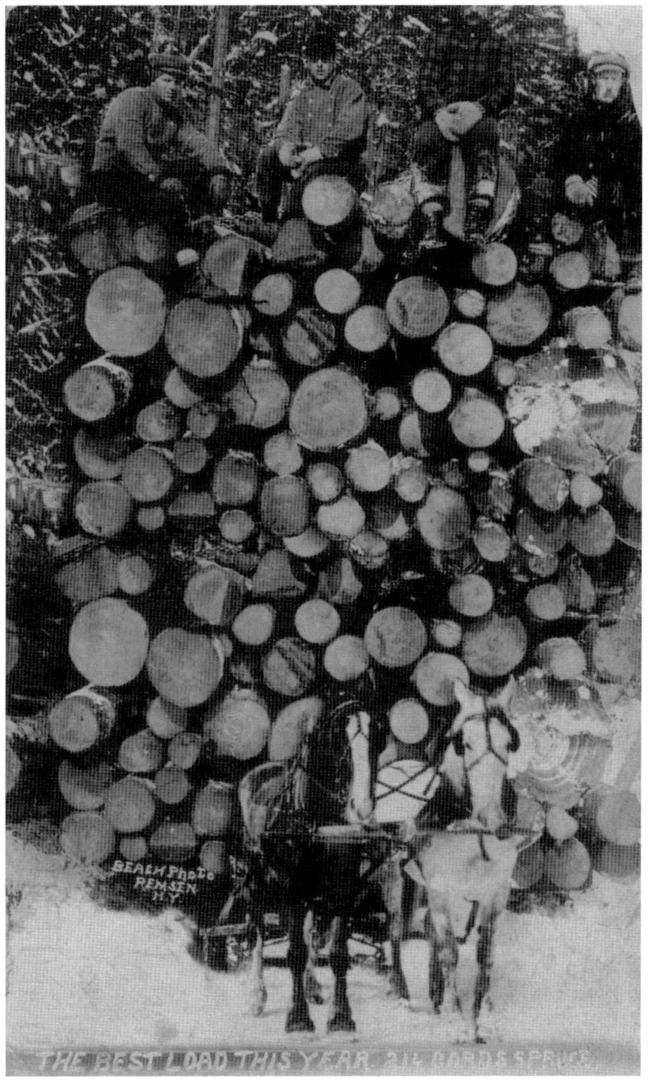


9.10. "The Best Load This Year," ca. 1914. Spring Coll.

Beach's classic, dramatic head-on shots of teamsters atop heavy loads were routine compositions.

The next step for the teamster was to pilot the heavy sleigh along the long, icy run to the banking grounds, or flow ground, where the load was dumped (illus. 9.11). "Banking grounds" refers to the areas on or beside frozen waterways where logs were stored. The logs stayed there until the spring melt provided enough water to fill the lakes, ponds, and rivers and propel the logs downstream to the mills by means of the legendary river drives (illus. 9.12).

## Mechanized Logging

By the time Beach entered the most productive phase of his career, successful logging companies had expanded their operations and had built, or were in the process of building, railroad extensions (spurs) in places where the timber was cut (illus. 9.13). Although river drives did not end until 1950, they were gradually replaced by mechanical means of transporting logs (Welsh 1995, 16). Increased mechanization led to a qualitatively different timber harvest than Beach photographed earlier in his career. Fewer men were needed in the woods. As the industry became more competitive, volume, efficiency, and cost saving resulted in fewer independent loggers and more tied directly to large companies and motorized equipment. The mechanization first took the form of steam-powered log loaders that accompanied the flatbed railroad cars (illus. 9.14).

There were other labor-saving innovations tied to the railroad. "Jackworks" were locations on railroad lines where flatbed cars were loaded using conveyor-belt ramps (McMartin 1994, 36) (illus. 9.15).

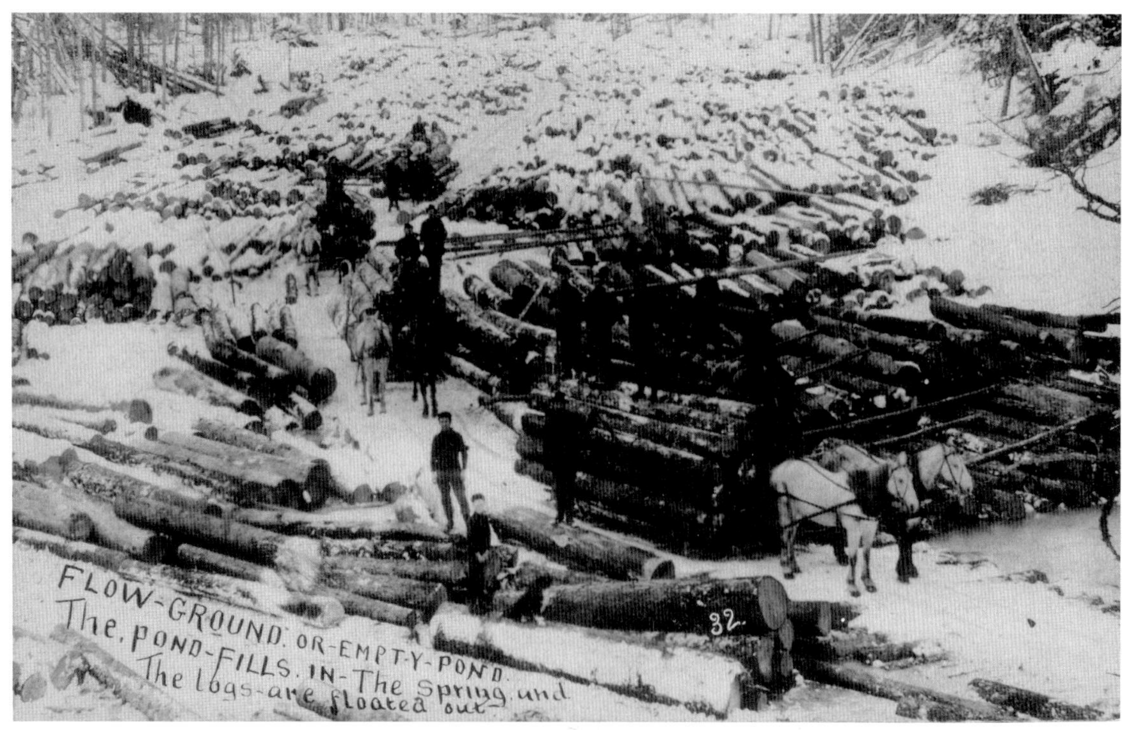


9.11. Flow ground or empty pond, ca. 1908. The pond fills in spring, and the logs float out. Getman Coll.

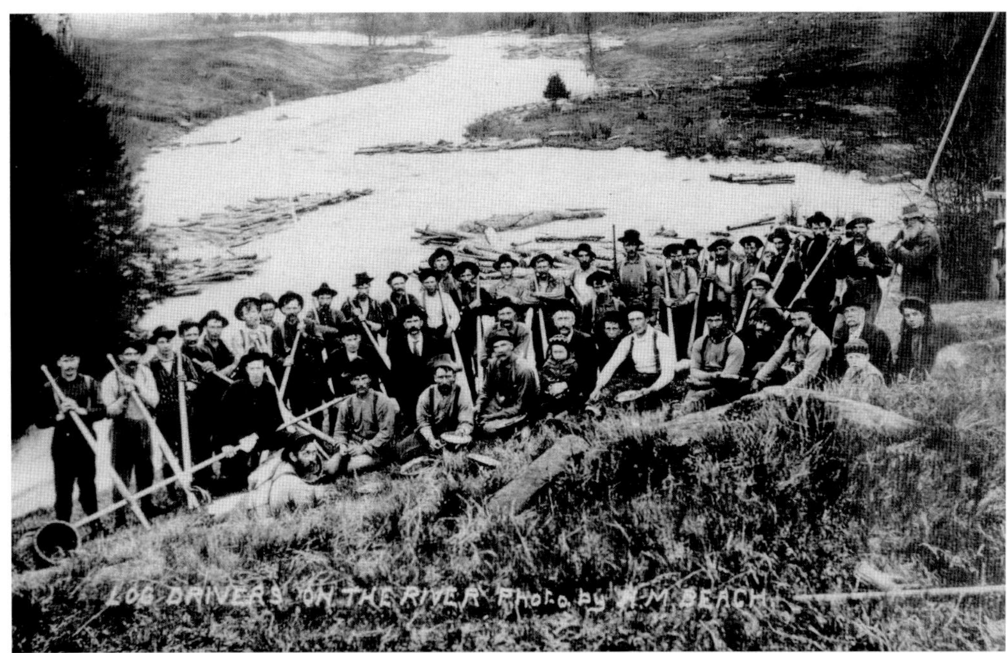


9.12. Log drivers on the river, ca. 1908.
Courtesy of the Adirondack Museum.

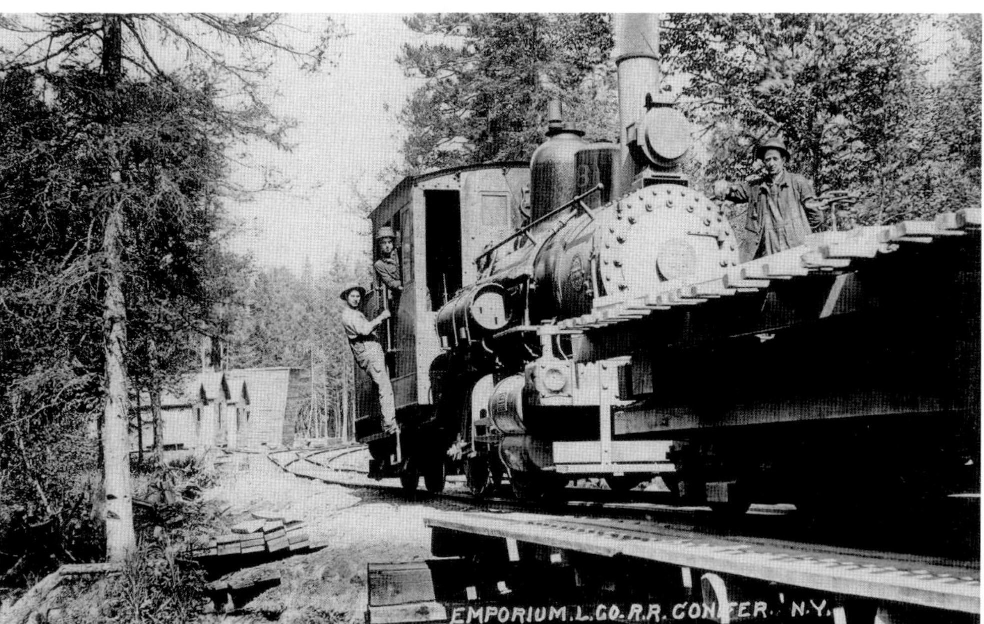


9.13. Emporium Lumber Company Railroad,
Conifer, N.Y., ca. 1917. E. Pierce Coll.

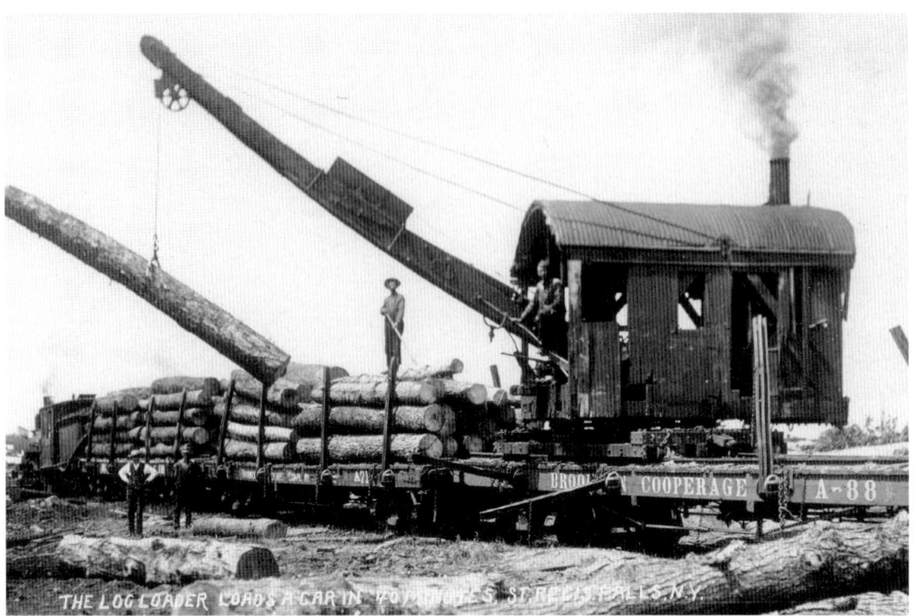


9.14. "The Log Loader Loads a Car in 40 Minutes," St. Regis Falls, N.Y., ca. 1915. Courtesy of the Adirondack Museum.

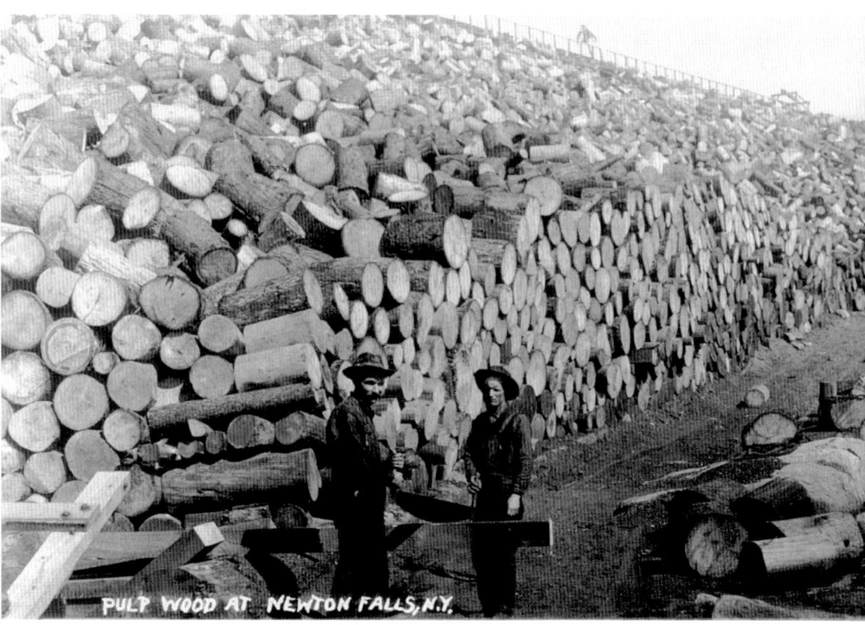


9.16. Pulpwood at Newton Falls, N.Y., ca. 1914. Davis Coll.

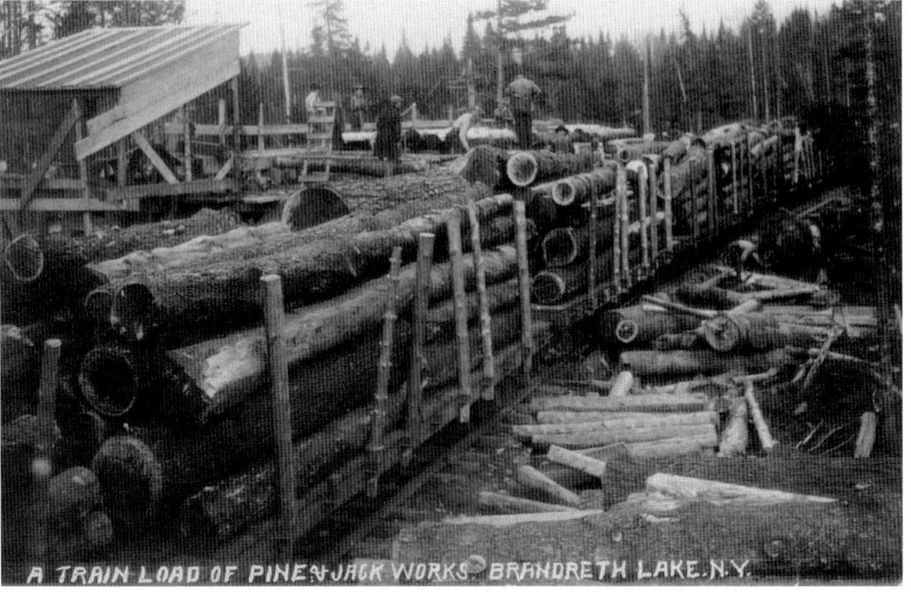


9.15. A trainload of pine and jackworks, Brandreth Lake, N.Y., ca. 1920. Myers Coll.

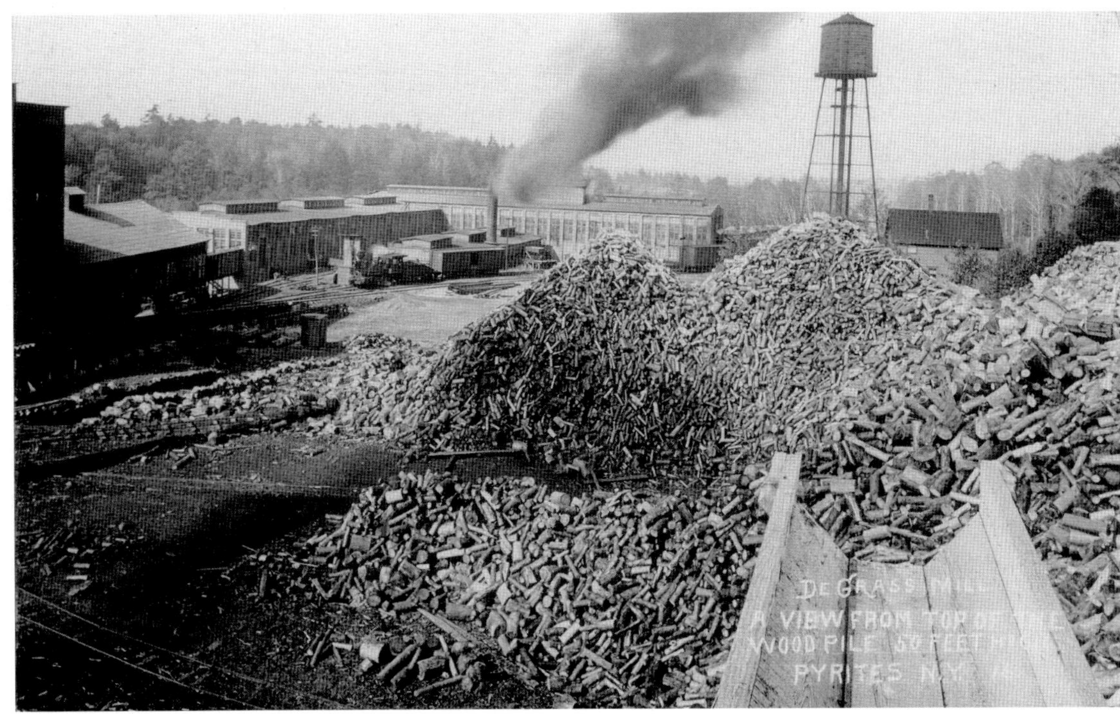


9.17. Degrasse Mill, Pyrites, N.Y., ca. 1920. A view from the top of the wood pile, fifty feet high. Rollins Coll.

## Paper Mills and Sawmills

The pulpwood and timber were delivered by river drive, railroad, and, later, truck to wood-product mills (illus. 9.16). In what is now the Adirondack Park, places such as Pyrites, Piercefield, Conifer, Newton Falls, McKeever, St. Regis Falls, and Childwold all had wood-processing plants. So did towns around the park's periphery, including Lyons Falls, Beaver Falls, Carthage, Newcomb, Norwood, and Norfolk.[7] Although mills differed in size, operation, and what they produced, they all provided employment for local people. They also belched polluting exhaust and in other ways were an ugly blight on the environment.

Beach produced postcards of every mill in his territory, at different angles and from different distances. Although they were not major items on his sales list, he did produce some industrial-mill panoramics as well. He probably never thought of his mill landscapes as social criticism or as conservationist commentary on the excesses of industry, but today his images are powerful reminders of the hazards of unregulated commercial development.

The contents of Beach's paper-mill pictures are all similar: mountains of pulpwood accompanied by iconic smokestacks spewing heavy black fumes. Illustrations 9.17 and 9.18 are of the mills at Pyrites and at Newton Falls. With Henry's photos as step-by-step illustrations, you could trace the processing of the pulpwood from its arrival at the plant to its shipment as paper products.

The pure bulk of the tonnage arriving at the plant is astonishing. The logs were moved by the conveyer system to chippers and other machines that mechanically reduced the wood to small pieces (illus. 9.19). Changing wood into slushy liquid pulp was the next step in paper making. Aided by mechanical

7. Not all these locations had paper mills. There were other types of wood-process industries besides paper mills.

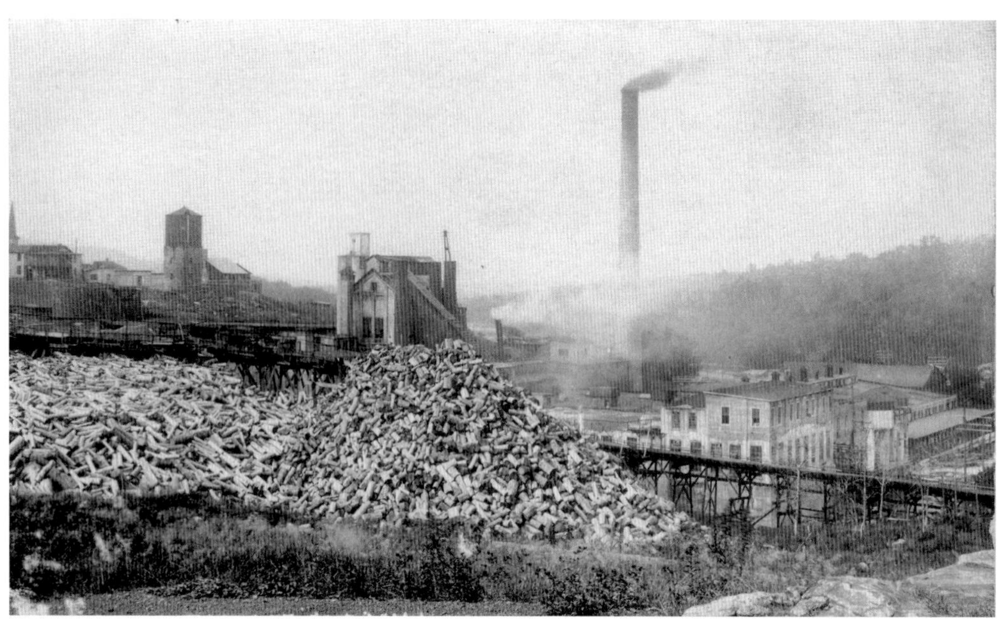

9.18. Pulpwood and mill, Newton Falls, N.Y., ca. 1920. Courtesy of the Adirondack Museum.

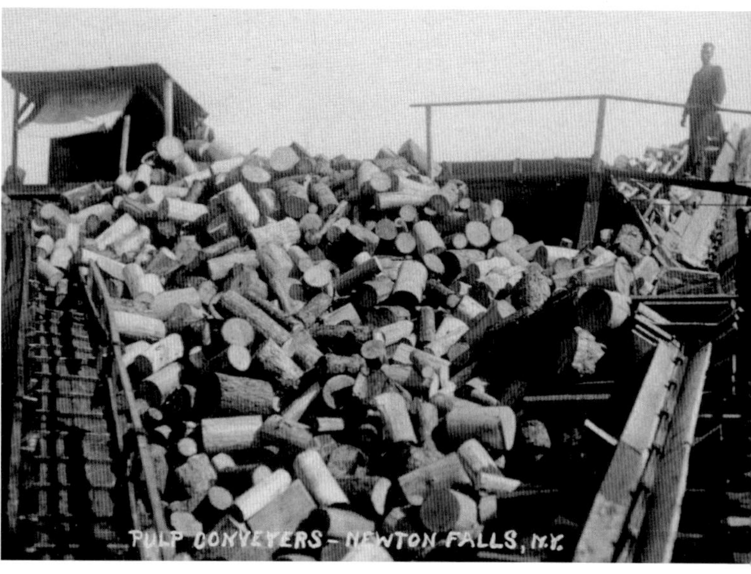


9.19. Pulp conveyers moving wood into mill, Newton Falls, N.Y., ca. 1920. Courtesy of the Adirondack Museum.

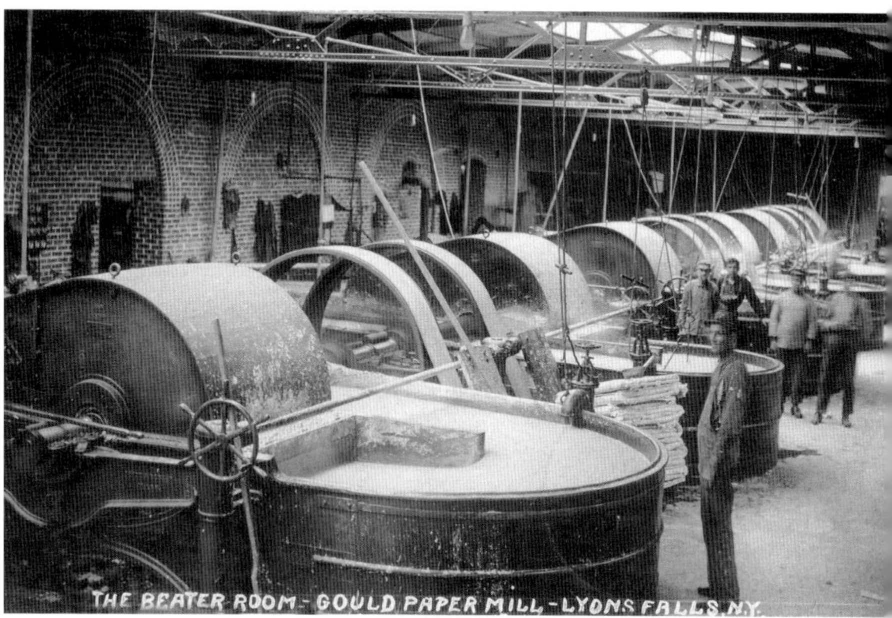


9.20. The beater room, Gould Paper Mill, Lyons Falls, N.Y., ca. 1910. Author's Coll.

agitators, the wood fibers were dislodged in chemical baths. A "beater" was a large tub equipped with moving bars that rubbed and pressed the washed cellulose fibers, creating clean slurry (illus. 9.20).

To make paper from slurry, the cellulose fibers that were suspended in the water were deposited on screens to start the drying process (illus. 9.21). The mass passed over suction boxes that drained out most of the water. It was then squeezed between press rolls and passed over a number of steam-heated dryer cylinders. The paper then passed through a processor that produced a smooth surface. Finally, the sheets were wound into large rolls. The final step in the paper production process was the finishing room where paper was cut and wrapped for shipping (illus. 9.22).

All paper-mill machines were not as large as the ones at Pyrites and Norfolk, however. Mills such as the one at McKeever were smaller and their final products of lesser proportions (illus. 9.23).

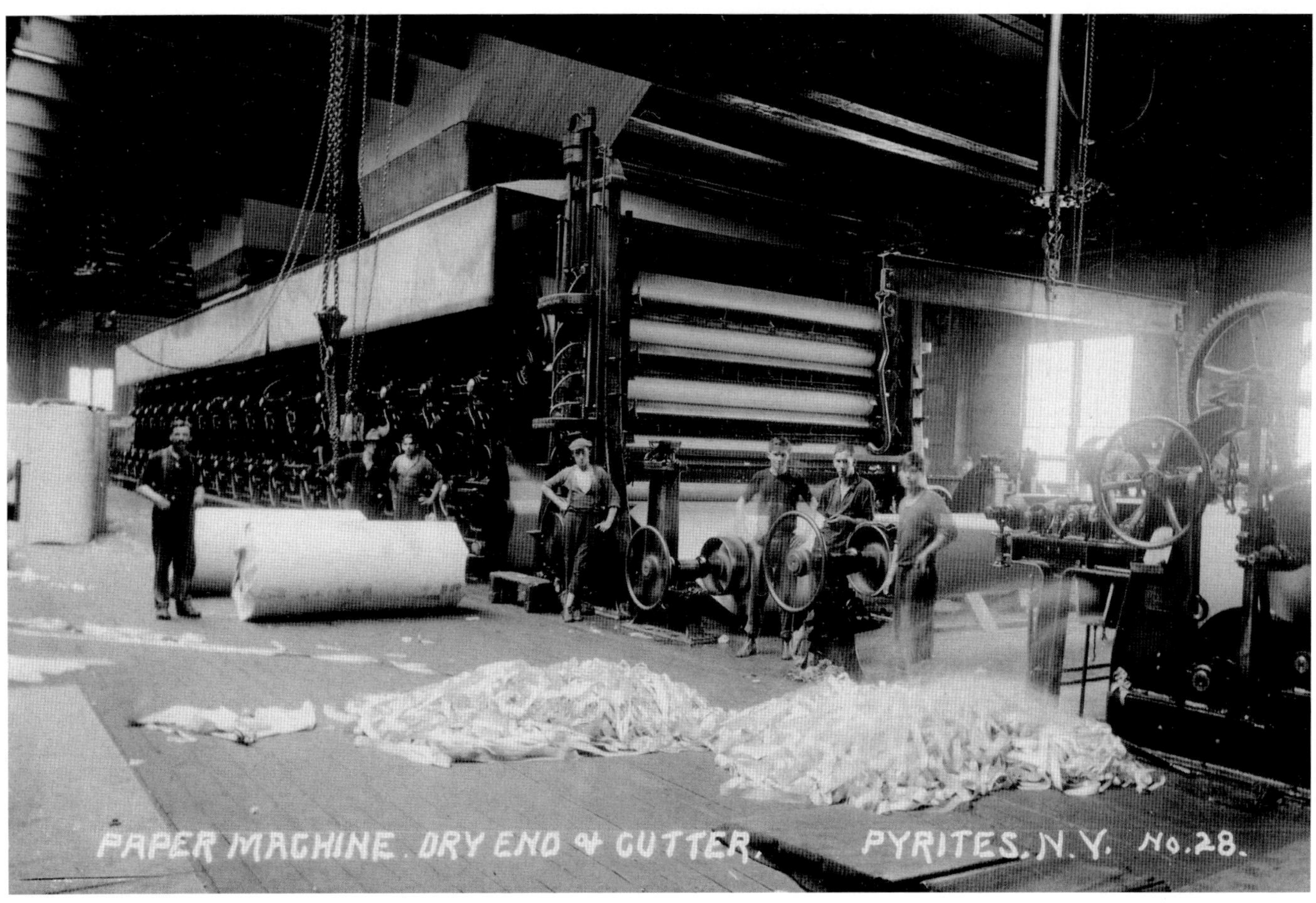


9.21. Paper machine, dry end and cutter, Pyrites, N.Y., ca. 1914. Courtesy of the Adirondack Museum.

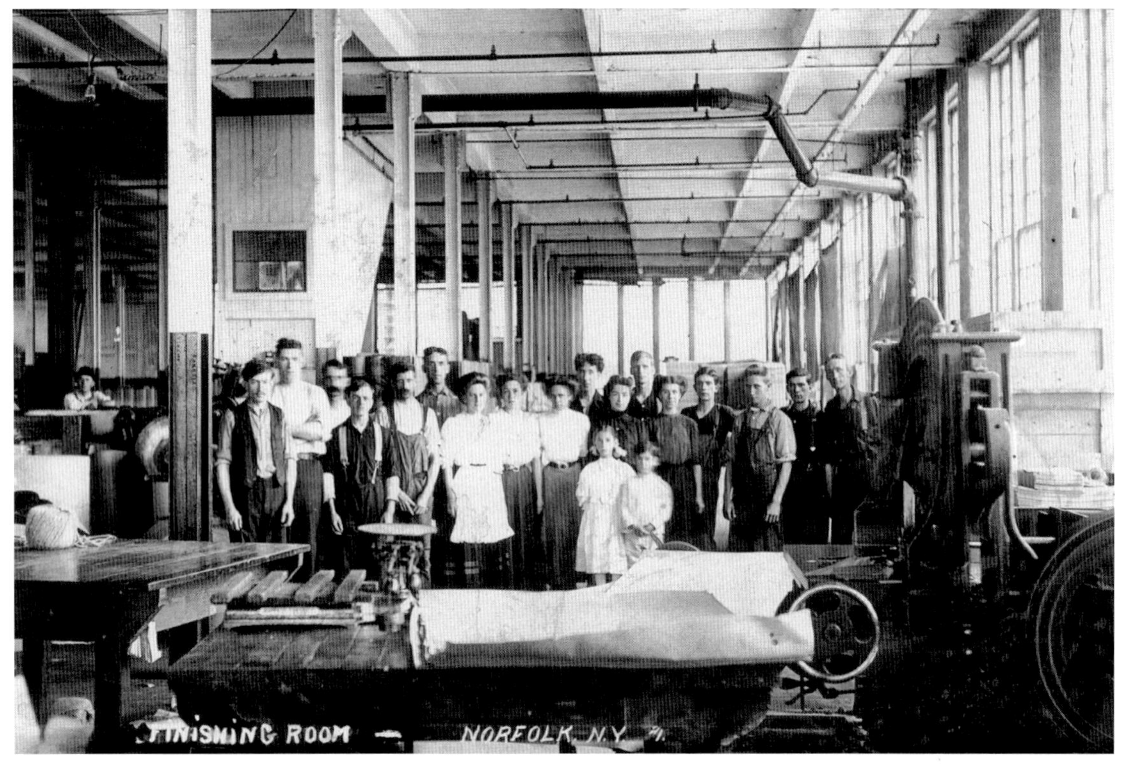


9.22. Finishing room, Norfolk, N.Y., ca. 1914. Author's Coll.

The views Beach took of the interiors of mills did not sell very well. Some document child labor and the hazardous work environments, but those elements probably did not impede sales. Such conditions were taken for granted as part of North Country life. Although locals bought them, the pictures just were not the cheery presentations of life in the great outdoors that tourists wanted. Henry seemed to be engrossed with the subject matter, though. Perhaps he was lured by the power of machinery or the mills' mechanical intricacies, or maybe it was just that mills were so central to Adirondackers' lives (illus. 9.24).

## Mill Towns

Some companies built their mills in isolated areas and erected towns around them. In some large population centers the mill was not the only employer, but in the rural settings the plant dominated every aspect of life. Beach made a series of pictures of these population centers. One mill town he photographed extensively was Piercefield (Fowler 1968; Hyde 1974) (illus. 9.25).

Prior to the 1890s Piercefield was a backwoods haunt for hunters and anglers, a few miles east of Tupper Lake. Its industrial development started slowly. At

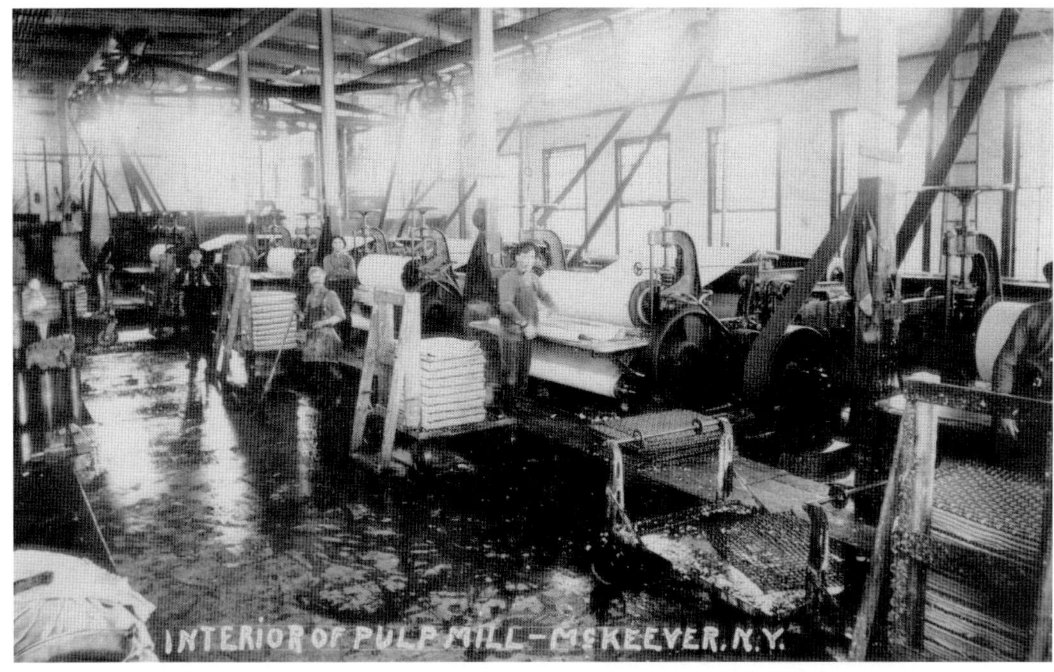


9.23. Interior of a pulp mill, McKeever, N.Y., ca. 1920. Courtesy of the Adirondack Museum.

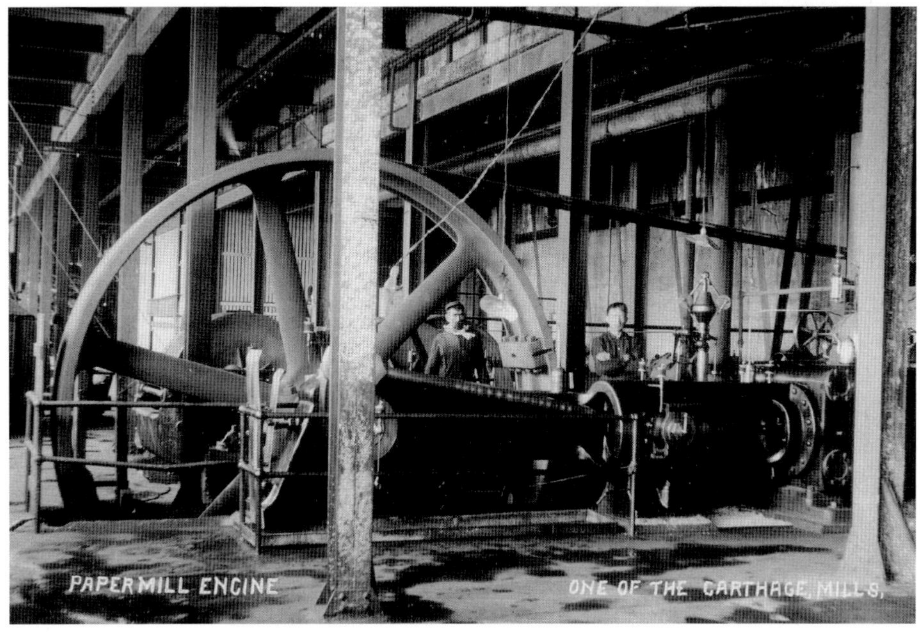


9.24. Paper mill engine, Carthage, N.Y., ca. 1908. Courtesy of the Adirondack Museum.

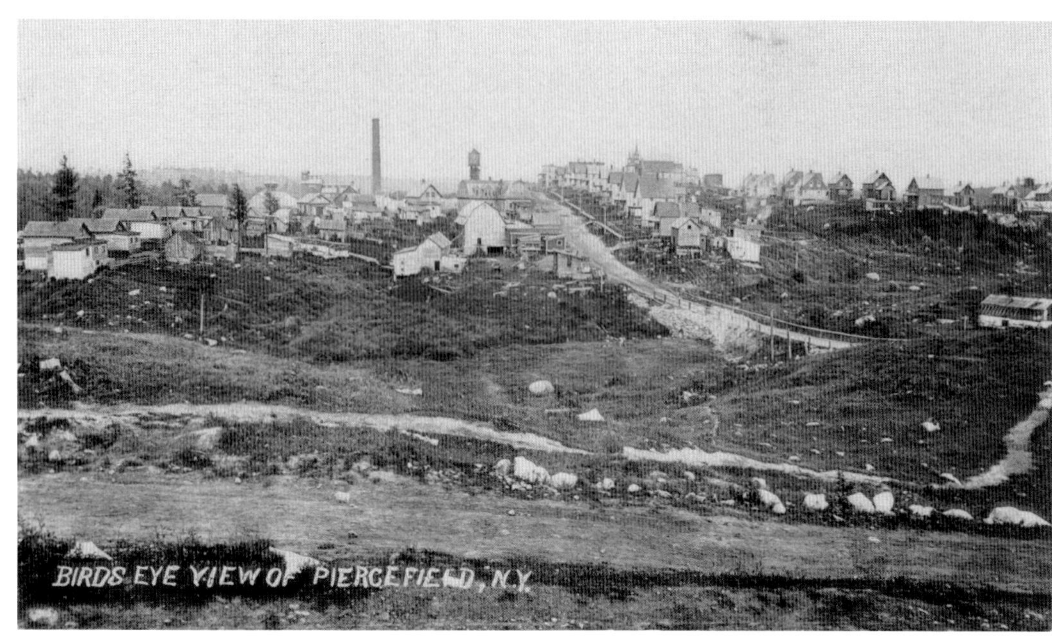


9.25. Bird's-eye view, Piercefield, N.Y., ca. 1909. Rollins Coll.

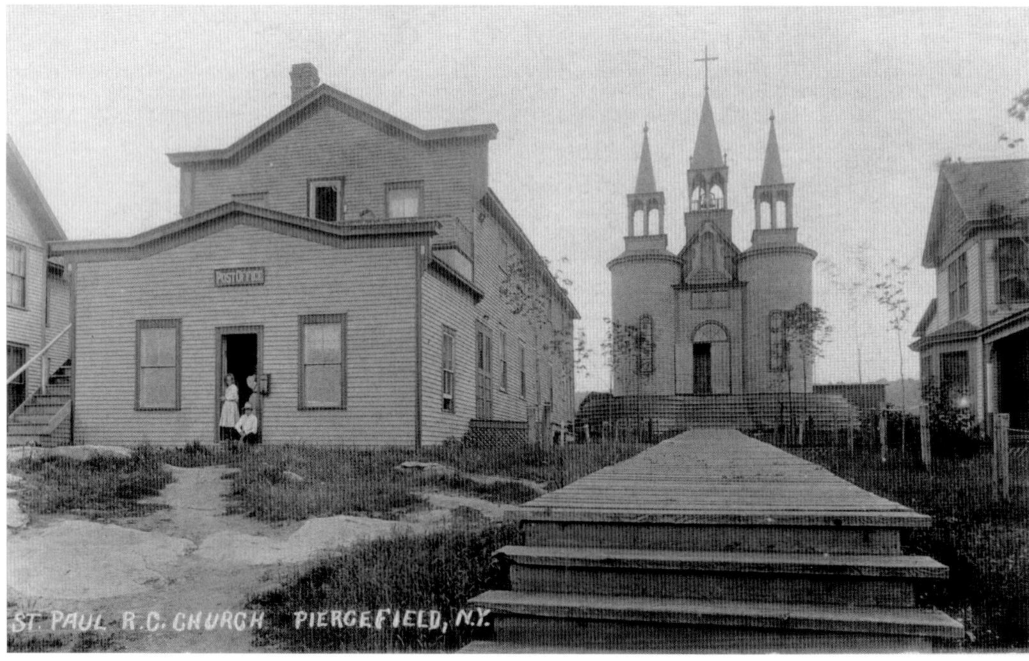


9.26. St. Paul's Catholic Church, Piercefield, N.Y., ca. 1908. Rollins Coll.

first it was a small locally owned mill called the Piercefield Paper and Manufacturing Company with a few houses around it. After the turn of the century when it was bought and expanded by International Paper, it became one of the largest consumers of pulpwood in New York State. The town itself grew quickly from a few families to a population of one thousand with two churches, a school, a large hotel, and rows of company-supplied housing. The mill closed in 1933.

Logging operations started near the mill but drifted outward, creating barren areas of clear-cut in what was once a sea of green. In Beach's bird's-eye view of Piercefield we see what resembles a bombed-out war zone more than a community in the wilderness. The smokestack and the water tower on the left of Main Street and the church spire on the right are the triple towers that appear against the sky. The upper terrace to the right is the workers' housing.

If you feel that Beach's portrait leaves a bad impression of Piercefield, bleak and foreboding, look at some of the views he took of the town itself. They are dreary and barren, almost Gothic renderings. His view of St. Paul's Roman Catholic Church taken from Main Street gives the feel of a scene from an early Frankenstein movie (illus. 9.26). The church is a characteristic example of nineteenth-century Quebec vernacular-style architecture and reflects the presence of a large number of French Canadian families in town. The building on the left, the one with the two girls in the doorway, is the company store and post office. The dominating wooden walkway leads your eye up the barren hill to the church against the sky. The second scene of the town of Piercefield looks down Main Street, an empty dirt road (illus. 9.27).

Another paper-mill town that Henry photographed was Newton Falls (Hyde

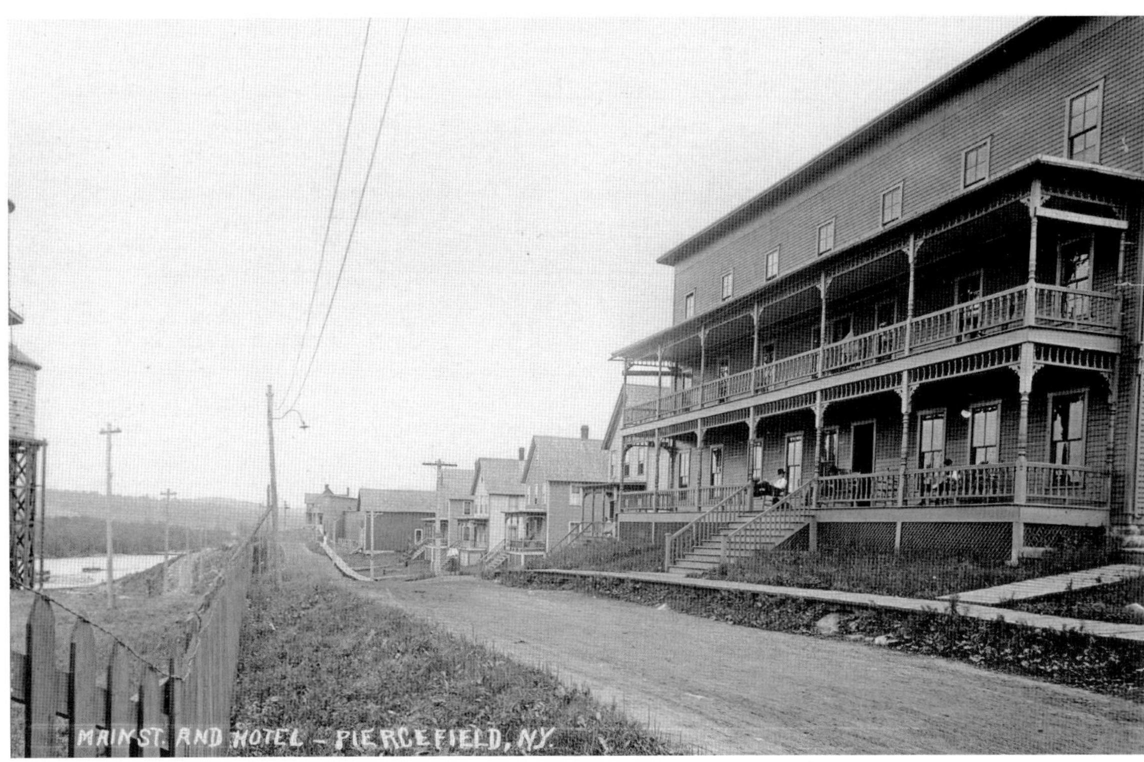


9.27. Main Street and hotel, Piercefield, N.Y., ca. 1914. Rollins Coll.

1974; Fowler 1968) (illus. 9.28). Although Newton Falls never reached the size of Piercefield, the pattern of industrialization was the same. Before the mill was built, the land was hidden deeply in the woods. In 1894 locals established a small low-tech mill. Taken over by International Paper after the turn of the century, Newton Falls quickly evolved into a mill town with company housing, a company store, and hundreds of mill workers and their families. In the days that Beach photographed the mill they produced paper for paper bags, butcher wrap, light cardboard, and, coincidentally, printed postcards.

It is futile to try to guess what Beach was thinking and what, if anything, he hoped to accomplish in taking any particular picture. We are too far from him, his surroundings, and his mentality to know, for example, whether he was critical of the large companies that came to dominate the Adirondack economy and alter its landscape. This remark having been made, in the picture of Newton Falls from a distance he seems to be calling out to the viewer to acknowledge the rape of this land.

It is difficult to believe that this bleak view with the tearlike squiggly drips descending from the letters in the caption is not at least a personal expression of critical commentary if not despair. The same is so of the next view taken from the depot (illus. 9.29). It shows the boardwalk stretching over barren ground in the direction of the row of company houses on the crest of the hill.

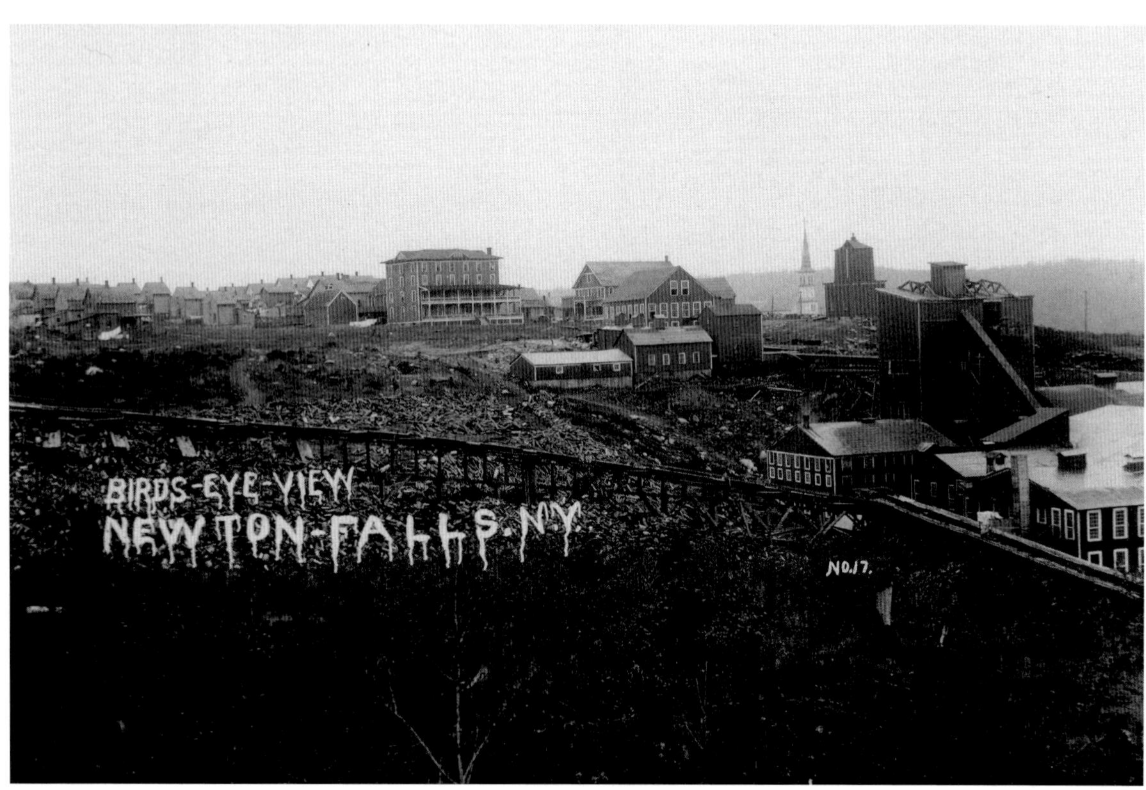


9.28. Bird's-eye view, Newton Falls, N.Y., ca. 1908. Rollins Coll.

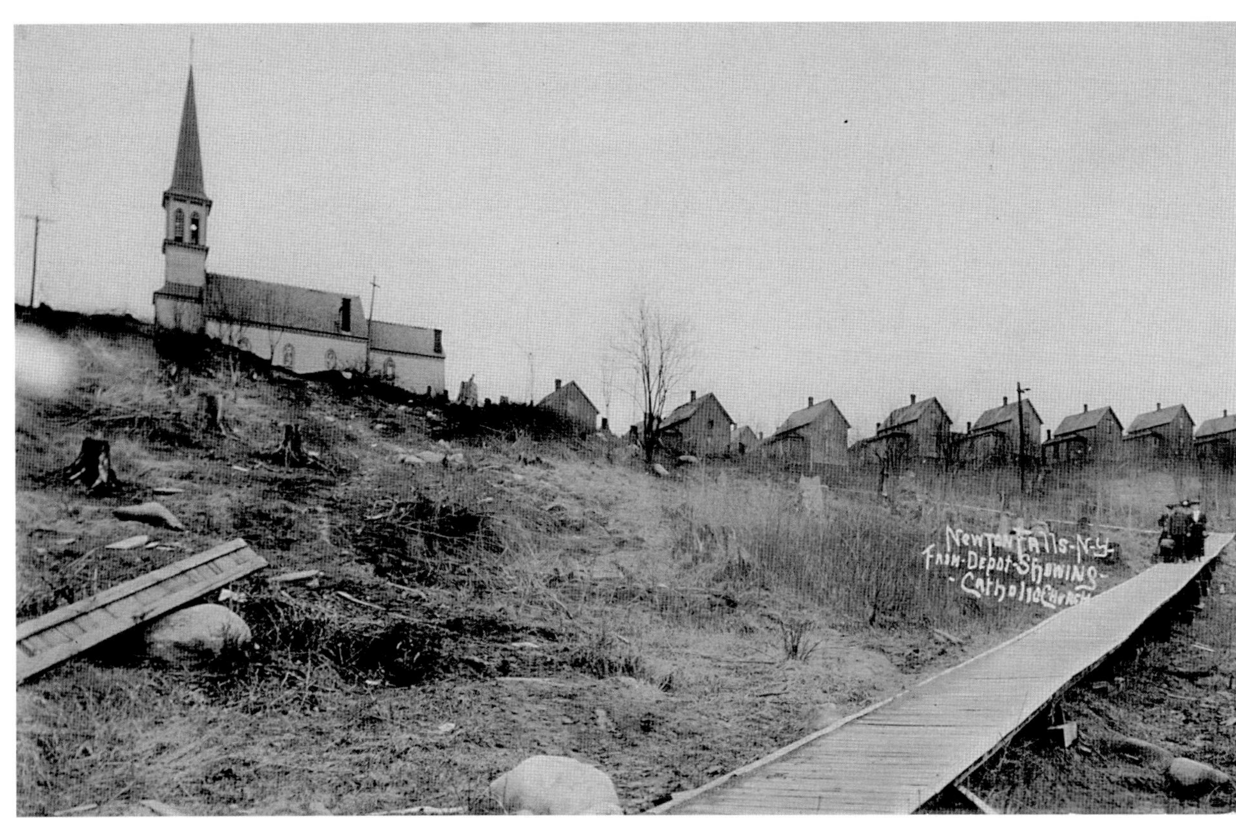


9.29. A view of Newton Falls, N.Y., from the depot, showing the boardwalk, ca. 1909. Rollins Coll.

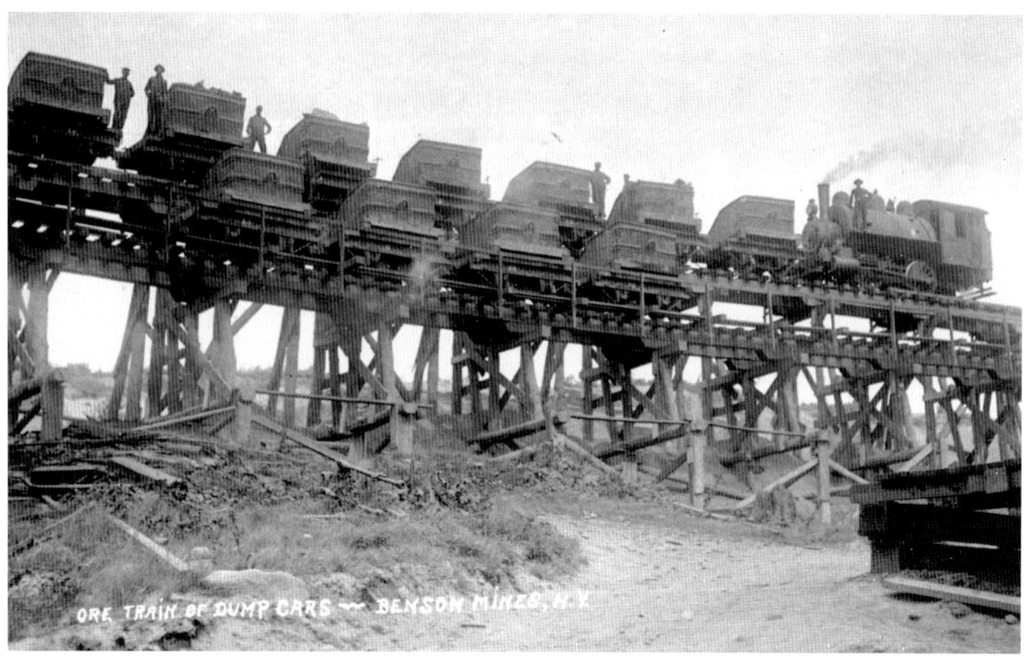


10.1. Ore train of dump cars, Benson Mines, N.Y., ca. 1909. Smeby Coll.

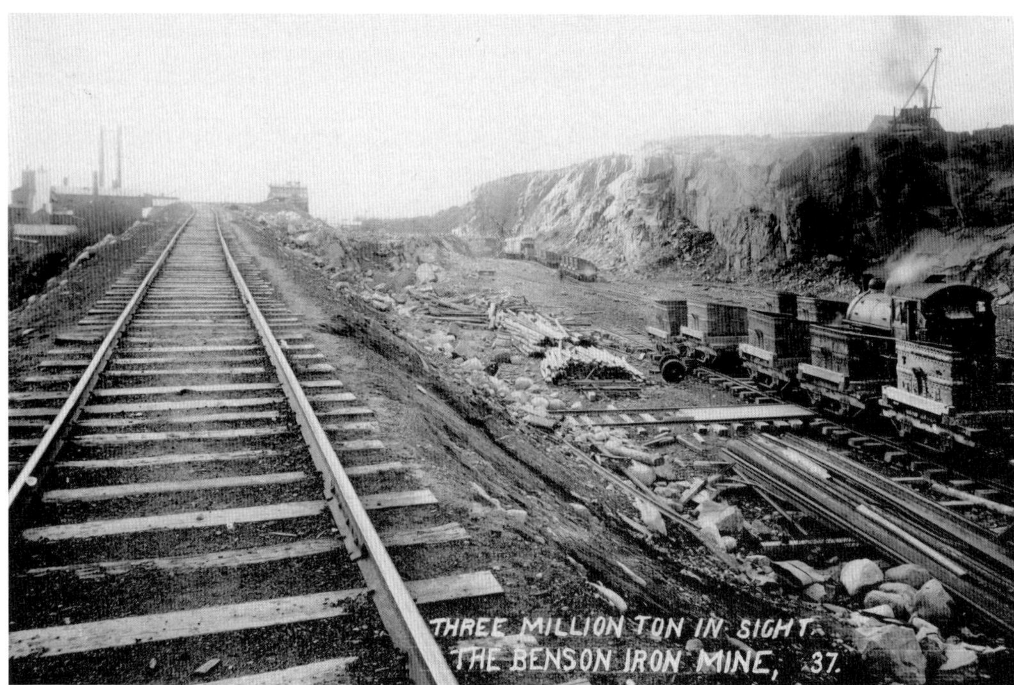


10.2. "Three Million Ton in Sight," Benson Mines, N.Y., ca. 1909. Courtesy of the Adirondack Museum.

10

# Benson Mines and Other Industrial Sites

Seven miles south of the mill at Newton Falls was Benson Mines, an industrial site of a sort different from the ones that processed trees (illus. 10.1). It handled the earth itself, iron ore. Beach visited Benson Mines many times and constructed an intriguing and powerful series of industrial photos. Although I will show you only a few of the ones he took, this chapter contains more photographs from a single location than any other does. I want to illustrate that if you take Beach's work from a particular site and look at it in context, as a series, it becomes a photo essay that provides a different visual experience than looking at photographs in isolation.

When Beach photographed Benson Mines in the early decades of the twentieth century, it was a large open-pit excavation with an adjacent processing plant. Although surveyors discovered the deposit in 1810 (Hyde 1974, 176), mining did not start until toward the end of that century.[1] In 1907 the Benson Mines Company bought the operation and expanded it with hopes of making it into a major producer. In the early years, the financial security of the company was precarious, but during World War I times were good.[2] In 1919 increased costs and declining demand resulted in its closure.

The mining process was simple but dangerous. Using an unwieldy steam drill, workers bored holes into the exposed surfaces of the deposit, packed them with explosives, and blasted large chunks from the earth's crust. Steam shovels loaded the hunks into "hoppers" (railroad cars designed to carry the ore) that brought them to powerful crushers, then massive machines separated the iron from the waste. Large kilns heated the concentrate into nodules that were then cooled and shipped by rail to steel manufacturing plants in Pennsylvania.

The assault on the earth's surface soon created a gaping black scar that was incongruent with the forest surrounding it. When Beach visited between 1908 and 1917, Benson Mines was a bustling but dirty and grim place, a company town loaded with heavy equipment, railroad facilities, and huge smelting machinery. The upper village was residential and included about twenty-five company-owned workers' homes, a school (see illustration 11.14), and two churches. The lower village had a large hotel, a department store, a railroad station, and a line of stores, dwellings, and saloons along the railroad tracks.[3]

## The Mining Process

Beach's pictures provide an overview of the mining operation, details about the work, and town views. Though he delivers straightforward documentation, some of his images are complex. We see this evidence in the photo postcard

1. The Magnetic Iron Company first successfully extracted ore in 1889. The railroad made industrialization at the turn of the century possible.

2. It closed afterward, at least until the start of World War II when it was taken over by Jones and Laughlin Steel Corporation and had a rebirth. The company enlarged the mine, taking over part of the village of Benson Mines. The school and other buildings were demolished. The Catholic church along with its rectory were moved to Star Lake. After a period of prosperity, the mine eventually closed in the 1970s (Linney 1943).

3. In its peak years Benson Mines had nine saloons that were infamous as a rollicking retreat for not only miners and plant workers, but lumberjacks and mill workers as well. Neighboring Wanakena was dry.

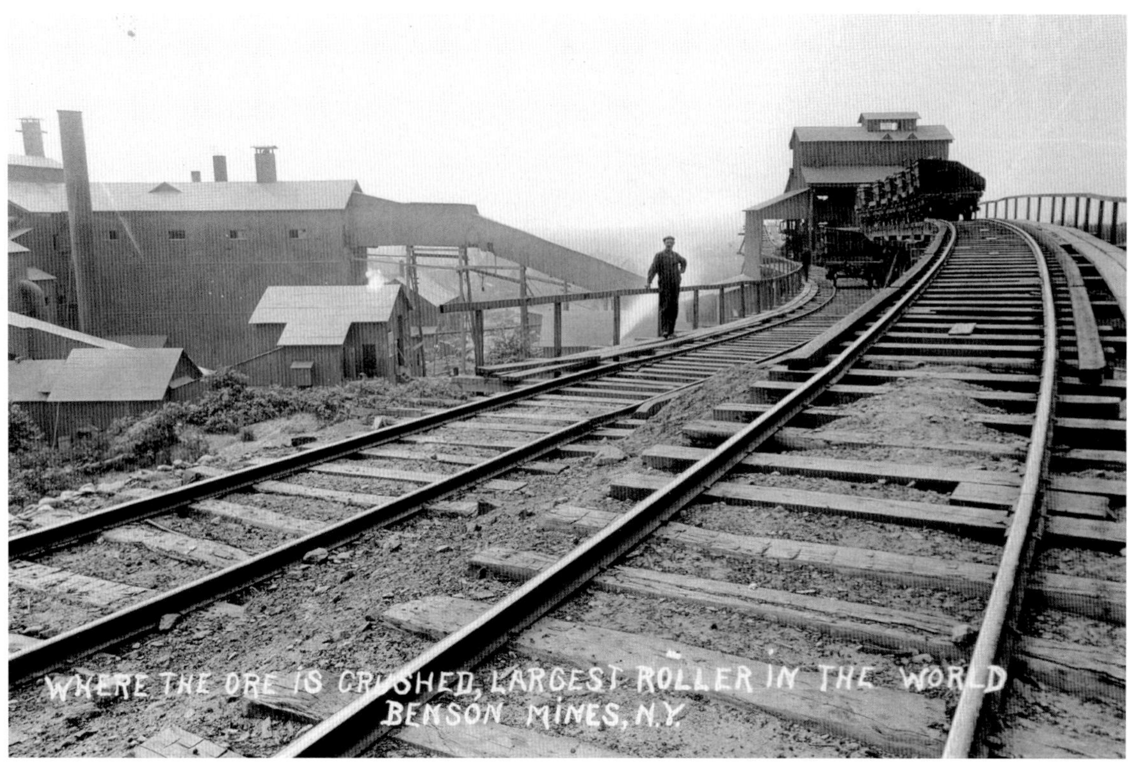


10.3. Largest roller in the world used to crush ore, Benson Mines, N.Y., ca. 1915. Rollins Coll.

titled "Three Million Ton in Sight" (illus. 10.2). The tracks dominate as they pull the viewer's eyes to the distant, misty processing plant in the background. The massive open-pit mine on the right competes for attention. The locomotive, hopper cars, tracks, and disorderly debris in the broad ditch that cuts across the center of the picture add unsettling confusion. The gray tones, barren content, and dearth of people communicate a forewarning of pending misfortune.

Illustration 10.3 is taken down the tracks, closer to the crushing plant. A lone man stands in the center. Idle, his hand on a railing, it is not clear why he is there or what he is doing. There is a sense of anticipation. He is prominent in the picture but diminutive compared to the massive elements that surround him.

In "Birds Eye View of the Mill" we get a broad take of the processing facility with the extended conveyor moving waste from the factory and dumping it on the mountain of residue (illus. 10.4). Although the industrial complex in the back dominates the picture, the disheveled children and the shack in the foreground remove us from it and provide a human touch in an otherwise bleak scene. The children create a tension as well as a yardstick to measure and appreciate the mammoth mound of waste.

Henry took pictures inside the buildings that we have seen thus far only from a distance. They reveal the mechanical secrets hiding within: massive kilns and processors. The juxtaposition of the worker in the background with the colossal machinery drives home the idea that we are dealing with a substantial industrial site (illus. 10.5).

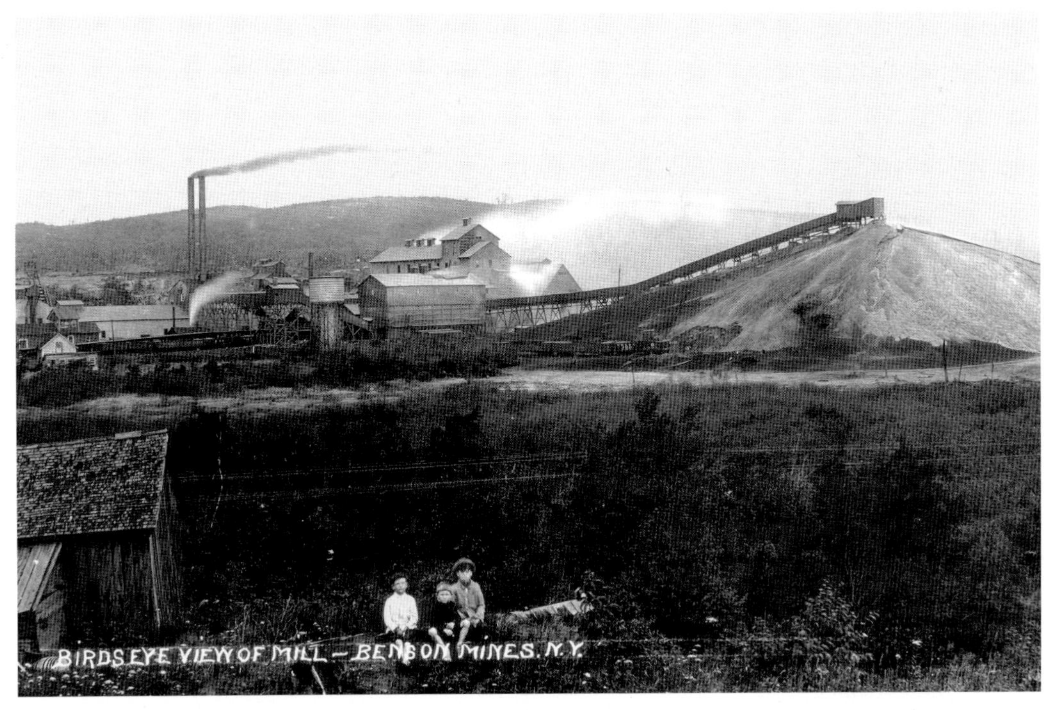


10.4. Bird's-eye view of the mill, Benson Mines, N.Y., ca. 1909. Courtesy of the Adirondack Museum.

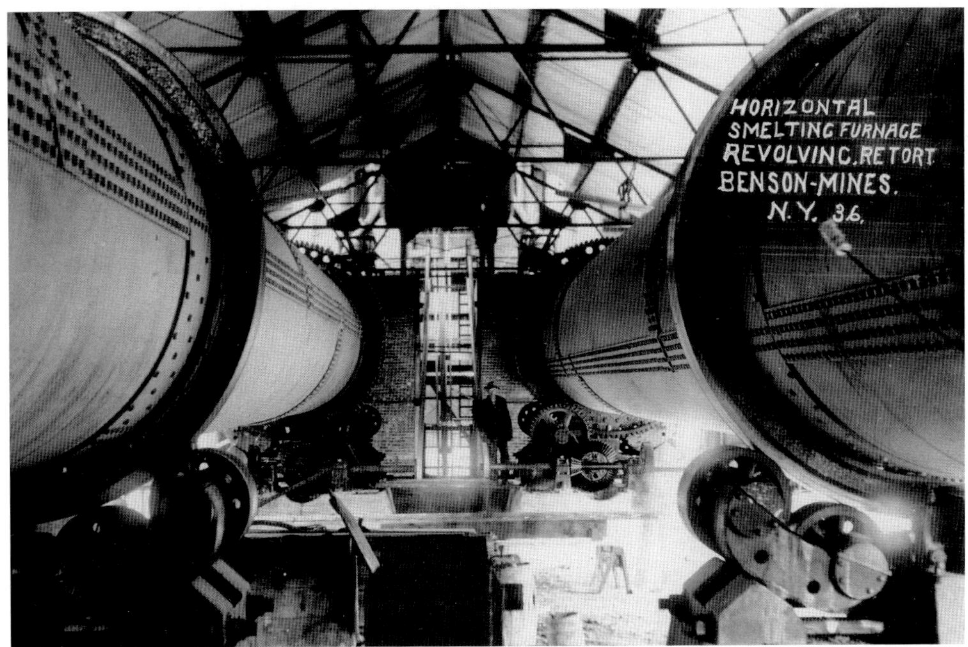


10.5. Horizontal smelting furnace with revolving retort, Benson Mines, N.Y., ca. 1914. Courtesy of the Adirondack Museum.

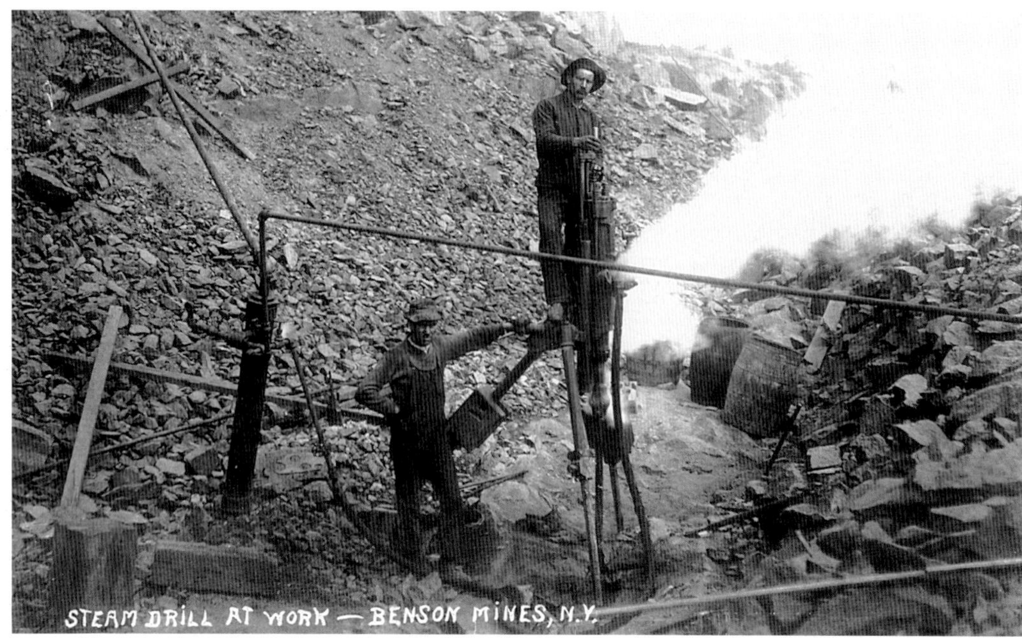


10.6. Steam drill, Benson Mines, N.Y., ca. 1911. H. Slusarczyk Coll

In illustration 10.6 we are again outside, this time up close to the actual labor done in the pit. Two workers, covered with sweat and dirt, operate the steam drill, prepping for blasting. Looking at their faces we are drawn to ask: "What was it like working and living in this isolated Adirondack mining town in the early decades of the twentieth century?" Beach's pictures and a few accounts left by the town's inhabitants and visitors are all that exist to help us answer the question. At times, combining written stories with a series of Beach's photos provides us an in-depth experience unavailable with one medium alone or with scattered views. This circumstance is the case with what happened on August 15, 1908.

## Tragedy

On August 15, 1908, just before noon, a small crew of men, mainly Catholics of French Canadian origin, were filling their drilled holes with powder. A premature explosion literally blew four of them to pieces, scattering their body parts over a radius of a hundred feet. When the wives and children of the dead men heard the news, they were overwhelmed with grief, screaming and sobbing. Their expressions of suffering fanned the anxiety and frustration of the entire community. Exaggerated rumors about the number of victims added to the confusion and volatility. Though conflicting reports exist about how precarious the situation was, some reported that the company officials feared riots (Fowler 1968, 54).

A young priest, Father Bergeron, who had recently been called as cleric of the new Benson Mines Catholic church, St. Hubert's, went from home to home, consoling the distraught.[4] The remains of the dead were taken to the parish house where Father Bergeron watched over them. The next morning they were put in caskets and placed in a line down the center isle of the church. Approximately one thousand mourners came to the memorial service, a crowd that was much beyond the sanctuary's capacity. The overflow remained outside as Father Bergeron conducted the service (Reynolds and DeCrosse 1976).

Henry Beach photographed Benson Mines around the time of the accident and produced a number of photo postcards of St. Hubert's (Reynolds and

4. St. Hubert is the patron saint of hunters.

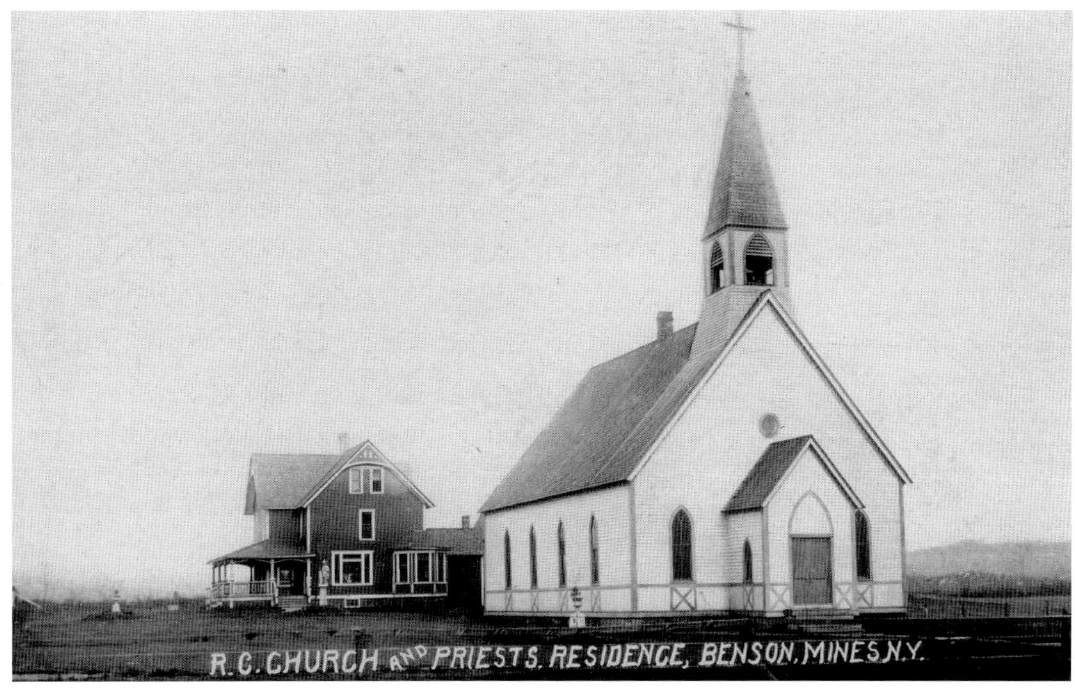


10.7. Catholic church and priest's residence, Benson Mines, N.Y., ca. 1909. Note the urns and religious statues on the lawn. Holstein Coll.

DeCrosse 1976, 17). The first is of the church and the parsonage, where the bodies were kept on the night of the accident (illus. 10.7). The solemn composition is fitting for the subject and the story and is typical of Beach's architectural photography. The other two photographs are taken inside the church. In one, Henry shot the sanctuary from the rear, producing an expansive interior view (illus. 10.8). The window at the left sprays soft light across the altar, creating a feeling of sacred space. Examining the photo more carefully you can see Father Bergeron, dressed in white robes, standing near a life-size statue of Christ on the cross. The lighting on the objects up front draws you past the large metal stovepipe running vertically through the picture. In the second picture Beach moved to the right of the crucifixion to take a close-up photograph of Father Bergeron at the altar (illus. 10.9). The hand of the statue of Christ is barely visible. There is a disturbing, sad, intense feeling on the face of Father Bergeron, the young man who played such a significant role in the town's tragedy (Fowler 1968, 55).

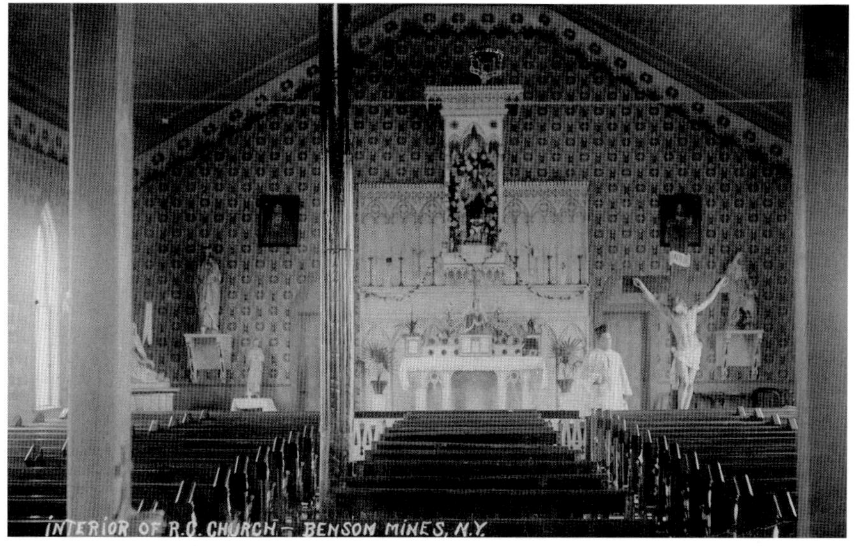


10.8. Interior of Catholic church, Benson Mines, N.Y., ca. 1908. Author's Coll.

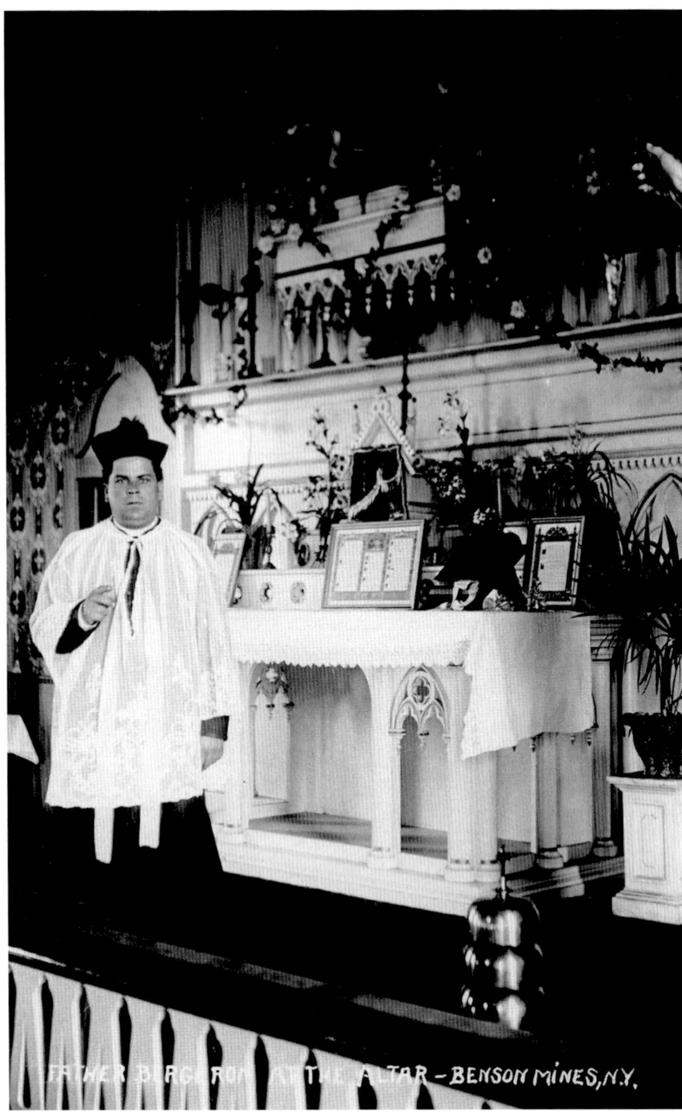


10.9. Father Bergeron at the altar, Benson Mines, N.Y., ca. 1908. Courtesy of the Adirondack Museum.

## Other Industrial Photographs

Henry's Benson Mines photographs are his most extensive coverage of an industrial site outside the wood-processing plants. But Beach photographed people working in other factories in other parts of the Adirondack region. The knitting mill at Port Leyden was a place he visited and photographed throughout his life. The two illustrations of the interior of that facility are taken in about 1906 and in the mid-1920s (illus. 10.10, 10.11).

## Electricity and Dams

The rivers provided power to run the machines that produced the lumber, paper, cloth, and other products. In the nineteenth century the energy was mechanical: rushing water moved wheels that turned gears that made the machines work. By the new century the water was turning generators that produced electricity. The power plants contributed to the region's industrialization and made life more comfortable for the citizens in the surrounding towns (illus. 10.12).

Moving into the twentieth century, huge concrete dams were constructed to increase electric production and to serve other functions. They were needed to control flooding and to keep the Erie and Black River Canals filled during the summer. The dams and the new bodies of water they created significantly altered the landscape, communities, and ecosystems.

Beach arrived in Remsen in time to photograph the massive dam construction in the southern Adirondack region. Prior to his move, the Utica Electric Light and Power Company had built a dam and power plant on the West Canada Creek at Trenton Falls, not far from Remsen.[5] In 1901 it began supplying Utica with power. Expansion and renovations of these facilities occurred while Beach lived in the area.

5. The facility changed the historically significant Trenton Falls from an attractive resort community that had lured painters, writers, and other travelers to a power plant supplying electricity to the Mohawk Valley.

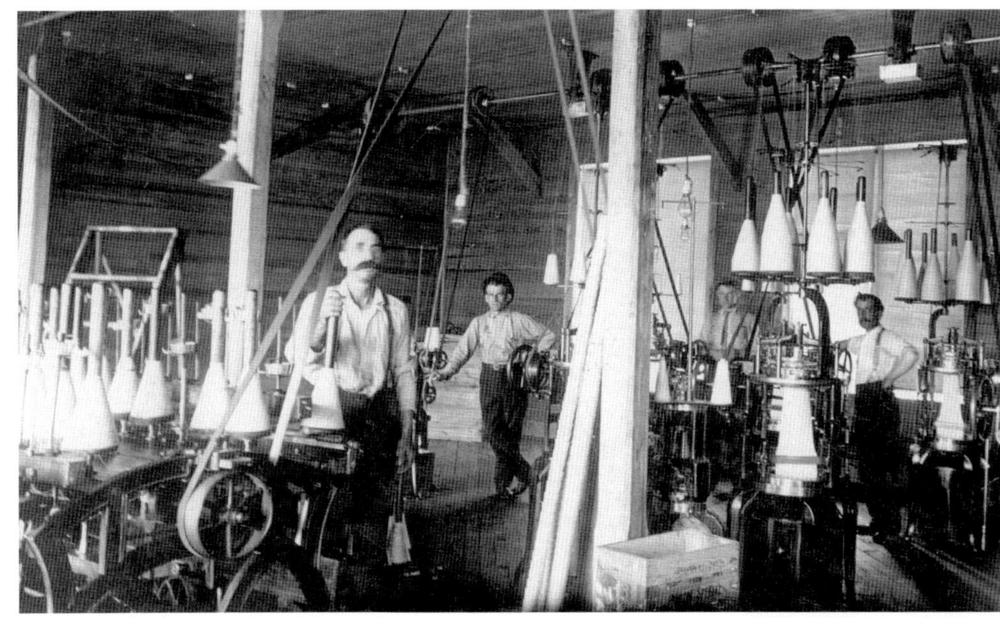

10.10. Inside Port Leyden knitting mill, Port Leyden, N.Y., ca. 1906. Author's Coll.

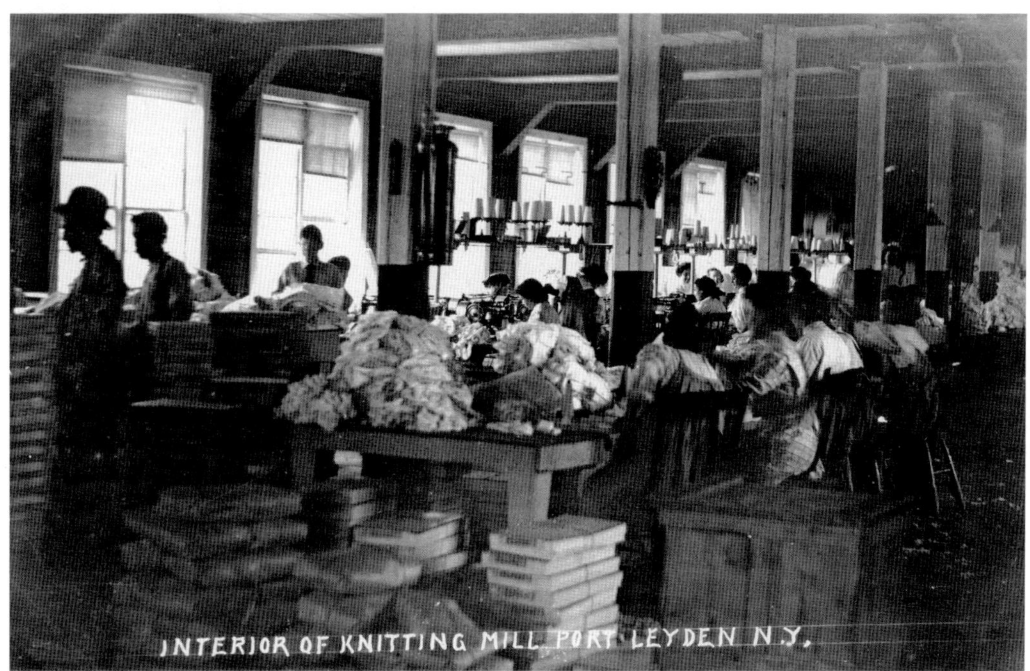


10.11. Inside the knitting mill, Port Leyden, N.Y., ca. 1926. Author's Coll.

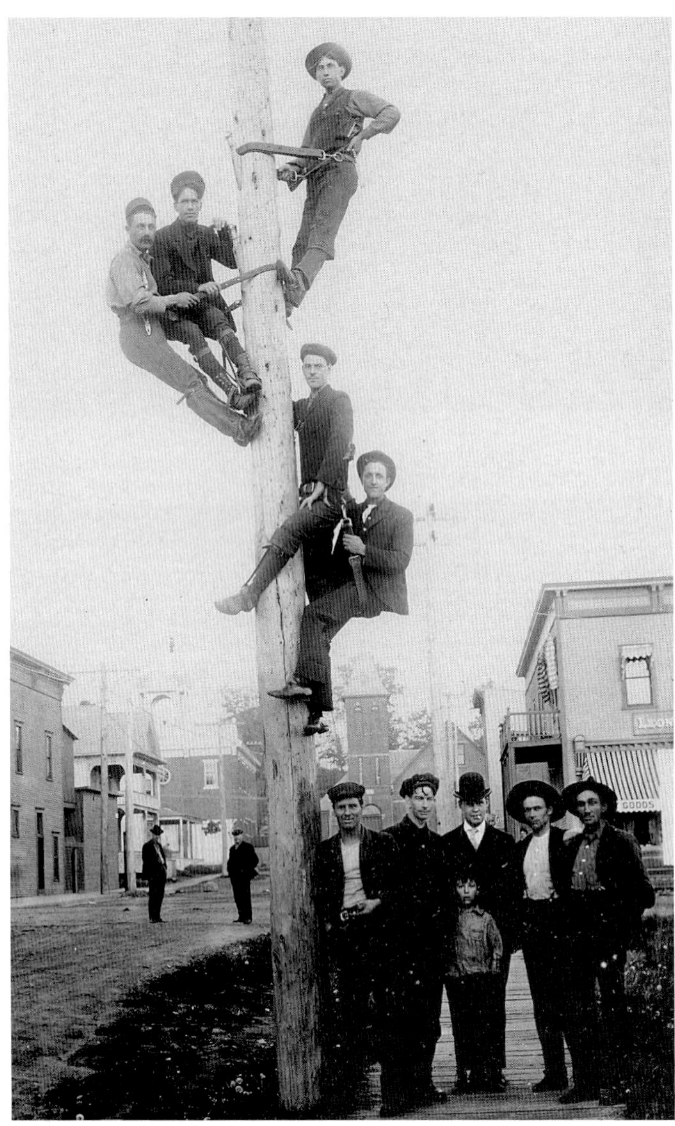

10.12. Installing the electrical lines, location unknown, ca. 1909. Courtesy of the Adirondack Museum.

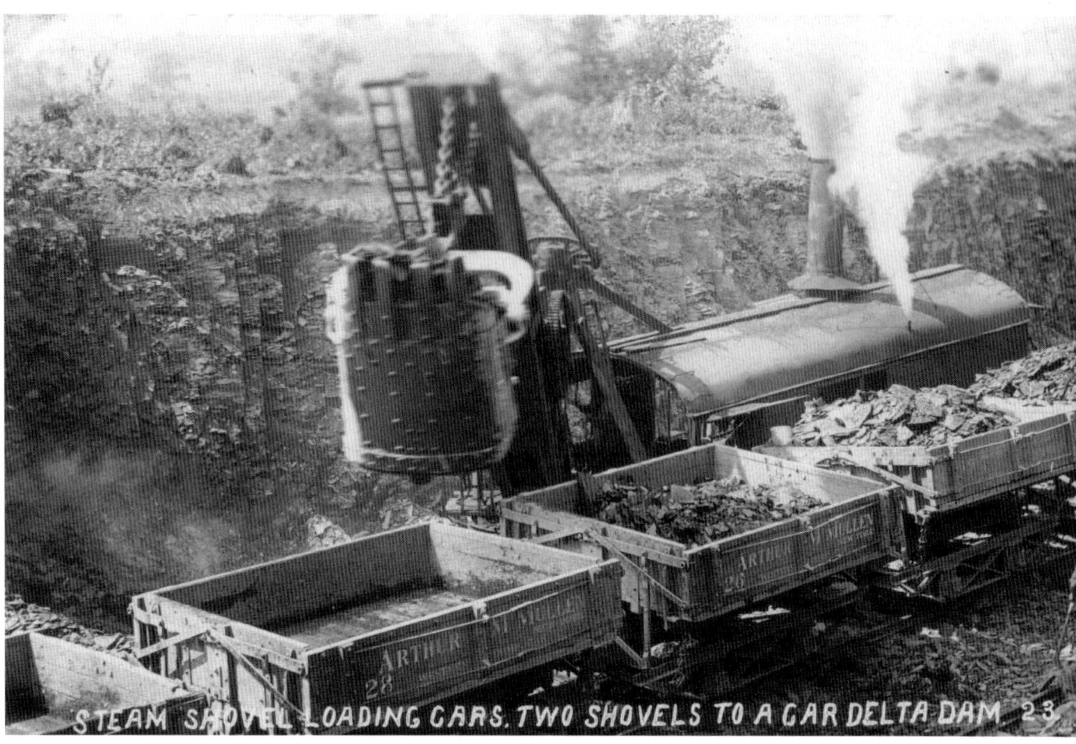


10.13. Steam shovel loading cars, with two shovels to a car, Delta Dam, ca. 1912. Author's Coll.

Not far from Remsen, north of Rome, the state of New York built the huge Delta Dam in 1912.[6] Two years later it completed the equally impressive Hinckley Dam. The former blocked the Mohawk River above Rome, and the latter was built across the West Canada Creek near Trenton Falls (Thomas 1951; Utica Gas and Electric Company 1922). Henry photographed all of this development, starting with the Delta Dam and continuing with the Hinckley construction project (illus. 10.13, 10.14, 10.15, 10.16).

6. I thank Mary Joan Centro for information in this section.

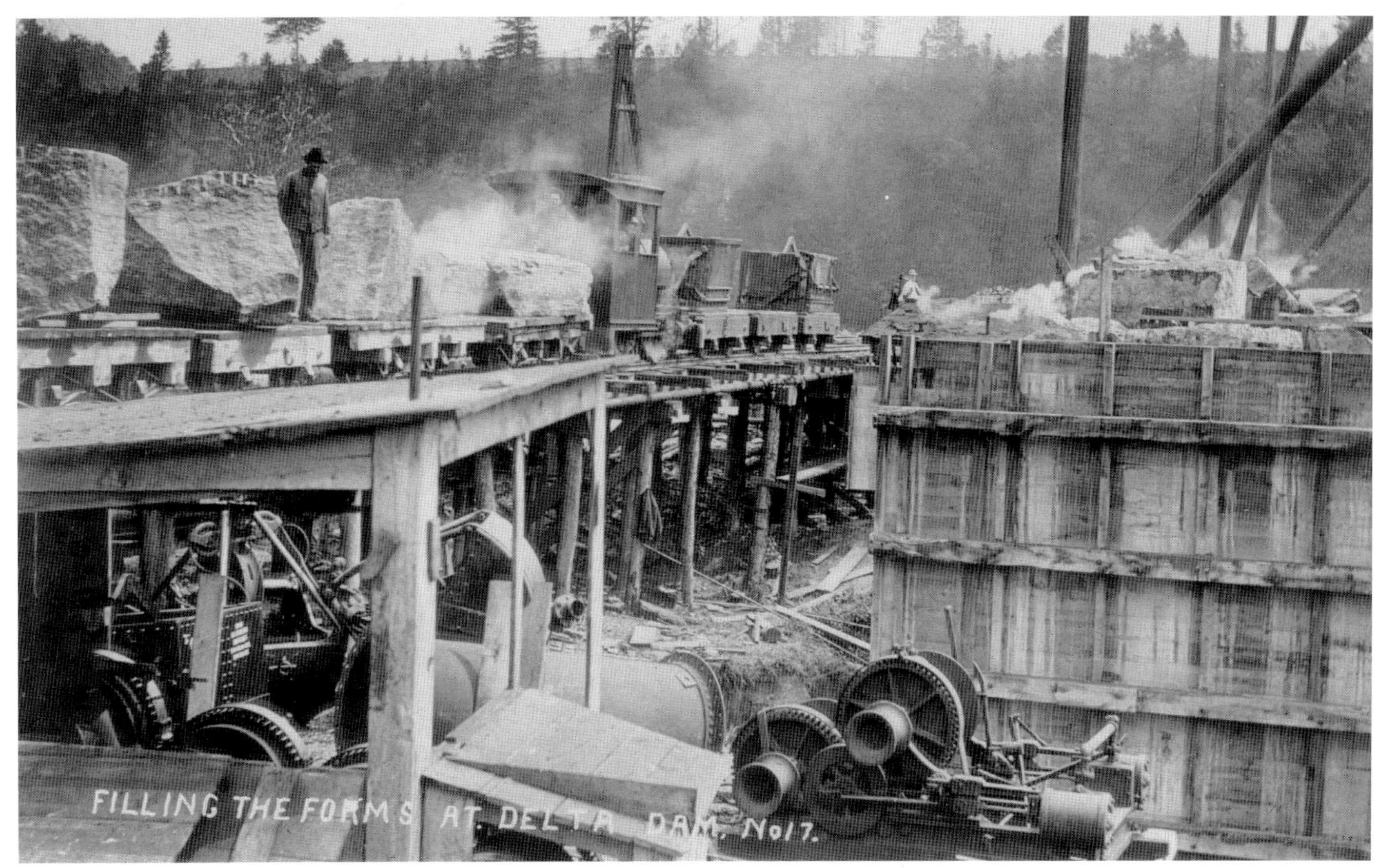


10.14. Filling the forms at Delta Dam, ca. 1912. Author's Coll.

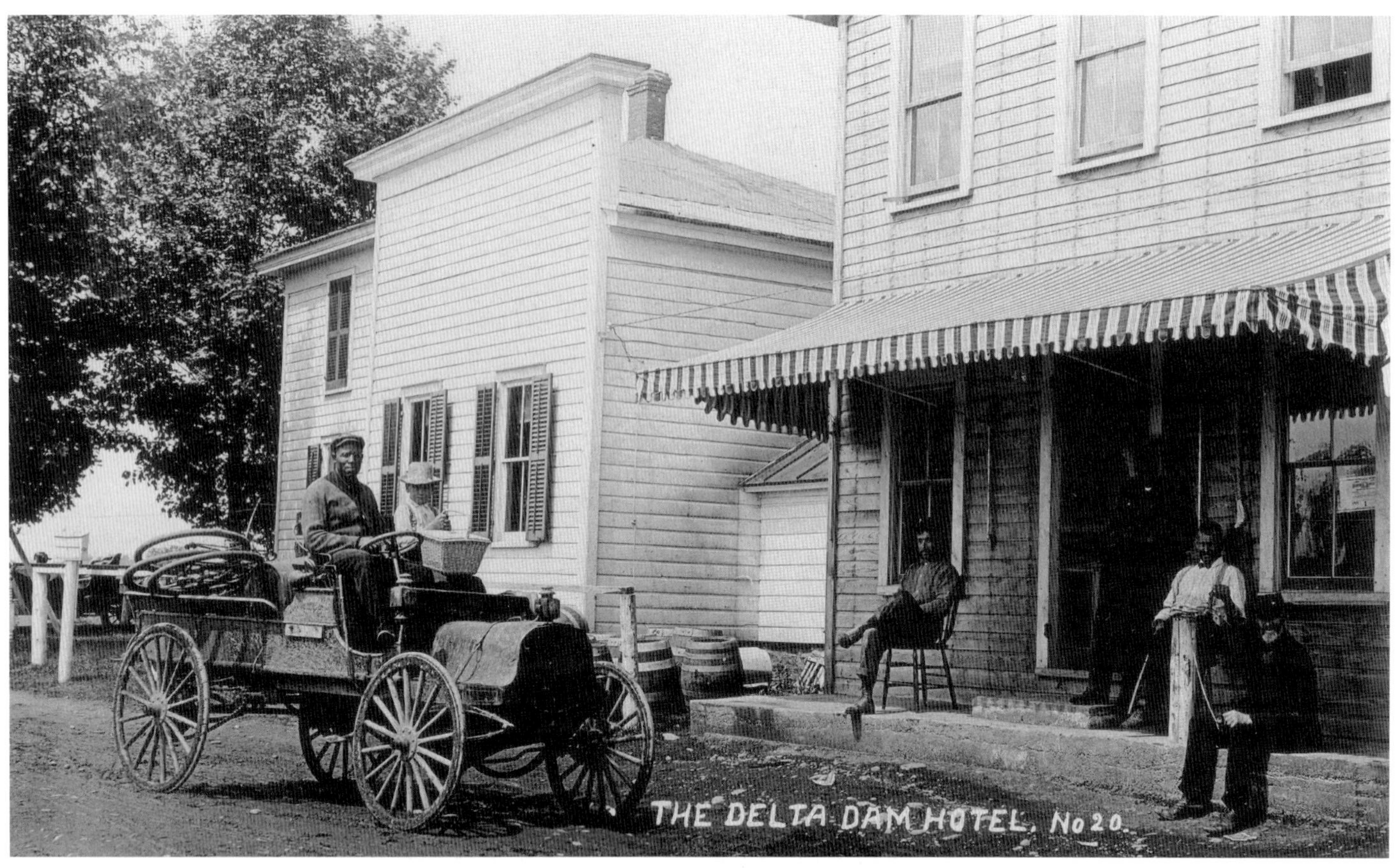


10.15. The Delta Dam Hotel, ca. 1912. Monroe Harris is the African American construction worker picking up lunch to take to the construction site. He worked as a driver for the McMullin Construction Company, the firm that had the contract to build the dam. Author's Coll.

In the late twenties, the growing need for electrical power caused power companies to explore new sources of hydro-generated electricity or to expand existing facilities. Construction of the Moshier power development project was begun in 1928 by the Northeastern Power Corporation on the Beaver River (illus. 10.17). By area standards the project was immense, consisting of a dam located about twenty-five miles from Lowville, in the Adirondack Park. The Moshier plant was the last of a chain of eight hydroelectric plants built below the Stillwater Reservoir. Beach was in his sixties when he took on the job of photographing the construction. It was his last major project.

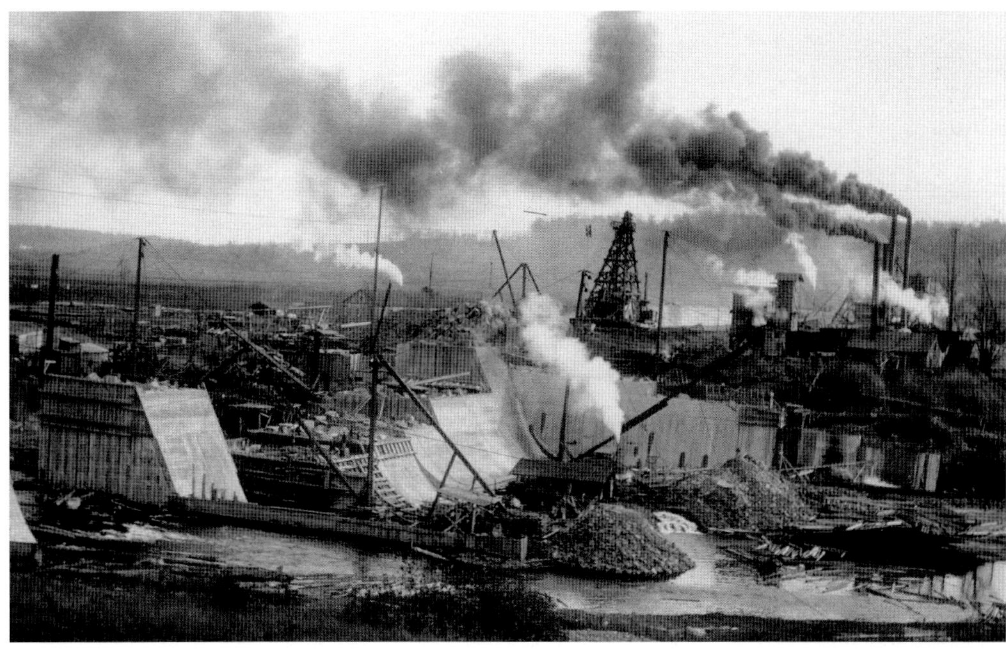

10.16. Hinckley Dam construction, ca. 1914. Author's Coll.

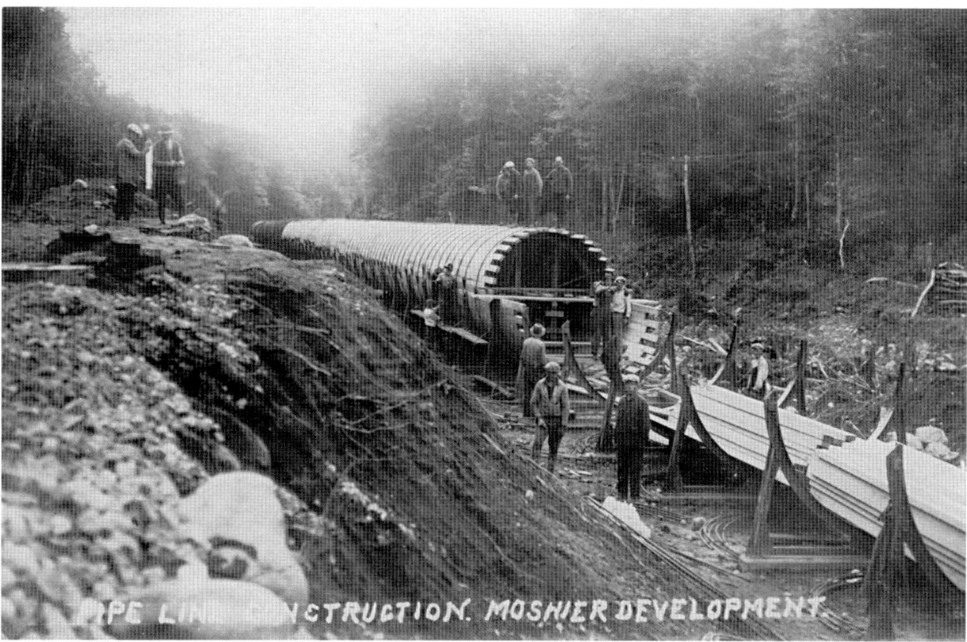


10.17. Pipeline construction, Mosier Project, ca. 1929. Author's Coll.

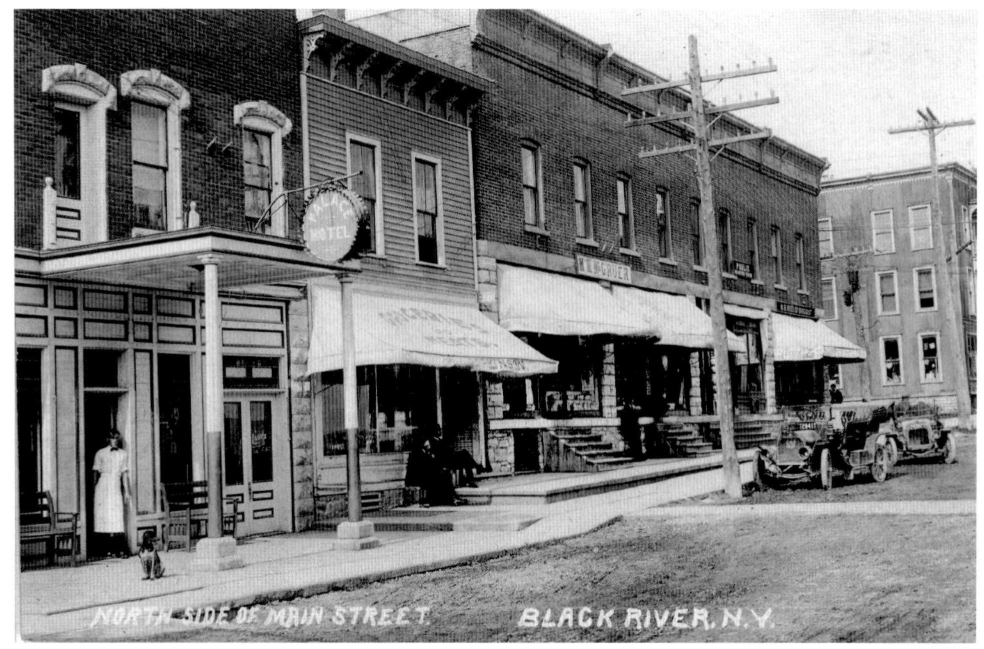


11.1. North side of Main Street, Black River, N.Y., ca. 1912. Author's Coll.

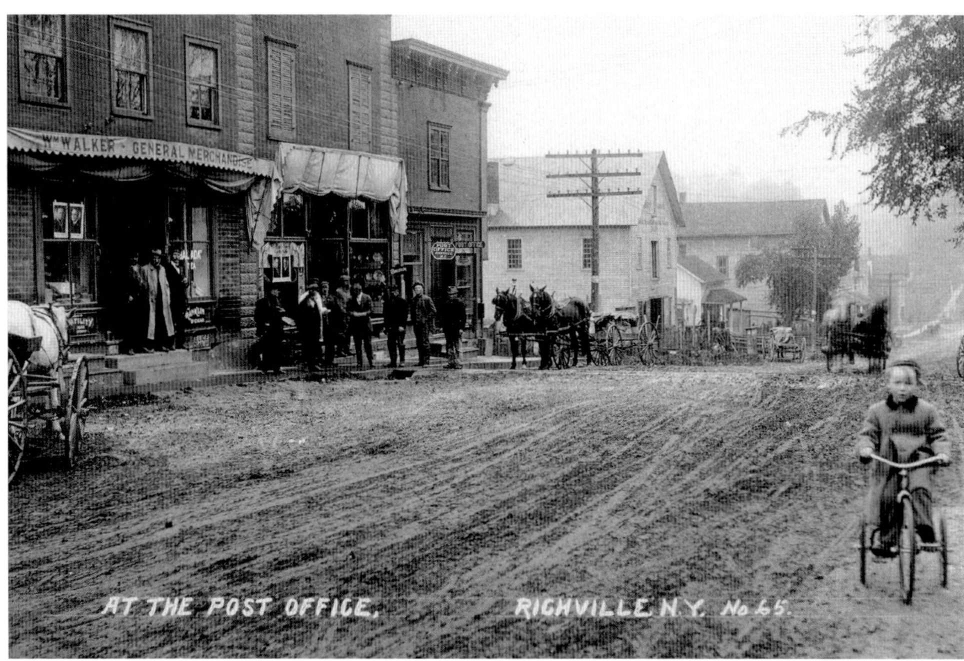


11.2. At the post office in Richville, N.Y., ca. 1908. Courtesy of the Adirondack Museum.

11

# Towns, Villages, and Hamlets

Although Henry was not a town photographer, he did take pictures of population centers. In fact, taking town, village, hamlet, and settlement photo postcards and selling them to general stores and other local retail outlets were necessary to his prosperity. He took as many town photographs as any other subject, including hotels and resorts.

The number and geographic range of this work were extensive: more than two hundred and fifty locations. In addition to the area that now lies within the Adirondack Park he traveled from Lake Champlain, across the St. Lawrence Valley, along the edge of Lake Ontario past Oswego, down to Syracuse, and down the Mohawk Valley. While working out of Fort Plain, he even photographed in and around Oneonta. The areas he photographed the most were Lewis, Herkimer, Oneida, Jefferson, Franklin, and St. Lawrence Counties. He saturated these places with his postcards.

The subject matter of most of Beach's town photographs was not that different from other photographers': main streets, village squares, local businesses, schools, and other civic gathering places. Many are indistinguishable from others done by technically competent town photographers, but some grab one's attention because of the mood they convey, the composition, or the choice of elements or subjects included.

## Streets

The photo of the young waiter in the doorway of the Palace Hotel in Black River, with a dog sitting nearby, on the otherwise empty street, produces the feel of morning in a sleepy town in the North Country (illus. 11.1). Seeking detail makes looking at Beach's town pictures a treasure hunt. Look at the decorative painting on the facade of the hotel and at the sign out front. The door to the right of the waiter is marked "Ladies Entrance." The various shops and what they are selling can be identified. A small sign on the wall to the right reads "Public Reading Room." On the W. R. Wheeler Druggist facade, at the far right, there is a Coke sign.

Quite a different mood is provided in "At the Post Office" (illus. 11.2). Rather than a lazy morning, the scene is of bustling commercial activity, albeit in a tiny rural location where the center of commerce is a post office and a few stores. The boy riding the bicycle speeds up the scene.

## Stores

Henry was at his best when he was photographing the commonplace of town life. Some of his finest town views are of storefronts. Many show a striking resemblance to pictures taken by famous documentary photographers of the 1930s.

"W. B. Hill's Store and Post Office" provides a good example of an early postcard (illus. 11.3). Self-satisfied Mr. Hill stands outside the entrance to his prosperous-looking general-merchandise store that includes a post office. He reaches out to a hand-lettered sign promoting "nine pounds of sweet potatoes for twenty five cents." Likely, those gathered to his right are family and perhaps an employee. Like all good documentary the photo is loaded with detail. In the window on the left, somewhat obscured by a display of gloves, is a campaign poster for William Taft's 1908 run for president. His running mate, also pictured, is James Sherman, a Utica native and local favorite.

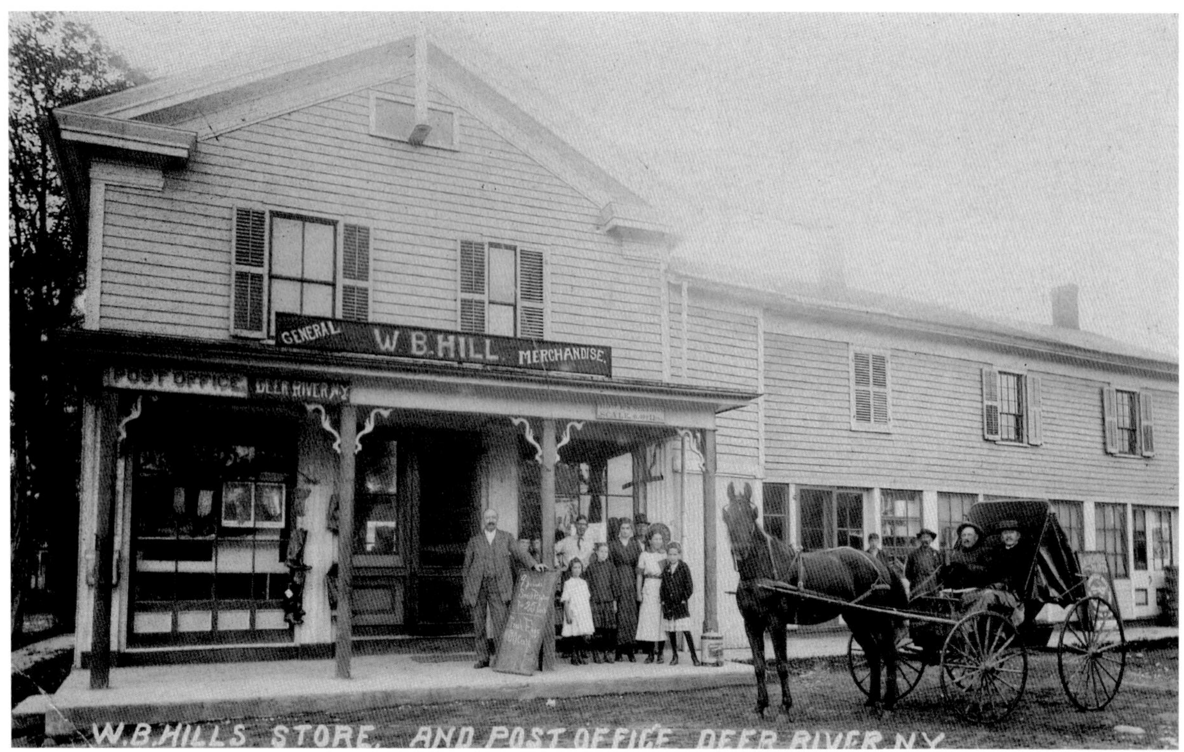


11.3. W. B. Hill's store and post office, Deer River, N.Y., ca. 1908. D. Pierce Coll.

Given Beach's reliance on natural light and knowing how difficult it was to photograph within a confined space, we can appreciate how wonderful the pictures of interiors of stores are.[1] Although I cannot show you what it was like inside Hill's store, it probably looked something like the store down the road in Westernville, New York (illus. 11.4). The way Beach handled the light coming from both the front and the back provides evidence of his mastery of the old glass-plate view-camera technology as well as of his eye for composition and minutia. Not only does he provide a feel for the place, but he also presents a visual inventory of the stock.

The family-run general store was the backbone of the retail trade in the North Country. In Henry's photograph of the R. C. Jones Store in Remsen the owners are out front, and Mrs. Jones is holding her daughter (illus. 11.5). It is a close-up portrait of a small, successful family-run business. Tomatoes, potatoes, and other produce displayed in baskets were an inviting soft-sell approach to advertising. The goods in the front of the store give rich texture to the photograph.

1. Views of the inner spaces of commercial establishments did not sell as well as photos of the facades. The faces of stores defined a town's landscape and therefore were most appropriate for display on correspondence. Given the drawbacks, Henry did not take many interior pictures of stores.

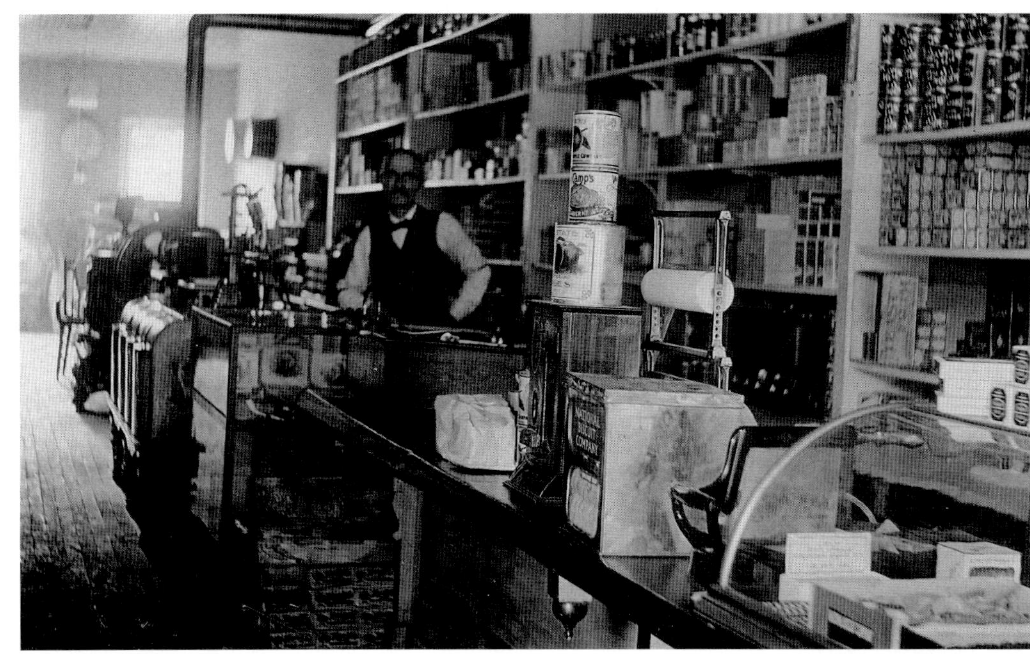

11.4. Interior of general store, Westernville, N.Y., ca. 1910. Gates Coll.

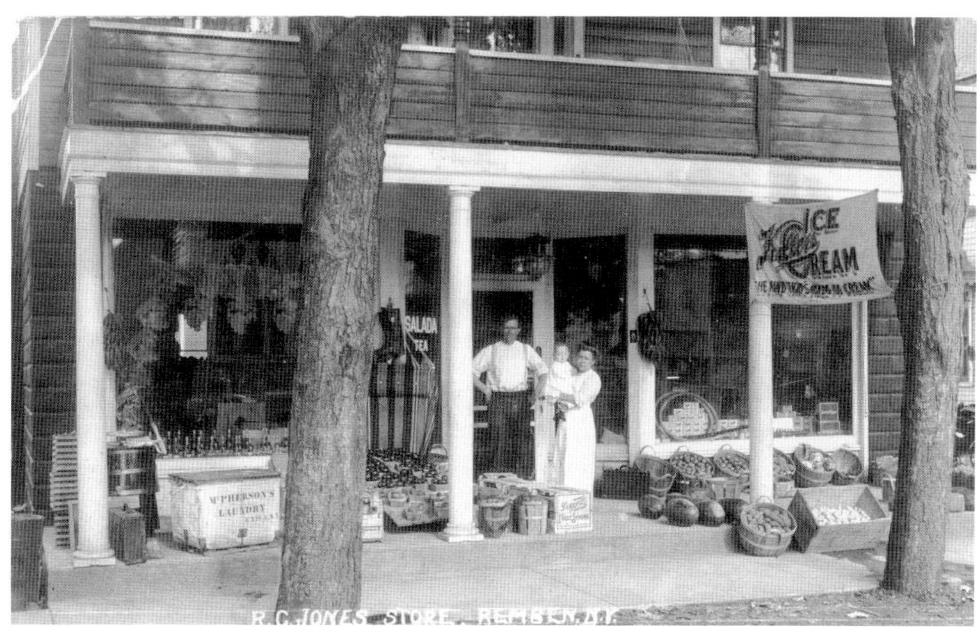


11.5. R. C. Jones's store, Remsen, N.Y., ca. 1915. G. Jones Coll.

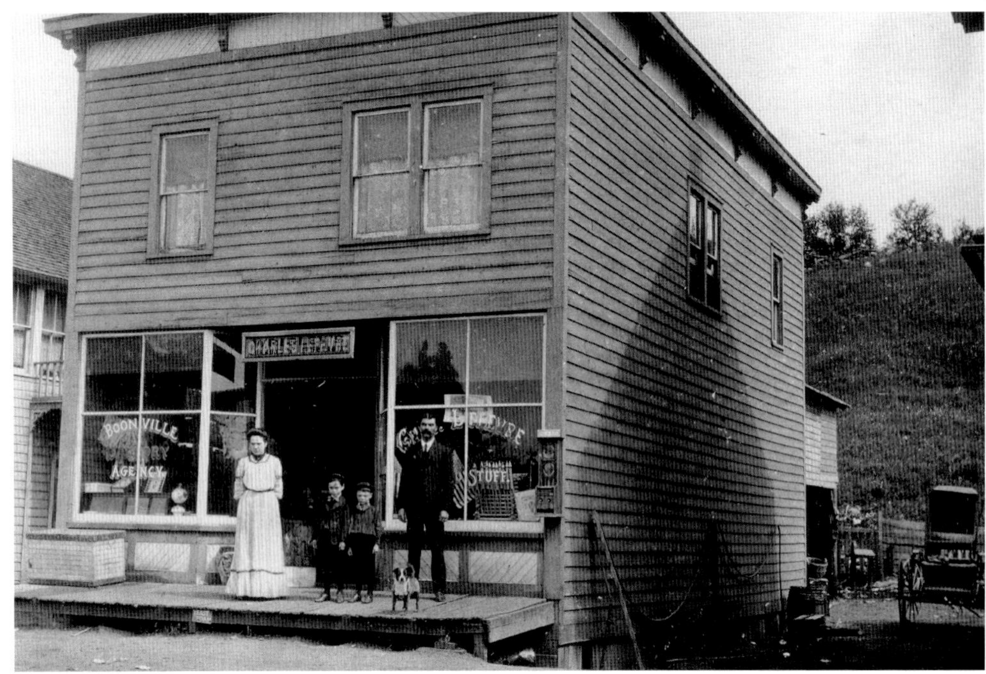


11.6. Family in front of store near Boonville, ca. 1908. Look in the window for details. Courtesy of the Adirondack Museum.

Another family store with mom, pop, and the children in front—the dog is there, too—is found in illustration 11.6. But the LeFevres (the name in the window at the right) are not keeping up with the Joneses. We see a porch in disrepair, a building in need of paint, and a sparse assortment of products for sale (fireworks, an American flag, and gas-lighting fixtures are in the window). The text in the window on the left reads "Boonville Laundry Agency," suggesting that the establishment functioned as a pickup and delivery station for a clothes-cleaning business in Boonville.

Another struggling merchant is pictured in the uncaptioned photograph in illustration 11.7. The subject is a young man, dressed in a suit, on a dilapidated porch of a makeshift dry goods store. The chalkboard sign leaning against the window is an ad for a spring hat-and-coat sale, but there does not appear to be much merchandise. If we were to caption it, it might read "On the Verge of Bankruptcy."

Although family-run general stores dominated the retail trade market in small North Country population centers, larger towns had specialty stores. The

11.7. Young merchant outside dry goods store, location unknown, ca. 1910. Courtesy of the Adirondack Museum.

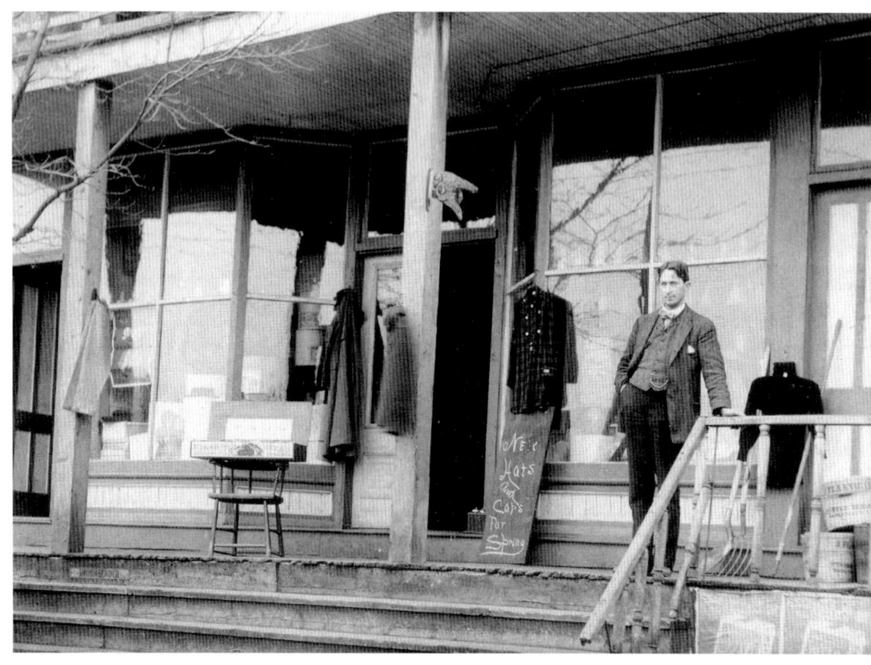

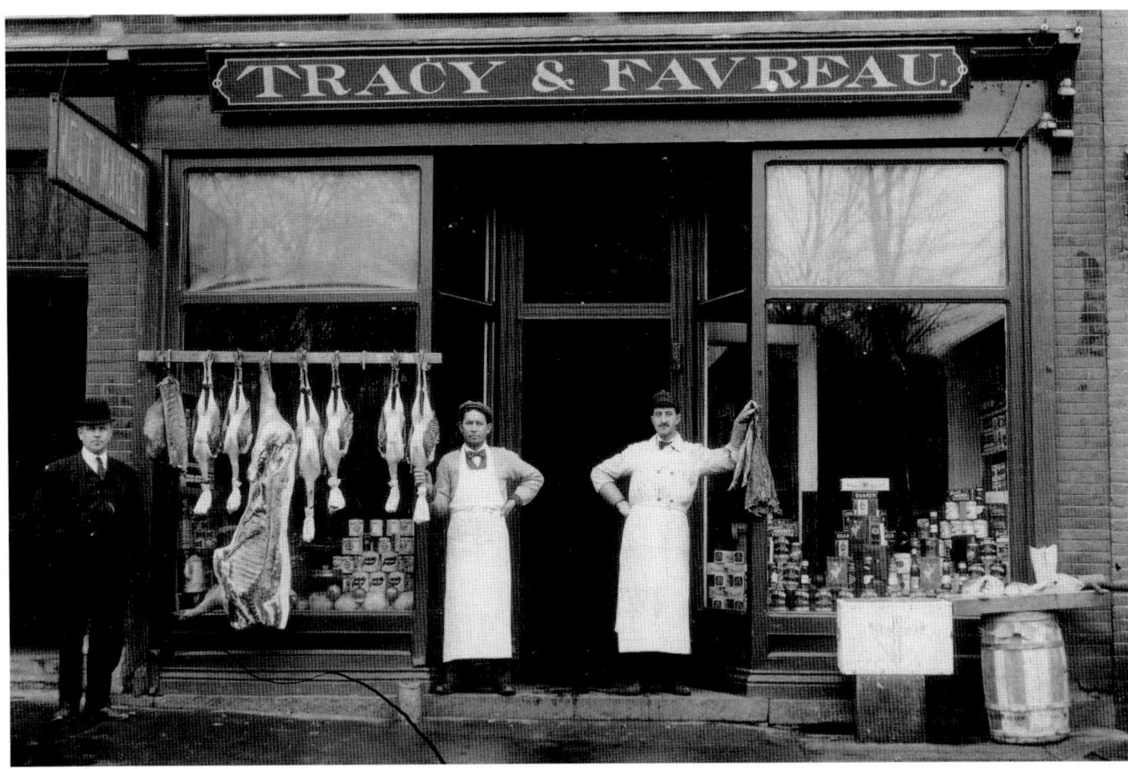


11.8. Tracy & Favreau Meat Market, location unknown, ca. 1910. Courtesy of the Adirondack Museum.

picture of Tracy & Favreau's Meat Market is not captioned, but it was probably taken in one of the large population centers such as Saranac Lake, Carthage, or Malone (illus. 11.8). Whether the man standing on the left is an owner or the two men with aprons are Tracy and Favreau is not clear. Although the sign over the person in the suit reads "Meat Market," the merchandise in the window (such as Quaker Oats) suggests a wider range of products. Notice the butcher in the center-left holding the large goose by the neck and the dead birds' heads covered with paper bags.

The Old Forge Hardware Store is a landmark to people familiar with the central Adirondacks. Today this establishment is seen as a quaint throwback to an earlier time and a marketplace for Adirondack-style eclecticism. When first established in the early twentieth century it represented modernity, the coming of up-to-date merchandise to the North Country. Henry's picture was probably taken a few years after the store was built (illus. 11.9). There was not a proper sign on the facade identifying the business, so Beach hand-lettered the name on the building in the negative. In this view a couple, likely Moses Cohen, the store founder and local entrepreneur, and his second wife, Sarah, stands in the doorway (Wessels 1963).

Although illustration 11.10 is not the inside of the Old Forge establishment, it provides a good idea of what the interior of a large general store in the North County looked like. It shows the interior of the company store at Piercefield. The neatly arranged candies inside the cabinets (note the sign for Schrafft's Chocolates in the center) along with packaged foods lined up on shelves create a geometric design.

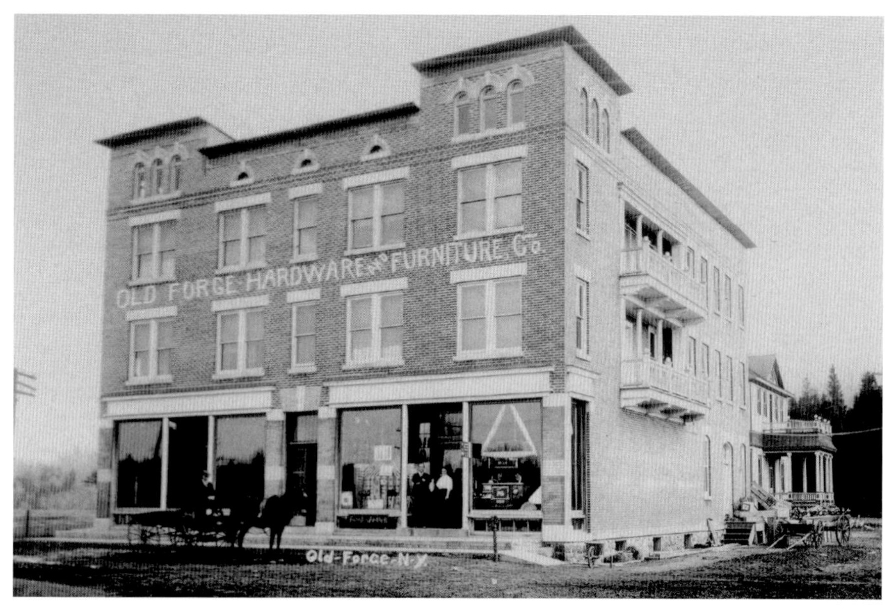


11.9. Old Forge Hardware and Furniture Company, Old Forge, N.Y., ca. 1907. Courtesy of the Adirondack Museum.

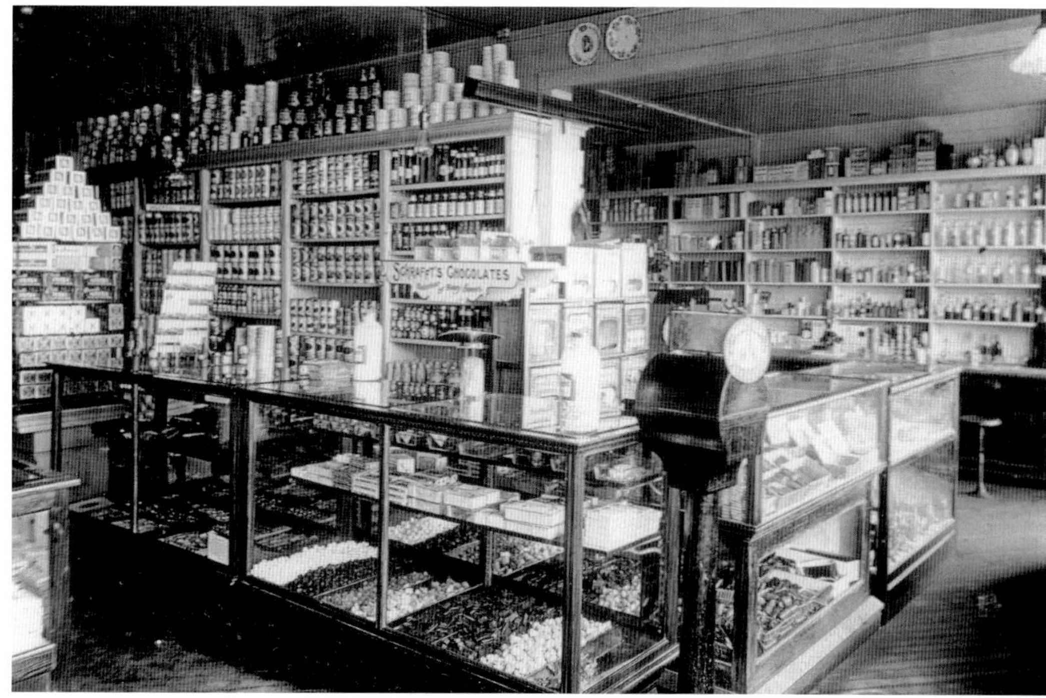


11.10. Interior of company store, Piercefield, N.Y., ca. 1908. Courtesy of the Adirondack Museum.

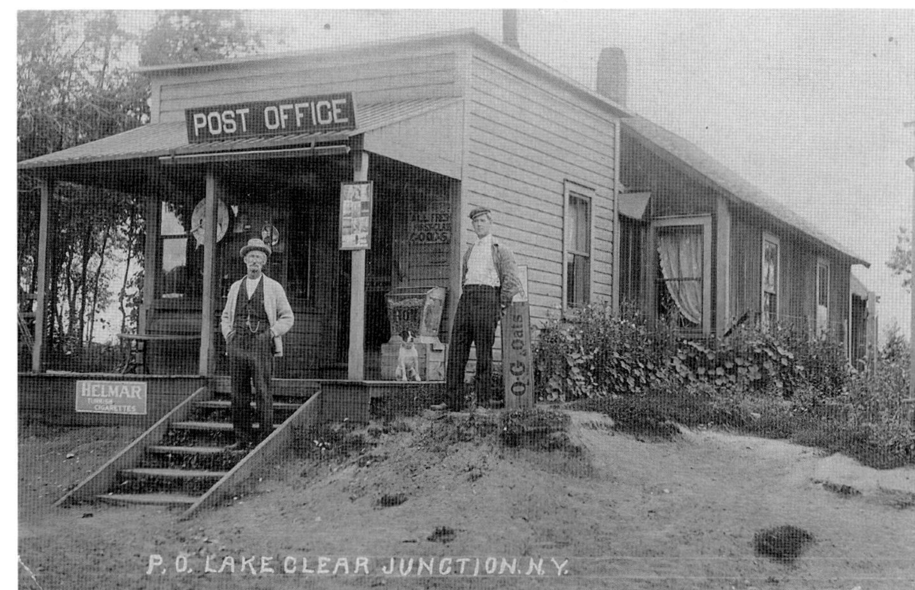


11.11. Post office at Lake Clear Junction, N.Y., ca. 1908. E. Pierce Coll.

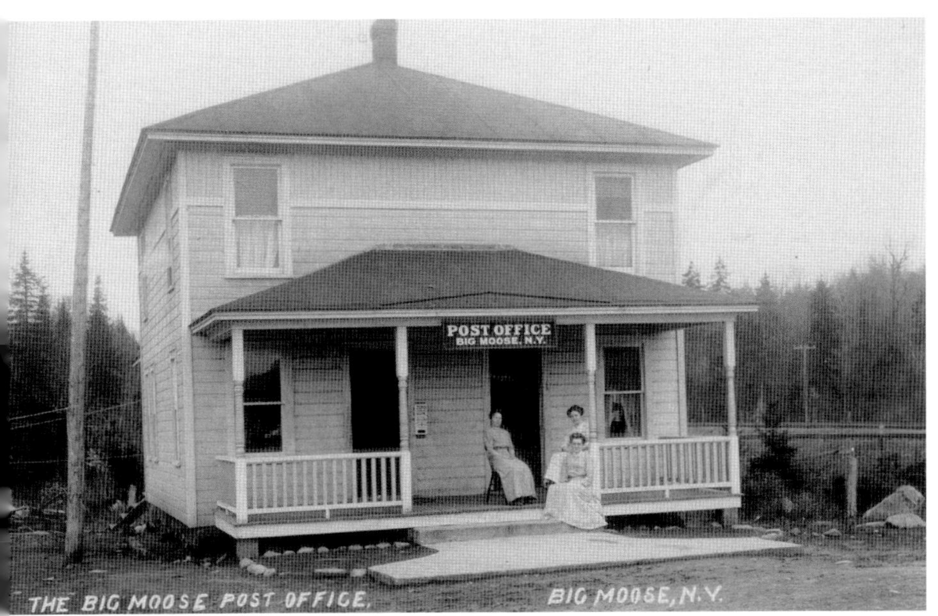


11.12. Post office at Big Moose, N.Y., ca. 1915. Gates Coll.

In the heart of the Adirondacks, settlements were scattered and retail stores simple. Often, the proprietor of an unassuming store held the job of postmaster. Not on salary, these retailers earned their living in part by commission from the government tally on the amount of postal business they did. This income was augmented by what they could make from other sales. Postcards were a good item to sell because people who came in to buy stamps were ready customers. Beach photographed these minimart precursors and sold his postcards to their proprietors. The post office and general store at Lake Clear Junction, east of Saranac Lake, fits the description well (illus. 11.11). Note the array of commercial advertisements. On the pole is a framed display of postcards, likely the work of Henry.

Henry photographed all kinds of post offices. The Lake Clear Junction variety may have been more like a store than a post office, but in some hamlets, such as Big Moose, the post office was located in a private residence (illus. 11.12). It was a tranquil setting where locals and summer people greeted each other as they took a break from their divergent activities. His photograph is notable not for the detail as much as for the atmosphere of a lazy day in summer that it depicts.

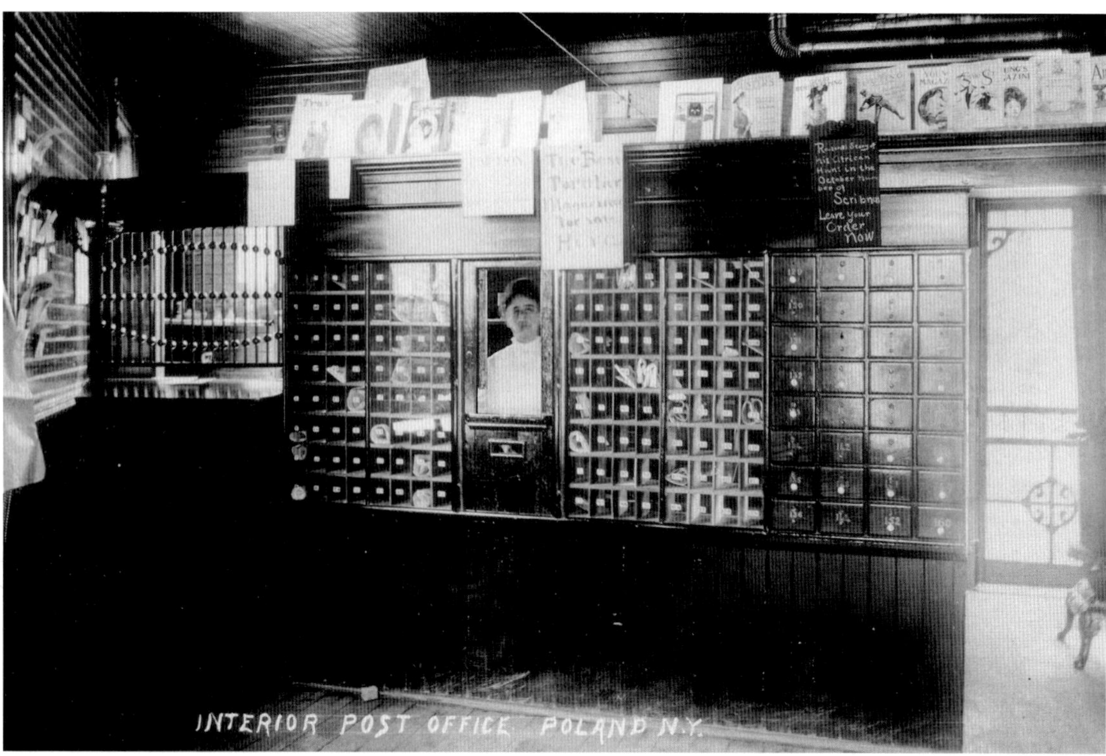


11.13. Interior of post office, Poland, N.Y., ca. 1910. Courtesy of the Adirondack Museum.

Interior photographs of the type of the post office at Big Moose were almost impossible to shoot because the areas were so poorly lit. That fact did not stop Henry from getting the post office at Poland, New York, on film (illus. 11.13). Though mail is clearly the main item of business, a generous lineup of magazines, including an early issue of *Good House Keeping,* is displayed overhead, revealing the entrepreneurial bent of the owner. The display of shapes and light with the woman framed in the center is a visual treat.

## Schools

I could fill a large book with Beach's school photographs. Important to his business, photographs exist of every school in his region. Many are stark, with no teachers or students visible. Others have a few children as props to add interest. His picture of the school at Benson Mines is one such example (illus. 11.14). The scuffed flagpole and the poorly tended grounds, combined with the barren surroundings, reflect the context of the mining community to which it belonged (see chapter 10).

Beach also took school pictures that included the entire student body and staff. As with the school at White Lake, they were sometimes one-room common schools with fewer than twenty students (illus. 11.15). Others, like the school that served the sons and daughters of lumber-industry workers at St. Regis Falls, were quite large even by urban standards (illus. 11.16). Identifiable faces in photo postcards boosted their sales because the children's parents wanted them for the family albums. The picture of St. Regis must have been

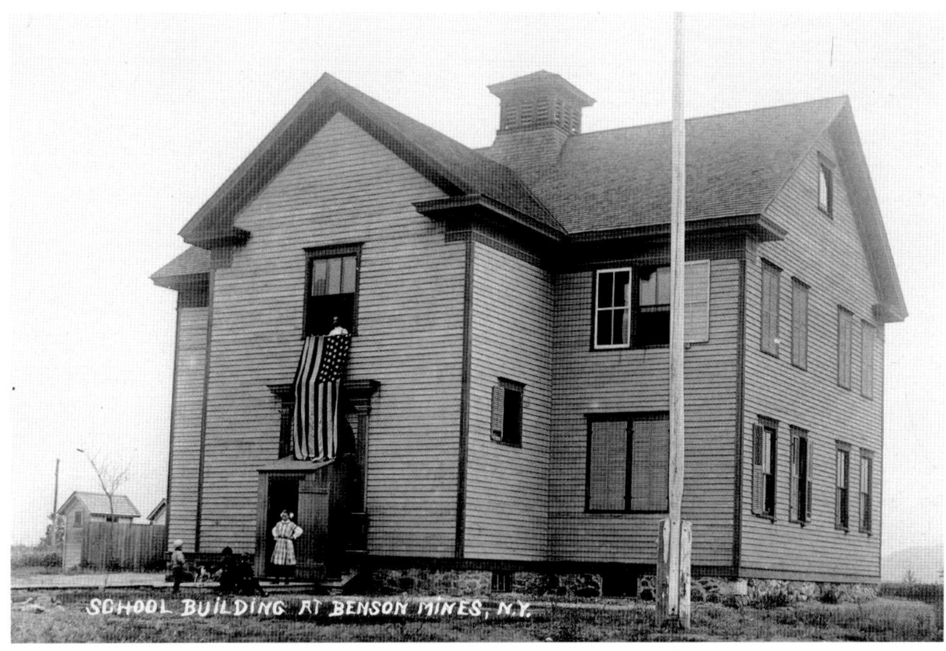


11.14. School at Benson Mines, N.Y., ca. 1910.
Courtesy of the Adirondack Museum.

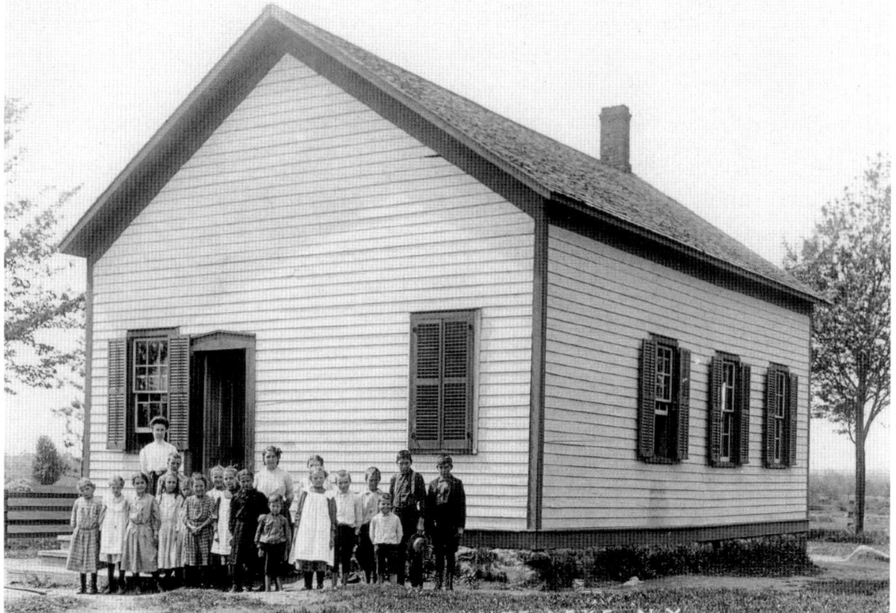

11.15. School at White Lake, N.Y., ca. 1912.
Courtesy of the Adirondack Museum.

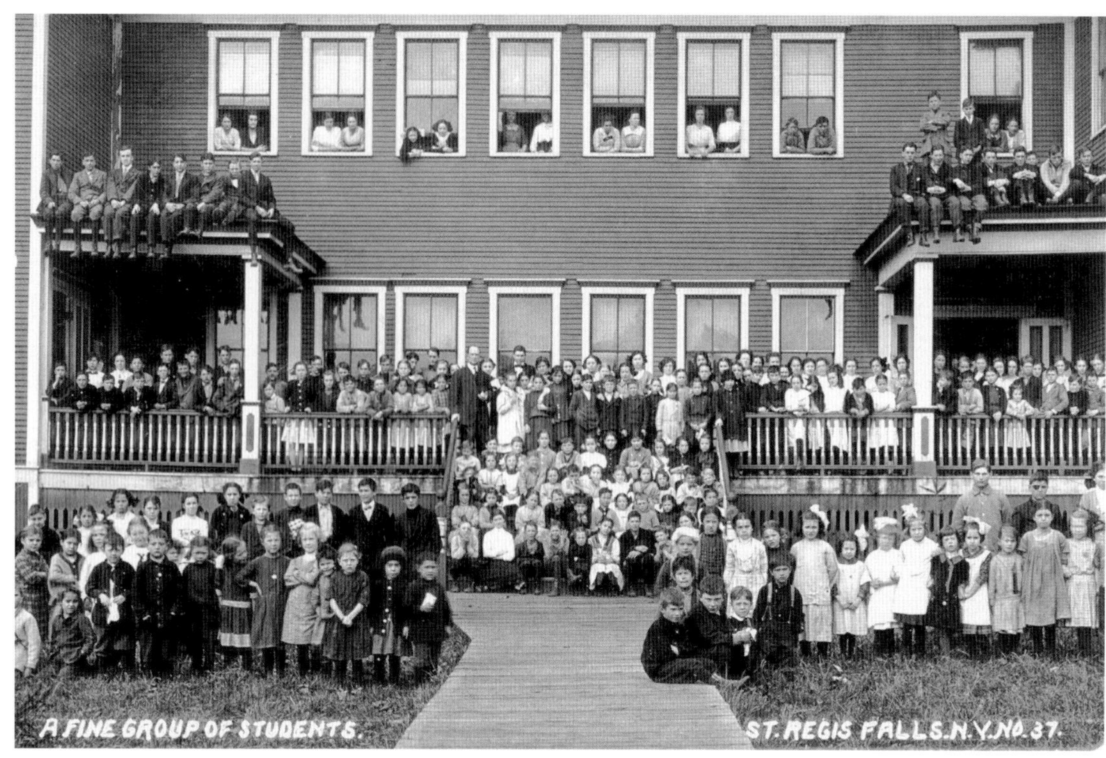


11.16. Group of students, St. Regis Falls, N.Y., ca. 1914. Author's Coll.

quite a moneymaker. Beach actually took four different views of the school on that day. The one shown here as illustration 11.16 is a close-up of the center portion of the school.[2] Henry also produced a single postcard of the whole school. Notice how the text at the bottom praises the students. When captioning school photographs Henry was lavish with his praise, using such expressions as "The North Country's Finest," "The North Country's Best," and "An Elegant Group of Students." In truth, Beach was fond of children and included many in his nonacademic photographs. The complimentary remarks also promoted sales.

Not all North Country students attended public schools. Parochial-school education was widely available for children whose parents wanted and could afford the modest fees (Taylor 1972). Most Catholic schools were in larger towns and their students were locals, but some schools took boarders as well. One such academy was St. Joseph's in Malone (illus. 11.17). The academy consisted of a large coeducational day school plus boarding arrangements for a dozen or so girls.[3] The administration probably hired Henry to produce a series of photographs. His outside views were taken in late fall, when the trees were leafless. That element, combined with the stark institutional architecture, resulted in a dreary set of pictures.

Although the varied dress and the few half smiles on the boarders' faces pick up the mood of this series a little, the brick wall in the background and the orderly composition contribute to the feel of gloomy confinement (illus. 11.18).

2. There are two others, one of each end. As the instructions in the captions on the side pictures indicate, if held side by side they formed a panoramic view of the entire setting.

3. The academy was founded in 1898 by Sister Stanislaus, an Ursuline nun. The Ursulines are an order that caters to the educational needs of girls, although their school in Malone was coeducational (Taylor 1972).

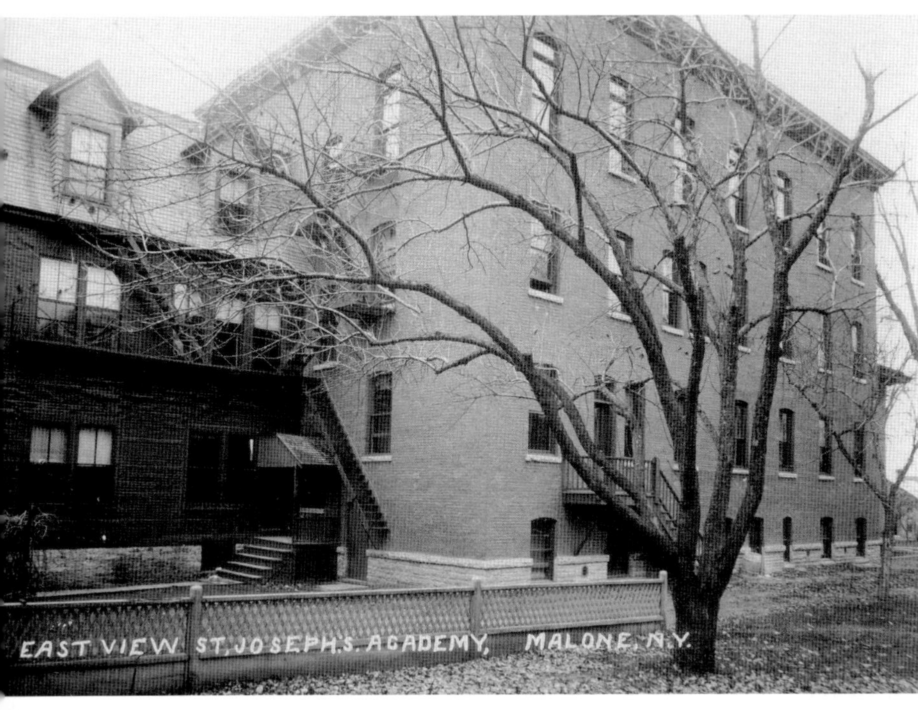


11.17. St. Joseph's Academy, Malone, N.Y., 1909. Courtesy of the Adirondack Museum.

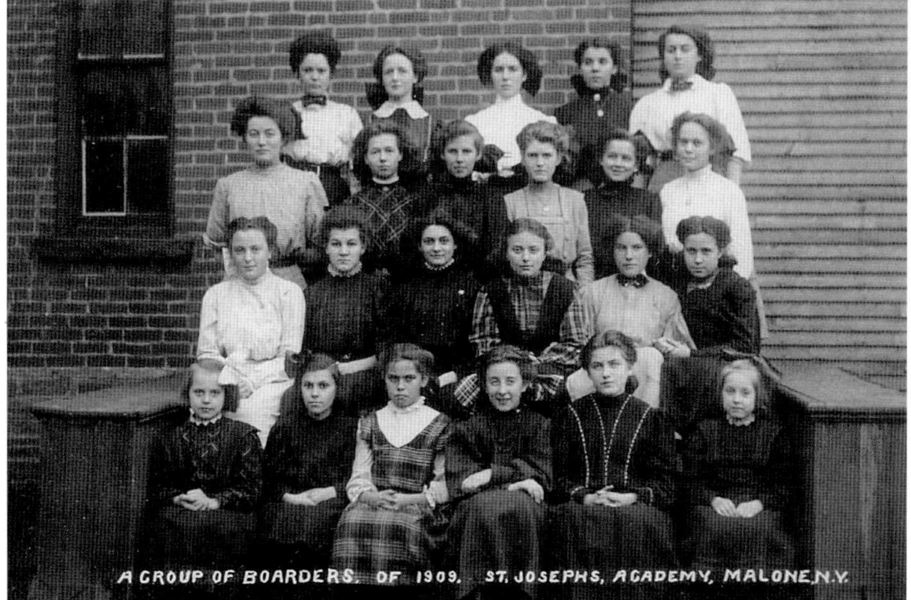


11.18. Group of boarders, St. Joseph's Academy, Malone, N.Y., 1909. Courtesy of the Adirondack Museum.

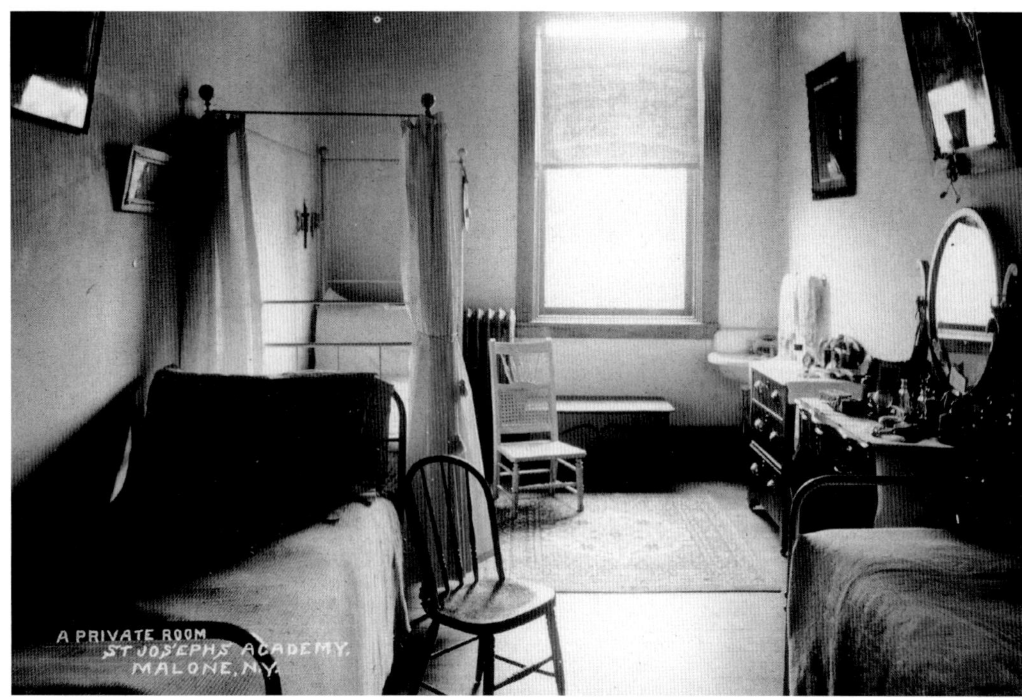


11.19. Private room, St. Joseph's Academy, Malone, N.Y., 1909. Courtesy of the Adirondack Museum.

Likewise, in spite of Henry's magic in handling the light, the interior shots suggest more of the same dullness (illus. 11.19, 11.20).[4] In these photographs, as in so many others, Beach provides not only aesthetically striking pictures but also detail unavailable from any other historical sources.

## Festivals and Celebrations

Besides superior quality, there are other differences between Beach's village work and the work of other town photographers. Henry did not concentrate on photographing annual commemorations, festivals, or celebrations such as the Declaration Day parades, Fourth of July activities, or picnics organized by the Daughters of the American Revolution. Because he was not a resident in most of the towns he photographed, these events passed him by. But even for his own towns, Lowville, Remsen, and Fort Plain, he took very few pictures of festive occasions.

The lively crowd and street-fair strength-testing device in the center-left of "Boonville on a Busy Day" are dead giveaways that the picture was taken during some special event (illus. 11.21). It might have been a fair or celebration, but Beach chose not to tell us what we are observing. Part of the reason is commercial. More generic captions provided pictures with a longer shelf life. After

4. Apparently, there were two levels of boarders: students who had private rooms and students who stayed in the dormitory. In an apparent contradiction, the "private room" appears to have three beds. Probably, "private" meant compared to the dormitories that were dense with beds.

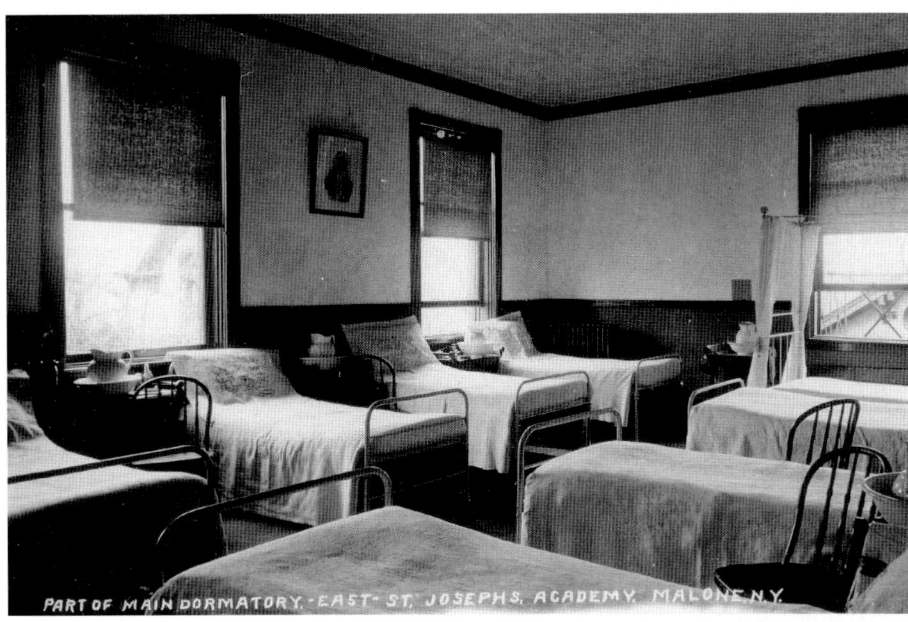


11.20. Part of main dormitory, St. Joseph's Academy, Malone, N.Y., 1909. Courtesy of the Adirondack Museum.

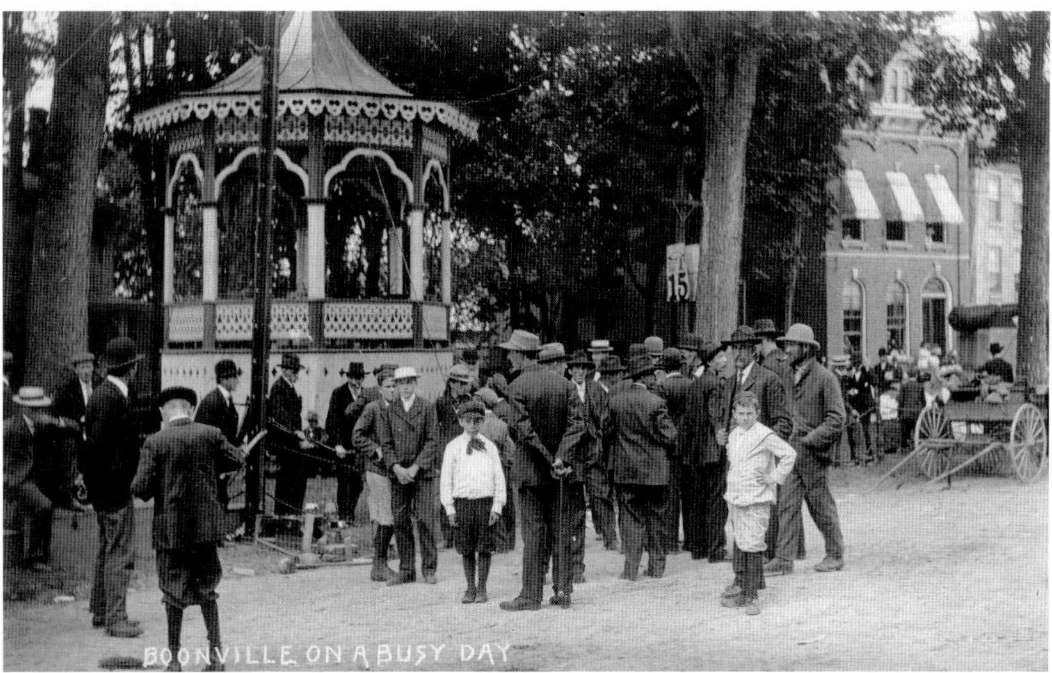


11.21. "Boonville on a Busy Day," Boonville, N.Y., ca. 1909. Holstein Coll.

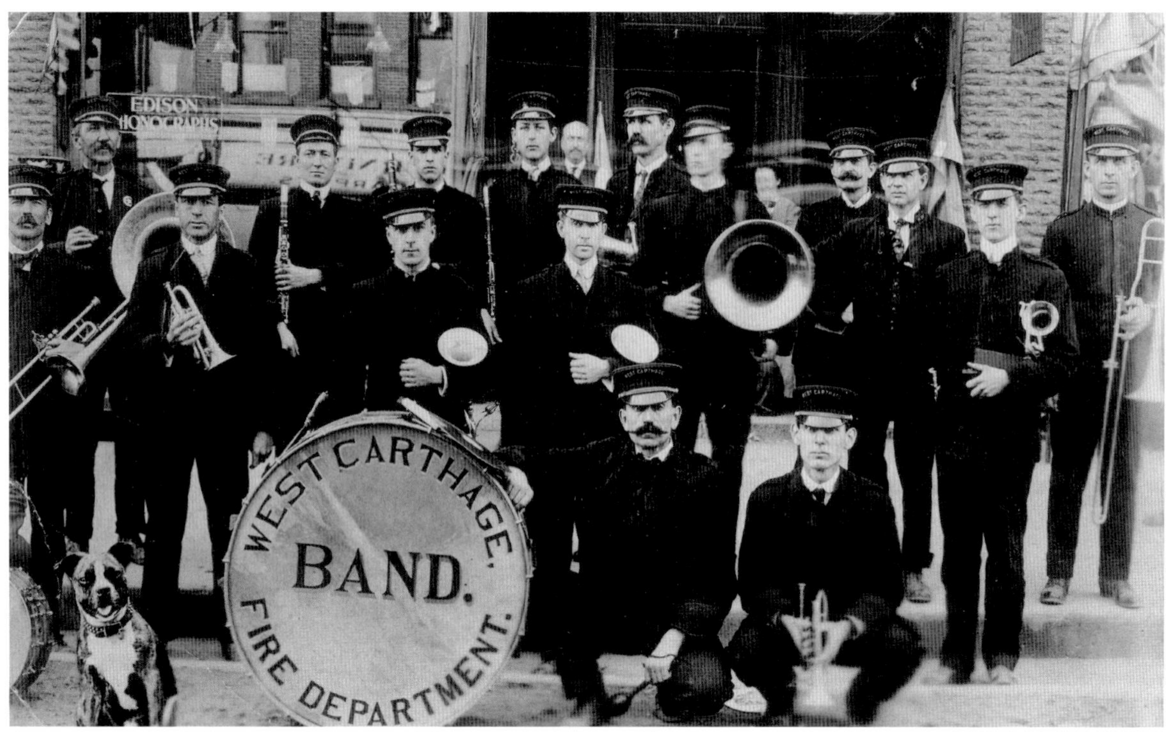


11.22. West Carthage, N.Y., Fire Department Band, ca. 1911. Author's Coll.

a few days of brisk sales, people lost interest in annual-event shots. Another explanation is Henry's ironic sense of humor. There were very few days in a year when a crowd of people would assemble in downtown Boonville. The caption, "Busy Day in Boonville," could be interpreted to imply that busy days in Boonville were few and far between.

The West Carthage Fire Department Band must have assembled for some special occasion when Henry took illustration 11.22. But, again, he chose not to provide the specifics in a caption. Nonetheless, his group portrait of these men and their dog catches a local tradition that was central to village-life celebrations.

The scope of a topic such as "Town Views" is so expansive that it is impossible to provide even a superficial sampler of all the topics that could be included. I left out graveyards and municipal parks, for example. Henry Beach took hundreds of photographs of town buildings in addition to the stores and schools, including town halls, Masonic temples, libraries, factories, jails, hospitals, and private homes. Without knowing it, he created an archive of North Country structures. For many buildings, Beach's clear, straightforward images are all we have left of what were once the towns and villages of the North Country.

12

# Disasters

Floods, tornadoes, blizzards, earthquakes, fires, wrecks, and explosions—all forms of natural and human-made catastrophes were of special interest to postcard photographers of Beach's generation.[1] Shooting them, or more often their aftermaths, was an opportunity to make an extra buck. Local photographers were right there to catch the moment, quickly process their film, and have cards to sell shortly after the event.

Henry was not what we would call an ambulance chaser, but he took absorbing and well-composed disaster photos. At least on one occasion, he traveled out of the North Country in pursuit of a frightful event. For another calamity, it appears that he sold pictures of an event he pretended to have witnessed, but in fact had missed.

Let us deal with the second case first. Sometime after March 29, 1911, Beach went to Albany to photograph the results of a dramatic fire that destroyed the newly built state capitol building. The postcards he produced make it appear that he was actually at the fire. In reality, he took negatives of the charred remains and altered them by stroking in the raging fire with a brush.[2]

1. Although Beach never took pictures of gross human brutality such as the mass executions during the Mexican Revolution and lynchings of African Americans, these atrocities produced fast-selling postcards in other parts of the country (Allen et al. 2000).

2. In February 1911 Beach sent panoramic photographs he had taken in Albany to the Library of Congress for copyright protection. In one of the panoramics, the new state capitol building is prominent. He may have transformed pictures from that trip into photographs for his Albany fire collection.

Why Beach selected the 1911 Austin, Pennsylvania, flood to photograph is unknown, but it likely had an Adirondack connection. W. L. Sykes, owner of the Emporium Lumber Company in Conifer, New York, near Tupper Lake, had hired Henry to photograph the company's expanding northern New York facilities (Welsh 1995, chap. 9). Emporium was originally a Pennsylvania firm and operated mills in and around Austin. Henry's flood photographs, some of which are of Sykes's mills, are well composed and helpful in understanding Henry's attempts to market to a broader audience than his northern New Yorker clientele.

In "Selling Their Relicks [*sic*] of the Flood," Beach produced a distressing vista of a flood-ravaged house with its surviving former occupants marketing their salvageable personal goods to well-dressed sightseers (illus. 12.1). The open trunk and other household items in the foreground segmented from the debris-littered landscape in the background give tremendous depth to the view. As with many of his documentary photos, Beach conveys a concern for the victims, but the social message, if there is one, is muddled. Is he merely empathizing with the victims, or is he pointing out exploitation?

Henry took many views of the flood and promoted them with Pennsylvania merchants. He mailed a postcard advertisement to store owners in which he offered a large-size panoramic view free as a bonus for buying large lots of cards. His Pennsylvania-flood postcard views are hard to find today, indicating that he may not have been successful with his sales tactics.

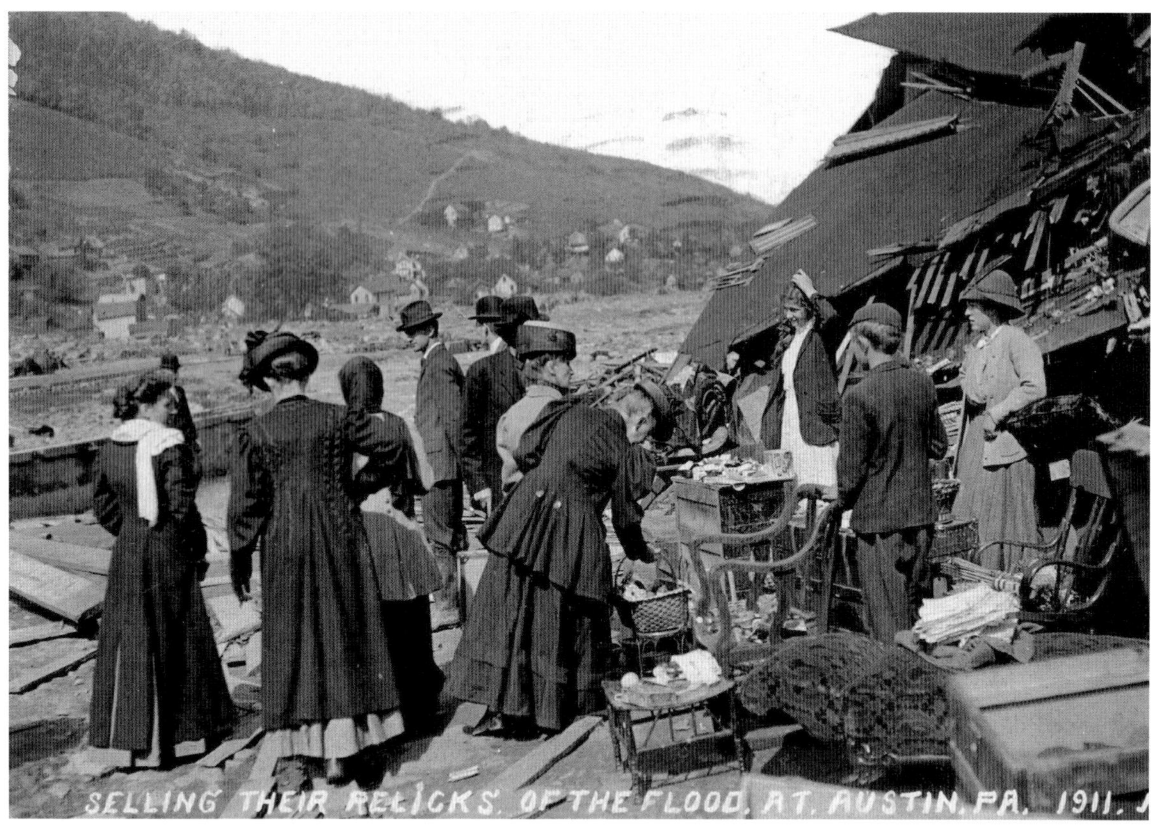


12.1. After the flood at Austin, Pa., 1911. Author's Coll.

## Local Floods

Beach had floods to photograph closer to home, too. Every few years, in early spring, many Adirondack rivers produced floods. The cause was too much rain, temperatures rising too quickly, and the thick ice that covered the rivers not having sufficient time to melt or break into small chunks. Rushing water thrust huge ice slabs onto the land, smashing structures and blocking roads.

In 1914, Henry took a series of pictures at Deer River, a hamlet north of Lowville, in which he documented an ice-jam flood. In "The Power of Water" and "Ice and Iron," Beach seems bent on impressing the viewer with the strength of the waterway (illus. 12.2, 12.3). Nature, Beach tells us, has the upper hand over human-made structures, but the pictures also convey a nonchalant acceptance of the whole occurrence. Beach accomplished this feat by including locals who posed casually with the damage as if they were proud of the destruction. In another folksy but less dramatic shot, captioned "A Cold Spell (Ice) in Our Neighbor's Garden," Beach jokes about the gargantuan ice blocks on the lawn of the property owner who is barely visible in the center-left of the picture (illus. 12.4).

Henry's covers this North Country flood as if it is a normal occurrence rather than an unusual calamity. Many Adirondack locations that had ice jams were not densely populated, so flooding and damage were relatively inconsequential. But when towns and villages were involved, it was another matter. Take the great flood of 1910 that brought devastation to the town of Herkimer.

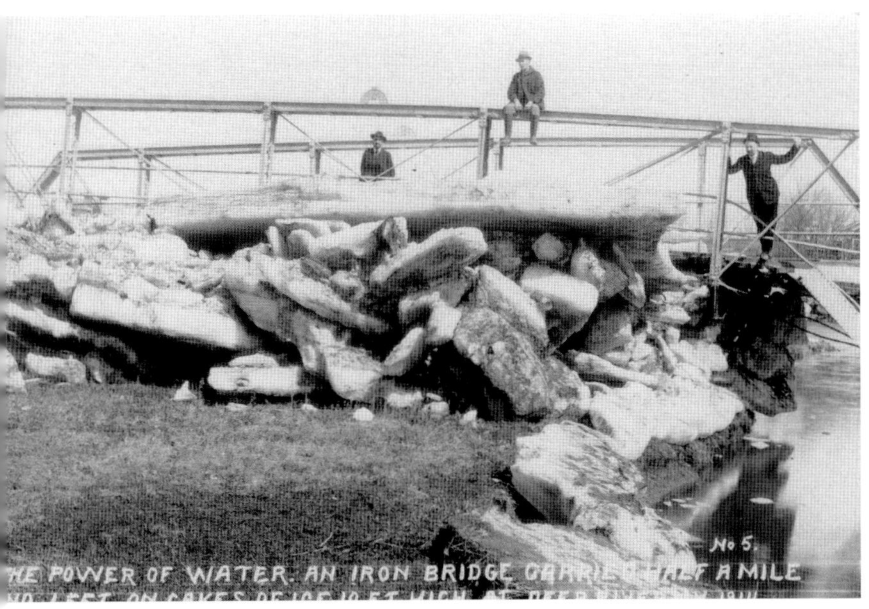


12.2. "The Power of Water," Deer River, N.Y., 1914. An iron bridge floated one-half mile, leaving ice ten feet high. Davis Coll.

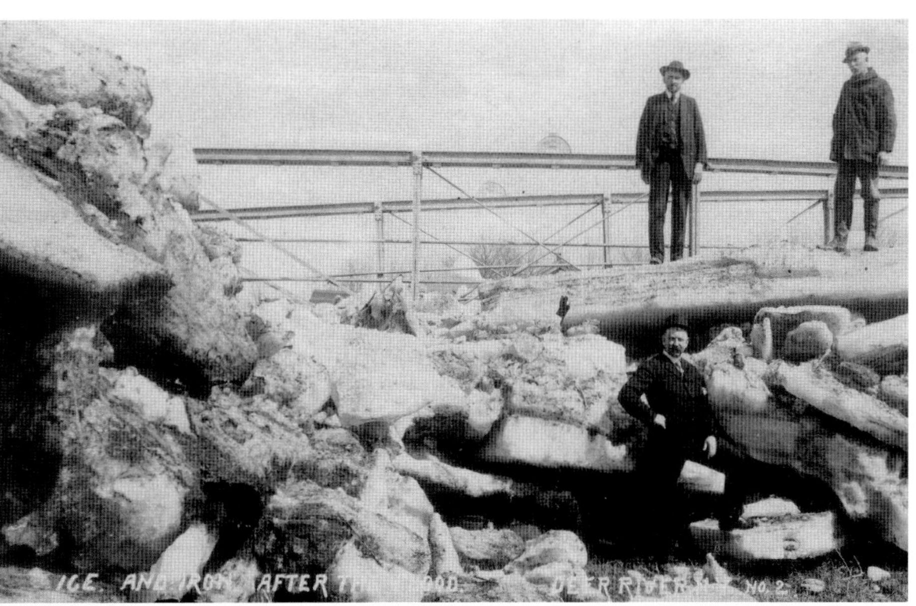


12.3. "Ice and Iron After the Flood," Deer River, N.Y., 1914. Author's Coll.

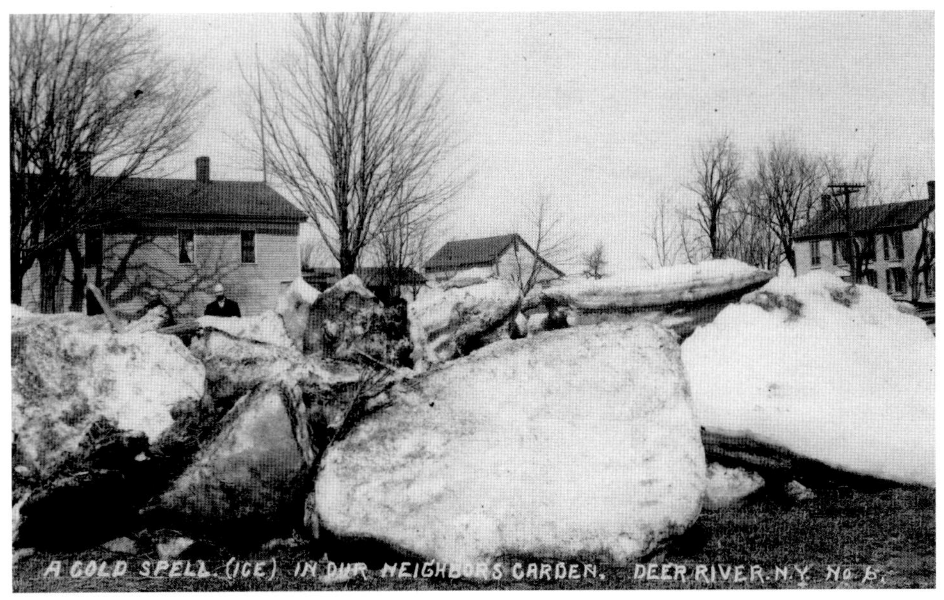


12.4. Blocks of ice in garden, Deer River, N.Y., 1914. Author's Coll.

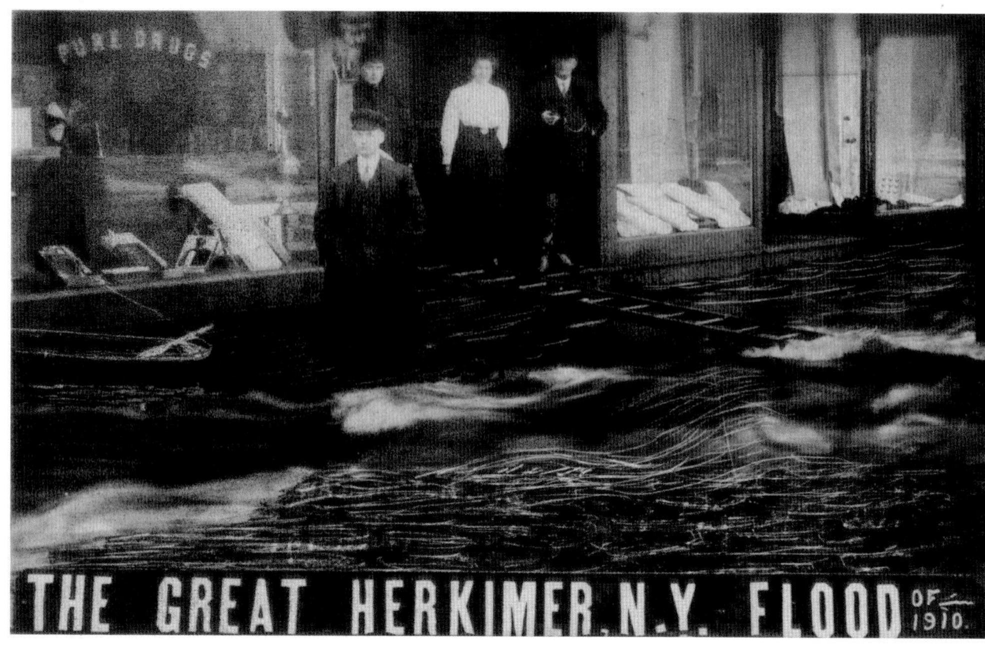


12.5. The great Herkimer, N.Y., flood, 1910. B. J. Slusarczyk Coll.

## The Great Herkimer Flood

Herkimer is located fifteen miles south of the Blue Line and a short ride from Remsen by train (Utica Gas and Electric Company 1922).[3] The circumstances surrounding the "Great Flood," as locals called it, were a little different from the normal spring ice jams. The winter of 1909–1910 had been unusually cold, and the ice on the waterways that led to the village was uncommonly thick. In late February, a warm spell with heavy rains caused creeks and streams to overrun their banks. The real problem started when a large ice jam formed near where West Canada Creek, a river that originates deep within the Adirondacks, enters the Mohawk River. The West Canada burst its banks, carrying massive ice blocks into Herkimer.

Word of the catastrophe reached Remsen, and Beach arrived on the scene, camera in hand. Sections of the village were three feet underwater. Houses were knocked off their foundations, businesses were flooded, and all transportation was halted. Eventually, officials used dynamite to dislodge the ice jams, and the river receded. After three days of flooding, the cleanup work began.

Apparently, Henry got there while there was still flooding. He took a variety of views. Some focused on the water in the downtown. He singled out one image to feature, labeling it with an unusually large caption (illus. 12.5). It was probably a lead card for a packaged series. Look carefully at this example of folk photography, and one can see that Henry embellished the scene by brushing in strokes to ruffle the fast-moving current. In addition, he inserted a crudely drawn rowboat. Although he wanted to increase the drama, the result is clumsy if not surreal. Cards of the great Herkimer flood detail the damage and cleanup of the downtown as well as show a train equipped with a mighty plow clearing ice at the railroad yard (illus. 12.6).

As with the Pennsylvania flood coverage, there are a few images that capture a particular moment that puts the viewer in touch with the human dimension of the catastrophe. My favorite is "Came Back after Her Treasures" (illus. 12.7). It shows a battered family dwelling unmoored from its foundation in a sea of

3. Herkimer is the county seat for Herkimer County, the county where Big Moose, Beaver River, and a substantial portion of the Fulton Chain are located.

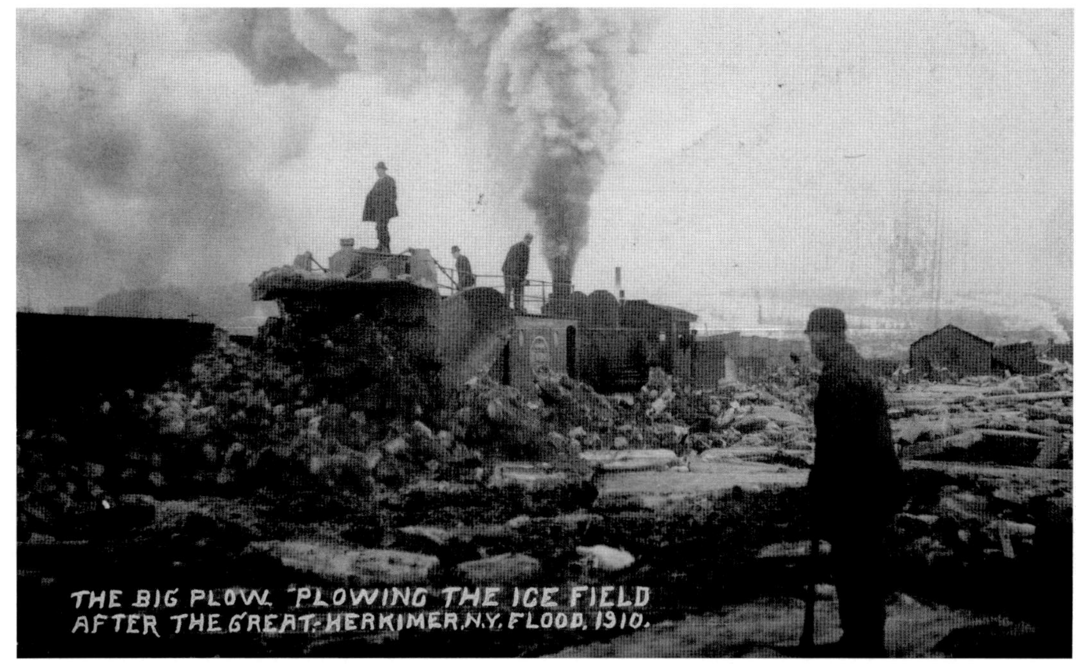


12.6. Plowing the ice fields after the great Herkimer flood, Herkimer, N.Y., 1910. Author's Coll.

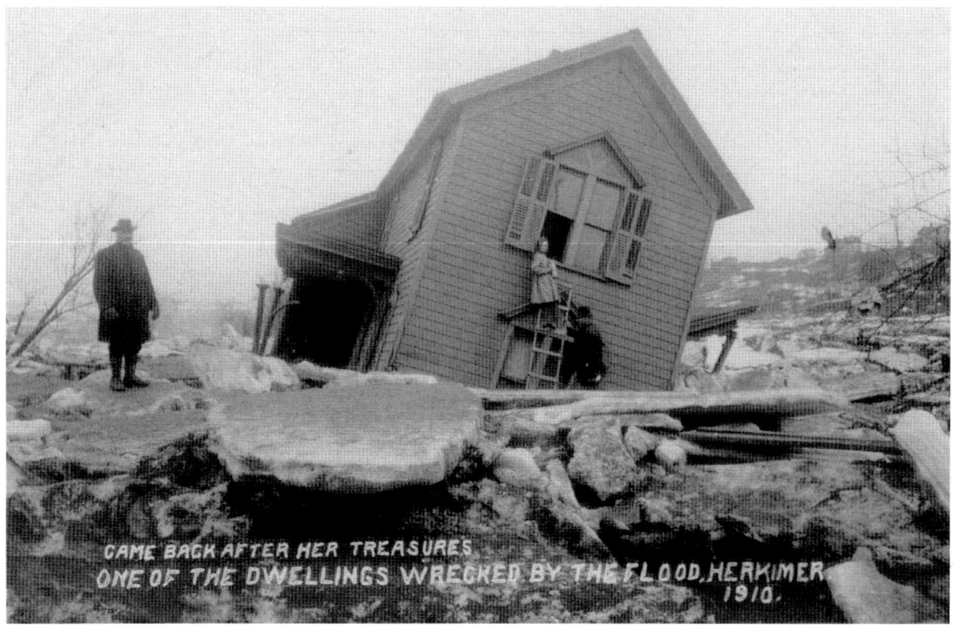


12.7. "Came Back after Her Treasures," Herkimer, N.Y., 1910. One of the dwellings wrecked by the flood. B. J. Slusarczyk Coll.

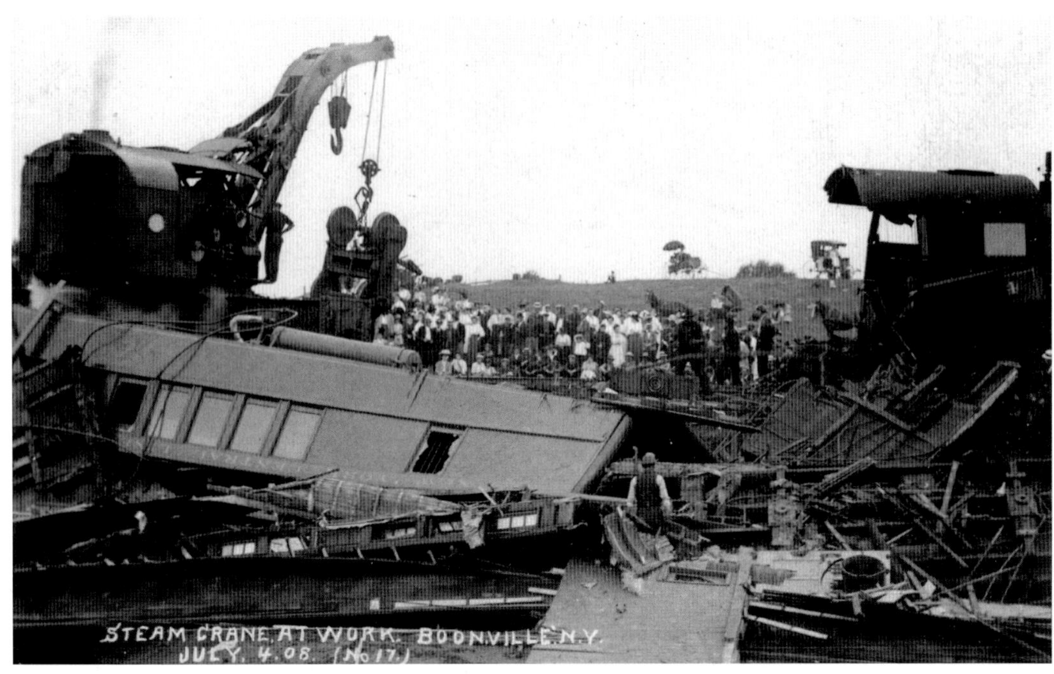


12.8. Steam crane at work, Boonville, N.Y., 1908. Myers Coll.

ice slabs. A little girl, assisted by a man holding a makeshift ladder, appears to be climbing to the window on the second floor in an effort to retrieve her personal property. The second adult, standing by, adds another touch of compassion to the scene. Beach's sentimentality is inconsistent. Another picture of the same dwelling, taken from a different angle and with no people present, is captioned "The Dizzy House."

## The Great Boonville Train Wreck

Beach took other disaster photographs closer to home. One of his earliest, largest, and most visually exciting series is of the great Boonville train wreck of July 4, 1908.

Although the catastrophe occurred one mile north of the village proper, the sound of the early-morning collision could be heard in the business district. A freight train loaded with lumber, dairy products, and cattle coming from Lowville smashed head-on into a passenger train coming from Utica. That train was carrying summer residents and visitors from New York City to the North Country. Most were snoozing in sleeping cars at the moment of impact.[4]

The collision threw an engine into the Black River Canal and killed the crew. A total of five died, and twelve were seriously injured. These numbers seem small when viewing the extensive damage and the tangled mess depicted in Beach's photos.

Henry arrived a few hours after the crash. He set up his tripod and went to work. I am unsure how many pictures he took, but he published a Boonville train-wreck series that has at least seventeen different shots.[5] His bird's-eye views provide an overview of the accident, whereas his medium-range and close-up shots give us the specifics (illus. 12.8, 12.9, 12.10, 12.11, 12.12).

Among the twisted parts are train-company workers studying, cleaning up, and restoring the site. Others, the survivors, try to recover possessions and to

4. A human error in adjusting the signal light caused the tragedy.

5. He numbered the series. Seventeen is the highest number that I and other collectors have seen.

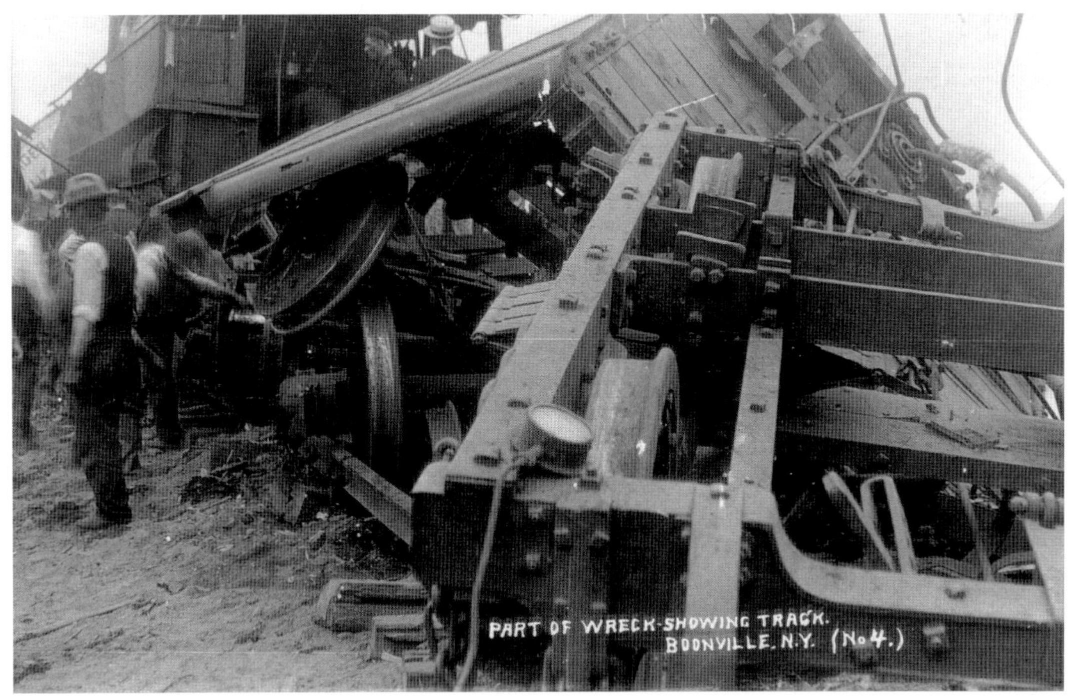


12.9. View of tracks after train wreck, Boonville, N.Y., 1908. Author's Coll.

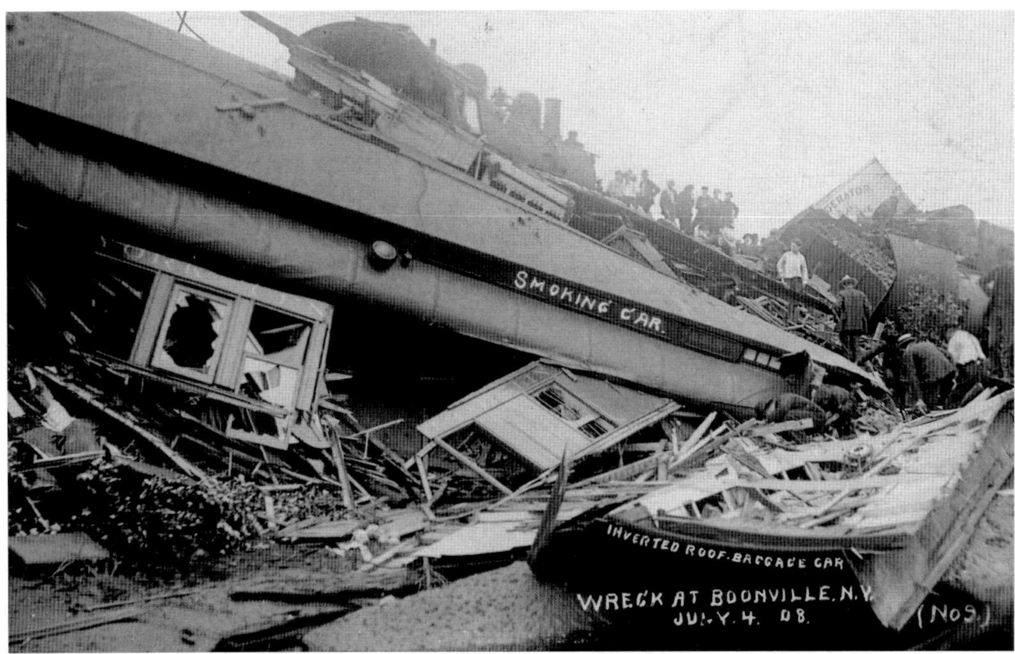


12.10. Wreck at Boonville, N.Y., 1908. Note Beach's lettering on the cars. Author's Coll.

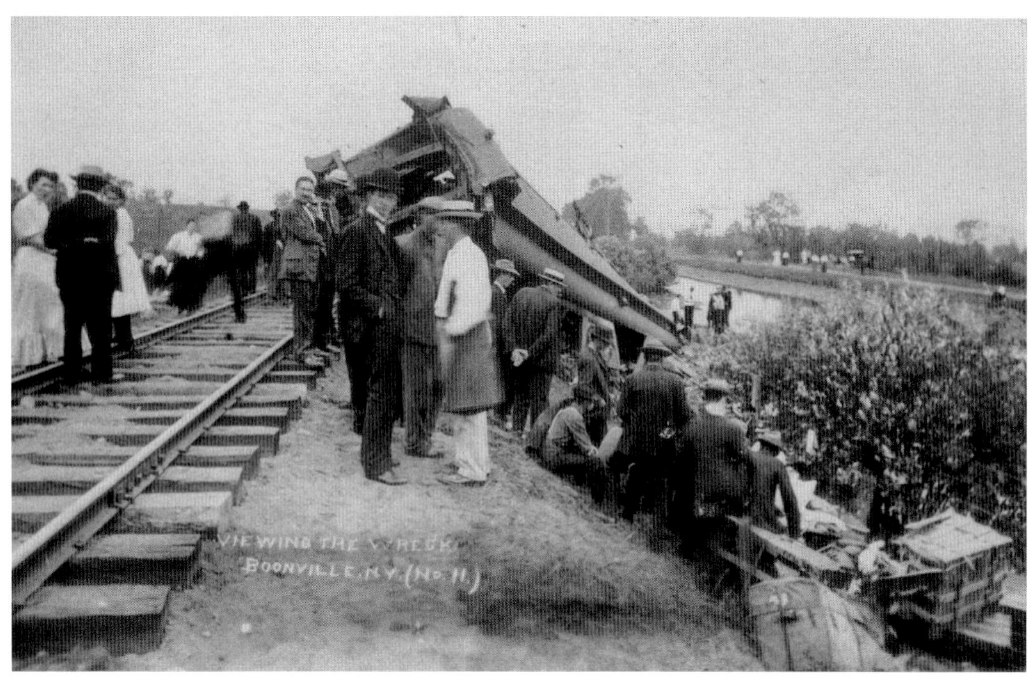


12.11. Viewing the wreck, Boonville, N.Y., 1908. Myers Coll.

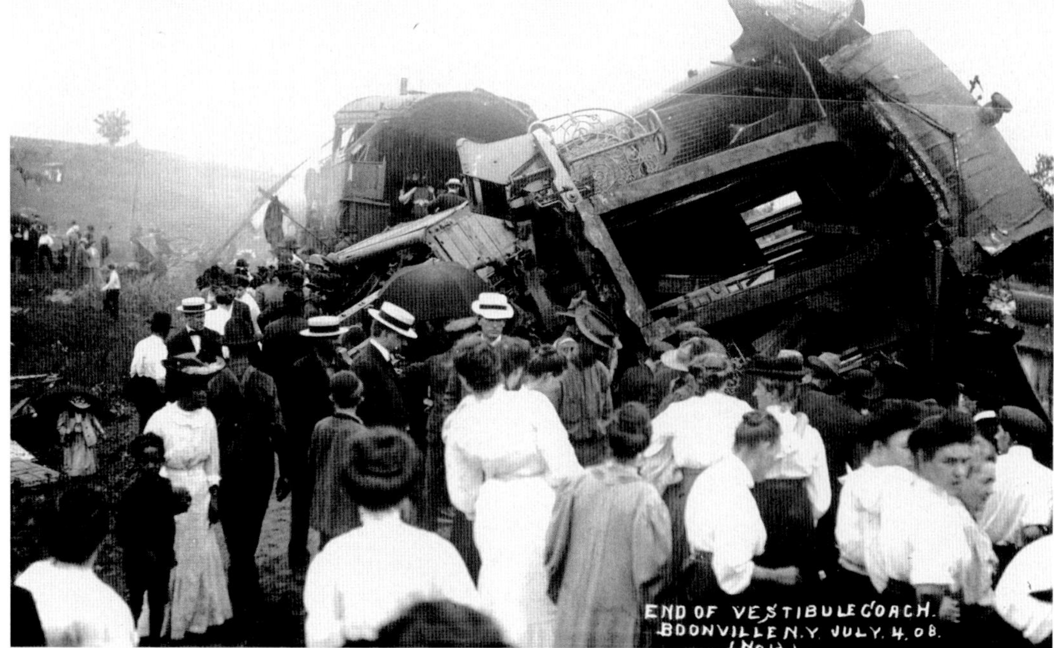


12.12. End of the vestibule coach, Boonville, N.Y., 1908. Author's Coll.

understand what they had been through. And then there are the morbidly curious. Through captions and labels Beach attempts to help the viewer understand the accident. To some extent he is successful in conveying information about the physical aspects, but the series creates, as well as captures, an unsettling feeling of chaos. Who exactly are the people? What are they doing? Is anyone in charge? How soon after the accident were the shots taken? Where are the injured? Are the people in shock? This mass of heavy, tangled metal just seems out of place in Boonville. All of the questions, combined with Beach's use of the local phrase "The Great Train Wreck," create a sense, probably unintended by the photographer, that we do not know what is going on and do not belong there.

## Minor Disasters

Beach took other photos of Adirondack accidents and damage, albeit of a magnitude less than the Boonville train wreck. In these pictures, as well as in the other disasters covered in this chapter, Henry played the role of an early newspaper photographer. The pictures were not published in local dailies; they were sent or placed in the purchaser's own album where they served as markers in the person's own visual biography.

Surprisingly, Henry's portfolio, or at least the photos I have seen, does not include pictures of forest fires, logging mishaps, or industrial accidents. These tragedies were common in the Adirondacks. Either Beach was not there to take them or they did not fit his ideas of a photo opportunity.

Beach took pictures of logging camps that showed the buildings covered with huge mounds of snow. On some of them he gave a measure of its depth. He also took pictures of trains with huge plows pushing through massive snowdrifts. These recordings of the aftermath of blizzards are not dated in the captions, which suggests to me that deep snow was so common that Beach and others just took it for granted.

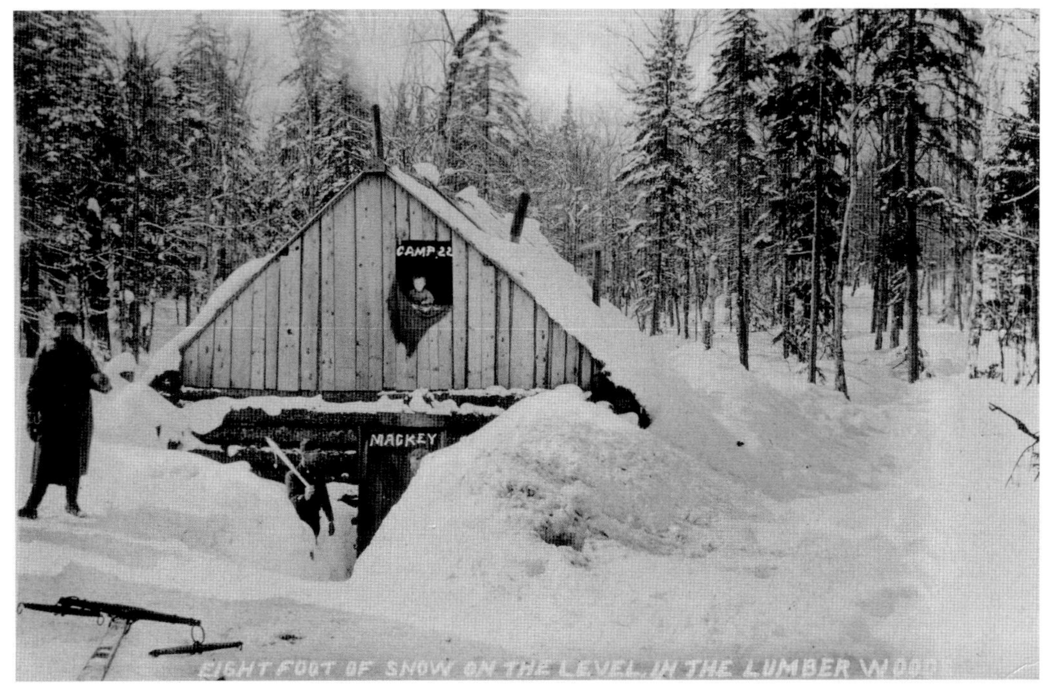


12.13. Eight feet of snow, in the lumber woods, ca. 1908. Author's Coll.

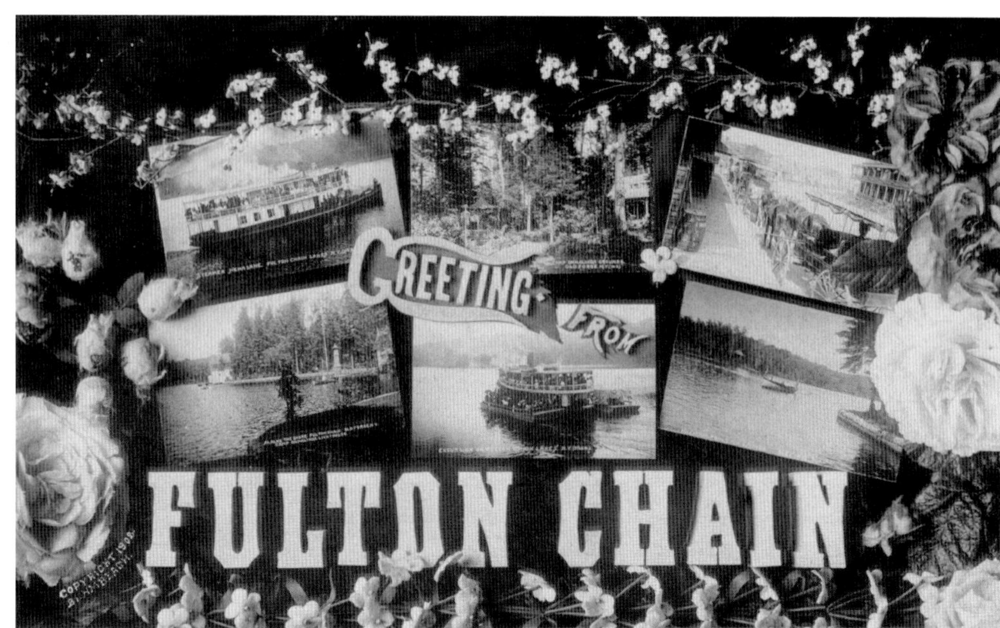


13.1. "Greetings from Fulton Chain." An example of a montage card, ca. 1908. Burhans Coll.

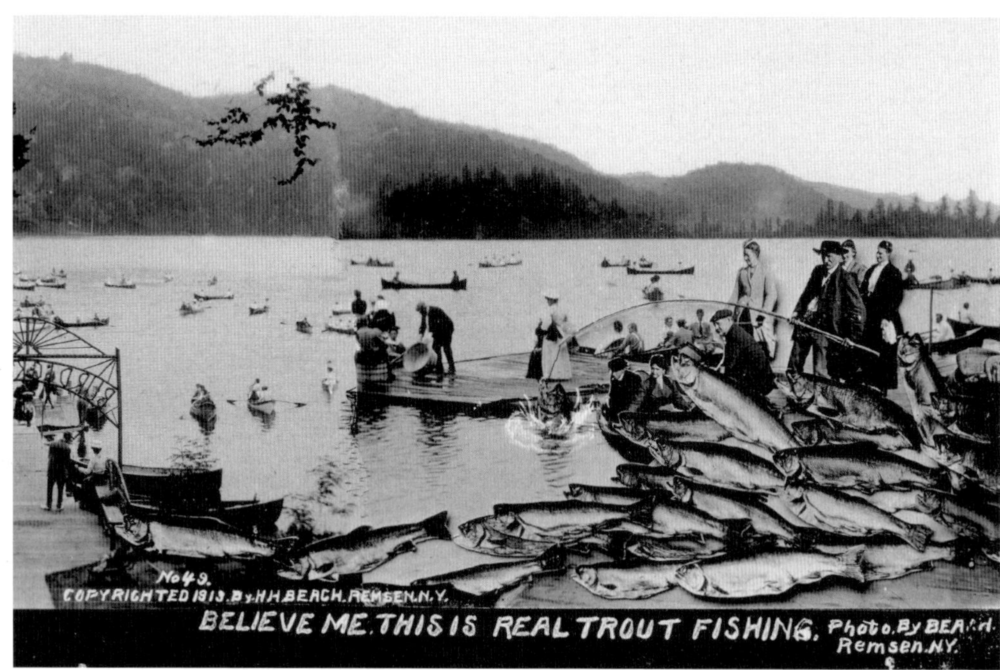


13.2. One of Beach's freak cards. Background photograph taken at Burdick's, Big Moose Lake, N.Y., ca. 1913. Courtesy of the Adirondack Museum.

13

# Montage and Whimsical Postcards

In addition to his ordinary single-picture postcards, Henry produced a composite variety. What I am referring to are multiple pictures and cut-up images juxtaposed with various graphic embellishments (large letters, pictures of flowers, flying fish, and other objects) on a single card.[1] Some, like the one of the Fulton Chain, were just decorated assortments of pictures (illus. 13.1). Others were surreal pasteups known among postcard collectors as exaggeration cards. Beach referred to them as "freak" cards (illus. 13.2).

It was unusual for North Country photographers to produce this variety of photo postcards. Beach was the only one who included them as a standard part of his stock. He strayed from what we typically think of as commercial photography into a funky, whimsical art form that required creativity and innovation.

Beach's montage work can be divided into three categories: advertising cards, produced for business owners; scenic views, meant for the general customer; and exaggeration, or freak, cards, novelty items produced for the tourist market.

1. Beach produced montage cards by taking the various elements—cutouts, lettering, flowers, small and large photographs, calendar pages, and the like—arranging them on a large flat surface, and taking a picture of the collage. It was like taking a picture of a bulletin board he had decorated. He used a similar technique for doing freak cards, except the parts were cutouts from other photographs superimposed on the original image. Montage and composite cards tend to be slightly more blurred than Beach's other images because each is a picture of a picture.

2. Examples of these self-promotion pieces are hard to find. I have seen only six different examples.

## Advertising Cards

By "advertising cards," I mean advertisements, postcards made for businesspeople and civic figures for publicity purposes or to solicit business. Henry produced advertising postcards for his own business.[2] (Examples were included in chapter 2, illustrations 2.12 and 2.13.) His trademark self-portrait is on the majority, but the lettering and the composition vary. The first illustration shows a simple formal style, a large business card (illus. 13.3). The next example is much more quirky and cluttered. It includes his wholesale price list (illus. 13.4). Beach violates all the rules of modern advertising design. He is trying to accomplish so much in such a small space that the contents seem to be bursting their seams. Space is so tight that when printing it he erred slightly, cutting out some of the letters on the left side. Notice the spider-web design near his portrait, the ten miniature scenes, and the informal lettering in the text. Seriously flawed? Unrestrained brilliance? Take your pick!

Henry created montage advertisement postcards for hotels, restaurants, stores, and other commercial establishments. A fine example is the postcard he made for Mrs. I. G. Barrows's Hair, Millinery, and Ladies Furnishings shop in Utica, New York (illus. 13.5). Typical of his work, the Barrows example contains bold lettering, photographic inserts with their own captions, and a greeting, all garnished with a rose. In addition to being a piece of vernacular advertising, it is also a revealing visual document containing details of all aspects of the hair and millinery business. Included is a room with women making hairpieces from

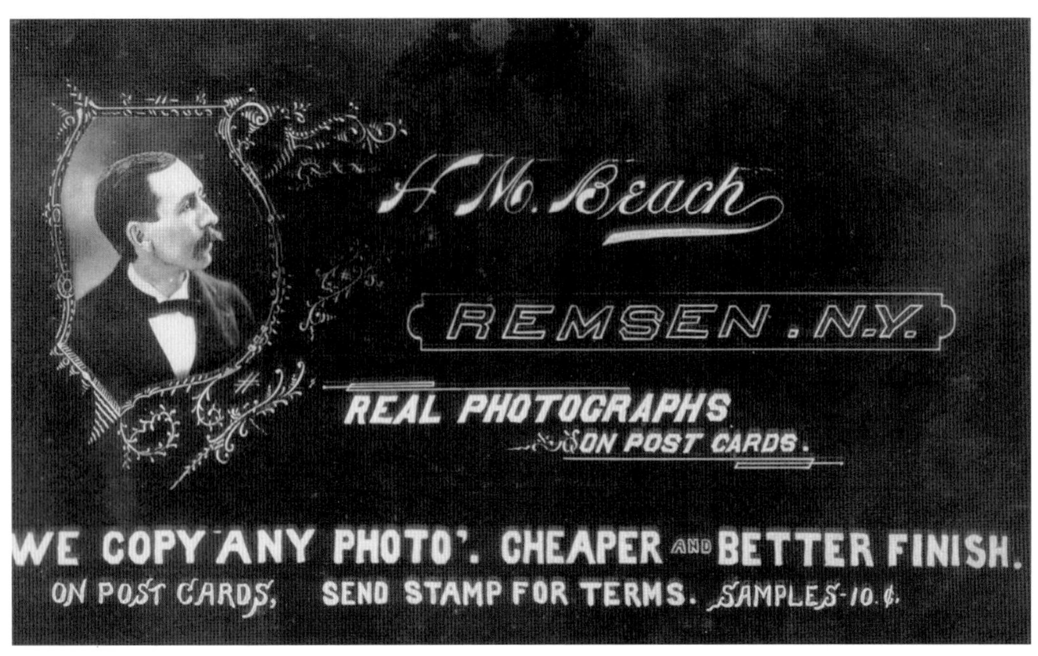


13.3. Beach advertising postcard, ca. 1910. Henry's signature is on the top line. R. Jones Coll.

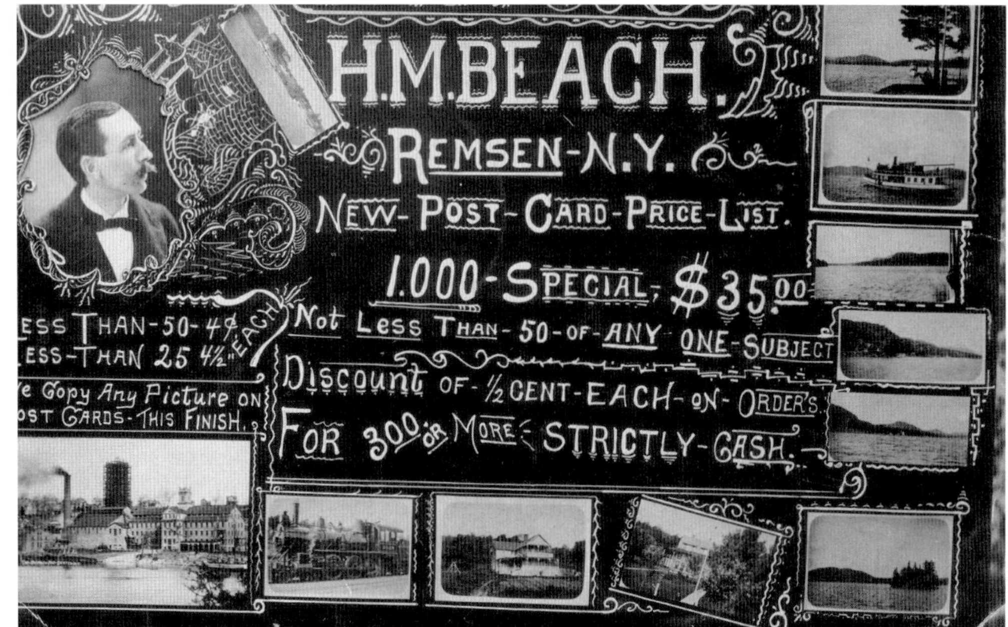


13.4. Beach advertising card with new wholesale postcard price list, ca. 1912. Author's Coll.

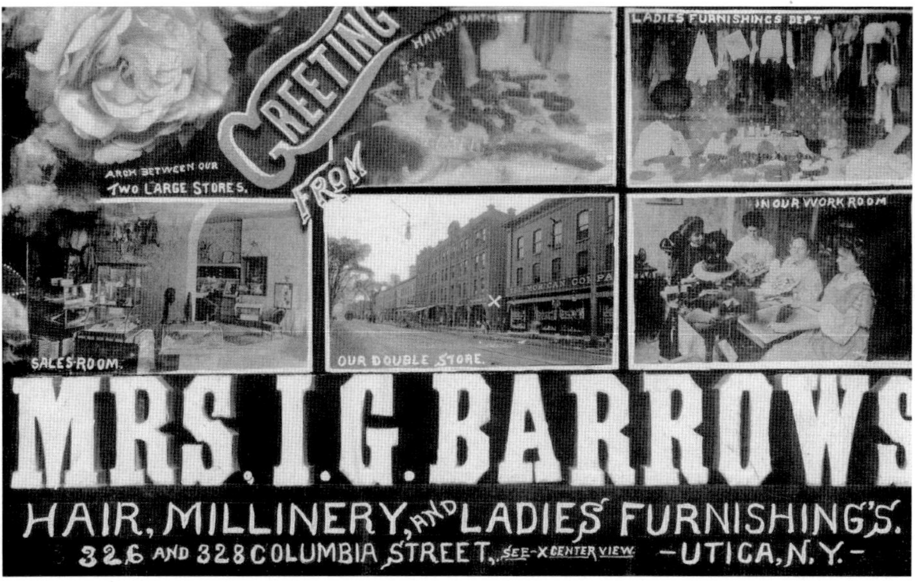


13.5. Mrs. I. G. Barrows's Hair, Millinery, and Ladies Furnishings advertisement card, ca. 1911. Author's Coll.

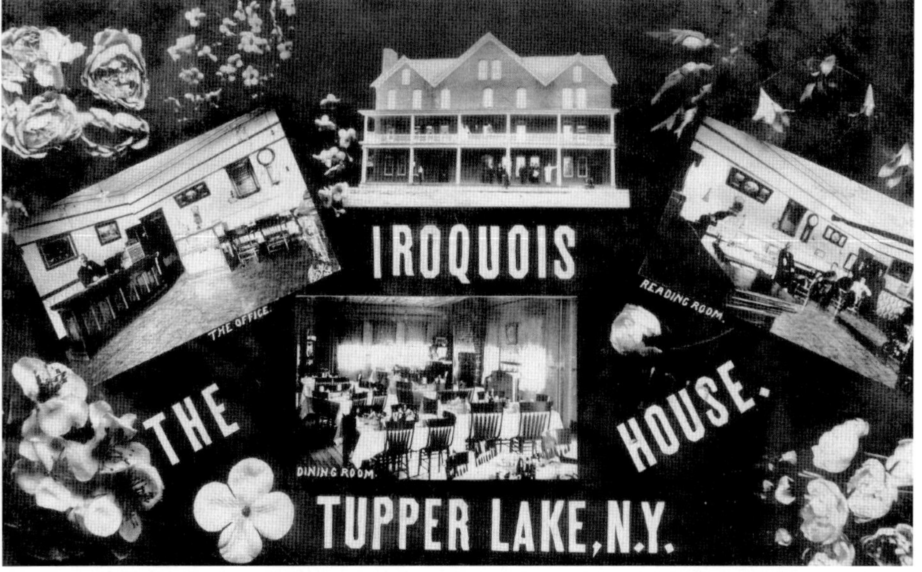


13.6. Montage of Iroquois House, Tupper Lake, N.Y., ca. 1910. Author's Coll.

real hair. Note how Henry marked the storefront with an X on the image in the center.

Although he did ad cards for merchants, his most frequent customers were North Country hotel and resort owners. The Iroquois House advertisement features interior views (illus. 13.6). Notice the pictures of the proprietor at the main desk, the guests in the lobby, the dining room, and groupings of flowers. More common of his tourist-oriented promotional pieces were postcards featuring a particular hotel with views of surrounding lakes and mountains, such as the one for the Eagle Bay Hotel on Fourth Lake (illus. 13.7). Another North Country resort example shows yet another design. This variety has one view, in this case of the Seventh Lake House, and many supplemental inserts, including pages from the 1911 calendar, fish, and people in a rowboat in the foreground (illus. 13.8).

Some images Beach produced roughly fall under the heading of commercial montage, but they are even more unconventional than the previous examples and more difficult to interpret. The postcard for the Hurley House in De Kalb Junction is a case in point (illus. 13.9). Although at first glance it may seem uncomplicated, closer inspection creates a brainteaser. For one, the train and the people to the right have been superimposed on the image. The railroad did not run next to the hotel, and the train is much out of proportion to the building. W. H. Miller, the proprietor, is in the insert. The gleam in his eye and his smile are difficult to decipher. Though the reproduction here is not of sufficient quality to read the title of the book he is holding, in the original it is easy to read: *Therapeutic Notes.* Add the phrase in the caption, "Special Service to Traveling Men," to the puzzle, and we are really in a tangle.

Try this one: a cow superimposed on a lawn in front of a well-manicured house, with a caption bragging about milk production (illus. 13.10). Your guess is as good as mine! Part of the joy of viewing Beach's photography is that some of it is so outrageous, so out of our realm of logic, that we have to throw up our hands and give in just to enjoying the image.[3]

3. Although it may be difficult to interpret this card, it is probably of a champion milk producer. The details in the caption probably include her name and the amount she produced. Who the picture was taken for and why are a mystery. It may have been an ad for the owner. Why the cow is superimposed on the lawn is also a mystery.

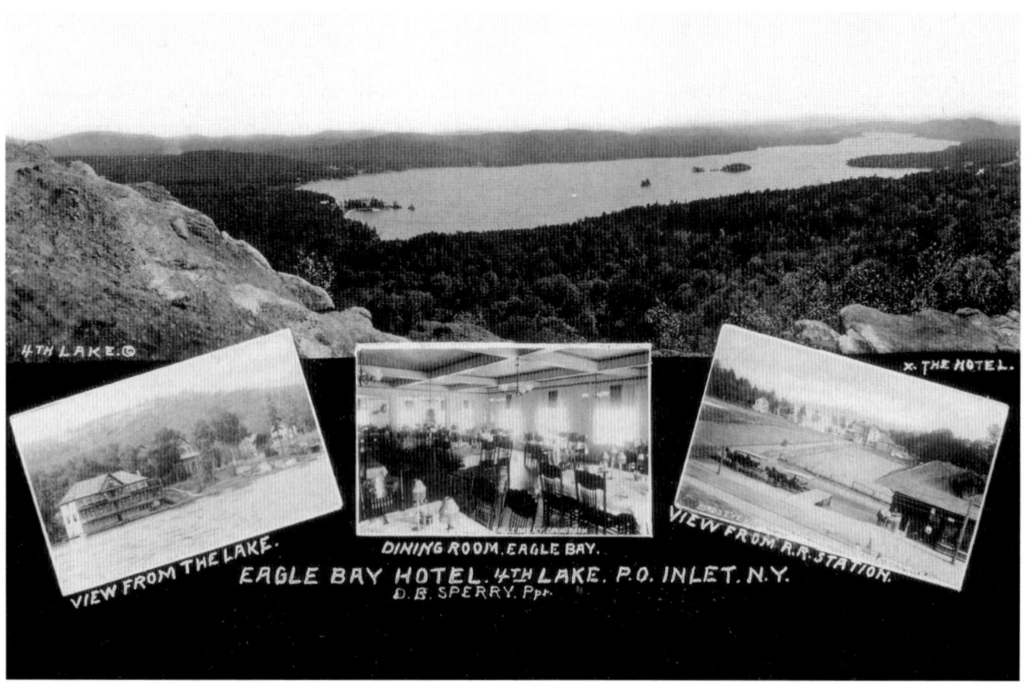


13.7. Eagle Bay Hotel, Fourth Lake, advertising card, ca. 1912. Note that the miniature view on the right is illustration 4.9. Courtesy of the Adirondack Museum.

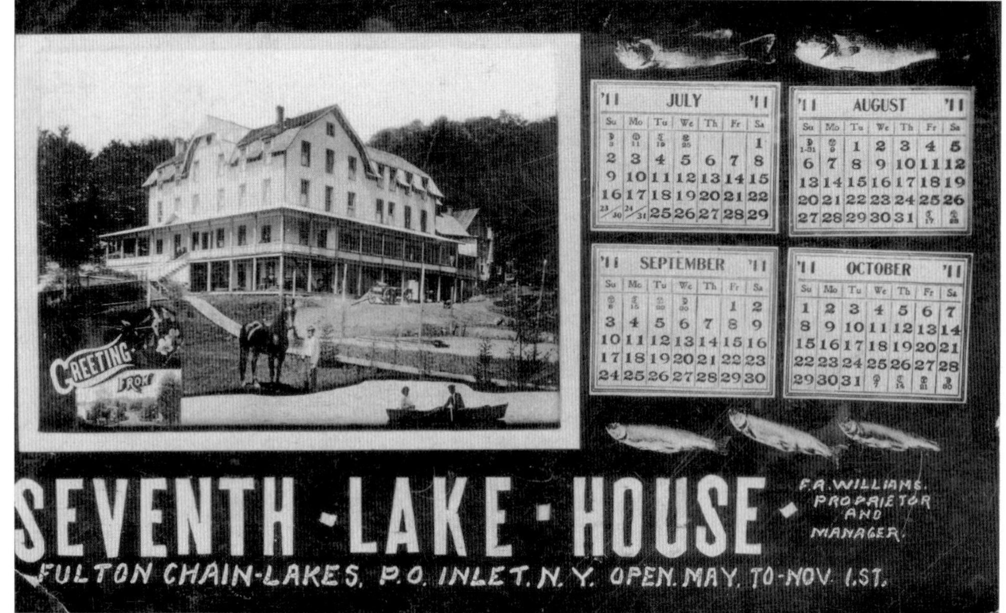


13.8. Seventh Lake House, Inlet, N.Y., ca. 1911. Author's Coll.

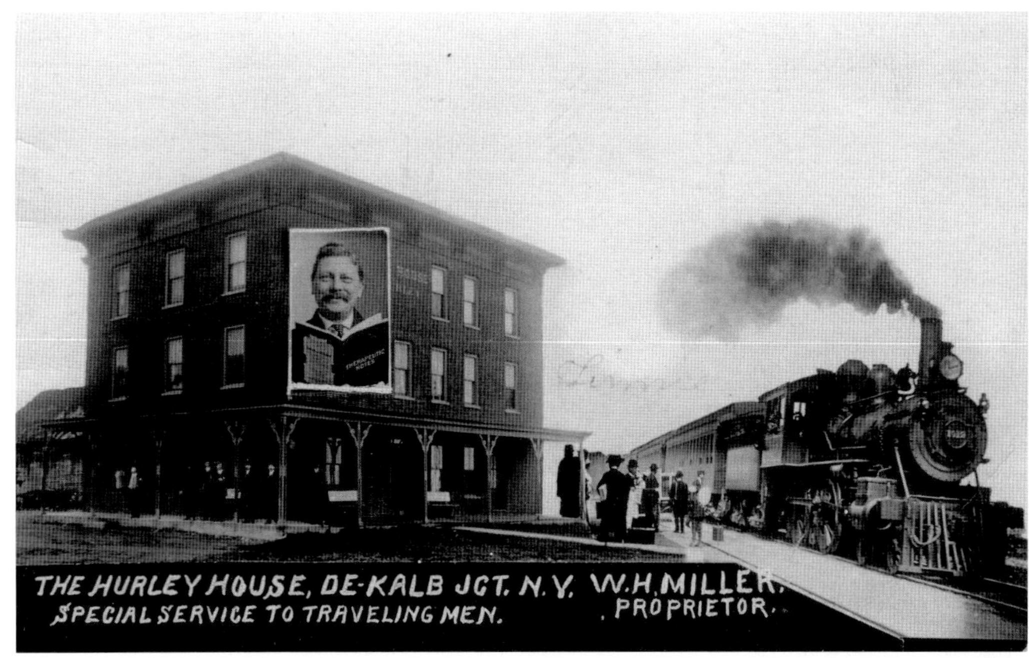


13.9. Hurley House, De Kalb Junction, N.Y., ca. 1914. Author's Coll.

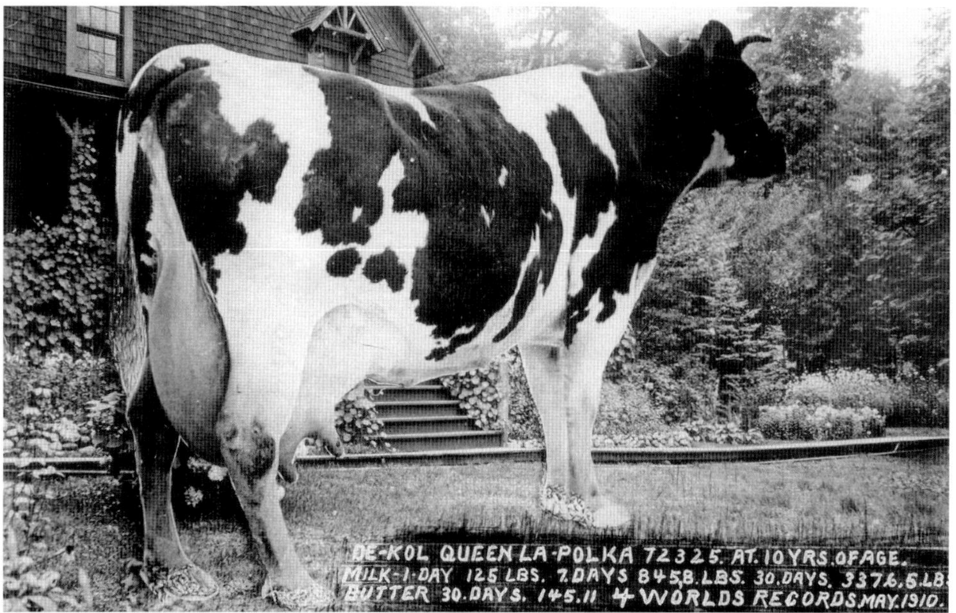


13.10. De-Kol Queen La-Polka, winner of four world records, 1910. Author's Coll.

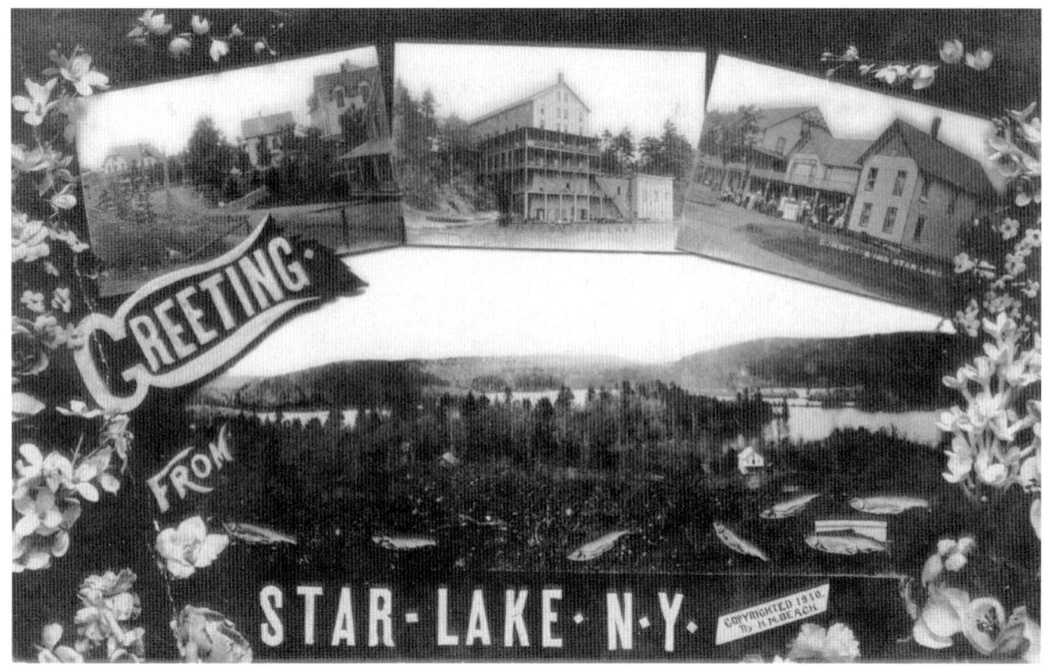


13.11. Montage card, Star Lake, N.Y., ca. 1910. Davis Coll.

## Scenic Montage

Beach produced general scenic montage cards, too. Rather than advertisements for particular hotels or resorts, they were just composites of scenes of towns and vacation spots where he did a lot of business. The scenic card of the Fulton Chain, illustration 13.1 above, is one of Henry's most carefully crafted scenic cards. As you can see, there are many similarities between it and his advertising cards. The scenic composite cards were attractive to customers who wanted to send a card that showed a sampling of views. Beach produced some to serve as the capstone of a series sold in sets. The miniatures that were part of the composite were produced as full-size cards, too. The card of Star Lake is a classic (illus. 13.11).

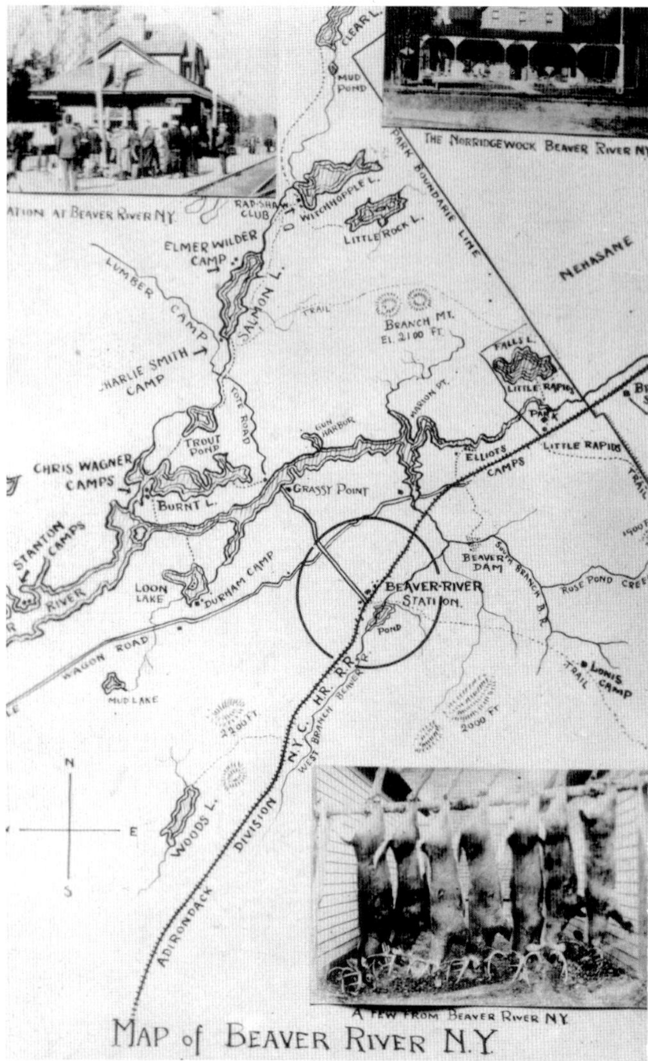


13.12. Map of Beaver River, N.Y., ca. 1912. Author's Coll.

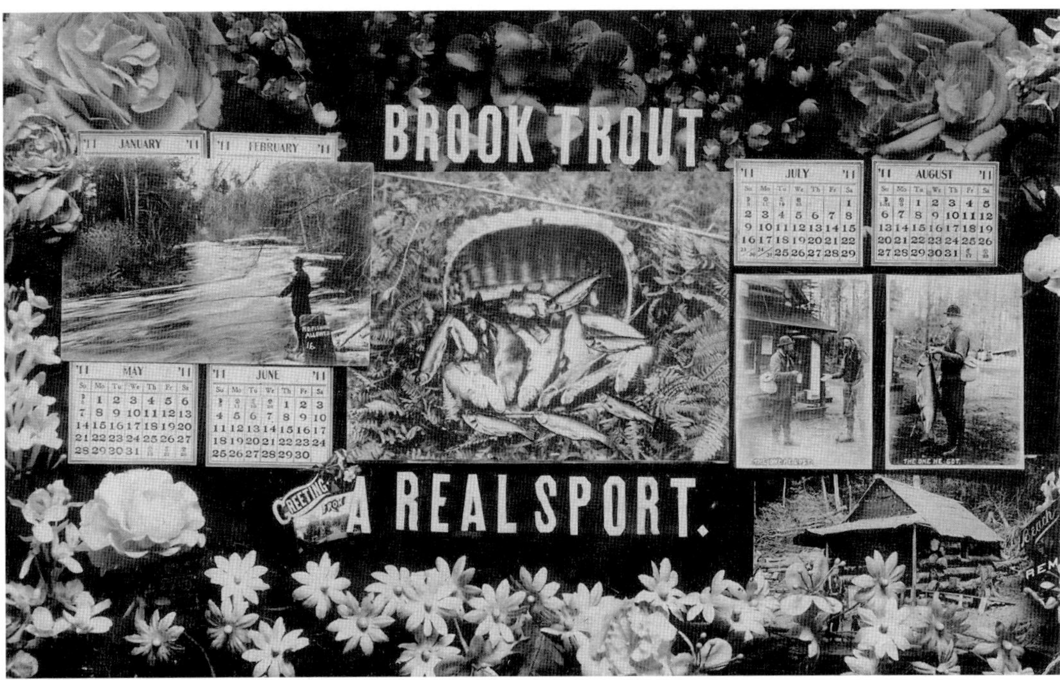


13.13. Montage card, "Brook Trout, Real Sport," ca. 1911. Note that the miniature view on the right is illustration 2.2. Davis Coll.

Henry also made montage postcards consisting of small photos scattered about a hand-drawn map. Some, like the one of Beaver River, focus on a particular area (illus. 13.12). Included are pictures of killed deer, the Beaver River railroad station, and the Norridgewock Hotel.[4] Other map cards were produced as advertising cards for resorts. In those cards the map might include the whole of New York State with arrows on the main roads pointing out the directions to the resort. Far from professional cartography, Beach's maps are crudely drawn by hand.

Henry produced generic scenic Adirondack montage postcards such as his "Brook Trout, a Real Sport," too (illus. 13.13). The detail is difficult to make out, but the small pictures retain their own captions. The one on the left reads "No Fishing Allowed," and the second one from the right is of a man showing with his hands the size of the fish that got away. It is captioned "The One He Lost." The image on the right is of a man with a pipe holding a huge fish, "The One He Got." I recently came across a slightly different copy of that picture in full-size postcard form (see illustration 2.2). Upon closer inspection we see that the man is none other than Henry M. Beach. The fish in the original is much smaller, though. In the montage version the catch's size was exaggerated by photographic manipulation. Henry's tongue-in-cheek humor, creativity, visual resourcefulness, and manipulation are shown in many of his images. Study all of his pictures carefully, or one will be fooled rather than amused.

4. For other pictures and more information on the area, see chapter 8 and illustrations 6.21 and 6.22.

## Freak Cards

Beach produced a line of exaggeration, or freak, cards in which the tampering is much more blatant than in "Brook Trout" or in any of the other images shown thus far. The best way to describe this variety is to look at one. Rather than Henry printing an unadulterated picture from a single negative, he manufactured an implausible synthesized composite. Parts of two or more photos were combined and superimposed on a photo background. Purposefully distorted, the alterations are so obvious that their fabrication was apparent to all but the most gullible viewer. Not realistic depictions, they were Barnumisms, designed to poke fun, to engage in overstated humorous visual rhetoric (Rubin and Williams 1990). The effect is embellished by outlandish captions such as the one in the example: "Believe Me, Some Big Fish Come Up the River. We Caught Several of Them Just Below the State Dam" (illus. 13.14). These cards force us to expand our vision of who Beach was.

With his freak cards, Beach was a spinner of visual tales that originated in logger's bunkhouses, general stores, and other places where Adirondackers sat around swapping stories. For outsiders, "Adirondack humor" may be an oxymoron. The popular notion is that local Adirondack people are uncommunicative, reticent, and highly unlikely to tell jokes (Bethke 1981). But, as Beach knew from a lifetime of sitting around woodstoves, there were many North Woods dens overflowing with laughter.

Robert Bethke in *Adirondack Voices* (1981) relays a story of an Adirondack woodsman spinning a tale about the remarkable two-foot-long bullhead he landed near St. Regis Falls. A logger listening to the story contributed: ". . . just liable to catch anything up there. I went fishing there . . . and my line hooked on something that I didn't know what it was. I pulled it up. It was a lantern. And it was lit." The first storyteller called the interloper a "goddam liar!" In defense, the logger retorted: "Well, I tell you what I'll do—you shorten up your fish and I'll blow out the lantern" (27).

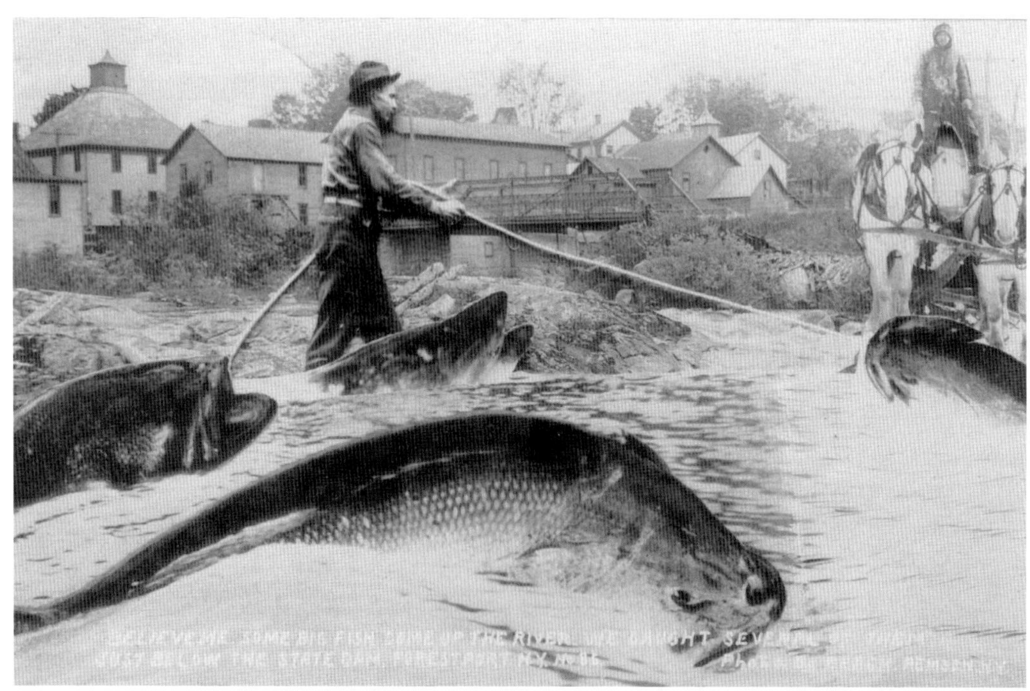

13.14. Fishing freak card, Forestport, N.Y., ca. 1914. Courtesy of the Adirondack Museum.

As the story suggests, Adirondackers were not exempt from exaggeration nor the tendency to laugh about it. It was common to add inches when reporting snowfalls, degrees to how cold it was, extra points to the number of spikes on a buck's rack, and inches (and sometimes feet) to the size of the fish. This boastfulness was the basis for a good deal of humor. The history of the Adirondacks is filled with tongue-in-cheek, larger-than-life creatures and events. With his tall-tale cards, Beach both celebrated and poked fun at this leaning.

Being an avid fisherman, it is not surprising that Beach's most common exaggeration-card subject was fishing (see illustrations 13.2, 13.13, and 13.14). Encounters with wild, and presumably dangerous, animals were another frequent topic. The bears in illustration 13.15 loom large. The caption reads, "Too Scared to Shoot He Droped [*sic*] His Gun and Gave One Some Tobacco."

The third-most-common exaggeration involved the logging industry and the size of the timbers that were harvested. As you saw from the chapter on the logging industry, horses could move enormous loads, but not as large as the one in the card captioned "Rolling the Big Pine to Sleighs" (illus. 13.16).

Forest themes were not the only subjects of his freak cards. Beach pasted urban components on rural and small-town photographic backdrops, thereby creating composites with incongruent urban–North Woods elements. Illustration 13.17, "The Busy Corner," is typical of this genre. Henry superimposed cutout images of trolley cars, a large touring car, and pedestrians on a photograph of Main Street in Piercefield, a location that never saw such things.

In another example, Henry created quite a commotion in the sleepy town of Old Forge, with crowds and ferryboats competing for space at the dock (illus. 13.18). All of it, including the contemplative African American woman in the left front of the view, is part of a composition of cutout parts.

In his small-town fantasy cards he captured and capitalized on a tension that characterizes Adirondack culture. Residents of the area are both insecure and

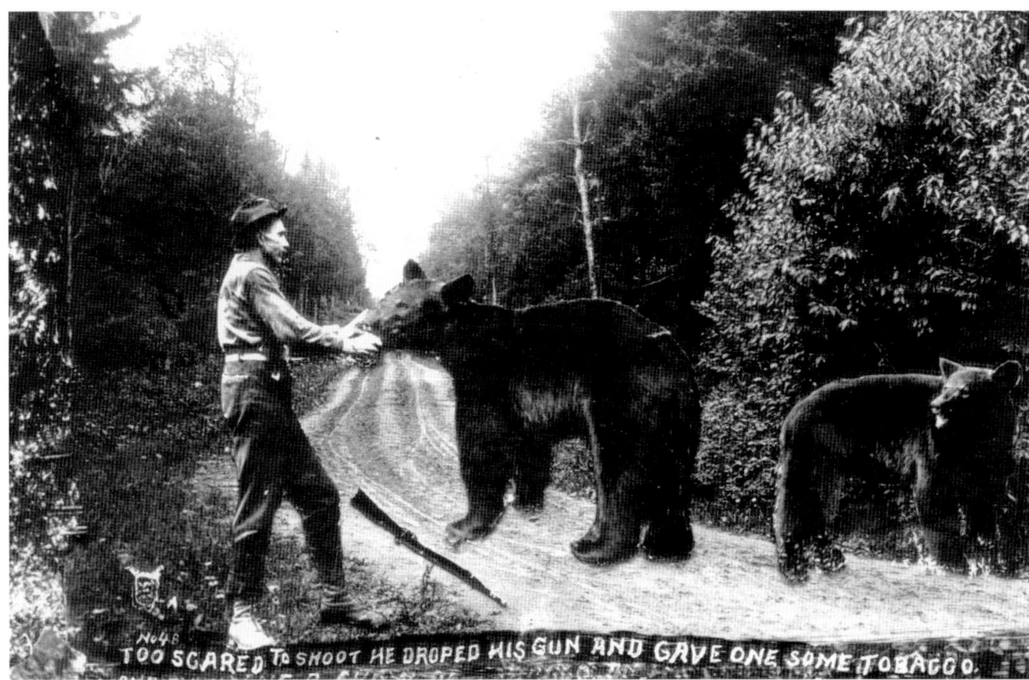


13.15. Bear exaggeration card, ca. 1912. Davis Coll.

proud of being rural. In his "Busy Day" cards Beach makes fun, while warning us about urban progress. What makes Beach freak cards special is that Henry seemed to be a quiet, unassuming man, not prone to loud talk and overstatement. In his cards his humor is deadpan. He becomes the wise yarn spinner with a twinkle in his eye, laughing at, or perhaps laughing with, us and his customers, be they local or up from the city on a visit to the North Woods.

The composite card combined Beach's penchant for inventiveness and his whimsical personality with his need to turn a profit (Rubin and Williams 1990). Rather than being confined by a narrow, stuffy convention of photography, Beach's rural location and self-styled business gave him license to experiment. He could play with different visual forms and thereby enlarge his product list. Sometimes his oddball formats and innovations found an audience with paying clientele. Freak cards touched the funny bone of the potential buyers, persuading them to purchase extra cards.

Whereas we look at Beach's freak cards as down-home artifacts, produced by a relatively uneducated rural artist, these compositions have many of the same elements found in the so-called sophisticated work of contemporary artists operating in urban art centers and referred to as surrealists (Teitelbaum 1992). It is obvious that his intention is not to fool us. Henry is telling us, "Don't take it seriously" (Rubin and Williams 1990). Beach crudely but purposely blurred fantasy and reality as well as the credible and the incredible.

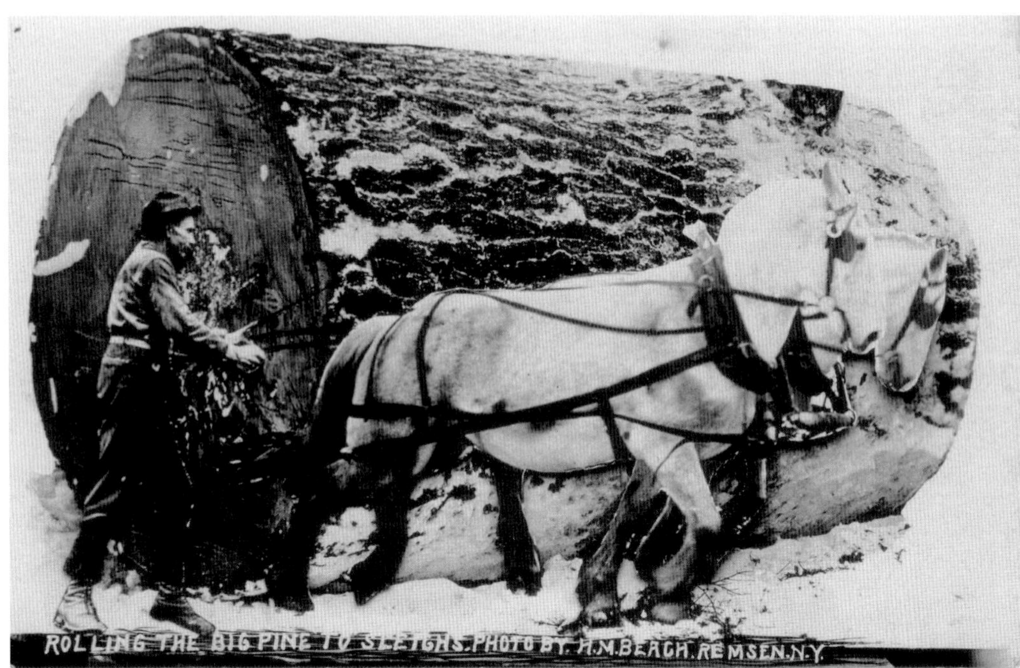


13.16. Logging exaggeration postcard, ca. 1924. Author's Coll.

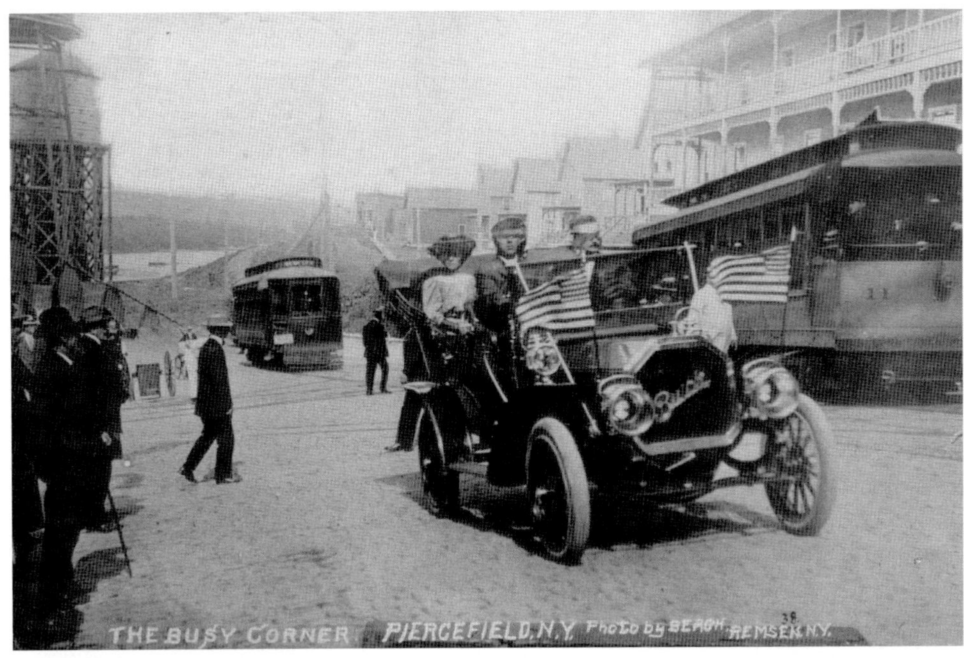


13.17. "The Busy Corner," Piercefield, N.Y., ca. 1910. H. Slusarczyk Coll.

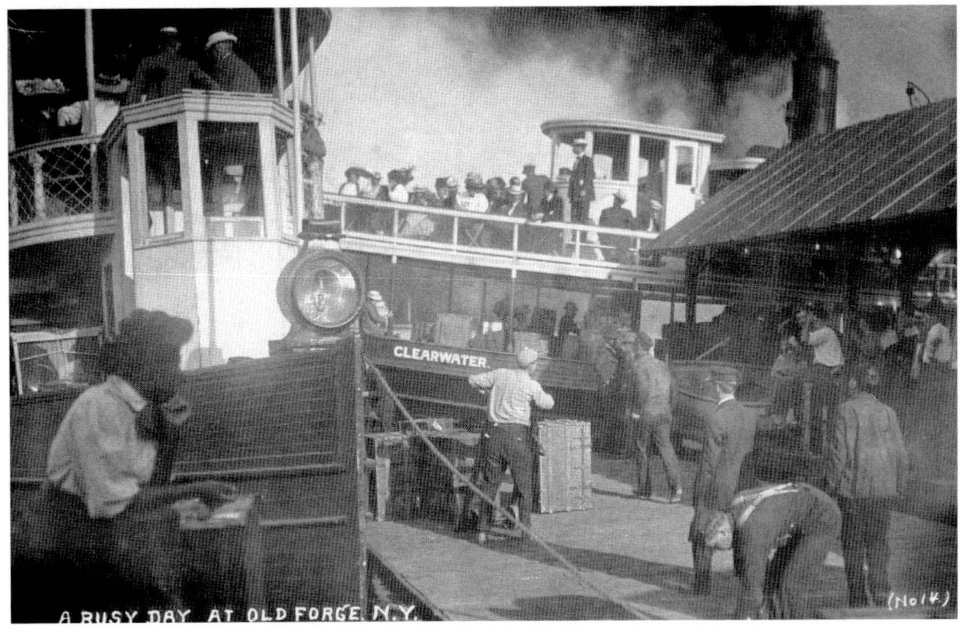


13.18. Busy day at Old Forge, N.Y., ca. 1912. D. Jones Coll.

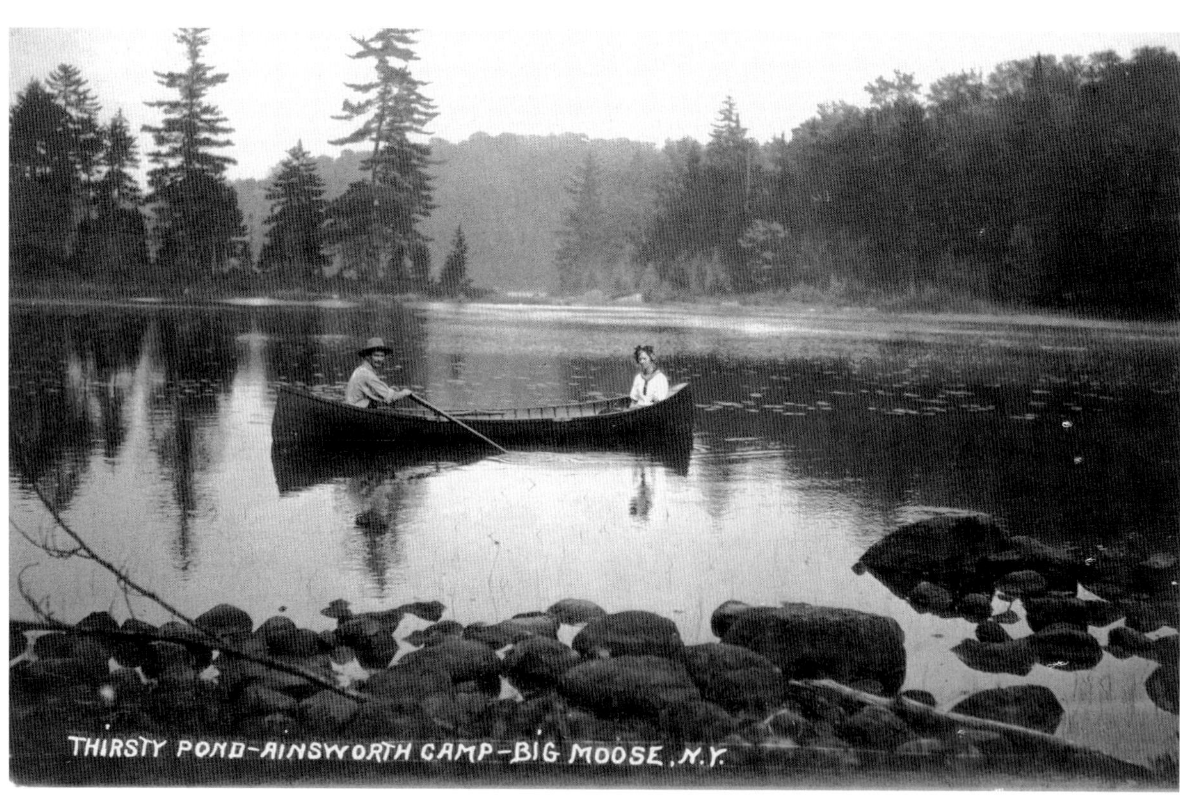


14.1. Thirsty Pond, Ainsworth Camp, Big Moose, N.Y., ca. 1910. Winter Coll.

14

# Conclusion
## Vernacular Photography

We have traveled through the North County with Henry Beach as our guide, stopping at Remsen, Thendara, Big Moose, Benson Mines, Tupper Lake, Saranac Lake, Mountain View, and other locations. He took us to railroad stations, garages, scenic spots, resorts, hotels, hunters' and anglers' haunts, logging camps, mills, mines, main streets, general stores, and disaster sites. The trip was far-reaching, but the pictures we have seen are merely a selection from Beach's vast bequest.

We know Henry, his terrain, and his times and work better now. Beach was intimate with the places we have been. Because he was our escort, we went to spots and met people most visitors never get to see. But a local guide, no matter how authentic, can bring us only so close. As some of Henry's pictures remind us, we remain outside of Beach's world—tourists without a deep grasp of what his pictures meant to him and to his people.

Henry M. Beach was a man who had a steadfast dedication to his trade, an exceptional photographic eye, and a great sensitivity to the ordinary parts of his and his neighbors' way of life. I conclude with reflections on what Henry has to teach us about a special kind of picture taking: vernacular documentary. In addition, I touch on the difficulties of and opportunities for learning about the Adirondacks and its people by studying his work.

### Thirsty Pond

I mentioned the problem with the term *scenic* for classifying Beach's photographs in the chapter on that topic. That chapter was slim because *scenic* did not capture much of Henry's work. I push this discussion further with another card, "Thirsty Pond" (illus. 14.1).[1] When I first saw this picture, I automatically classified it as a beautiful Adirondack scenic. It seems obvious to do so. After all, Beach created a lovely, peaceful landscape. Included is a couple, perhaps girlfriend and boyfriend, in a guide boat on the calm pond. With reflections in the water, trees silhouetted against the sky, and stones in the foreground, the picture is lovely to the eye. But, as I discovered, considering it a romantic, pretty picture is just one way of looking at it.

I was jolted into a different understanding when I visited Big Moose on an August afternoon last year. I was sitting with Ida Winter, a longtime resident of the area and collector of antique postcards, going over her collection. When we came to the card in question, I made a fuss about how lovely it was. Not responding to my enthusiasm, she was quiet, and then she spoke to me about the card.

1. Thirsty Pond was renamed Ainsworth Pond.

The man in the boat was not just anyone, she said; it was her father, Danforth R. Ainsworth Jr. (1879–1931). In 1913, when the picture was taken, Dan and his wife had taken over the Ainsworth Camp from his parents and were in the process of developing it into a modestly prosperous family resort. As part of the personal service Dan provided guests, he took new arrivals out on a maiden boat ride on the pond, which is what we see in the picture.

Now the sad part. Ida told me about her father's death. Dan Ainsworth was in the process of setting up camp for a group of sport hunters who had hired him to be their guide when he fell out of his boat. Unable to swim, he drowned.[2] Ida and I had just met, but, from the tone in her voice and the quiet in the room, I realized that our postcard viewing had switched from hobbying to something much more personal. To Ida, the postcard of Thirsty Pond is beautiful and touching, but not the way a scenery card is to an outsider like myself. Its meaning for her is intimate, tied to a particular location and her own biography.

Henry did not approach this photographic opportunity with "scenic view" in mind, either. Dan Ainsworth was a regular customer, and the two men were old acquaintances. Dan sold Beach cards in the office. The Ainsworths originally came from the Port Leyden area, just south of Lowville, and they knew many of the same people. Beach was not taking a picture of "*a* pond" and "*a* person"; rather, he was engaged with a particular place and a camp owner whom he knew. Of course, after Dan's tragic drowning the meaning of the card changed substantially for both Ida and Beach. "Scenic view" is an outsider's translation of the card, not Ida's or Henry's.

## Huckleberry Charlie

As I did when I saw the picture of Thirsty Pond, when we do not know much about a picture we read it in our own outsider way. But some of the Beach pictures I showed you—for example, the ones of the oldest stage driver, Thomas Harmer (see illustration 4.5), and Mr. Shannon, the blind newspaper seller and his dog (see illustration 4.26), as well as others—are more difficult to interpret. Another example is Henry's picture of Huckleberry Charlie (illus. 14.2).

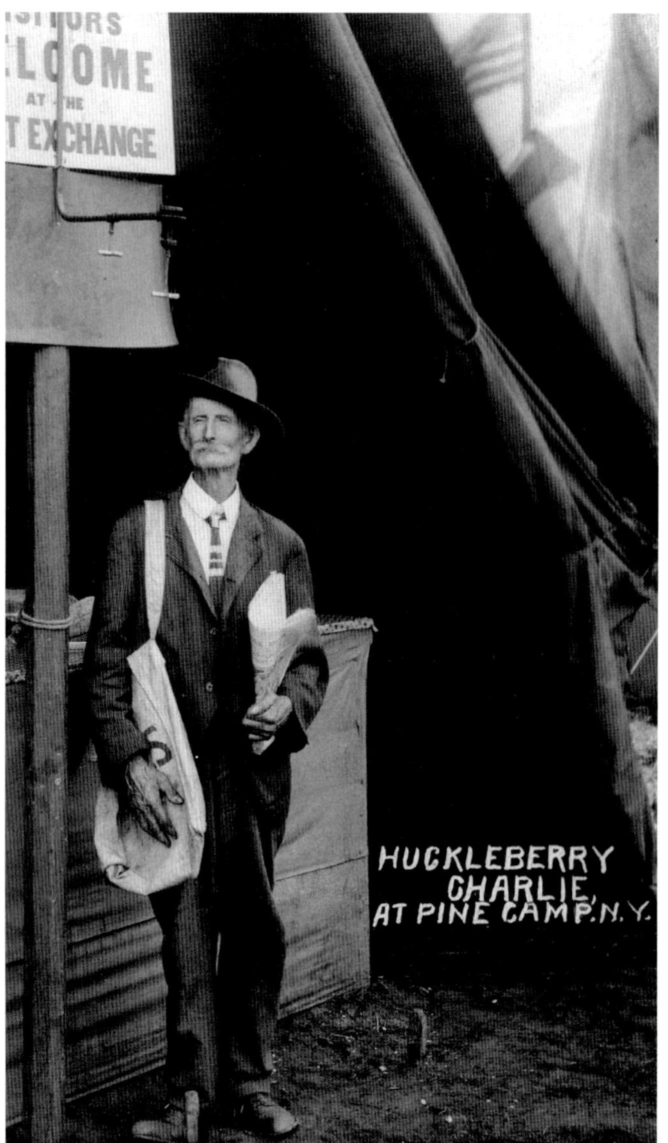


14.2. Huckleberry Charlie, Pine Camp, N.Y., ca. 1908. Author's Coll.

2. Wanda's father was fifty-two on the day of his death. The accident happened on Big Moose Lake in 1931. Afterward, the Great Depression set in. Ida recalls her mother's fortitude in holding the family and the business together against strong odds. Eventually, Thirsty Pond was sold and the resort passed on to other hands.

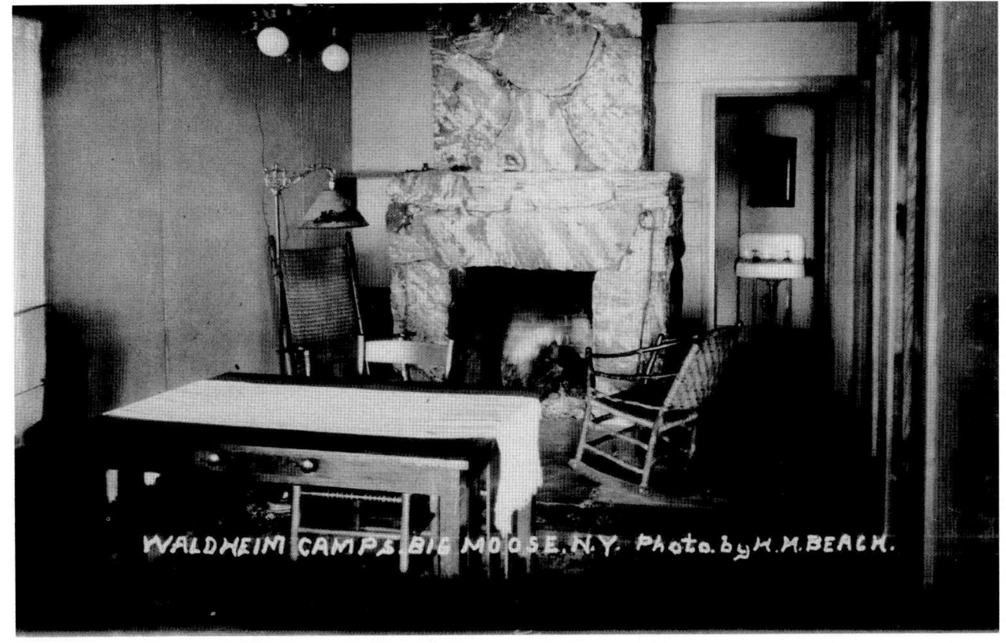


14.3. Waldheim Camp interior, Big Moose, N.Y., ca. 1924. Martin Coll.

I was drawn to the image when I initially saw it, even though I could not figure out who Charlie was or the occasion and context that prompted the shot. The caption provides some help. Pine Camp was an old military training site on the edge of the Adirondack Park.[3] But even with that information, I viewed the picture impersonally as interesting in the abstract.

To Henry and other North Country residents, Huckleberry Charlie was not a mysterious figure, and the postcard was not an abstraction. As Beach might have relayed, Charlie's full name was Charles R. Sherman, and the picture was taken in 1908 at a visitors' day military show.[4] Henry knew Charlie personally, and he knew what North Country residents thought of him. They were sympathetic, amused, and appreciative.

Charlie was a local eccentric whose reputation stretched across the North Country. He made money selling newspapers, but he also peddled sauerkraut, horseradish, and, in the berry season, huckleberries. Charlie was known for his nonsensical, riddlelike talk, and locals held mixed opinions as to whether he was crazy, feebleminded, or just wildly unconventional.[5] An incident that sealed his status as a character happened around the time of the photograph. As he had on many occasions, Charlie was selling newspapers at an open house at Pine Camp. Army units were staging war maneuvers, with one unit hiding in

3. It straddles Lewis and Jefferson Counties. The eastern boundary is approximately five miles from the Blue Line. It is now called Fort Drum.

4. The information reported here on Mr. Sherman comes from clippings in the files at the Jefferson County Historical Society in Watertown, N.Y. They were not dated, nor were the newspapers they came from noted on the clippings.

5. Mr. Sherman was sixty-six at the time of the picture. Legend has it that he was born in Watertown to one of the oldest and wealthiest families in the area. He lived in Great Bend, not far from Pine Camp. He dressed in gaudy clothes and eagerly played tunes selected from his five-tune repertoire on his banjo.

the brush. Charlie interrupted the mock battle by running toward the troops flailing his arms, warning them of the pending attack.[6]

Knowing all this history helps us to read the picture within the North Country context. It brings us closer, but all the information provided is no substitute for an insider's understanding of the man, the events, and the picture.

## The Bathroom at the Waldheim

One more visual puzzle! It is a picture of the interior of a cabin at Waldheim Camp at Big Moose Lake (illus. 14.3). I could have included it in the chapter on family camps and hotels. I show it now not because of the quality of the picture, but because when I first saw it I wondered why Beach took it. From discussions with insiders I have come to believe that the picture's appeal was that the bathroom door was open and showed that the cabin had inside running water and electric lights. The Martins, who owned the Waldheim, were proud of this fact, and Beach, accommodatingly, appreciated their point of view.

## Vernacular Photographer

The postcards of Thirsty Pond, Huckleberry Charlie, and the Waldheim cabin illustrate an important point. Photographs do not possess their own meaning. We take photos, see them, interpret them, and feel them differently depending on our background and experience. Although there is variation within any group, people who take and look at pictures of their own culture take different pictures and see what is taken differently from outsiders.[7] Beach was of the North Country, a native in the sense that the term is used in those parts. He worked within a particular visual language that was part and parcel of the Adirondacks. Many of his photographs were for his own people. He was a vernacular photographer.[8]

Henry was an insider to the world he photographed. He knew the people and places of the Adirondacks firsthand and intimately. In addition to shooting as a local, he was not formally schooled as a photographer and lived far enough away from mainstream society that his work was not dominated by national photographic styles and trends. The result is a different rendering of the region than we get from other photographers.

Beach took pictures of different people, objects, and places than an outsider might. Some of these decisions were simply because he knew the nooks and crannies and could go places nonlocals just did not know. He was familiar with the full complement of people and personalities, the old-timers and the children, the resort employees and owners, the lumberjacks, and all the characters of his culture, the respected and the ridiculed alike. Who else but Henry, or someone of his stripe, would have taken pictures of Huckleberry Charlie, Dan Ainsworth, or the other people—and dogs—we have viewed in this book? Beach's celebrities were the local characters, like Charlie, and men and women of modest achievements, like the people who built family resorts and were guides and trappers.[9]

Unlike visitors who see only what is at hand, and what is important to them, insiders are there day after day, year after year, and have different sensibilities. Insiders are more often naturally comfortable around their subjects. Knowing the social etiquette of the locale, Beach genuinely knew how to fit in while taking pictures. This fact, on occasion, might have constrained him, but more often it allowed him to shoot where outsiders might be reluctant to tread. Henry did not have to worry about establishing rapport, knowing how to behave, or not being trusted. His clientele were not reluctant. They were not worried about what Beach would do with the pictures he was taking. They knew.

The chapters in this book are filled with examples of photographs only an insider would and could take: the Catholic church at Benson Mines, St. Joseph's

6. The area around Pine Camp was an outstanding place for berry picking, and Charlie's obituary claimed that he was "the champion huckleberry picker of the United States." The dark color of his left hand gives away the season in which the picture was taken.

7. Interestingly, it is conventional in the art world to call indigenous artists outsiders (as in "outsider art") rather than insiders.

8. *Vernacular* is a word used by people who write about art photography to refer to a particular style of documentary personified by the work of Walker Evans. The term is used in that context to refer to images that have a realist or vernacular feel. My use of the term is different. In my way of thinking the work of people like Beach is authentic vernacular, whereas "vernacular style" is an attempt to create the feeling of the local color.

9. The closest Henry got to people of national stature was James Sherman, a Utica major who served as vice president under Taft. He also photographed General Fredrick Dent Grant at Pine Camp. He was the son of Ulysses S. Grant.

Academy in Malone, the local hunters and anglers, the logging camps, the wood mills, the no-trespassing signs, and the details of mom-and-pop-run camp life. The same is true of the range of small stores, as well as schools, residences, railroad depots, churches, and on and on. So many of the pictures he took were about local peoples' lives and aspirations. This subject matter is neglected in outsiders' visual accounts of the Adirondacks.

Not only was the subject matter of Beach's work different, but he shot and configured his pictures in a different way than a spectator would. His aesthetic was homegrown. Although in his youth he referred to himself as an artist, he had few artistic pretensions.[10] His pictures came out of the subject rather than being derived from training in a particular approach to image making. His technique was laid-back. His compositions and position in relation to the subject matter were unintentional, and less controlled by a uniform style. His visual language was the everyday images the people he photographed saw. His tendency was not to force the photographic moment, pushing for a preconceived composition in order to produce a heightened documentary experience. His respect for the people is evident, too. Some of his pictures are candid, catching his subjects off guard, but they are not stark portraits of alien beings, the kind of voyeuristic images the subjects might be uncomfortable with.

Being a commercial photographer profoundly shaped what Henry did, too. Although there were some negative consequences, mainly the quality of his prints and the unevenness of his portfolio, overall being a small-time entrepreneur enriched rather than undermined his contribution. The niche he found in the market required that he produce and sell many pictures over a long period of time. Postcard and panoramic formats fitted that requirement nicely and became his ticket to a prolific career. We would not have Henry's incredible documentary legacy if he had not been a nickel-and-dime picture taker and the postcard format were not available.[11]

10. When stylized artistic pretension appears in his pictures, it is so obvious that it is encompassed as part of the local idiom.

11. Although the formats he worked in (postcards and panoramics) have been maligned by some as cheap commercial products—artifacts of popular culture—taste about importance and aesthetics of such forms is changing. Henry's position as an authentic vernacular photographer, combined with the increased appreciation of the postcard genre, may turn what some might think as a shortcoming into a plus.

The postcard marketplace was crowded and competitive. Henry had to contend not only with other local photographers but also with large companies that made printed cards. This competition pushed him not only to produce in quantity, but also to innovate, to make different products, to create styles and unusual compositions. The variety in his regular views and an abundance of montage and freak cards were the result. Rather than the economic contingencies restraining his style, he took what others might make a routine task, producing objects to sell to the general public, and created outlandish, flamboyant photographs.

Beach's captions are an outgrowth of his business approach, too, but their funky form is linked to the fact that he was a local photographer. In elite photography circles, an image is supposed to stand alone without an explanation of context, with only the briefest captioning. Beach's photographs could stand on their own, too, but his work is greatly enhanced by extensive knowledge of how the subject matter fitted into Adirondack culture. Vernacular photography is improved by captions, and, as is the case with Beach, the more down-home the caption, the better. Misspelling, quirky wording, insider terms, and particular styles of lettering should be viewed not as mistakes or flaws, but as part of the total visual experience.

## No Respect

With few exceptions (Johnson, Rice, and Williams 1999; Sandler 1989), people have not championed vernacular photographers' work.[12] The products, like Beach's regatta picture (see illustration 1.1), have been seen only in passing, not as objects to be studied in their own right, not as photographs produced by a particular photographer. I have tried to counter that trend here.

One problem in remembering a photographer like Beach is that there is not an art-world category in which to place him, not one that provides visibility, honor, and respect. Beach and his ilk have had a precarious relationship with

12. A number of commercial and local photographers have found a place in the written history of photography. The French photographer Eugene Atget is perhaps the most celebrated (Abbott 1964). William Henry Jackson is a well-documented American commercial photographer (Hales 1988).

people who aspire to be art, documentary, fashion, news, architectural, landscape, or some other kind of respected photographer. Although I think his work stands up well under any standard, the lack of a genre to place him in has motivated me to push this idea of "vernacular photographer."

I have not developed this classification just to honor Henry Beach and his work. In order to fully appreciate the distinctiveness of what he produced, we need to look at it from a different point of view. We need to remember that insiders' photographs contain information that is not easily read or understood by outsiders. Although their work can bring us closer to the local experience, they are never a substitute for having been there, and we should never assume that the way we see their photographs is the way the insider does.

The job of the viewer of a vernacular photograph is not only to appreciate the picture in terms of his or her own aesthetic, but also to try to understand it from the insider's perspective, from the point of view of the photographer's culture.

## Meanwhile, in New York City

As Americans moved into the twentieth century, devotees of the art world in New York City were arguing about the place of photography in "high culture" (Becker 1982). Practicing his trade in rural upstate New York, Beach was not privy to, or interested in, such debates. Alfred Stieglitz, the chief proponent of photography as art, was making inroads in convincing some tastemakers that photography should be taken seriously as an art form (Szarkowski 1995; Trachtenberg 1989; Whelan 1995). As part of the campaign, he and his colleagues self-consciously produced images that resembled paintings (Lowe 1983; Norman 1973; Szarkowski 1995). Later, Stieglitz and other art photographers moved to a more direct form of visual representation that is referred to as "realist." By the 1930s this style evolved into a form that came to be called "documentary photography."

While these developments were taking place in urban cultural centers, Beach and other local, small-time commercial photographers were producing postcards and other photographic products. Although not classified as documentary photographers by people who write the history of photography, the best of some of these commercial photographers, Beach being the case in point, took pictures of the same subject matter and in a style similar to what would later be called "documentary."

In the art world, the term *documentary* is not just descriptive; it is honorific as well, bestowed on images that experts deem "important" (Becker 1982). Beach and people like him remained out of the loop. But Walker Evans (1903–1975), the person whom many consider the creator of the documentary style, began collecting postcard views when he was twelve years old (Hambourg et al. 2000). Late in his life he used examples from his postcard collection as illustrations to accompany a lecture he gave at Yale University. He had been asked to talk about the origins of his approach to picture taking. In his talk titled "Lyrical Documentary," he attributed his direct realist method to his attempt to emulate postcards (Fineman 2000, 133).[13]

Henry M. Beach and others like him are more consequential in the history of fine photography than they are given credit. The quality of their best documentary images compares favorably to photographers whose work we canonize. By concentrating on a few elite photographers, the history of photography has kept us from examining the broader scope of documentary work, such as the vernacular photography of Henry Beach.

13. By the time of his death Evans had a collection of more than nine thousand postcards (Rosenheim 2000, 66). The postcard collection and the speech he gave at Yale are in the photography room archives at the Metropolitan Museum of Art in New York City.

# References


Abbott, Bernice. 1964. *The World of Atget.* New York: Horizon.

Adler, Jeanne Winston. 1997. *Early Days in the Adirondacks: The Photographs of Seneca Ray Stoddard.* New York: Harry N. Abrams.

Allen, James, et al. 2000. *Without Sanctuary: Lynching Photography in America.* Santa Fe: Twin Palms.

Battani, Marshall. 1997. "Striking the Artist's Pose: The Emerging Field of Photographic Practice in the Nineteenth-Century United States." Ph.D. diss., Univ. of California at Davis.

Beach, Elmer Taylor. 1923. *Beach in America: Containing General Information Regarding the Three Brothers Richard Beach, John Beach, and Thomas Beach, Planters in the Original Settlements of New Haven Colony, Wallingford Colony and Milford Colony, Connecticut, 1638 to 1641, and Genealogical Record on a Portion of the Descendants of Richard Beach, Together with Notes on Pioneer Beaches of Michigan, and an Index of All Known Male Descendants of Planter Richard Beach, Signer of the Fundamental Compact of New Haven Colony, 1639.* Kalamazoo, Mich.: Ihling Bros. Everard.

Becker, Howard S. 1982. *Art Worlds.* Berkeley and Los Angeles: Univ. of California Press.

Bethke, Robert D. 1981. *Adirondack Voices.* Urbana: Univ. of Illinois Press.

Blake, Jody, and Jeanette Lasansky. 1996. *Rural Delivery: Real Photo Postcards from Central Pennsylvania, 1905–1935.* Union County, Pa.: Union County Historical Society.

Bogdan, Robert. 1999. *Exposing the Wilderness: Early-Twentieth-Century Adirondack Postcard Photographers.* Syracuse: Syracuse Univ. Press.

Bond, Hallie E. 1995. *Boats and Boating in the Adirondacks.* Blue Mountain Lake, N.Y.: Adirondack Museum; Syracuse: Syracuse Univ. Press.

Borsavage, Kim. 1979. *L. L. McAllister: Photo-Artist.* Burlington, Vt.: Robert Hull Fleming Museum.

Bowen, G. Byron, ed. 1970. *History of Lewis County, New York, 1880–1965.* Willard, N.Y.: Board of Legislators of Lewis County.

Bowes, Anne. 1965. "The Beaver River Flow Country: The Lumberjacks Are Long Gone but Their Stories Color a Backwoods Retreat." *Conservationist:* 18–20.

Brandon, Craig. 1986. *Murder in the Adirondacks.* Utica, N.Y.: North Country Books.

Brumley, Charles. 1994. *Guides of the Adirondacks.* Utica, N.Y.: North Country Books.

Burleson, Clyde W., and E. Jessica Hickman. 1986. *The Panoramic Photography of Eugene O. Goldbeck.* Austin: Univ. of Texas Press.

Covey, Frances Alden. 1964. *The Earl Covey Story: A Biography.* New York: Exposition Books.

Crowley, William. 1982. *Seneca Ray Stoddard: Adirondack Illustrator.* Blue Mountain Lake, N.Y.: Adirondack Museum.

Cunningham, Michael. 2000. "Ahead of Their Time." *Adirondack Life* 21: 66–71.

Davis, Margaret P. 1976. *Honey Out of the Rafters: A Pictorial History of the Settlement and Growth of Steuben and Remsen, N.Y.* Remsen, N.Y.: Remsen-Steuben Historical Society.

DeSormo, Maitland C. 1972. *Seneca Ray Stoddard.* Saranac Lake, N.Y.: Adirondack Yesteryears.

Donaldson, Alfred L. 1921. *A History of the Adirondacks.* Vol. 1. New York: Century.
Donnelly, W. B. N.d. *A Short History of Beaver River.* Beaver River, N.Y.: Beaver River Property Owners Association.
Dreiser, Theodore. 1925. *An American Tragedy.* New York: Horace Liveright.
Duquette, John. 1991. "The Wawbeek." *Saranac Lake Adirondack Daily Enterprise.*
Edey, Maitland. 1978. *Great Photographic Essays from Life.* Boston: New York Graphic Society.
Fineman, Mia. 2000. "'The Eye Is an Inveterate Collector': The Late Work." In *Walker Evans,* by Maria Morris Hombourg, Jeff L. Rosenheim, Douglas Eklund, and Mia Fineman, 130–41. New York: Metropolitan Museum of Art.
Fowler, Albert. 1968. *Cranberry Lake: From Wilderness to Adirondack Park.* Syracuse: Syracuse Univ. Press.
"Funeral Held." 1973. *Lowville (N.Y.) Journal and Republican.*
Galassi, Peter. 1995. *American Photography, 1890–1965.* New York: Museum of Modern Art.
Gilborn, Craig. 1987. *Adirondack Furniture and the Rustic Tradition.* New York: Harry N. Abrams.
———. 2000. *Adirondack Camps: Homes Away from Home, 1850–1950.* Syracuse: Syracuse Univ. Press.
Grady, Joseph F. 1933. *The Adirondacks: Fulton Chain–Big Moose Region, the Story of the Wilderness.* Little Falls, N.Y.: Courier.
Hales, Peter. 1988. *William Henry Jackson and the Transformation of the American Landscape.* Philadelphia: Temple Univ. Press.
Hambourg, Maria Morris, Jeff L. Rosenheim, Douglas Eklund, and Mia Fineman. 2000. *Walker Evans.* New York: Metropolitan Museum of Art.
Haynes, Wesley. 1990. "So Close to Nature: Rustic Architecture at the Club." In *The Adirondack League Club, 1890–1990,* edited by Edward Comstock Jr., 197–245. Old Forge, N.Y.: Adirondack League Club.
Higby, Roy C. 1974. *A Man from the Past.* Big Moose, N.Y.: Big Moose Press.
Hochschild, Harold K. 1962a. *Adirondack Resort in the Nineteenth Century: Blue Mountain Lake, 1870–1900, Stagecoaches and Luxury Hotels.* Blue Mountain Lake, N.Y.: Adirondack Museum.
———. 1962b. *Life and Leisure in the Adirondack Backwoods.* Blue Mountain Lake, N.Y.: Adirondack Museum.
———. 1962c. *Lumberjacks and Rivermen in the Central Adirondacks, 1850–1950.* Blue Mountain Lake, N.Y.: Adirondack Museum.
Horrell, Jeffrey Lanier. 1999. *Seneca Ray Stoddard: Transforming the Adirondack Wilderness in Text and Image.* Syracuse: Syracuse Univ. Press.
Hough, Franklyn. 1883. *History of Lewis County.* Syracuse: D. Mason.
Hyde, Floy S. 1970. *Water Over the Dam at Mountain View in the Adirondacks.* Mountain View, N.Y.: Floy S. Hyde.
———. 1974. *Adirondack Forests, Fields, and Mines.* Lakemont, N.Y.: North Country.
Johnson, William S., Mark Rice, and Carla Williams. 1999. *Photography from 1839 to Today: George Eastman House.* Cologne: Taschen.
"Killed in Auto Wreck." 1917. *Lowville (N.Y.) Journal and Republican.*
Kudish, Michael. 1996. *Railroads of the Adirondacks: A History.* Fleischmanns, N.Y.: Purple Mountain Press.
Landon, Harry F. 1932. *The North Country: A History, Embracing Jefferson, St. Lawrence, Oswego, Lewis, and Franklin Counties, New York.* Indianapolis: Historical Publishing.
Lesy, Michael. 1997. *Dreamland: America at the Dawn of the Twentieth Century.* New York: New Press.
Linney, J. R. 1943. "A Century and a Half of Development Behind the Adirondack Iron Mining Industry." *Mining and Metallurgy:* 480–87.
Lowe, Sue Davidson. 1983. *Stieglitz: A Memoir/Biography.* New York: Farrar, Straus, and Giroux.
Margolies, John. 1993. *Pump and Circumstance: Glory Days of the Gas Station.* Boston: Little, Brown.
McMartin, Barbara. 1992. *Hides, Hemlocks, and Adirondack History.* Utica, N.Y.: North Country Books.
———. 1994. *The Great Forest of the Adirondacks.* Utica, N.Y.: North Country Books.
Meehan, Joseph. 1990. *Panoramic Photography.* New York: AMPHOTO.
Mihalyi, Louis. 1998. "Special Delivery: George Burke and the Red Mail Sled." *Adirondack Life:* 10–14.
Morgan, Hal, and Andreas Brown. 1981. *Prairie Fires and Paper Moons: The American Photographic Postcard, 1900–1920.* Boston: David R. Godine.
Naef, Weston. 1980. "'New Eyes': Luminism and Photography." In *American Light: The Luminist Movement, 1850–1875,* edited by John Wilmerding, 267–91. Washington, D.C.: National Gallery.
Nickel, Douglas R. 1998. *Snapshots: The Photography of Everyday Life, 1888 to the Present.* San Francisco: San Francisco Museum of Modern Art.
Norman, Dorothy. 1973. *Alfred Stieglitz: An American Seer.* New York: Random House.
"Obituary: Henry M. Beach." 1943. *Lowville (N.Y.) Journal and Republican.*

O'Leary, Ann Stillman. 1998. *Adirondack Style.* New York: Clarkson Potter.

Pilcher, Edith. 1992. *The Constables: First Family of the Adirondacks.* Utica, N.Y.: North Country Books.

Reynolds, Jeanne, and Bessie DeCrosse. 1976. *Two Towns, Two Centuries.* Clifton, N.Y.: Clifton-Fine Bicentennial Committee.

Rosenheim, Jeff L. 2000. "'The Cruel Radiance of What Is': Walker Evans and the South." In *Walker Evans,* by Maria Morris Hambourg, Jeff L. Rosenheim, Douglas Eklund, and Douglas Fineman, 54–106. New York: Metropolitan Museum of Art.

Rosenheim, Jeff L., and Douglas Eklund, eds. 2000. *Unclassified: A Walker Evans Anthology.* New York: Metropolitan Museum of Art.

Rubin, Elyce, and Morgan Williams. 1990. *Larger than Life: The American Tall-Tale Postcard, 1905–1915.* New York: Abbeville.

Samson, Harold E. 1971. *Tug Hill Country.* Utica, N.Y.: North Country Books.

Sandler, Martin W. 1989. *American Image.* Chicago: Contemporary Books.

Scheffler, William, and Frank Carey. 2000. *Big Moose Lake, New York, in Vintage Postcards.* Charleston, S.C.: Arcadia.

Schneider, Paul. 1997. *The Adirondacks: A History of America's First Wilderness.* New York: Henry Holt.

Stieglitz, Alfred. 1980. "Pictorial Photography." In *Photography: Essays and Images,* edited by Beaumont Newhall, 163–66. New York: Museum of Modern Art.

Szarkowski, John. 1995. *Alfred Stieglitz at Lake George.* New York: Museum of Modern Art.

Taylor, Sister Mary Christine. 1972. *The History of Catholicism in the North Country.* Ogdensburg, N.Y.: Diocese of Ogdensburg.

Teitelbaum, Matthew. 1992. *Montage and Modern Life.* Cambridge: MIT Press.

Terrie, Philip G. 1990. "A Park for the Adirondacks." In *The Adirondack Park in the Twenty-First Century,* edited by the Commission on the Adirondacks in the Twenty-First Century, 10–23. Albany: State of New York.

Thomas, Howard. 1951. *Trenton Falls: Yesterday and Today.* Prospect, N.Y.: Prospect Books.

Thompson, Pat. 2000. *Beaver River: Oasis in the Wilderness.* Beaver River, N.Y.: Beaver River Press.

Trachtenberg, Alan. 1989. *Reading American Photographs: Images as History, Mathew Bardy to Walker Evans.* New York: Hill and Wang.

Utica Gas and Electric Company. 1922. *The Upper Mohawk Valley: A Land of Industry.* Utica, N.Y.: Utica Gas and Electric Company.

Welsh, Peter C. 1995. *Jacks, Jobbers, and Kings: Logging in the Adirondacks, 1850–1950.* Utica, N.Y.: North Country Books.

Wessels, William L. 1963. *Moses Cohen: Peddler to Capitalist.* Lake George, N.Y.: Adirondack Resort Press.

Whelan, Richard. 1995. *Alfred Stieglitz: A Biography.* Boston: Little, Brown.

White, William Chapman. 1985. *Adirondack Country.* Syracuse: Syracuse Univ. Press.

Willumson, Glenn. 1992. *W. Eugene Smith and the Photographic Essay.* New York: Cambridge Univ. Press.

# Index

*Note:* Page numbers in italics indicate a photograph on that page. Page numbers in the form *pan. 1* are in the panoramic foldouts.